MANAGING MEDIA SERVICES

MANAGING MEDIA SERVICES

Theory and Practice

Second Edition

WILLIAM D. SCHMIDT
Central Washington University

DONALD A. RIECK
Iowa State University of Science and Technology

2000
LIBRARIES UNLIMITED
A Division of Greenwood Publishing Group, Inc.
Greenwood Village, Colorado

LIBRARIES UNLIMITED
A Division of Greenwood Publishing Group, Inc.
7730 East Belleview Avenue, Suite A200
Greenwood Village, CO 80111
1-800-225-5800
www.lu.com

Library of Congress Cataloging-in-Publication Data

Schmidt, William D.
    Managing media services : theory and practice / William D.
Schmidt, Donald A. Rieck. -- 2nd ed.
        p.   cm.
    Rev. ed. of: Managing media services / Charles W. Vlcek. 1989.
    Includes bibliographical references and index.
    ISBN 1-56308-530-5
    1. Audio-visual library service--United States. 2. Instructional
materials centers--United States--Administration. 3. Media programs
(Education)--United States--Administration. 4. Audio-visual
education--United States. I. Rieck, Donald Arthur. II. Vlcek,
Charles W.   Managing media services. III. Title.
Z692.A93S36   1999
025.17'7--dc21   99-23361
                                                        CIP

Contents

ILLUSTRATIONS

FIGURE

FIGURE

FIGURE

PREFACE

When Drs. Charles W. Vlcek and Raymond V. Wiman departed this life, they left behind a rich legacy. They were both very prolific writers, the first edition of this book being one of their contributions. That work, *Managing Media Services: Theory and Practice,* won the Association for Educational Communications and Technology's Outstanding New Publication of the Year award after it was published in 1989. Vlcek wrote widely in the copyright field and Wiman in the field of media production, theory, and practice.

They were outstanding media professionals. Their contributions to the Association for Educational Communications and Technology and other organizations are noteworthy; Vlcek in the early years of educational television and later in the copyright arena and Wiman in history and archives, student media festivals, and a myriad of other areas of interest.

They were superior teachers. Many of their students are still making significant contributions to the media and technology field, and, as such, they still live on.

Finally, they were both great friends of each other and of this writer. In chapter 10 of the first edition, Vlcek and Wiman made this statement: "Not all conflict is bad. Research provides evidence that some conflict between people working together increases productivity and creativity. Studies indicate that some divergence and conflict can serve as a stimulus and remove people from their personal comfort zones, forcing them to change their viewpoints and assumptions." As I stated, Charlie and Ray, as they were fondly called, were my friends. We did things together socially and we worked together for many years. On the job and in media associations, however, we did come in conflict at times, but this conflict led to the process of making a better decision. It forced us to reexamine our philosophies and assumptions, and we were almost always able to arrive at a compromise. In the end, we always remained very good friends.

I undertook this second edition because of that friendship, working with them on writing and production projects, joining them in furthering goals of media associations, and being a colleague as a teacher. Additionally, I knew of Charlie's wish to involve Don Rieck in this project, and I honored that desire. Charlie and Don were classmates during their master's degree programs at the University of Wisconsin–Stout. Don's significant contributions would have pleased Charlie. The children of the two dynamic authors of the first edition have endorsed this effort, and that has also been an incentive to move forward.

Charlie and Ray, friends and colleagues, as much of the essence of the two of you is embodied in your former students, may your contributions also live on through this revised edition of your work.

WILLIAM D. SCHMIDT

ACKNOWLEDGMENTS

It is appropriate for each generation of media specialists to pay tribute to those who helped develop the field they entered. The present writers have used this work to quote many of the leaders who gave birth to and/or led early formative efforts in the audiovisual, media, and technology field. These individuals' comments are on the title pages of many of this book's chapters. Using this tactic, we run the risk of omitting some of the key contributors to the field. If we have erred in that regard, it was not intentional, but simply the result of not always being able to find the appropriate quotations to capture the flavor of each chapter.

We also acknowledge the many contributions made by media professionals and others in K-12, college, and corporate organizations. It would be impossible to recognize all contributors, but we do want to recognize the following who had a hand in this effort: Bruce Eyer, Yakima School District, Yakima, Washington; Richard Ruggeriero, California State University, Northridge; Donald Murphy, Central Washington University, Ellensburg; Richard Gilkey, Portland Public Schools, Portland, Oregon; William King, Miami University, Oxford, Ohio; Ruth Ann Jones, American Library Association; Judy Gaston, University of Minnesota, Minneapolis; Michael Albright, University of California, Monterey Bay, California; Orville Stout, Pierce College, Tacoma, Washington; Ann McLean, Puget Sound Educational Service District, Burien, Washington; Montgomery College, Takoma Park, Maryland; Apple Computer Company, Cupertino, California; TiltRac Corporation, Carrollton, Texas; Crestron Electronics, Rockleigh, New Jersey; Media Minder, Tallahassee, Florida; VanSan Corporation, City of Industry, California; Waveguide Consulting, Decatur, Georgia; Iowa State University, Ames; and Central Washington University, Ellensburg.

INTRODUCTION TO THE REVISED EDITION

Drs. Charles W. Vlcek and Raymond V. Wiman did an admirable job in writing the first edition of this book. They strived constantly to balance the practical side of management with the human considerations. Vlcek and Wiman shared with all of us knowledge based on a combined fifty years of media management. As a consequence, the present writers made a conscious effort to retain as much of their collective wisdom as was possible.

We have also had a similar tenure in working in the media field as managers. We both have had the fortunate experience of working beyond the time of Vlcek and Wiman, when some of the most powerful instructional technologies have emerged. Consequently, we have done a significant amount of updating of the text in regard to the great changes that have taken place in the past decade. New text is included in all chapters. Many new illustrations and photographs are used throughout the book. Some of the chapters have been altered rather significantly.

In some respects, this is a major period of transition. Many of the old technologies are being used less and less, while computers, CD-ROMs, and video race ahead at an alarming but exciting pace. At times, we were in a quandary as to how much of the old technologies should be omitted from the text. In the end, we decided that while we work our way through this great period of change, we would retain some of the information on the older, established technologies, but balance that with a major emphasis on the newer technologies.

We hope that we have achieved a blend of the accepted knowledge of the past with a blend of the vibrant, ever-changing rush of new methods and technologies.

MANAGING MEDIA SERIES

MANAGING MEDIA SERVICES

An Overview

The director of instructional technology must have bifocal vision, with one focus on the ends to be achieved and the other on the means to achieve them. If he sees only the future, he becomes a visionary with no firm base in reality. If he becomes too concerned with means, he gets lost in the trivia of daily routines or becomes hypnotized by hardware.

Edgar Dale, *Audiovisual Methods in Teaching*, 1969

OBJECTIVES

At the conclusion of this chapter you should be able to

1. Review the history of the instructional/industrial media field.

2. List and describe seven major categories of tasks that media managers may be expected to perform.

3. Define and explain the functions of a media center.

4. Describe the purpose of instructional development units within a media center.

5. Explain why a public relations program is important to a media center and list and describe public relation vehicles that can be employed effectively.

IN THE BEGINNING

Any discussion about the emergence of media centers must touch upon the attempts of prehistoric human beings to preserve for posterity their sacred rituals and culture. Some of these early pages in the book of humanity still exist, and traces of early visual records have been discovered in Europe, Africa, Australia, and the Western Hemisphere. Paintings and rock carvings executed by our prehistoric ancestors provide some tantalizing looks into the past. Lancelot Hogben (1949, 16) has some unique observations on early humans: "When modern man appears on the stage of pre-history, he is a picture making animal, the only picture making animal which has ever lived on our planet, maybe the only picture making creature in the universe."

Australia's earliest aboriginal "creation saga" may date back some 35,000 years (Breeden 1988). Paintings found in the caves of France and Spain are estimated to be about 30,000 years old, and some discoveries in Africa also go back about that far (Hogben 1949, 15–33). Petroglyphs in the United States and the hewn rock stela found in Central and South America appear to be somewhat younger (Matheny 1987). These "picture libraries" are found in protected places around the earth, chiseled out of, inscribed into, or painted on rocks. Following spoken language, pictures were among our ancestors' first communication tools, for through pictures they developed the ability to communicate across time and over long distances.

Early Advances

Progress was practically undetectable for thousands of years, but then slowly, and later at an ever more rapid pace, the changes came. Advances in communications technology have outdistanced all of our other achievements save the development of weapons for war. There is a definite link here, however, for as weapons developed so did the need for ever faster and far-reaching communications.

After the entry of the picture maker on the scene, it took thousands of years for languages to develop and thousands more for alphabets to be perfected. The process continues today. Stone and clay tablets came into use and were discarded to make way for paper, pen, and ink. A key invention at this point in time was the invention of paper, for it was to become essential in the coming information revolution. More hundreds of years passed as books, if they were to be reproduced at all, were laboriously copied by hand. The major breakthrough came some five hundred years ago with the invention of movable type. Paper and printing came together and information began to move with phenomenal rapidity. The chronology runs something like this:

The first book, the Gutenberg Bible, was printed in 1546.

In 1621 the first news sheet appeared.

One hundred ten years later the first magazine (in the modern sense) was published.

Printing technology steadily improved, and by 1814 steam-powered printing presses were in use.

1850–1950

The last half of the nineteenth century saw the development of paper made from wood pulp, the perfection of photographic processes, the typewriter, telegraph, gramophone, the automobile, the motion picture, the wireless, and more. More progress was made during these fifty years than had been made in the preceding five hundred. The pace quickened again during the first half of the twentieth century as the airplane, the electric light, safety film, transcontinental telephones, radio, sound films, phototelegraphy, animated cartoons, tape recorders, television broadcasting, and microgroove recordings emerged. It must be noted here that the two wars fought during those years gave a decided push to the development of communications devices and techniques, particularly during the frantic efforts expended during World War II to speed the training of large groups of men in the shortest possible time. Evidence that these efforts were successful is found in a comment by the chief of the German General Staff: "We had everything calculated perfectly except the speed with which America was able to train its people. Our major miscalculation was in underestimating their complete mastery of film education" (Olsen and Bass 1982, 33). Many of those who led this effort were directors of departments of audiovisual instruction on leave from their regular jobs in U.S. schools.

Toward the Twenty-first Century

As soon as some semblance of normalcy was achieved after the cessation of hostilities, educational developments fostered by the military began to spill over into civilian classrooms, where progress had been at a standstill. The pace of innovation picked up quickly, and each step forward seemed to lay the groundwork for the next. In 1952 the first crude videotape recorders were developed and by 1956 had been refined to the point where they could be used for television broadcasting.

The catalyst that set off the twentieth century's biggest advances in instructional technology, however, was the orbiting of the Soviet satellite Sputnik I in 1957, a severe blow to American pride. After the shock of being beaten into space by the Soviets waned, America's first reaction was to enact the National Defense Education Act (NDEA) of 1958. Four of the titles within the act directed attention to the media field and funded research and experimentation in more effective utilization of all types of media designed for educational purposes. Further, the act provided funds for the purchase of instructional equipment and materials to be used in instruction.

The private sector also became heavily involved by setting up a variety of organizations: the Educational Facilities Laboratories, the Educational Media Council, the National Science Foundation, the Learning Resources Institute, and others. Their major emphasis was investigating the use of media, equipment, and facilities in new ways to improve educational processes. Some of the areas explored included educational television, electronic learning laboratories, teaching machines and programmed learning, massed film series, and instructional systems.

Each advance in space technology seemed to spin off a corresponding advance in communication devices. The early vacuum tube computers soon gave way to transistorized units and then to silicon memory chips. These new computers were smaller, more reliable, and performed their tasks many times faster. Prices came down as computers proliferated and soon were within reach of schools and individuals. The development of viable programs to guide the computer and the user, plus the low cost and improved reliability of the hardware, ushered in the computer age.

Computers made space travel possible, for with them people could make calculations with a speed and accuracy that had been impossible before. One result was that the first human space traveler circled the globe in 1961. The following year the first telestar satellite went into orbit, relaying television signals across the Atlantic Ocean. More satellites followed quickly and a few short years later, when human beings set foot on the moon, this fantastic accomplishment was seen around the world—as it happened. In slightly over a century, mankind had progressed from reliance upon surface transportation and the written word to disburse information to the electronic transmission of events, from wherever they took place, to viewers around the world.

One must not assume that this is the end, however; the millennium in inventions has not arrived as predicted in 1870 by Bishop Milton Wright. Bishop Wright proposed that flight was reserved for the angels and that "Man has invented everything that can be invented" (Cole 1958). Thirty-three years later his sons Wilbur and Orville flew their airplane into history at Kitty Hawk.

Early Audiovisual Departments

By 1910, only fifteen years after the first film showing, the firm of Kline, Selig, and Spoor issued a catalog listing more than one thousand films for "Universities, Colleges, Scientific and Literary Institutions, and Traveling Lecturers" (Elliott 1948, 4). Thus the first film library came into being. At about the same time the superintendent of the New York City Schools was recommending that motion picture projectors be installed in the city's schools, but it was 1920 before a "Director of Public Lectures and Visual Education" was appointed. New York City did not lead the way, however; that honor belongs to the city of St. Louis. St. Louis capitalized upon the Louisiana Purchase Exposition held there in 1904 and established an educational museum, using, in part, some of the displays from the exposition (Saettler 1955, 111). Within one year, the Department of Instruction was delivering materials (media) to classrooms by horse and wagon. Thus the first department in the United States had its beginning under the name "Educational Museum." During the next twenty years, seventeen public school departments were established across the country. The first department identified specifically with visual instruction was created in 1917, when the city of Chicago appointed Dudley C. Hays to the post of Director of the Bureau of Visual Instruction.

Though the growth of media service centers may have appeared to be rather slow, this was not the case, as was noted by F. Dean McClusky (1962, 502), one of the movement's pioneers.

> Organized professional interest in our field emerged during 1918–1924. In this six year period, the first formal credit courses in Visual Education were offered at the University level, the first research was reported, the first books published, and the first classroom films produced. Also fine professional visual education organizations of national scope appeared along with many at state and local levels.

At about this time institutions of higher education began to set up film and slide libraries, which became, in essence, the first state and regional educational film rental libraries. Two of these early film libraries were established at Indiana University in 1912 and the University of Iowa in 1914. Later as film utilization grew, it became necessary to establish film libraries at state, county, regional, and local school district levels.

The number of media centers, or departments of visual instruction, as many came to be called, grew slowly through the 1920s and 1930s, but progress came to a complete halt during the 1940s—except in the military, where research into the use of media fostered a succession of improvements in equipment, materials, techniques, and production processes. To a certain extent this progress was paralleled in industry, where thousands of men and women learned unfamiliar production processes and work techniques in the aircraft, shipbuilding, and light and heavy arms manufacturing industries. Here, as in the military, training tools had to be created and put to use. This spillover continued after the war as the private sector wrestled again with peacetime training and selling problems. Competition was fierce and companies with the best-trained workers were the ones that eventually came out on top. Many companies, such as Caterpillar Tractor, Boeing Aircraft, the telephone companies, insurance companies, and fast-food companies, created media service and production units to help solve instructional and training problems. The result was the development of media service centers in both the public and private sectors.

A National Organization and a Field in Transition

The Department of Visual Instruction (DVI) of the National Education Association was formed in 1923, but this name gave way in 1948 to the Department of Audio-Visual Instruction (DAVI) as sound made its contributions to the field and was recognized. By 1974 that name too was no longer suitable because it did not identify the field. New parameters and definitions were in order to better identify what it was that the field covered. Thus the organization gave up departmental status in the National Education Association, became independent, and changed its name to the Association for Educational Communications and Technology (AECT). In 1977 the association published a monograph entitled *The Definition of Educational Communications and Technology* in an attempt to identify more closely the field and its activities (AECT 1977). The entire definition is made up of sixteen parts and, according to the text, must be considered in its entirety. Our purpose here is not to delve into all of the details, but rather to boil the overall definition down into manageable proportions. AECT's initial statement defines educational technology as:

> a complex, integrated process involving people, procedures, ideas, devices and organization for analyzing problems and devising, implementing, evaluating and managing solutions to those problems involved in all aspects of human learning (Seels and Richey 1994, 20).

In other words, educational technology is the creative application of man, machines, and materials to solving instructional problems. That really is what the media field has been all about since its inception, and that is what it is continuing to do even as advances in hardware and software and how we think about learning come about.

Seels and Richey (1994, 1) reexamined the 1977 definition and surveyed new developments in theory and practice in the instructional technology field. Their definition is as follows:

> Instructional Technology is the theory and practice of design, development, utilization, management, and evaluation of processes and resources for learning.

They point out the terms *educational technology* and *instructional technology*, as used today, are pretty much synonymous.

In any discussion of the formation of the instructional technology field, it is important to focus on some of the most significant writings that helped lead this development. In 1996 Ely and a colleague conducted a survey to determine the writings on educational technology that collectively lay out much of the conceptual base of the field. These very difficult-to-locate writings are found in *Classic Writings on Instructional Technology* (Ely and Plomp 1996). Included in the book are sections on definition and conceptual background, design and development functions, evaluation, delivery options, and the profession. A well-grounded media manager would do well to review these foundation writings.

This text focuses upon the theory and practice involved in the administration of media centers. The services provided by such audiovisual or media units are many, ranging from the circulation of materials to the creation of materials designed to meet specified problems. It goes almost without saying that wherever one finds people involved in skills development and knowledge transmission and who are facing the communication problems involved in teaching, training, telling and selling, media is being created and used to facilitate the process. The fact that the contributions made by media units to their parent organizations are valuable and important can usually no longer be called into question. They have been funded because their contributions were found to be necessary and timely.

WHAT'S IN A NAME?

In a 1984 study by the Division of Educational Media Management of AECT, it was found that 54 different names were used to identify 196 media units in higher education (Albright 1984). The six most common names listed by respondents were Audiovisual Center, Learning Resources Center, Media Center, Instructional Media Center, Audio Visual Services, and Media Services. Albright and Milet did a more recent survey of college media centers. In that study, Media Services was clearly the most prevalent name for the media unit (Albright and Milet 1997). One of the writers of this book did an analysis of the job title listings in the 1996 membership directory of the AECT (1996). AECT is the oldest and one of most prominent of associations representing a broad spectrum of media and technology resources and specialists from K-12; community colleges; four-year colleges and universities; and military, government, and commercial organizations. It was found that *media services* or *media center* were the two most common terms used in titles in the approximately 4,000 entries. The word *media*, by a three-to-one margin, was the most common word used in titles, followed by *technology*. The word *resources* was third and *audiovisual* was fourth.

It is hoped that the use of various configurations of titles using *media* and *technology* is transitional. The use of a single title, like Instructional Technology, as proposed by Seels and Richey (1994), would give the field the more coherent look it had several decades ago, when all similar programs in this field were called audiovisual. The use of Instructional Technology Center or Services could replace the well over fifty different titles for media and technology programs used in the AECT directory. But in reality, today, the word *media* with other word combinations is far and away the most predominate term still in use. As a consequence, throughout this book, *media center* will be used to identify audiovisual, media, and technology facilities.

WHAT IS A MEDIA CENTER?

In general, a media center provides the instructional materials and support services required by an institution for its instructional and training programs. Some may also provide library-type services related to the circulation of print materials such as books, periodicals, and other documents. The authors' intent in this text is to concentrate upon the administration of nonprint materials and services. There is plenty of literature readily available in the library field, but very little is available for media center administrators.

A media center, for our purposes, is defined as a service facility housing various instructional materials collections, equipment collections, media development facilities, and a trained staff. The center's basic function is to facilitate the integration of various communication resources into instructional learning situations so that those resources become an integral part of the teaching/training/learning environment. The kinds of materials circulated by a center may include films, videotapes, CD-ROMs, videodiscs, computer software, graphics, still photos, transparencies, slides, audio materials, and others. Further, the center must provide the equipment necessary to display those materials before an audience, whether a large group or one person. In recent years, technology classroom design and support, designing and operating distance education systems, and providing technology training have become important services in rapidly evolving media and technology centers. Finally, media professionals in the center consult with clients regarding their media needs and may also direct the design and production of specialized materials and systems. In essence, these are the common functions that appear to exist in all media centers, regardless of the entity funding the activity.

As has been noted, media centers are found in organizations representing almost any type or kind of endeavor one can name. Depending upon their focus, media centers may serve children, adults, teachers, trainers, trainees, workers, salesmen, military personnel, and so on. Regardless of the type of institution or the clients served, the successful media center is basically a service organization charged with the job of providing cost-effective, high-quality instructional services where and when required by that center's clients.

To provide a high level of service requires good management of all available resources, and this involves many tasks. Programs must be planned, services must be delivered, budgets formulated and presented, and staff supervised. The media center should focus primarily upon service. This philosophy of service must be reflected in the actions of the entire media center staff if the center is to fulfill its mission successfully.

Johnson (1994, 23), in a survey of ninety colleges and universities, synthesized his findings into a "typical" profile of a media services department. This profile was based on "the most commonly reported situation" in the various categories:

> The typical department would be housed in one location. It would be named media services and administered by a full-time director. The media administrator would have been in his or her position from 6 to 10 years and have completed a master's degree. The degree would not likely be in instructional media or a closely related technology or media field. The administrator and department would be structurally aligned within the university library administrative system. Department staff would most likely include one additional professional (either an assistant director or media specialist), two technical support people (possibly equipment maintenance and production technicians), and one secretarial or clerical person. The department staff would also include 10 to 15 student workers, covering 100 to 150 work-hours each week. The average departmental support to instruction would include: (1) the maintenance and circulation of a video and film collection, (2) rental of additional titles from outside sources, (3) the local production of media materials, (4) photographic support for instruction, (5) video production, and (6) satellite video reception. Photographic services would include location photography, copywork, and black-and-white film and print processing. The department also would have its own television studio, but support video field production and editing.

Albright (1991, 18–19) provided further information on what a media center involves. In a survey in which 221 four-year college and university media services' directors responded, he reported information that is germane here. He found that among the main activities of a media center were circulating media equipment, assisting faculty in finding resources and using them effectively, consulting on classroom design, and repairing media equipment. While the type of services Albright listed were most prevalent in 1991, a survey today might include some newcomers, such as distance education, multimedia production, high-tech classrooms, Web site development, facility design, and others. In fact, a recent survey confirmed that (Albright and Milet 1997). In the same survey, Albright and Milet found that, among other arrangements, media directors reported to library, chief academic, and chief information service or technology administrators. There appeared to be a trend toward media service programs reporting to information service or technology administrators.

Keeping the Center Current

While it is important to provide all traditional media services that are still needed, it is also important that the media center stays current with new developments in instructional technology. The center that is perceived to be largely committed to old technology and not embracing many of the new developments may soon lose much of its support. This may result in consolidation with some other technology-related service, absorption by some other program, or, at worst, elimination as a service program.

The main way to avoid such scenarios is to constantly gather feedback through informal and formal evaluation. Evaluation will be discussed in detail in a later chapter.

WHAT DO MEDIA MANAGERS DO?

Seels and Richey (1994, 48–52) divided the domain of instructional technology management into four subcategories: Project Management, Resource Management, Delivery System Management, and Information Management. The domain of instructional technology management evolved at first from the management of media centers and later from the disciplines of information science; at the present, quality improvement and quality management principles from industrial settings are being tried in educational settings.

The tasks performed by media managers are diverse, and the good manager does whatever, within reason, is necessary to get the job done. Not all of the tasks that one may be asked to handle can be classified as media tasks, nor are some of them very exciting. When you are asked to cover a display case in a boardroom within the next thirty minutes so that its contents can be revealed at the right time, it is difficult to reason that this is a media task. However, when the person asking is in upper management and indicates that you have a reputation for being resourceful, then you do the job quickly and with a smile. Who knows, perhaps in the future you may need this person's support for a proposal.

While it would be difficult to list all of the tasks that involve media managers, the major tasks can be identified and grouped under headings for various areas of responsibility. Within this text, the tasks that will be discussed are as follows:

Media program management
- sets goals and objectives
- establishes long-range plans
- devises programs and projects to meet center goals and objectives
- plans and implements procedures to provide efficient media services
- identifies, acquires, and manages appropriate instructional resources
- develops appropriate delivery and information management systems
- develops appropriate media design and production facilities
- devises and implements periodic evaluations of service

Personnel management
- determines personnel requirements
- prepares job descriptions
- recruits, hires, and dismisses personnel as needed
- supervises staff
- provides staff training
- evaluates employee job performance
- works with employees to develop job satisfaction

Fiscal program management
- determines fiscal needs
- prepares budgets
- justifies budgets
- develops cost-effective procedures
- monitors the center budget and department budgets

Public relations management
- promotes media service programs to the administration
- works to develop good relations with other administrators
- attends all meetings pertinent to the center
- develops inservice communication programs for staff
- develops and distributes client orientation programs about center services

Instructional development
- assists instructors in analysis of learner characteristics
- assists instructors to clarify objectives
- assesses and recommends teaching/learning strategies
- considers and recommends appropriate media
- evaluates teaching/learning design

Media facility design
- advises or is a member of building committees
- consults with administration on media design requirements
- develops minimum media standards for classrooms
- consults with clients on special media facility needs
- develops specifications for media facilities and equipment
- consults with architects on media facilities

Professional responsibilities
- reads appropriate publications and journals
- collects and analyzes appropriate data
- applies relevant research findings to problems
- evaluates results
- conducts appropriate research
- develops and maintains professional contacts
- is active in appropriate professional organizations
- keeps up with the changing technology

Job Satisfaction

Prospective media managers will be interested in what recently employed college and university media managers report about their job satisfaction. Doyle (1994) reports the results of a study that found, among other things, that in the "Work Itself" category most reported average to above-average job satisfaction. They were generally less satisfied with the other two categories: "Physical/Economic" (physical environment, job security, and equitable financial rewards) and "Human Relations" (supervisor and co-worker relationships, opportunities for staff participation, supportive management, and trust).

FUNCTIONS OF A MEDIA CENTER

As will be seen below, media centers provide a variety of services and serve a wide spectrum of instructional functions. The manner in which these services are delivered will depend in part upon the focus of the parent organization, in part upon the philosophy of the media center director, in part upon how well the media center staff has been trained, and finally in part on how adequately the media center is funded. Because of these factors, no two situations are alike, even though they may offer the same range of services.

Materials Selection and Acquisition

The selection of materials to be circulated from a media center is a critical responsibility. Media collections are usually developed to meet the specific instructional needs of an organization or institution. The quality and usefulness of the materials collection is determined by the policies and procedures set up for the development of the collection. No single list is appropriate or adequate for all media centers; while a collection may be ideal for one organization, it may not be adequate for a similar entity for a variety of reasons. Collection requirements and needs will differ greatly, depending upon factors such as subject areas and levels, geographic location, availability of commercial materials, and the perceived needs of users. The purpose of any media collection should be to meet the needs of patrons, either by supplying materials from the center's collections, renting them from other sources, or creating them. Most nonprint materials, such as films, videotapes, audio materials, slide programs, and computer software, are expensive; therefore the selection procedures and criteria must be carefully and precisely drawn. Media centers cannot afford to have films and other costly materials sitting unused on their shelves.

Equipment Selection

Equipment must be selected that will be dependable, easy to use, and will serve organizational needs. If it is possible, managers should attempt to standardize equipment brands in order to provide clients with equipment they know how to operate and to facilitate maintenance and repair.

Circulation

A primary function of most media centers is the circulation of materials and equipment among its clients. To accomplish this function, procedures must be developed that will enhance the movement of both as required. This means that the manager is faced with a host of logistical problems ranging from reserving materials and equipment for someone weeks or months in advance, supplying them immediately upon demand, arranging for long-term loans, and securing the return of materials and equipment to the center so they can be readied for the next user. This entails setting up several different but interlocking systems for materials, equipment, and maintenance so that the center staff will be able to keep track of all of the various elements involved.

Maintenance and Repair

Audiovisual equipment and materials require meticulous maintenance if maximum dependable use is to be obtained from them. Preventive maintenance will appreciably extend the usable life of equipment and materials, an aspect that is critical in determining the cost effectiveness of services offered by the center. Users' enthusiasm for using media in their work can be very quickly destroyed if equipment and/or material failures happen very often. Repeated breakdowns embarrass the user and will translate into pressure upon the center manager. Thus, a comprehensive maintenance and repair program is essential if the center is to offer high-quality services.

Design and Production Function

The design and production of instructional materials that meet specified objectives is another function of many media centers. The size and scope of units to meet this need vary, depending upon the kinds of services required by the institution. The basic mission of most design and production units is to design and create graphic, photographic, and audio materials for use in teaching, training, telling, and selling activities that are not available from any other source. In finished form, these materials may be used alone or in films, videotapes, slides, transparencies, filmstrips, charts, graphs, print materials, photographs, CD-ROMs, videodiscs, computer diskettes, and more. The possibilities can go on and on. The skills required of a design and production staff will vary, depending upon institutional requirements. Media design and production will be discussed in depth in chapter 7 under the broader concept of media development.

Video/television materials may be required in order to fill needs for materials that are not available from other sources. Design and production units may range from those capable of producing single-camera video programs, to very complex video productions involving multiple cameras and elaborate special effects, to multimedia productions. The main advantage of having such facilities within a media center is that instructional materials of a very specific nature can be produced to meet identified needs. Video equipment can also be used to provide individuals with an opportunity to "see themselves in action" as they prepare for sales demonstrations, lectures, speeches, and other presentations. However, media managers must keep in mind the fact that video/television design and production is an expensive business. Not only is the equipment costly, but producing a program requires many people, which raises production costs considerably. If needed instructional materials requiring motion are not available from other sources, a television production unit can be cost-effective and make valuable contributions to the institution's overall instructional programs.

Computer-based design and production is the newest and potentially most powerful technology available to the media center. Software is available to make the preparation of flyers, posters, banners, slides, overhead projector transparencies, and many other materials a relatively fast and simple process. Design software is available to produce storyboards and scripts. From the design, authoring software can be used to develop multimedia productions for instruction, training, promotion, and sales. Authorware and Macromind Director are some of the current high-end software programs, while HyperStudio and Digital Chisel represent some software that have a low learning curve and are user-friendly to the instructor or trainer with a moderate amount of computer skills.

Facility Design

In recent years, there has been a big demand in institutions to design various types of facilities, e.g., technology classrooms or distance education facilities and systems. Media center personnel should work closely with the end users of each facility to ensure they get what is needed. They can serve as a valuable link with outside architects and builders and, in the process, build up valuable credits applied toward a positive perception of the media center.

Instructional Development

If mediated instructional activities are to have the desired effect upon learners, appropriate materials and activities must be carefully selected and integrated into the teaching/learning environment. In the past few decades methods and techniques bearing names such as (1) Systems Approach to Learning and (2) Instructional Development have received a great deal of attention. Whatever the name employed, the basic purpose of such programs is to develop teaching/learning strategies, programs, and materials that facilitate learning or training performance. These plans also incorporate more thorough and effective evaluation techniques than have been employed in the past, thus both instructor and student receive feedback regarding their performance. While there has been some confusion over the use of the phrases *instructional design* and *instructional development*, the Heinich, Molenda, and Russell (1989, 439) definition of instructional development is used throughout this book: "The process of analyzing needs, determining what content must be mastered, establishing educational goals, designing materials to help reach objectives, and trying out and revising the program in terms of learner achievement."

This approach to instructional planning brings together a variety of experts to work in concert to develop valid instructional strategies that use a wide spectrum of materials and hardware. The objective is to produce more efficient learning situations derived through effective teaching methods, materials, and carefully stated objectives measuring performance skills, knowledge acquisition, and attitudes.

Some institutions have created instructional development units within their media centers in order to make the best use of the people and resources available. In most media centers, one finds creative professionals conversant with message design as well as talented graphic artists and technicians who can create instructional materials designed to meet specific needs. Here, in the media facility, all of the elements needed to develop effective teaching/learning strategies and materials can come together in synergistic combinations as content experts, instructional staff, and production staff work together in a search for solutions to instructional problems. An examination of figure 1.1, page 16, showing elements usually involved in an instructional development model, illustrates the complexity of the process. Here is perhaps the most exciting and rewarding area of endeavor in a media center; an area media managers must know well if they are to be effective as leaders in instructional development. Some institutions may not assign responsibility for instructional development to the media center, preferring to establish a separate unit or to provide such services informally, or, in some cases, to rely upon teachers to do the job. Whatever the case, if instructional development takes place in an institution, the media center will become involved in one way or another as instruction and/or training is brought to users through traditional modes as well as through newer modes engendered by the explosive growth in communications technology. Newer strategies now include interactive videodiscs, computer multimedia, CD-ROM (read only or recorded), to name a few, as well as instructional programs transmitted to distant learners via microwave link or satellite. Looking further ahead, one finds high-definition television and digital videodiscs ready to enter the instructional scene.

Faculty/Staff Development and Training

With the advent of new technologies for teaching and training and the complexity of some technologies, there is an accelerating need to provide instructional/training sessions for faculty and trainers. Topics of these sessions range from how to operate a computer to how to design and produce a multimedia production. In between, there is a need for information on how to teach by distance education, how to design a Web home page, and how to make a CD-ROM.

Evaluation

On a practical level, media center staff are always evaluating services performed. We check with users on how equipment is functioning, how well a product designed and produced in the center works, and how employees render services to users.

But to be truly accountable, some formal evaluation needs to be performed. Some examples are:

a periodic, unbiased evaluation of the center's performance;

formative and summative evaluation during product development;

periodic evaluation of the performance of employees; and

problem analysis techniques to gather information on problems and formalize decision-making strategies.

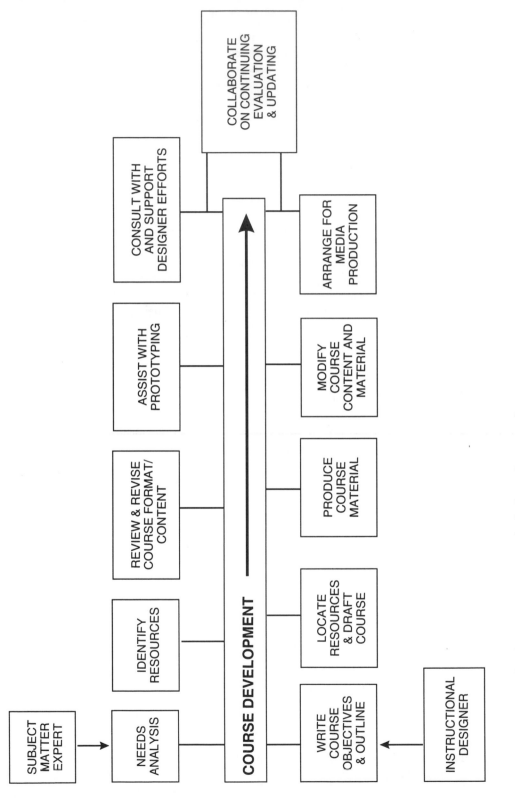

Figure 1.1. Course development process typical of a major manufacturer.

BLOWING THE CENTER'S HORN

All institutions, public and private, are involved to some extent in the promotion of their particular products, services, or programs. Public schools, for instance, engage in a continuous program of communication with parents and the public to ensure they know what the school is doing for their children and what kinds of services are available. It is also necessary that taxpayers be made aware of the ways in which school programs and activities benefit the community, in order to gain support for those school programs and activities. Business and industry also let their customers and the general public know what they have to offer using a wide variety of strategies.

It stands to reason, then, that the media center in an organization must also advertise its services if it is to have the opportunity to make the maximum possible contribution to that institution's instructional activities. A resourceful media manager will use a number of promotional techniques to sell the center's services to ensure that the center gains support wherever possible. Programs and services are "sold" at conferences, in departmental meetings, meetings with upper management, workshops, and the like. Informally, the selling may be accomplished over coffee, lunch, on the golf course, and elsewhere. Posters, brochures, catalogs, reports, computer home pages, and the services themselves all play an important role in disseminating information about and promoting media center services. While a media manager may develop and implement planned promotional programs, the center's best advertisers will always be their clients. High quality programs, services, and materials will do more to sell the media center concept to users than anything else, but one cannot rely upon that alone; always to be considered is the matter of reaching potential users who do not know about the center's services.

More information about public relations and communicating with various audiences appears in chapter 12.

WHAT'S NEXT?

In following chapters, the tasks, functions, responsibilities, and problems faced by media center executives will be discussed. Management ideas, models, policies, procedures, forms, and many other items pertaining to managing media centers will be presented for consideration. The basic purpose is to develop understandings from which one can develop operational plans to fit particular situations. The text may well raise more questions than will be answered. Perhaps this is as it should be, for management requires continual decision making, and the ability to find creative solutions for problems is based upon asking appropriate questions.

SUGGESTED ACTIVITIES

1. Describe the earliest use of visual media to communicate, and list and describe ten inventions and/or events that advanced the media field to its present state.

2. List the departments in a media center with which you are acquainted and describe the functions each department performs.

3. Interview a media manager and prepare a written report on the responsibilities and tasks that the manager performs.

4. Make a list of departments within a hypothetical media center and describe the functions of each department.

5. List six public relations vehicles that may be effective in publicizing a media center.

REFERENCES

Albright, Michael J. 1991. "A Profile of the Profession as We Enter the Last Decade of the Century." Proceedings from the meeting of the Consortium of College and University Media Centers, May 31–June 2, 1991, at Philadelphia, Pennsylvania.

———. 1984. "The Status of Media Centers in Higher Education: DEMM Task Force Report." *Media Management Journal,* 3, no. 3: 4–18.

———, and Lynn Milet. 1997. "Media Centers in Transition: Results of a 1997 CCUMC Member Survey." *College and University Media Review*, 4, no. 1: 11–41.

Association for Educational Communications and Technology. 1996. *AECT Membership Directory.* Washington, D.C.: AECT.

———. 1977. *The Definition of Educational Communications and Technology.* Washington, D.C.: AECT.

Breeden, Stanley. 1988. "The First Australians." *National Geographic*, 173, no. 2: 266–89.

Cole, Walton. 1958. "Man's Limitations." *Phi Delta Kappan*, 39, no. 5: back cover.

Dale, Edgar. 1969. *Audiovisual Methods in Teaching.* 3d ed. New York: Holt, Rinehart and Winston.

Doyle, Robert G. 1994. "Job Satisfaction Levels of U.S. and International College and University Media Specialists." *College and University Media Review*, 1, no. 1: 89–96.

Elliott, Godfrey M., ed. 1948. *Film and Education.* New York: Philosophical Library.

Ely, Donald P., and Tjeerd Plomp. 1996. *Classic Writings on Instructional Technology.* Englewood, Colo.: Libraries Unlimited.

Heinich, Robert, Michael Molenda, and James D. Russell. 1989. *Instructional Media and the New Technologies of Instruction.* 3d ed. New York: Macmillan.

Hogben, Lancelot. 1949. *From Cave Painting to Comic Strip.* New York: Chanticleer Press.

Johnson, Larry. 1994. "Characteristics of Media Service Departments at Mid-size Universities." *Tech Trends*, 39, no. 6: 20–23.

Matheny, Ray T. 1987. "An Early Maya Metropolis Uncovered: El Mirador." *National Geographic*, 172, no. 9: 317–39.

McClusky, F. Dean. 1962. "The Coalition of 1932." *Audiovisual Instruction*, 7, no. 7: 502–7.

Olsen, John R., and Virginia B. Bass. 1982. "The Application of Performance Technology in the Military, 1960–80." *Performance and Instruction*, 21, no. 6: 32–36.

Saettler, Paul. 1955. "History of A-V Education in City School Systems." *Audio-Visual Communication Review*, 3, no. 2: 109–18.

Seels, Barbara B., and Rita C. Richey. 1994. *Instructional Technology: The Definition and Domains of the Field*. Washington, D.C.: Association for Educational Communications and Technology.

MEDIA RESOURCES

Alan November on Technology, the Learning Process, and a Vision for the Future. Technology in Today's Classroom Series. KOCE-TV (PBS affiliate), 70 minutes. Santa Monica, Calif.: Canter & Associates, 1997. Videocassette.

Educational Technology: Linking Schools to the Future. National Alliance of Business, 60 minutes. Washington, D.C.: U.S. Department of Education, 1995. Videocassette.

SELECTED BIBLIOGRAPHY

Anglin, Gary J., ed. *Instructional Technology: Past, Present, and Future*. 2d ed. Englewood, Colo.: Libraries Unlimited, 1995.

Bailey, Gerald D., and Dan Lumley. *Technology Staff Development Program: A Leadership Sourcebook for School Administrators*. New York: Scholastic, 1994.

Bozeman, Bill, and Donna Baumbach. *Educational Technology: Best Practices from America's Schools*. Princeton, N.J.: Eye on Education, 1995.

Brody, Philip J. *Technology Planning and Management Handbook: A Guide for School District Educational Leaders*. Englewood Cliffs, N.J.: Educational Technology Publications, 1995.

Brown, James W., Richard B. Lewis, and Fred F. Harcleroad. *AV Instruction: Technology, Media and Methods*. 6th ed. New York: McGraw-Hill, 1983.

Dills, Charles R., and Alexander J. Romiszowski, eds. *Instructional Development Paradigms*. Englewood Cliffs, N.J.: Educational Technology Publications, 1997.

Gentry, Castelle B. *Introduction to Instructional Development: Processes and Techniques*. Belmont, Calif.: Wadsworth, 1994.

Hackbarth, Steven. *The Educational Technology Handbook: A Comprehensive Guide*. Englewood Cliffs, N.J.: Educational Technology Publications, 1996.

Heinich, Robert, Michael Molenda, James D. Russell, and Sharon E. Smaldino. *Instructional Media and Technologies of Instruction*. 6th ed. Upper Saddle River, N.J.: Merrill, 1999.

Inglis, Fred. *Media Theory: An Introduction*. Cambridge, Mass.: Basil Blackwell, 1990.

Jonassen, David H., ed. *Handbook of Research for Educational Communications and Technology*. Old Tappan, N.J.: Simon & Schuster, 1996.

Kearsley, Greg, and William Lynch, eds. *Educational Technology Leadership Perspectives*. Englewood Cliffs, N.J.: Educational Technology Publications, 1994.

Marlow, Eugene. *Managing Corporate Media*. Rev. ed. White Plains, N.Y.: Knowledge Industry Publications, 1989.

Moller, Leslie. "Working with Subject Matter Experts." *Tech Trends*, 40, no. 6 (1995): 26–27.

Morris, Betty J., John T. Gillespie, and Diana L. Spirt. *Administering the School Library Media Center*. 3d ed. New Providence, N.J.: R. R. Bowker, 1992.

Newby, Timothy J., Donald A. Stepich, James D. Lehman, and James D. Russell. *Instructional Technology for Teaching and Learning: Designing Instruction, Integrating Computers, and Using Media*. Columbus, Ohio: Merrill, 1996.

Olive, J. Fred. *The Educational Technology Profession: A Bibliographic Overview of a Profession in Search of Itself*. Englewood Cliffs, N.J.: Educational Technology Publications, 1995.

Plomp, Tjeerd, and Donald P. Ely. *International Encyclopedia of Educational Technology*. 2d ed. New York: Pergamon Press, 1996.

Ritchie, Mark L. *Quality Management for Educational Technology Services*. Washington, D.C.: Association for Educational Communications and Technology, 1994.

Rudin, Claire. *The School Librarian's Sourcebook*. New Providence, N.J.: R. R. Bowker, 1990.

Saettler, Paul. *The Evolution of American Educational Technology*. Englewood, Colo.: Libraries Unlimited, 1990.

———. *History of Instructional Technology*. New York: McGraw-Hill, 1968.

Wilson, Brent B., ed. *Constructivist Environments: Case Studies in Instructional Design*. Englewood Cliffs, N.J.: Educational Technology Publications, 1997.

Yesner, Bernice L., and Hilda L. Jay. *Operating and Evaluating School Library Media Programs: A Handbook for Administrators and Librarians*. New York: Neal-Schuman, 1998.

2

PHILOSOPHICAL PERSPECTIVES

. . . this is not to imply that only when all else fails should the communications worker rely on philosophy. Rather, it underscores the utility of philosophy as a starting point—as, in fact, the alternative to wild extrapolation from scientific data or to mindless improvisation based on incoherent impulses.

A. W. Vandermeer, in *Educational Media: Theory into Practice*, edited by Raymond V. Wiman and Wesley C. Meierhenry, 1969

OBJECTIVES

At the conclusion of this chapter you should be able to

1. Describe how a media manager's personal philosophy will serve him or her in managing a media service program.

2. Describe some useful steps in developing your own media management philosophical statements.

3. State seven or more philosophical tenets that managers have found useful.

4. Develop a philosophical foundation upon which to base your career as a media service program manager.

5. Describe some of the key elements of the philosophy of working media managers.

This chapter focuses upon an important element with which media managers must concern themselves early in their career, namely, the philosophical framework within which they operate. Most people will agree that getting a handle on philosophy is sometimes difficult but that the task is an essential undertaking for executives in any field. The old saying, "If you don't know where you are going, any place will do," can be applied to management with some minor changes if one keeps in mind that philosophy is a major guide for managers. The statement then becomes, "If you don't know where you are coming from, how can you lead and manage the activities of others?"

Contrary to some popular thought, philosophy does not belong in or to the past; nor is it the property of the great thinkers and writers through the ages. Philosophy is a part of all of us; it is a vital part of managing oneself and an essential element in the management of almost any kind of unit, company, or institution.

VALUE OF A PHILOSOPHY

Media administrators face continuing as well as unexpected problems requiring decisions that are consistent and straightforward. Therefore, practitioners must work from a sound, stable base and framework from which decisions can be made; otherwise, those decisions may prove to be unworkable and inconsistent. It is easy enough to come up with unworkable decisions even when one has a pretty good idea of what one believes, but the problems are greatly exacerbated if one does not have a well-developed set of principles.

Everyone operates from a personal philosophy which, stated or unstated, written or unwritten, comprises his or her personal guidance system. Thus one's beliefs, concepts, attitudes, and values express the basic philosophy that has been growing and developing within for years. Certainly philosophy is never static; it must of necessity grow and change as new, different, and more difficult challenges are met. Reading what others have written about themselves and their thoughts and philosophies is well worth the time because such expositions may raise thoughts, ideas, and concepts that might not have occurred to the reader otherwise. Thus others can contribute a great deal to the development of one's own philosophy. Life forces each of us to formulate a philosophy to guide us along our respective ways. In essence, regardless of whether you have read or thought much about philosophy, your belief structure is your philosophy!

Michael Hammer, in *Beyond Reengineering* (1996, 133), lays out his thoughts about a philosophical framework:

> Through personal example, direct interaction, and endless communications the leader fosters the attitudes and spirit that a high-performance organization requires. Reduced to short phrases, the messages can sound simplistic and cliched: your work matters; we are all on the same team, the customer pays our salaries. But brought to life by a true leader, they are uplifting and inspirational. There is no substitute for sincerity; simply mouthing politically correct platitudes does not make for inspiration or leadership. The true leader must express his or her own inner visions and beliefs, not simply cite the conventional wisdom.

Stephen R. Covey and his associates, in *First Things First* (1994, 116), added these thoughts:

> Vision is the fundamental force that drives everything else in our lives. It impassions us with a sense of the unique contribution that's ours to make. It empowers us to put first things first, compasses ahead of clocks, people ahead of schedules and things.

Clearly, what you believe affects everything you do. Thus from a managerial standpoint, it is essential for managers to know with some surety just where and how he or she stands; otherwise thoughtful action is impossible. As leaders, executives must know what they believe in and can support. Of course, individuals must believe in themselves above all, but beyond that, as Thomas J. Peters and Robert H. Waterman observed in their book *In Search of Excellence* (1982, 280):

> Every excellent company that we studied is clear on what it stands for, and takes the problem of value shaping seriously. In fact, we wonder whether it is possible to be an excellent company without clarity on values and without having the right sorts of values.

So it seems that the ancient Greek admonition to "know thyself" holds true, not only for individuals but for other kinds of entities as well. As often as one hears this piece of advice, seldom does the person giving the advice offer any clues as to how to go about the *knowing*. The discovery process is not all that difficult, though it does require that one be totally honest with oneself, and that perhaps is the most difficult part of the task. The writers would like to propose that there is little to be gained by trying to put one's entire philosophy down on paper. There is too much involved, and the philosophy will probably change in some respects even as it is being written. However, setting down in outline form the specifics of a limited area of philosophy can contribute materially to the process of determining the best route to follow when making decisions. The ultimate objective of this kind of exercise is to enable one to make decisions and set policies that all concerned—the boss, yourself, your "clients," and your staff—can live with.

Perhaps at this point it would be a good idea to take a look at a well-known philosophy that began with one simple, basic idea. This is an example of a good working philosophy because over the years the related thoughts, values, concepts, and ideas that developed from the initial concept have been shaped and modified as the times and conditions warranted. If modification of a philosophy is not possible, that philosophy is either dead or not a philosophy at all.

Most philosophies will never become nearly as complex as the example at hand, but in this case, though simply stated at the outset, the philosophy serves millions of people and thus of necessity has become much more complex as the philosophy and the people it serves have grown and developed. Its antecedents extend to England and the Magna Carta, but Patrick Henry gave the concept a different twist as he stood before the Virginia Convention in 1765 and gave voice to his desire (and the desire of most colonists) to be free from an oppressive British rule:

> Is life so dear, or peace so sweet, as to be purchased at the price of chains and slavery? Forbid it Almighty God! I know not what course others may take, but as for me, give me liberty or give me death! (Bartlett 1901)

This speech set in motion events that eventually resulted in the writing of the Declaration of Independence. The Declaration started the American Revolution, and the colonists wrote a new set of laws, the Articles of Confederation, which were formulated to support their newly won "freedom" philosophy. These articles were brought forth, tried out, and found to be sadly wanting. Shortly they were discarded to make way for the Constitution of the United States. As needs were discovered and changes indicated, a bill of rights was adopted and other laws enacted. For over two hundred years the Constitution has been amended and laws interpreting it have been passed to give continuing life to our ever-growing, changing philosophy of freedom; and the process is still going on. That is a very short exposition of a philosophy that grew. Today, as we know and live this philosophy, so should we also know the aspects of the other philosophies by which we work and live.

DEVELOPING YOUR PHILOSOPHY

It is imperative that one know the philosophies that surround him or her and how those philosophies will affect all concerned. There is a pencil-and-paper process that can help to determine the guiding philosophies that influence managerial decision making. Looking at management from a problem-solving standpoint requires several steps: (1) identify each problem as it occurs as precisely as possible and write it down; (2) note in outline form the major guiding philosophy of the company or institution for which you work; (3) determine what your personal philosophy is and how it relates to the institution's philosophy; and (4) specify the mission of your unit and how it relates to the mission of the institution. With all of the pertinent elements and philosophies identified and outlined on paper, it is much easier to get down to specifics and begin to analyze how one element affects or is affected by another and what the best course or courses of action might be for solving each specific problem as it occurs.

The guiding philosophy of an institution or company is usually pretty clearly defined. For a Maytag employee, for instance, the guiding philosophical statement would be "Ten Years Trouble-Free Operation" (Peters and Waterman 1982, 174). On the surface this seems to be a simple statement, but upon examination one finds that it is more than adequate owing to the implications that can be drawn from it when one gives the statement some thought. In practice this company philosophy not only controls what goes into its product but also how the workers are to do the job of assembly. The statement assures that the product is good, simple, durable, and properly assembled. Maytag's advertising is also extracted from the simple five-word statement; witness the television ads about the "lonely Maytag repairman"—no one calls him because so little goes wrong with their Maytag machines.

For an employee of McDonald's, the guiding philosophy is Q, S, C, and V, which stands for "Quality, Service, Cleanliness, and Value" (Peters and Waterman 1982, 172). Managers who do not pay enough attention to this corporate philosophy stand the chance of being fired or losing their franchise. Again, the guiding philosophy is stated in a simple and direct manner, but keep in mind that these "philosophical" slogans are the product of some rather careful thought. A slogan that can express a corporate philosophy in a few well-chosen words is the result of reflective rather than "off the top of the head" thinking.

For most educational institutions, the guiding philosophy might be something like the following statement: "The needs of the student come first!" Thus your job as a media manager must involve finding out what those needs are and how you and your unit can best meet those needs.

One must look beyond the surface meaning when examining a philosophy, because the implications inherent in the words may not leap forth initially. For instance, the McDonald's philosophy reveals that there is much to be drawn from Q, S, C, and V. Each of the key words can provide guidance in depth and dictate both thought and action.

Quality: The *public* looks for quality. This means that quality must permeate everything: the foods used, the food handling, and the physical setting in which the food is produced and consumed. Certainly the term also bears on the attitude expressed by the employees.

Service: The *public* looks for quick courteous service and smiling people, ready and willing to meet requests with pleasure.

Cleanliness: The *public* expects the restaurant that they patronize to be clean. Thus one would expect the employees, from the boss on down, to use idle moments to clean things up in front of and behind the counters as well as in the yard and parking area.

Value: Very simply, *customers* want their money's worth; they do not want to be overcharged.

The above does not exhaust the possibilities, but it is apparent that with thought this philosophy is certainly adequate to guide everyone in the corporation, from the chairman of the board to the counter workers. Everyone knows what to look for, and if something is not clear one needs only to go back to what he or she has outlined on paper and refine the outline further, looking for facets of the philosophy that were not evident before.

In a sense a philosophy is much like a diamond—it is three-dimensional, with a multitude of facets covering its entire surface. A diamond reflects light in all directions, as does a philosophy. Through its facets, a philosophy reflects thoughts, feelings, attitudes, and values. These philosophical facets fit together closely, one juxtaposed to another, with each contributing to the brilliance of the others, and all facets coming together to make up the complete philosophy. Each facet reflects one aspect of the total and represents something to which one can commit oneself and be able to live with, day by day and decision by decision. Each facet of the philosophy contributes a measure of understanding to and about other facets. When one has a good understanding of one's philosophy, hidden uncertainties regarding the value of one's goals and actions are greatly reduced and thus the decision-making process is enhanced. This does not mean that life will be easier, however, for honestly held and defended beliefs may well bring one into conflict and disagreement with others holding contrary views.

The philosophy of a group, an institution, a corporation, or some other entity usually stems from the personal philosophies of the leaders within. The key to determining and understanding a philosophy or philosophies involves, for the most part, careful, conscious thought about stated beliefs in a manner that draws specifics from broad generalizations. The importance of this kind of philosophical digging and thinking must not be underestimated, because it is through such critical examination and the understandings gained from it that one fosters the long-term survival of self and job in this highly competitive world.

The formulation and growth of the philosophy that guides an individual, a group, an institution, or a business calls for an ongoing dialogue with oneself or among some aggregate of people brought together to believe something or to achieve something together. In other words, one has to ask many questions or make many statements and then question them in order to develop and refine a working philosophy.

From a survival standpoint, the question to be asked as one examines all, or parts, of a philosophy is simply, "Can I live with this?" If, upon examining the philosophy of the entity for which one works, one answers "No, I cannot live with this" in response to a major tenet of the philosophy, it may be necessary to find work elsewhere. At the least, it means that the search for a philosophical tenet that one can live with continues. Being able to live with something does not always mean that the course selected is easy or comfortable. In fact, *living* might be viewed as a continuum that is rated as happy at one end, comfortable in the middle, and difficult on the other end. Many times the philosophical tenet that one feels compelled to champion may be located on the difficult end of the continuum. When it comes to managerial decisions, the critical question to be asked changes ever so slightly. Now the manager should ask, "Can *we* live with this?" because the company or institution, the administration, the internal units, and the employees will all be affected and must be considered prior to any decision making. If, after decisions have been implemented, it is found that things do not function as expected, some changes may be indicated and should be undertaken following a careful review and analysis. This might be identified as the refining phase in the development of a working philosophy and, to a greater or lesser extent, the process should be continuous.

Usually, as one works to make a philosophical concept or idea operational, a more complex design evolves. The elements can be easily isolated for study, understanding, and/or dissemination if all of the elements of the philosophical tenet under review are stated in outline form using short, simple, understandable statements. Thus a complex philosophical entity is taken apart and disassembled into simpler concepts, ideas, and values. After due consideration the entity may be assembled again, with perhaps something deleted and something added to take its place. This process of adding and deleting continues until the philosophy becomes tuned more finely and reflects more closely those whom it serves.

USEFUL PHILOSOPHICAL TENETS

There are many general philosophical facets that might well fit into a sound management philosophy. Only a selected few will be presented in this chapter for consideration. Some you may agree with in whole or in part, and some you may not agree with at all. This is as it should be; as you read, you may want to note your reactions to the ideas set forth and perhaps create some of your own. To some, you may comment "Well, I knew that!" The question is, have you considered it as part of a philosophy? A great deal of what follows has been proposed by people who are rated as good executives.

A primary tenet or facet in management is "Knowledge precedes action." Perhaps this concept should be number one on any list of philosophical tenets, but wherever it is placed it cannot be ignored. One of the highest accolades that one hears about a manager is often, "He does his homework," or "She knows her stuff," or perhaps "She's always prepared." Having done one's homework usually means that one has not only developed a comprehensive background in a field but also stays current and on the cutting edge of that field. Managers who prepare themselves after the fact, after a need has been demonstrated, all too often find that it is too late and that someone has stolen the march on them. Many excellent opportunities can be lost this way. Managers should prepare ahead, insofar as is possible, for meetings, conferences, the unexpected, and the future. The Boy Scouts covered this with one simple statement: "Be prepared." A scout was to be well versed, not only in the general area of scouting, but also in specific areas of knowledge related to scouting. "Be prepared," and perhaps "Plan ahead," should certainly be part of an active working philosophy.

Looking at the matter of decision making and implementing action, managers must endeavor to "Be proactive." Good management practices dictate that managers are leaders and therefore must be ready to take action. Proactive managers do not wait for things to happen, rather they try to anticipate and, to a certain extent, create what their unit will be doing. Forward-thinking managers will try to foresee problems with a view to taking care of them *before* they present themselves for solution. Reactive managers, on the other hand, lean toward the idea that one can succeed by evading difficult decisions, the premise being "If you don't do anything, you can't do anything wrong." This idea may work for a while, but in the long run the unit will become less and less productive and upper management will do something about it. Proactive managers more than likely figure that "If you aren't making mistakes now and again, you aren't doing anything." Proactive managers are reactive, however, to the extent that they become very good at handling problems and emergencies quickly and effectively as soon as they arise. One thing is inevitable: Emergencies and foul-ups will occur just as surely as day follows night. "Anything that can happen, will!" is an axiom that most managers live by, and thus they must be proactive/reactive in their thinking. This is particularly true for managers who work for clients. In the media field, the writers know of no managers in either the public or private sector who do not work for clients coming from within or outside of the "company."

One aspect of being proactive, however, is that one must use care to avoid trying to see too far ahead, thereby wasting creative energies worrying about problems that have not arrived or that may not exist. The caution here is "Don't borrow trouble," but be prepared to meet and handle it whenever it arises.

Following a little further along this line of thinking, one must recognize when a cause is lost and be prepared to drop it once he or she is sure that there is little or nothing to be gained by pursuing it further. Hearkening back to the events that precipitated the American Revolution, Benjamin Franklin observed that the revolution could have been avoided if England, under George III, had not been so committed to the enforcement of policies that obviously did not work! When a cause has lost out, for whatever reason, it is time to move ahead without regrets, as long as one can say, "I gave it my best shot and this is what I learned." The guideline then, in the words of the immortal baseball player Satchel Paige, is "Never look back."

Managers must not put off or avoid making difficult decisions. The manager who procrastinates will usually find that problems that are initially small quickly grow out of proportion to their originally perceived importance. It is best to recognize and settle problems immediately, before they become too big to handle easily. Managers who operate in continual crises of their own making usually do not last very long. Thus the "administrators don't delay difficult decisions" concept should be a part of every manager's philosophy. Harry Truman is remembered as a president who believed in confronting problems early on by gathering as much information as possible, making a decision, believing in the position taken, and actively promoting it. The book, *Where the Buck Stops*, summarizes his philosophy (Truman 1989, 75–113). Prompt response to problems is only one small aspect of a total philosophy; there is much more to be considered. It does not matter whether one is talking about media management in business, industry, or education, as there is a common thread of activities and problems that seem to run through all, wherever they are located.

Now a look at communication, an area that should hold considerable interest for managers. A continuous flow of information is essential to good management. Managers must be able to convey their thoughts, concerns, and ideas in the most easily understood form possible. Usually information will flow fairly well horizontally among those working at the same level, but the information flow vertically, up and down the organizational ladder, does not always take place as readily. The media manager must give this aspect special attention, for the manager is responsible for facilitating the flow of timely and accurate information in both directions. In their role as communicators, managers have to be effective simplifiers, so the philosophical guideline here might be "Keep it simple." A good executive will carefully extract essential information from its usually more complex matrix and present those essentials to others in an understandable and easily assimilated form. Doing so does not mean that everyone, particularly upper management, is going to listen and get the message, but careful attention to what you present will materially increase the possibilities for a favorable reception.

Richard Deupree, a past president of Procter and Gamble Corporation, demanded that P & G managers cut to the heart of a matter in their memos to him. He told memo writers to "Boil it down to something I can grasp!" and stated further that "I don't understand complicated problems, I only understand simple ones" (Peters and Waterman 1982, 150). What he was after were one-page memos that stripped ideas and problems down to their basics and made it necessary to deal with them before they became too complicated or involved, thereby reducing the possibility for sloppy thinking to arise. For Deupree, as it should be for most of us, simplicity is the key.

Many more simple but important guiding and managerial philosophical statements can be developed. A few additional examples are "Listen, listen, and listen some more," "Involve staff," "Stretch yourself," and "Delegate thoughtfully."

ELEMENTS OF WORKING MEDIA MANAGERS' PHILOSOPHIES

What elements make a good media center? Surely the philosophy of what drives a media center should include such elements. In a study by one of the authors, reported in *Learning Resources Programs That Make a Difference*, twenty-seven media programs at all educational levels around the nation were studied (Schmidt 1987). These exemplary programs were selected through a nominating process. During the interview process, each learning resources program's director was asked which single factor was the main source of the program's strength. It was not surprising that, in education as in private business, providing good service surfaced as one of the main sources of the strength of an organization. Peters and Waterman (1982) quote a large corporation's marketing vice president as saying: "It's a shame that, in so many companies, whenever you get good service, it's an exception" (14). They go on to say that is not the case in excellent companies. In the Schmidt study, another frequent response to the question regarding the source of a program's strength was a good staff, particularly professional and leader-manager types. Other responses were administrative support, good communication, and the right type of organizational arrangement. Following are the actual responses (Schmidt 1987, 109):*

Service

"A philosophy of ensuring client satisfaction."

"A long-time record of consistency of good service."

"Good service!"

"Responding to users' needs."

"Providing good service to the faculty."

"The ability to serve the entire institution and not just an elite part of it."

"Helping the vice-president to meet mission goals in public relations."

"A service philosophy that no problem is too big or too small."

"The ability of staff members to help the faculty and staff of the college."

Staffing

"A highly qualified professional staff."

"The leadership provided by eight professionals."

"The quality of the staff and their positive relationship with faculty at large (professionals having faculty rank helps achieve this)."

"The strength of the management people."

"A dedicated staff."

"Having a school library media specialist in every school in the district."

"The quality of the staff."

Administrative Support

"The support given by decision makers."

"The school board is very interested in students being trained to understand and use the newer technologies."

"The support of the administration."

"Having continued financial support with few cutbacks."

"Support from the administration."

"Administrative support in terms of budget for equipment and materials."

Communication

"Maintaining of close contact with users."

"Anticipating and meeting teacher and administrator needs."

"Communication with clients to assess their needs."

Organizational Arrangement

"Being able to report directly to the chief administrative officer of the agency."

"The centralization of all resources (rather than being fragmented)."

"The integration of all learning resources (including the training of media specialists) into one program."

Other

"The strength of our telecommunications distribution system using a regional microwave and earth station."

"Curriculum involvement making media program a viable and indispensable part of the school system."

"Gained credibility as a general consulting service for instructional problem solving."

"A cost recovery program (through charge-back and fees) that has enabled the center to continue to deliver services during times of cut-backs."

SUGGESTED ACTIVITIES

1. Reflect on some of your previous work experiences and list actions by managers that you perceived were good and bad. For each action develop a philosophical statement that would explain the manager's action.

2. Develop a list of philosophical statements to use in guiding the development of your management style.

REFERENCES

Bartlett, John. 1901. *Familiar Quotations*. 9th ed. Boston: Little, Brown, and Company.

Covey, Stephen R., A. Roger Merrill, and Rebecca R. Merrill. 1994. *First Things First: To Live, to Love, to Learn, to Leave a Legacy*. New York: Simon & Schuster.

Hammer, Michael. 1996. *Beyond Reengineering: How the Process-Centered Organization Is Changing Our Work and Our Lives*. New York: HarperBusiness.

Peters, Thomas J., and Robert H. Waterman, Jr. 1982. *In Search of Excellence: Lessons from America's Best-Run Companies*. New York: Warner Books.

Schmidt, William D. 1987. *Learning Resources Programs That Make a Difference*. Washington, D.C.: Association for Educational Communications and Technology.

Truman, Margaret. 1989. *Where the Buck Stops: The Personal and Private Writings of Harry S. Truman*. New York: Warner Books.

Wiman, Raymond V., and Wesley C. Meierhenry, eds. 1969. *Educational Media: Theory into Practice.* Columbus, Ohio: Merrill.

SELECTED BIBLIOGRAPHY

Boyer, Carlton H. *Philosophical Perspectives for Education.* Glenview, Ill.: Scott, Foresman, 1970.

Carter, Franklin. *Mark Hopkins.* Boston: Houghton Mifflin, 1892.

Dickens, Charles. *Hard Times.* New York: E. P. Dutton, 1916.

Elliott, Godfrey, ed. *Film and Education.* New York: Philosophical Library, 1948.

Herbert, Joanne M., and Robert F. McNergney. *Foundations of Education.* Boston: Allyn & Bacon, 1995.

James, William. *Talks to Teachers on Psychology.* New York: Henry Holt, 1916.

Jowett, Benjamin, trans. *The Dialogues of Plato.* Chicago: Encyclopaedia Britannica, 1952.

Laurie, S. S. *John Amos Comenius.* New York: C. W. Bardeen, 1892.

Pepper, William. *Benjamin Franklin: Proposals Relating to the Education of Youth in Pensilvania.* Philadelphia: University of Pennsylvania Press, 1931.

Thompson, Keith. *Education and Philosophy: A Practical Approach.* Oxford, England: Blackwell and Mott, 1972.

Twain, Mark. *What Is Man? and Other Essays.* New York: Harper & Bros., 1917.

Urquhart, Sir Thomas, and Peter Motteux, trans. *Francois Rabelais: Gargantua and Pantagruel.* Chicago: Encyclopaedia Britannica, 1952.

3

PLANNING MEDIA SERVICE PROGRAMS

*One overriding fact must be understood from the very beginning:
The structure and administration of American education is incom-
patible with technological innovation. The rigid curriculum, scheduling,
subject matter compartmentalization, lecture-print orientation, and
previous training of teachers and administrators all contribute to re-
sistance to change of any kind. When the threat of this change
shakes not one but all of these traditions, it becomes obvious that
innovations will be made only after considerable struggle and then
only in a piecemeal way.*

William H. Allen, "Audiovisual Instruction: The State of the
Art," in *The Schools and the Challenge of Innovation*, 1969

OBJECTIVES

At the conclusion of this chapter you should be able to

1. Describe the purpose of a needs assessment program.

2. List and discuss essential information that should be gathered in a needs assessment program.

3. Discuss the advantages and disadvantages of integrating print and nonprint collections and services within an institution.

4. Discuss some advantages and disadvantages of consolidating all media and technology services.

5. Discuss the reasons for centralized and decentralized media service centers and how they should be organized.

6. List the pros and cons of charging patrons for media services.

7. Name and discuss two inescapable limitations that must be addressed when planning media service programs.

8. Describe how those limitations can be addressed in a media service program proposal.

9. Describe the elements that should be included in a new or improved media service program proposal.

10. List and describe four major groups of individuals within an institution's power structure who must be identified and their support obtained if a proposal is to be funded and implemented.

William Allen's comment (page 33) about the difficulty of achieving techno-logical innovation in American education, though written in 1969, is still valid. Though computer-assisted instruction and advanced video technologies have made great inroads into education, the media manager must realize that some of the early biases remain and must proceed cautiously in planning and organizing media pro-grams. Always carefully examine the task at hand. What do my clients need? What kinds of technologies can I deliver to help meet those needs? What has happened in the past? Were there unmet expectations, examples of inferior service rendered, or inadequate staff and resources? Tread carefully into territories where some of the traditions Allen detailed may still exist, albeit in a dormant, covert state. Having said that, it must be stated there is more receptiveness to new technology at the present than has ever been true. Enjoy this new acceptance!

WHERE TO BEGIN

It is easy to understand why media managers ask many questions of others when one looks at the complex problems involved in directing the various activities found in most media centers. This is true for experienced managers as much as for beginning managers. It is doubly true for a manager moving into a new position. Still, the same questions are asked whether the information is elicited for an ongo-ing program or for setting up a new operation. To begin this chapter, let us establish a hypothetical situation:

> You have applied for the position of manager of a media center. Prior to being interviewed you reviewed the job requirements and job description and gathered information about the employing or-ganization from various sources. During the interview you asked questions about the services provided by the center, budget alloca-tions to support services, and staff and workloads. During a tour of the facility and the institution, you observed the staff at work, met the person to whom the media director reports, and devel-oped a generally favorable impression of the overall situation. Sev-eral weeks later you were offered the position and you accepted it. Now anticipation and anxiety creep in as you realize that whatever you know about the situation, it is not nearly enough! Questions begin to arise: When I start work, where do I begin? What do I need to know about the center's clients and their needs? Does the budget support the program? Are high-quality services presently provided? Have the existing services been evaluated? Do the services meet the needs of the clients?

As you can see, a media manager reporting to a new position faces a variety of tasks and concerns. There is, of course, a "honeymoon" period during which you will be expected to take up the reins of management of the unit. Answers to the previously posed questions, and more, must be found quickly if you are to establish a solid foundation of knowledge that will help to build and improve service programs. This chapter will provide some guidelines to help plan, implement, and evaluate service programs whether they presently exist or are being developed from scratch.

DETERMINING PROGRAM NEEDS

Effective media services cannot be developed unless the center's manager has acquired in-depth knowledge regarding both the media center and client needs. This chapter presents the collection of information that is necessary as one plans new programs or expands existing ones. For the most part, the same basic information is required for both planning activities. There are some differences, however, and the reader should keep this in mind when searching out information regarding what is required. In either case, the first step is to undertake a needs assessment that is designed to elicit information about the current status of the center and directions that the center should take in the future. Knowing where one is and where one needs to go is critical for the media manager. The following information is essential for conducting a needs assessment.

What media services are presently provided? This information can usually be elicited from a review of promotional materials, annual reports, discussion with center staff members, and a review of various circulation forms. An inventory of the center's equipment collections and departmental collections may also provide useful information (see figure 3.1).

Who uses the services? Find out who the center's clients are. Such data may be located in annual reports and other documents or files. Look for information that indicates which departments do or do not use media center services as well as for information regarding the extent of use by active departments. If no annual report is available, a review of past service request forms, while tedious, may provide some insights. Again, informal discussions with center employees may provide further information. Periodic program reviews and user surveys will also yield valuable information. As one reviews data gathered, it is a good idea to start thinking about what kinds of information to include in future annual summaries so that the machinery to collect the appropriate data can be put into operation. If information is not methodically collected, it may be impossible to collect the required data later. The ongoing collection and organization of data pertinent to the center's operation will be needed eventually to provide guidelines and information for various reports, plans, and projections.

How effective are the services presently being provided? If evaluations of the center's services have been administered, first study the instrument used to determine if the center is effective. The information requested should not be superficial or slanted. Assuming that the instrument is adequate, look at the results to determine the perceived strengths and weaknesses of the service programs. A new manager can look good quickly by correcting minor problems and weaknesses. Sometimes vexing problems will yield to small adjustments that other people might have missed. If no formal evaluation has been administered, then develop and administer one as soon as possible. You will gain valuable information and at the same time let your clients know that you exist and desire to offer the services they need. Here again, informal discussions with clients and potential clients will help to build goodwill.

	NUMBER	UNITS OWNED BY CENTER	UNITS OWNED BY DEPARTMENTS	YEAR PURCHASED
MEDIA EQUIPMENT:				
Projection Screens	_____	_____	_____	_____
Wall Type	_____	_____	_____	_____
Tripod Type	_____	_____	_____	_____
Film Projectors, 16mm	_____	_____	_____	_____
Slide Projectors	_____	_____	_____	_____
Sound/Slide Projectors	_____	_____	_____	_____
Opaque Projectors	_____	_____	_____	_____
Overhead Projectors	_____	_____	_____	_____
Record Players	_____	_____	_____	_____
Audiotape Recorders	_____	_____	_____	_____
Cassette	_____	_____	_____	_____
Reel to Reel	_____	_____	_____	_____
PA Systems	_____	_____	_____	_____
Compact Disc Players	_____	_____	_____	_____
Videodisc Players	_____	_____	_____	_____
Other: Attach List				
TELEVISION EQUIPMENT:				
Television Receivers	_____	_____	_____	_____
Television Cameras	_____	_____	_____	_____
Television Recorders				
Beta	_____	_____	_____	_____
VHS	_____	_____	_____	_____
U Matic	_____	_____	_____	_____
Other	_____	_____	_____	_____
Television Projectors	_____	_____	_____	_____
Studio Components: Attach List				
Other: Attach List				
MAINTENANCE AND REPAIR:				
Film Inspection Machine	_____	_____	_____	_____
Videotape Inspection Machine	_____	_____	_____	_____
Electronic Test Equipment: Attach List				
Fabrication Equipment: Attach List				
Other: Attach List				

(Figure 3.1 continues on p. 38.)

	NUMBER	UNITS OWNED BY CENTER	UNITS OWNED BY DEPARTMENTS	YEAR PURCHASED

PHOTO AND GRAPHIC PRODUCTION:

Cameras, Still	_____	_____	_____	_____
Cameras, 8mm	_____	_____	_____	_____
Cameras, 16mm	_____	_____	_____	_____
Cameras, Vertical	_____	_____	_____	_____
Cameras, Horizontal	_____	_____	_____	_____
Dry Mounting Presses	_____	_____	_____	_____
Laminators	_____	_____	_____	_____
Typewriters	_____	_____	_____	_____
Typesetters	_____	_____	_____	_____
Lettering Devices	_____	_____	_____	_____
Slide Mounter	_____	_____	_____	_____
Film Processors	_____	_____	_____	_____

Darkroom Photographic Equipment: Attach List

Other: Attach List

COMPUTING EQUIPMENT:

Microcomputers				
DOS/Windows	_____	_____	_____	_____
MAC	_____	_____	_____	_____
Other	_____	_____	_____	_____
CD-ROM Drives	_____	_____	_____	_____
Terminals	_____	_____	_____	_____
Scanners	_____	_____	_____	_____
Digital Cameras	_____	_____	_____	_____
Data Projectors	_____	_____	_____	_____
Multiscan Projectors	_____	_____	_____	_____
Multiscan Monitors	_____	_____	_____	_____
Printers—Types: Attach List				
Other: Attach List				

Figure 3.1. Media services equipment inventory.

What services do the center's clients require? Changes in existing media services cannot be made effectively without first determining client needs and wants. In most cases this means getting out and asking around. Employ every possible technique in gathering such information: Distribute questionnaires and meet with groups, administrators, department heads, and individual clients (see figure 3.2, page 40, and appendix 1, page 365). Carry your message to the users. Often potential users do not know what services are available or what they have a right to expect. The aforementioned techniques not only result in the collection of useful data but also serve as promotional tools for informing potential clients about available services. Involve your staff by asking for their observations regarding needed services or improvements. Ask all to prioritize their perceived needs. Then analyze the data and prioritize the needs as indicated by the collected body of information.

Who is not using center services? Why? Are there potential clients who for unknown reasons have not used the services? Perhaps they do not know about the center, have had a bad experience, or do not want to change the way they operate. Regardless of the reasons, try to determine who these people are and why they do not use the services. Again, appropriate surveys and informal interviews will prove useful in eliciting information and at the same time let others know that the center is there for them.

Are existing collections and facilities adequate? The big question here is, "What is adequate?" A center might have a large film library that is relatively unused because much of its collections are either out of date or are not appropriate for present needs. A much smaller collection of current, carefully selected materials on critical topics may prove to be more than adequate by comparison. The only way to obtain answers to such questions is to look at circulation records to determine what is used and how often. Such information should be available for all media center collections. Materials that do not meet existing needs should be identified, stored, or discarded, and equipment that continually breaks down should be replaced. A review of circulation and maintenance records should provide this information. Out-of-date materials and malfunctioning equipment will discourage interest in media use more quickly than almost any other problem. Adequacy of the center's collections is critical to its survival.

What personnel are available to provide services? Check job descriptions, review staff personnel files, and study the organizational chart to determine staff training, experience, skills, and placement of staff. Talk with individual staff members about their jobs. How do they view what they do? Do they have suggestions that will improve services? What are their complaints? Answers to these questions will assist in determining how to make the best use of staff.

What are the institutional expectations? Another way to phrase this is "What kind of program will the institution and its administrators support?" Unfortunately, in too many cases this becomes a budget matter. Administrators approve budgets and in that way express their support for service programs. The media manager must look at what administrators do, not what they say, as lip service seldom translates into dollars. It is a waste of time to attempt to develop a broad-based program if it is not supported. The needs assessment data and interviews with administrators should provide this kind of information prior to developing program plans. When

Institution/Branch_____ Department _____ Date _____

1. What do you consider to be the strongest features of the media services program?
   a.
   b.
   c.
   d.

2. What do you consider to be the limitations of the media services program?
   a.
   b.
   c.
   d.

3. How could those limitations be corrected?

4. What services would you like to have provided that are not now available?
   a.
   b.
   c.
   d.

5. Are adequate media resources easily available for your use? Answer yes or no.

   EQUIPMENT   **MATERIALS**
   _____ 16mm projectors   _____ Films
   _____ Filmstrip projectors   _____ Videocassettes
   _____ Sound filmstrip projectors   _____ Videodiscs
   _____ Sound/slide projectors   _____ Filmstrips
   _____ Overhead projectors   _____ CD-ROMs
   _____ Projection screen   _____ Slide sets
   _____ Audiotape recorders   _____ Transparencies
   _____ Compact disc players   _____ Records
   _____ Record players   _____ Audiotapes
   _____ PA equipment   _____ Compact discs
   _____ Camcorders   _____ Computer software
   _____ Television monitors   _____ Other: Please list
   _____ Videodisc players
   _____ Microcomputers
   _____ Scanners
   _____ Other: Please list

6. What facilities would you like to see added to the media center for your use?

7. Comments:

Figure 3.2. Media services user questionnaire.

planning for new programs or services, it may be necessary to pin things down as well as is possible regarding the dollar amounts that will be allocated. Remember that many administrators are not knowledgeable about media services and do not really know what to support. It is the media manager's job to inform, educate, and sell the programs. Usually this is a long-term effort that may take years. It is a task that is never finished. The manager must constantly provide information about the center's programs, needs, and clients. He or she should find out what other similar entities are doing and demonstrate a cost-benefit-value basis for the services the center provides. Certainly this is not an easy task when dealing in services and products that are used within the organization in ways that are difficult to measure. However, extensive information must be collected and presented to those who control the money. An example of a preliminary budget proposal by service levels for the purpose of obtaining administrative support is presented later in this chapter.

What are similar media centers doing? Given all of the preceding information, a media manager should visit other programs prior to making any formal proposals for media service program changes or development. Visitations and observation of other programs can engender new ideas and refine existing ones. The media executive who does not use and value the experience of others is overlooking a valuable resource. Why discover the wheel all over again when one can profit from the experience of others?

What existing standards or guidelines may support center needs? The existing literature within the media field contains a great deal of information that may relate to the goals and objectives of an institution's media center. The American Association of School Librarians (AASL) and the Association for Educational Communications and Technology (AECT) have developed joint guidelines for media services for K-12 public schools (AASL and AECT 1988). AECT has developed standards for higher education (AECT 1989). The National Council for the Accreditation of Teacher Education (NCATE) and U.S. regional accrediting bodies now have incorporated statements about technology needs. Standards or guidelines can be quite helpful in justifying materials, equipment, and personnel for service programs. Though guidelines have been developed for schools, none exist for business and industry owing to the diversity of needs found in the private sector. Still, existing standards may provide some useful guidelines.

Does the organization of the center lend itself to providing the client services, or could a different structure provide better and more efficient services? Does the structure lend itself to cooperation and coordination within the center? Without cooperation and coordination, wasteful duplication of effort could exist. Sometimes overdepartmentalization can result in too many service points requiring patrons to needlessly move from one area to another. Observation and careful study of the existing services may suggest a more efficient organization.

Do short-range and long-range plans exist to meet existing and future needs? A media center that does not have continually evolving short-range and long-range plans for improving services can soon become obsolete and fail to meet changing needs of patrons. Media managers must be constantly alert to changing curriculum needs, training needs, and other program changes which they now serve or could serve in the future. Short-term plans should exist for the next three to five years and long-term plans for the next six to ten years. Both long- and short-range plans are not static—they continually change. Both plans must be in agreement with the institution's expectation or mission of the media center.

It is worthwhile to reemphasize how important it is for a media manager to gather data regarding center services personally by talking with people who use or who might use the center's services. Evaluations and surveys will provide certain kinds of information, but nothing takes the place of personal contact. Information can be elicited in informal conversations that would never show up in a printed evaluation or survey. Again, this technique also puts the media manager before clients and potential clients in a very favorable way.

DECISIONS, DECISIONS, DECISIONS

Once all available information about a media service program and its clients has been collected, the manager is ready to analyze data and begin to develop program plans. Four issues regarding the center's organization may need to be considered before a plan of action can be prepared. It goes almost without saying that the center's service program must be organized in the manner that best meets client needs in an efficient and effective manner within available funding. How this is accomplished may involve some major decisions about the following questions:

If the institution has a library of print materials and the addition of audiovisual materials and services is under consideration, should the print and non-print (audiovisual software) services be integrated (intershelved) or organized separately?

Should a study of the need for consolidation (or, initially, cooperation among) all media and technology services be initiated?

Does the structure of the organization call for the centralization or decentralization of audiovisual services?

Should the center's services be provided without charge to its users?

Integrated Versus Separate Library/ Media Service Programs

This issue should be addressed early in planning. If a conventional print library and a media service program both exist, or if a media service program is being planned, should they be organized, housed, and managed together? The integration of library and media programs began in the late 1950s and has had a fairly extensive trial during the intervening years.

Many common functions are performed within both book libraries and media centers—the technical processing of acquisitions, cataloging, budgeting, and personnel management. There are also differences. Media centers provide a wide range of services not available from a traditional library, such as instructional development; media design; and graphic, photographic, video/television and multimedia production services. Other media center offerings are computer services as well as equipment and media circulation services that include making reservations for materials and equipment weeks in advance of their use. Even with these differences, it is difficult for many administrators to understand that the media personnel and budget requirements do not fit conventional library practices and formulas.

The concept that all teaching and training materials should be housed together for the convenience of the users has worked reasonably well, except in higher education. As one reads the literature and talks with media managers, it soon becomes apparent that integration efforts in higher education have experienced problems and that many efforts have failed to serve both interests well. On the other hand, some successful integrated programs do exist. Some have been developed at the higher education level, but they are much more prevalent in K-12 schools and community colleges. Why do some integrated library/media efforts succeed and others fail? A major reason seems to be the basic philosophy held by the person or persons directing the integrated organization. It is the director who is ultimately responsible for the development of the organizational structure and for shaping the attitudes of employees within the organization. Philosophy is critical. James W. Ramey, professor of library science in the graduate school at Drexel University, succinctly pointed out the difficulty:

> The plain truth of the matter is that most librarians are book oriented and plan to stay book oriented if they possibly can. Placing a book oriented librarian in a media center doesn't change a librarian. Unfortunately, all too often it does change the media center (Ramey 1971, 95).

The same can be true of a media-oriented person placed in charge of a book library. The director of an integrated library must not exhibit bias for or against any of the various collections, services, or programs within the unit. This is especially true when the nontraditional materials are brought into the library. The director must have a total view of media that does not allow undue emphasis to be placed upon one medium or another.

It has proven very difficult to find administrators who can administer the two types of programs without bias. Ideally such an administrator must have a working knowledge of both print and nonprint concepts, be an effective communicator, possess public relations skills, be a learning theorist, be a systems analyst, have administrative skills, and be dedicated to the integrated concept. Few programs to produce the requisite skills and knowledge in new graduates have been developed.

If the philosophy of the present library and media personnel within an organization does not seem conducive to successful total integration, a partial integration might be the answer. Some of the functions such as acquisitioning, cataloging, and circulating might be physically united, while the administration and budgets of the two programs remain separate. This approach could provide convenient services and at the same time eliminate any duplication of effort. Regardless of the option selected, decisions should be made on the basis of a needs assessment and the organizational structure selected that will best serve both library and media clients. The resulting organization must be one in which both services can flourish without undue restrictions.

Consolidation of All Media and Technology Services

In addition to and related to the library and media integration issue is the fact that during the last 10 to 15 years, there has been a marked trend in higher education to consolidate more media and technology services to avoid duplication. For example, two or more campus graphics units are consolidated into one. This has been driven by increasingly scarce funding. There has also been a trend to place all media and technology units under one administrator with the objective of reducing costs and fostering cooperation rather than competition. Basically, higher education is beginning to move toward more consolidated programs similar to those that have long existed in K-12 and community college media and technology programs. In a book entitled *Patterns and Options for Managing Information Technology on Campus* (Woodsworth 1991, vii), the challenge is laid out:

> As information technologies are integrated into the fabric of the campus, changes are inevitably introduced that alter the organization of the institution. Telecommunications networks, mainframe support of management, end-use microcomputers, scholars' workstations, and the library information system are new functions. Paradoxically, due to the increasingly inter-dependent yet decentralized nature of these technologies, the potential exists for either improved coordination or increased chaos in the management of the technology on campus. . . . How can visions of the ideal campus in the information age be realized: through the pervasive influence of groups of technologically literate leaders on campus? Or through strong central direction by a chief information officer (CIO)?

Consolidation, however, is a hard and bumpy road. Many of the program administrators affected fear it. Who will be in charge? Will the CIO be biased toward certain technologies? Consolidation usually has to come from the top down, or politics will preclude it from happening. Short of, or a step toward, consolidation, would be to create a mechanism by which the various media and technology units can cooperate for the benefit of their users. A new media manager in an institution would be unwise to advocate anything more than cooperation until the playing field is level.

Centralized or Decentralized Service Programs

No matter what the decision regarding the integration of print and audiovisual services or the consolidation of all media and technology services, in a large organization the question of centralization or decentralization of services must be considered. Should multiple service centers be developed or should all media services be housed in one central facility? The answer to this question can usually be found in the center's circulation statistics. If requests cannot be met because of delivery problems or extremely high utilization, then the establishment of smaller service centers throughout the institution may be indicated. There are two possibilities to be considered: (1) separate and independent media centers administered by the various departments of the institution or (2) multiple satellite centers administered from the institution's media center.

Let us look first at the option of establishing separate and independent media service centers administered by separate departments within an organization. As an example, we might consider that four departments within an institution are allowed to create their own individual graphics production units and collections of instructional materials. While the arrangement may allow maximum convenience for the users within these departments, it also creates a costly duplication of staff, equipment, facilities, and materials collections. In some cases such expenditures are justified. For example, this option exists in many medical training programs when the workload and specialty needs for artists, facilities, equipment, and materials are heavily used on-site to serve a particular function and training materials are so specific that they would not be used by others. In most instances, however, it is more efficient and economical to have media services emanating from one central unit instead of four. Experience indicates that a single graphics production unit is not only more economical in manpower and equipment but several artists can work together on rush productions. Fewer artists will be required because requests for work come from across the entire institution rather than a single department.

With regard to other services, similar savings are possible for centralized media collections—fewer staff members are required and the shared use of materials calls for fewer copies to be purchased. Similar savings can be documented for other units in a media center, such as in equipment circulation. In most cases, centralization will mean that services can be deployed more effectively and efficiently than decentralized services. Looking back at the four departments each with its own artist, two or three artists working together will, in all probability, accomplish as much or more than four artists working separately. Savings in purchasing costs can also be effected in centralized programs through discounts for quantity purchases. For instance, if the center provides rapid copy services, bulk purchases of paper from the factory can result in a saving of 25 to 30 percent over small-lot paper purchases from vendors supplying the same papers. Another advantage of a centralized program is that all of the resources of the media center are available to all departments in the institution. Departmental ownership of equipment and materials usually prevents shared use by others. The decision to centralize or to maintain centralized services depends entirely upon the individual situation, but, in general, when a department uses specific media resources daily in its program, then it makes sense to allow those particular collections of materials and equipment to be placed within that department.

The establishment of satellite centers administered by the media center is quite another story. When the various departments in an institution are heavy users of media and are separated from the center by an inconvenient distance, the logistics involved in getting materials and equipment to individuals on time and where needed becomes difficult and sometimes impossible. A further consideration is the wear and tear involved when moving equipment and materials from one place to another. In this case, the manager should consider establishing satellite service centers in those areas where the use justifies the duplication. A satellite center may possibly serve more than one department in its immediate area. The services are usually limited in nature and supply only materials and equipment. Production-type services are most often available only in the parent media center. A true satellite center is staffed with an attendant to book equipment, perform preventive maintenance, and receive and forward requests for other media services to the central media office.

In the K-12 schools, there has long been a pattern of having district media centers serve and coordinate functions performed by individual building (satellite) centers. This arrangement has never developed in higher education or in the corporate world. This stage in the evolution of media programs may be a good time for that to happen. With the powerful and often more complex new technologies, faculty, trainers, and other personnel at these levels need expert help at their workstations. Perhaps every building or large department should have an instructional technology specialist stationed in it to rapidly respond to staff needs.

A satellite center should not be confused with the practice of placing equipment on long-term loan within departments, which is a common practice and facilitates easy access for users. This system works well when equipment can be located in a secure place, the number of users is relatively small, and the users cooperate by signing the equipment out and returning it promptly when they are through with it.

Charge/No Charge

Another area of concern when developing media service programs is the matter of charging for the services rendered to clients. This is sometimes referred to as cost recovery. Let there be no mistake: Nothing is free, and somewhere a budget to cover the costs for the center's services must exist or the services cannot be provided. The issue here is how best to fund a media center's services. Should the budget be allocated to the media center so that services can be provided to users without charge, or should the budget be split among the various user departments so that the center can bill each department for services rendered? Both methods have advantages and disadvantages. The possible advantages of charging for services are:

Clients must make a judgment regarding the cost-benefit for the requested services.

Charging tends to reduce misuse of the services.

The disadvantages of making service charges may outweigh the advantages. Some of the disadvantages are:

The billing process requires additional personnel, forms, and procedures that contribute to increased operational costs.

If the retention of personnel depends upon income, and the income level varies from year to year, it may prove difficult to maintain a well-trained staff.

Service charges tend to inhibit client use. Charging adds one more level of red tape.

In most cases the disadvantages of billing for services outweigh the advantages to the extent that the authors recommend that, if at all possible, a budget be allocated directly to the media center to provide services to clients. Provision should be made for billing, however, if services are provided to clients outside of the funding organization. Sometimes other organizations may want to use materials that your center has obtained or produced. If institutional policy allows such services to be provided, then reimbursement is appropriate. However, a word of caution: Be very careful of providing services to the community, particularly if private firms may object to competition from a source that is tax-supported.

WHAT ABOUT LIMITATIONS?

In addition to the four issues just discussed that must be resolved early in the planning process, certain limitations also must be considered. Limitations crop up in everything one does. In a media center there will always be limitations that will affect the center's activities, whether it is a new center or one that has been in operation for a long time. Business, industrial, governmental, and educational institutions simply do not have unlimited resources and, therefore, constraints and limitations are a fact of life in the management of media centers.

Budget Limitations

Budgets control programs, and it is difficult for the media center director and his or her superiors to make intelligent judgments about program development without making some initial budget assessments. There is little use in planning for a wide variety of services if the institution can only afford a modest program. When planning for new or improved services, a good strategy is to prepare a proposal that details several levels of service ranging from a limited program to one that offers full services. The services that would be available at each level must be listed along with estimated costs. Those responsible for making funding decisions will then be better able to assess program possibilities before any money decisions are made.

Information for proposals should be drawn from all available sources, interviews, and evaluations. The proposals themselves must include pertinent information and should emphasize that cost estimates are preliminary and may be higher or lower when finalized. A 10 percent contingency budget, which means that the entire budget is increased by 10 percent, is normally acceptable at this stage of planning. The contingency figure should be clearly identified in the proposal. Careful attention to details at this stage puts the administration in a position to make its decisions based upon documented needs and available funds.

A wide variety of costs must be included when making budget estimates for levels of service. It would be impossible to cover everything, but as planning progresses the planners should try not to overlook any large items. The following example is a hypothetical preliminary program proposal for three levels of service: limited service, standard service, and enhanced full service. The amount of any proposed budget will depend upon the size of the organization for which the budget is made. In some organizations the expected outcomes or products of the service program must also be quantified (e.g., the number of audiovisual media units to be purchased or the number of circulations the requested budget will allow). Given this information the media manager's administrators should be able to make an intelligent decision regarding the level of service program they are willing to support. Once that decision is made, the media manager can begin to prepare a comprehensive proposal for a program at the designated level of funding. Estimated costs are provided as examples to demonstrate that costs increase as the service levels increase (see figure 3.3, page 48).

PROGRAM SERVICE LEVELS	CAPITAL BUDGET	OPERATIONAL BUDGET		
		MATERIALS/ EQUIPMENT BUDGET	PERSONNEL BUDGET	TOTAL YEARLY BUDGET
LIMITED SERVICE	$100,000	$50,000	$150,000	$200,000
STANDARD SERVICE	$175,000	$100,000	$300,000	$400,000
ENHANCED FULL SERVICE	$500,000	$200,000	$600,000	$800,000

Figure 3.3. Summary of service-level program costs.

Limited service: Estimated annual budget: $200,000
Provide a limited media service program to the clients of the institution. Services provided will be limited to two service units: (1) Media Materials Collection Unit and (2) Media Equipment Unit. The two units will provide the following services:

a.   limited acquisition of audiovisual materials

b.   limited circulation of media materials

c.   cataloging of the materials

d.   rental of materials

e.   instructional/training materials reference service

f.   limited inventory and circulation of audiovisual equipment

Standard service: Estimated annual budget: $400,000
Provide a high-quality media service program that will meet most needs of the institution's departments. Services will be organized into three basic units: (1) Media Materials Collection Services, (2) Media Equipment and Facility Design Services, and (3) Media Development Services. The three units will provide the following services in addition to those provided by the limited services program:

a.   expanded acquisition of audiovisual materials

b.   expanded rental of materials as needed

c.   maintenance of all materials

d.   expanded acquisition of audiovisual equipment to meet most client needs

e.   equipment will be placed within user departments when need dictates

f.   in-house maintenance of most audiovisual equipment

g.   delivery of audiovisual materials and equipment

h.   limited graphics, photo, audio, and multimedia production services

i.   video/television services limited to one-camera productions for client performance evaluation (mirror television)

j.   expanded media facility and systems design consulting with clients

Full service: Estimated annual budget: $800,000
Provide a high-quality, full-service media program that will meet the media needs of the institution's departments. The programs will be organized into five service units: the three service units proposed in the standard service program, plus (4) Video or Television Production Services and (5) Instructional Development Services. The following services will be provided in addition to those provided by the standard service program:

a.   expanded purchase of instructional/training materials and audiovisual equipment and rental of materials to meet nearly all the needs of media service users

b.   in-house maintenance of all audiovisual equipment

c.   provide operators for audiovisual equipment when requested

d.   full graphics, photo, audio, and multimedia production services to meet the instructional needs of users

e.   creation of a multicamera video/television production unit to produce instructional/training materials for clients

f.   development of an Instructional Development (ID) service to assist clients in the systematic design and evaluation of instructional/training units or courses

Space Limitations

Another constraint or limitation found in media service facilities is space. In most institutions, finding adequate space to house all of the institution's departments and programs is an ongoing problem. Other departments are constantly competing for available space, as well as for any new space that may be constructed. Even within the center, various service areas will be vying for additional space. Space is not free; it translates into a cost per square foot. Thus, obtaining adequate space to handle the media center's activities constitutes a major consideration. Every service function, such as circulation, media collections, equipment pool, maintenance, repair, previews, audio production, graphic production, photographic production, video/television production, and instructional development, requires space. Office and storage space are also required. Perhaps the most overlooked need is storage. About 10 percent of the available space for services should be allocated for storage.

In any proposal, space needs must be considered simultaneously with program approval. It does not help one's cause to have been given a green light to plan new programs if the space needed to implement them has not been allocated. It must be assumed that growth is going to take place if the media services are meeting client needs; thus one must develop total rather than fractional plans. Planning that does not include considerations for future growth and expansion is poor planning. If space requirements differ for the various levels of service, projections must be prepared detailing space requirements necessary for each level of service. A review of literature in the media field and visitations to existing media centers can provide some helpful space guidelines for various media functions.

DEVELOPING PROGRAM SPECIFICATIONS
FOR NEW OR IMPROVED SERVICES

Once the proposed program has been determined from needs assessments and interviews, and decisions regarding the integration, consolidation, centralization, and cost recovery have been made and support has been won, then planning can proceed. These plans must include all the details for the proposed program and be translated into specifications and cost estimates that include a time schedule showing how and when the program will be developed, assembled, and managed. Once in place evaluation procedures must be built into the scheme so that one can determine and disseminate how well the new service programs are meeting client and administration expectations. One must never assume that upper management will automatically know how things are going; it is up to the media manager to keep them informed. The elements that should be included in planning follow.

1. *Philosophy.* State the philosophical guidelines. As was discussed in chapter 2, the philosophy that guides the center's activities serves as the foundation for all programs and services offered by the center and must be developed and stated. For example: The guiding philosophy of the media service center is to provide high-quality, effective, efficient training and instructional support services to the center's clients.

2. *Purposes.* State the purposes of the service programs. Clear statements clarifying the media center purposes should be written. These purposes should interface with the philosophical statements already developed and should clearly describe programs and services provided by the center. For example, the media center

   a.   provides instructional and learning support services to its patrons

   b.   provides resources which should help patrons to expand *their* work potential

   c.   is concerned with learning as both a process and a product and is also concerned with providing multiple and alternative ways for learners to learn from instruction tailored to meet individual learning styles

   d.   collects and disseminates ideas, techniques, and concepts from outside the institution for consideration and possible use by clients within the institution

   e.   provides leadership in all areas of media service and helps clients with the evaluation, selection, and utilization of materials and equipment

   f.   supports the public relations efforts of the institution by assisting in the design and production of all types of promotional materials

3. *Specific program objectives.* For each of the program purposes listed in element 2, objectives should be developed. These objectives should be action-oriented and *measurable.* Measurability requires a certain amount of specificity that usually can be translated into numbers. This is not an easy task but it must be done if the objective is to be of any value to the program. Accountability for goals (or objectives) must not be so low as to be too easily attained; they must be attainable, however, and in concert with other objectives set forth by the organization as a whole. One must be careful not to overdo the matter of objectives. It is possible to set up so many objectives that they get in the way of achieving the tasks for which they were

promulgated. The watchword is to set a few key measurable objectives and then get on with the tasks at hand. Consider the Texas Industries motto, "More than two objectives is no objectives!" Perhaps the company did not intend to be quite that stingy with objectives, but the meaning is clear: The use of objectives can get out of hand.

Objectives and their measurement criteria must be stated clearly, understood easily, and simple to administer. The examples that follow present objectives and measurement guides for purpose (a) "provides instructional and learning support services to its patrons" (page 50). Assuming that these objectives are being established for a new program, one would not have any previous history or data to draw upon, so numbers to measure performance against will not exist. Therefore, during the first year of operation data must be obtained for use in following years to set more precise, measurable objectives.

If the media manager is taking over the direction of a program that has been in place for some time, accurate data may be available so that one can set objectives for the coming year. Some managers, however, may not have realized how important it is to obtain such information, and their records may be inadequate or inaccurate or may not exist at all. In fact, that may be one of the reasons that there is now a *new* media director!

These objectives do not deal with content quality. It is assumed that, because the users have reviewed and evaluated the materials prior to purchase, they meet instructional objectives.

> *Objective:* To build, maintain, and circulate a collection of instructional materials—films, videotapes, CD-ROMs, laser discs, computer software, slides, transparencies, records, tapes, kits, and others.

The following are examples of numerical measurements:

Measurement 1: Arrange previews of materials as requested by clients.

First year: List how many and what kinds of materials were previewed.

First year: List how many contacts were made with clients regarding new materials for preview.

The numbers used in the following examples come from a unit that has been in operation for a long time. The actual numbers used to measure fulfillment of the objectives would depend upon how long the unit has been in operation, the size of the unit, and the media *awareness* of the users. Once initial data have been collected, then precise objective measurements can be established. For instance, when setting objectives for the second year, the measurement criteria for the above might be as follows:

Second year: Arrange 400 media previews for clients.

Other measurements might include:

Measurement 2: Purchase materials requested and justified by previewers.

First year: Keep a tabulation of numbers, costs, and kinds of materials purchased.

Second year:	Purchase 200 new titles recommended by previews while maintaining a 15 percent purchase/preview ratio.
Measurement 3:	Circulate instructional materials to users.
First year:	Record total number of circulations to users. Individual booking statistics can be kept by client name, departments, schools, and so on.
Second year:	(1) Meet all requests for materials with less than a 2 percent "conflict in booking." (2) Eight thousand circulation bookings to clients will be made.
Measurement 4:	Procure materials from other sources when they are not available within the media service center.
First year:	Keep records of items obtained from other sources.
Second year:	(1) Meet all requests for materials with less than a 2 percent "conflict in booking." (2) Complete 250 rental transactions from other sources.

Looking further down the list of purposes (page 50), the following is an example of an objective and its measurement for purpose (e) "provides leadership in all areas of media service and helps clients with the evaluation, selection, and utilization of materials and equipment."

Objective:	Serve as an instructional/training media resource person to the institution's programs.
Measurement 1:	Media staff members, including the director, will meet requests to serve as resource person(s) or as guest lecturer(s).
First year:	Record the frequency of occurrence and number of times media service center staff successfully meet requests to serve as media resource persons within classrooms.
Second year:	(1) Media staff members will meet requests for their services as guest lecturers 95 percent of the time. (2) Media staff members will serve as guest lecturers in 30 classrooms during the year.

4. *Short- and long-range plans.* In order for programs to progress in an orderly and sequential manner, realistic plans must be developed and included in any service proposal. When proposed programs entail a large expenditure of funds, it is usually advisable to phase in the elements over a period of time, as funding will be easier to obtain in small increments than in one large amount. An example of this might be in establishing a media collection. This is a difficult and time-consuming task involving a number of factors, including the participation of those who will be using such materials. Clients must be contacted regarding their needs and wants; materials must be located, previewed, and purchased. When received, they must be cataloged, shelved, and material annotations prepared and inserted into a collection catalog.

All of this takes time, and everyone involved may also have other responsibilities. The process of building the media collection should not be forced at too fast a pace. If the process is spread over several years, the content of the collection will more nearly represent the needs of its users. Time frames extending over two to three years should be considered short range, while long-range plans extend over five or six years. Plans extending beyond three years should be considered tentative and subject to review as programs and services change and grow.

IDENTIFYING THE POWER STRUCTURE

Within every organization one finds two different power structures: one that makes things happen and one that prevents things from happening. It is essential to identify both elements prior to undertaking the selling or implementation of extensive service programs. To be successful in managing existing or in developing new media service programs, one must know who these people are and enlist their support. Winning the support of such leaders is just as important as planning. All too often proposals succeed or fail depending upon who in upper management is willing to defend them. The power structure in most institutions can be classified into four groups: (1) the formal leaders, (2) the informal leaders, (3) the gatekeepers, and (4) the innovators and the bottleneckers.

Formal Leaders

Formal leaders are those who hold official positions of authority within an institution, such as the president; vice presidents; and various managers, coordinators, and department heads. These are the people who officially approve or reject proposals for program changes or for new programs. Their support is critical, for without it enabling funds will most likely not be forthcoming. These are not the people that will, in most cases, "pick up on a proposal and run with it." They like to see hard data, realistic plans, and workable ideas well laid out. Usually they do not react favorably to wordy proposals.

Informal Leaders

Informal leaders do not hold official positions of authority but are able to influence attitudes and behaviors because they have earned the respect of others through their expertise, wisdom, ability to solve problems, and ability to express themselves clearly. They are often models others listen to and whose ideas carry weight.

Gatekeepers

Gatekeepers do not hold positions of leadership or authority but can be a great help or a hindrance, depending upon how well you get along with them. Gatekeepers usually work for or closely with the institution's formal leaders. Thus, the way gatekeepers handle items—that is, what they do with items that come across their desks—can facilitate or impede the progress of a project. A secretary, for instance, can lose a proposal or get it on the boss's desk immediately. Other gatekeepers who might help are budget officers, auditors, and clerks. People in other service centers who can be helpful at other stages in proposal implementation include carpenters, electricians, and custodians. If one can gain the support of such gatekeepers, things will flow more smoothly. It pays to give these people the respect and consideration that they deserve.

Innovators and Bottleneckers

Innovators are usually open to ideas and are willing to experiment and take educated chances. Their opposites are the bottleneckers, who resist or oppose new proposals regardless of origin, unless they originated the idea. Bottleneckers are easily identified by the way in which they can talk an idea into oblivion before it has been thoroughly reviewed.

Having identified as many individuals, groups, and other factions within your sphere that appear to support (or oppose) your ideas, it is time to prepare your strategies and move ahead. Don't make things too complicated!

CREATING AND PRESENTING
THE PROPOSAL

Just because a great deal of information has been collected and ideas have been developed does not mean that your supervisors will want to see them all in the written proposal. Actually most of the material collected is for the purpose of preparing yourself; what you have learned should be thought through, written down, edited, organized, and prepared for distribution as needed. Organize the arguments and justifications that will be employed to "sell" the proposal. If the data have been carefully collected, thoroughly analyzed, and interpreted, the final preparation should be relatively easy; clear and succinct data, properly presented, should go a long way toward gaining support for a project. At this point things are at the trial balloon stage, and proposals can be discussed with superiors informally over coffee or elsewhere to find out what they think. In this way most of the bugs can be worked out before any formal meetings are scheduled. If you have succeeded in selling the proposal informally, the task of obtaining formal approval may be quite easy. Your supporters may already have sold the concept for you.

Formal presentations are usually made in scheduled meetings. Remember to make the presentations as simple and straightforward as possible. Present your case and supporting data, answer questions, ask for suggestions and advice and, if possible, try to secure some kind of positive commitment from those present. Watch yourself, however; try not to press so hard that your audience becomes antagonized. Most superiors will not care for long, wordy reports or proposals; they will want to know the essentials only. Separate the materials into a series of short reports or sections that can be combined into a single report for selected individuals. When presenting a proposal to a group, distribute only the essential data initially and supplement with additional materials as the need arises. Thus, attention is focused upon the issues being discussed and people are not leafing through pages of extraneous material. With careful application, this strategy presents you as being well prepared.

SUGGESTED ACTIVITIES

1. Tour a media service center. Ask the center manager to explain the mission, goals, and objectives of the programs. Using that information, develop a needs assessment instrument that you would use if you were to become the media manager of that program.

2. Visit both an integrated and nonintegrated media service program. Ask the managers to tell you their perceptions of the value of integrated and nonintegrated programs and to explain what makes the programs successful or unsuccessful. Summarize your findings under four columns: (1) advantages of integrated programs, (2) disadvantages of integrated programs, (3) what is necessary if integration is to be successful, and (4) integration pitfalls to avoid.

3. Assume that you are the media manager in an institution where decentralized media service programs exist with many material and equipment collections and duplicate graphic, photo, and video/television production areas. Develop a rationale with strong arguments for centralizing these services within the media service center organization.

4. Recalling your previously developed personalized statement of philosophy, develop a policy statement regarding charging patrons for services.

5. Plan and develop a proposal for a media service program in a new institution. Specify who the program is to serve before you begin: (a) a large high school with 2,000 students, (b) an institution of higher education with a student body of 8,000, or (c) a business or industrial organization with 8,000 employees. Plan the media service program following the guidelines provided in chapters 2 and 3.

REFERENCES

Allen, William H. 1969. "Audiovisual Instruction: The State of the Art." In *The Schools and the Challenge of Innovation*. New York: McGraw-Hill.

American Association of School Librarians. Association for Educational Communications and Technology. 1988. *Information Power: Guidelines for School Library Media Programs*. Chicago: American Library Association.

Association for Educational Communications and Technology. 1989. *Standards for College and University Learning Resources Program: Technology in Instruction*. Washington, D.C.: AECT.

National Council for the Accreditation of Teacher Education. 1997. *Standards, Procedures, and Policies for the Accreditation of Professional Educational Units*. Washington, D.C.: NCATE.

Ramey, James W. 1971. "The Human Element: Why Nonprint Managers Turn Gray." *Drexel Library Quarterly*, 7, no. 2: 95.

Woodsworth, Anne. 1991. *Patterns and Options for Managing Information Technology on Campus*. Chicago: American Library Association.

MEDIA RESOURCES

Planning for Educational Technology. John Lawson, 120 minutes. College Park, Md.: University of Maryland Educational Technology Center, 1996. Videocassette.

SELECTED BIBLIOGRAPHY

Baule, Steven M. *Technology Planning.* Worthington, Ohio: Linworth, 1997.

Gagne, Robert M., ed. *Instructional Technology: Foundations.* Hillsdale, N.J.: Lawrence Erlbaum Associates, 1987.

Marcoux, Betty. "Information Literacy Standard for Student Learning." *Tech Trends,* 42, no. 1 (1997): 52–53.

Marlow, Eugene. *Managing Corporate Media.* Rev. ed. White Plains, N.Y.: Knowledge Industry Publications, 1989.

Morris, Betty J., John T. Gillespie, and Diana L. Spirt. *Administering the School Library Media Center.* 3d ed. New Providence, N.J.: R. R. Bowker, 1992.

National Center for Education Statistics. *Technology at Your Fingertips: A Guide to Implementing Technology Solutions for Education Agencies and Institutions.* Washington, D.C.: National Center for Education Statistics, National Cooperative Education Statistics System, National Forum on Education Statistics, 1997.

Picciano, Anthony G. *Educational Leadership and Planning for Technology.* 2d ed. Columbus, Ohio: Merrill, 1998.

Prostano, Emanuel T., and Joyce S. Prostano. *The School Library Media Center.* 4th ed. Library Science Text Series. Littleton, Colo.: Libraries Unlimited, 1987.

Schmidt, William D. *Learning Resources Programs That Make a Difference.* Washington, D.C.: Association for Educational Communications and Technology, 1987.

Stein, Barbara L., and Lisa W. Brown. *Running a Library Media Center: A How-to-Do-It Manual for Librarians.* New York: Neal-Schuman, 1992.

Toffler, Alvin. *Powershift.* New York: Bantam Books, 1990.

Wright, Kieth C. *The Challenge of Technology: Action Strategies for the School Library Media Specialist.* Chicago: American Library Association, 1993.

Yesner, Bernice L., and Hilda L. Jay. *Operating and Evaluating School Library Media Programs: A Handbook for Administrators and Librarians.* New York: Neal-Schuman, 1998.

4

MANAGEMENT BASICS

. . . it follows that the successful program is characterized by system, direction, and leadership. Order will eliminate otherwise inevitable confusion, duplication of effort, waste of time and money. Direction will channel the total effort toward purposeful and effective utilization. Leadership will change teacher apathy to enthusiasm for new techniques.

Ford L. Lemler, in *Audio-Visual Programs in Action*,
edited by Ford L. Lemler, 1951

OBJECTIVES

At the conclusion of this chapter you should be able to

1. Describe the characteristics that identify a manager's management style as open, closed or in between.

2. List the five major approaches to management and compare and contrast their theories, differences, and historical development.

3. State the purpose of an organizational chart.

4. Describe the relationship of positions in a line-and-staff organization.

5. Discuss chain of command, authority levels, responsibilities, and power of positions as identified on an organizational chart.

6. Describe how the departments of a media center can be identified on an organizational chart and list six typical media center departments.

7. Describe the purposes of and differences between rules, procedures, and policies.

8. Describe the differences between programmed and nonprogrammed decisions.

9. List and discuss five basic steps that facilitate effective decision making.

10. List and discuss five qualities that effective decision makers seem to possess.

The first section of this chapter discusses two topics, management styles and management organization. Thus this section is a prelude to other chapters that will deal in more depth with the human relationships that are so critical to effective management. One cannot look even superficially at management styles or organization patterns without considering people, for people are the heartbeat of any organization or unit within it. The Japanese see this very clearly. Japan is a small country with few natural resources, yet it is a major producer of high-quality goods for the world market. How did Japan achieve this? The Japanese attribute their success to the fact that their management makes the best use of their most important natural resource, the hard work of their people. The Japanese organize for, and their management style implements, a basic philosophy that values workers' contributions to the company as well as workers as individuals. It sounds simple, but the techniques employed are long range in nature and complicated.

MANAGEMENT STYLES

Every manager has a modus operandi, or operating style, which materially affects how things are done and what goes on within that manager's sphere of influence. One's management style is an outgrowth of one's basic philosophy regarding how things should be done. *Style* relates to how a manager goes about implementing this philosophy in the workplace; *management style* might be defined as an outward manifestation of a manager's basic philosophy.

Historical Perspective

There has been disagreement over the years on about just how many different approaches to management there are and what each approach involves. Certo (1997, 29–45) and other management authors have defined five approaches to management:

the classical approach,

the behavioral approach,

the management science approach,

the contingency approach, and

the systems approach.

Each of these five approaches has a historical context and set of management theories attached to its definition and use. The classical approach to management emphasizes using organizational efficiency to increase organizational success. Frederick W. Taylor, Frank and Lillian Gilbreth, Henry L. Gantt, and Henri Fayol are key people associated with this scientific method of management. From the late 1800s through the 1930s, this approach utilized time and motion studies, division of work, piece rates, and other organizational adjustments to improve productivity.

The behavioral approach to management, with its beginnings between 1924 and 1935, sought to increase organizational success by focusing on the human variable. The Hawthorne studies concluded that human factors could significantly influence work output. The study of human characteristics and their influence on work is still a major force in today's organizational research. Abraham Maslow and Douglas McGregor were advocates of this human relations approach in management theory.

The management science approach can be traced from World War II (1940s) to the present. This approach emphasizes the use of the scientific method and quantitative techniques to increase organizational success. Churchman, Ackoff, Arnoff, and Baldrige are associated with this approach. The primary characteristics of the management science approach are that it: (1) analyzes a large number of variables in a complex setting, (2) uses economic implications as a guideline for making management decisions, (3) uses mathematical modeling, and (4) uses computers. This approach is still evolving and, as more sophisticated analytical techniques are developed, is replacing the inventory control models, network models, and probability models in use today.

The contingency approach to management emphasizes that what managers do in practice depends on a given set of circumstances or situation. This approach, championed by Fred E. Fiedler, emphasizes "if-then" relationships in the organization. It suggests there is no one best way to solve a management problem in all organizations, but there is probably one best way to solve any given problem in any one organization. The contingency approach involves: (1) perceiving situations as they actually exist, (2) choosing tactics best suited to those particular situations, and (3) competently implementing those tactics. This approach is actively being implemented in many organizations today.

The systems approach to management is based on the idea that to understand fully the operation of an entity, the entity must be viewed as a whole. This requires understanding the interdependence of its parts. Ludwig von Bertalanffy and L. Thomas Hopkins are management theorists associated with this concept of wholeness in management. There are six guidelines for doing systems analysis management. They are: (1) the whole should be the main focus, with the parts secondary; (2) integration or interrelatedness is key; (3) possible modifications to parts should be weighed in relation to the effect on every other part; (4) each part has a role to perform so that the whole can accomplish its purpose; (5) the nature of the part and its function is determined by its position in the whole; and (6) all analysis starts with the existence of the whole.

Types

No two management styles will be exactly the same, even though the same elements may exist in both. There are too many factors interacting, and the overlap of such elements and factors will always differ among individuals. Overall, management styles might be seen as falling somewhere along a continuum that is labeled *closed* at one end and *open* at the other (figure 4.1). *Closed* and *open* identify how managers view and use, or apply, their authority. We will look at the effect that management styles have upon workers' attitudes and productivity in a subsequent chapter.

Toward the closed end of the continuum one will encounter style descriptors of a restrictive nature such as formal, autocratic, authoritarian, and exploitative. The philosophies of managers whose styles place them toward the closed end of the continuum would tend to believe that people are basically lazy, lack initiative, cannot make simple decisions, and avoid responsibility. Further, they would hold that all activities of workers at the job must be closely monitored and minor infractions of the rules noted. This type of manager usually has plenty of rules, most of which are negative in nature.

Figure 4.1. Management styles continuum.

As a manager's style places him or her toward the open end of the continuum, one finds that philosophies and therefore management styles become much more optimistic. The style descriptors used are more positive and indicate that people are viewed as capable, self-motivated, creative, and imaginative, and will seek out responsibility if given the reasons and opportunity to do so. In recent years, management styles have been moving away from the more formal, closed styles of management toward the informal, open, people-oriented styles. More and more, management is finding that cooperative, informative, sharing styles of management are not only more realistic and human but also more productive. This is due in part to the interjection of concepts that place high value upon the individual as a contributing member of a team rather than as a necessary cog in the machinery. Certainly Japanese management styles have received close attention around the world for this very reason. Words that might apply when locating the Japanese management style on the continuum include *paternalistic, benevolent, cooperative, teamwork, participatory decision making, open communication, praise*, and *recognition*. History has proven that the closed style of management prevailing at the beginning of the Industrial Revolution was too extreme. It did not work well, even though the workers were for the most part poorly educated and unaccustomed to what they were told to do. By the same token, a totally open style of management would not work well either, because the system would lack adequate direction. The answer lies somewhere between the two extremes. According to Peters and Waterman, modern management styles in America's best-run companies are grouped toward the open side of the continuum and emphasize respect for the individual and the contributions that he or she can make to the management unit involved. In discussing this concept, Peters and Waterman say:

> We are not talking about mollycoddling. We are talking about tough-minded respect for the individual and the willingness to train him, to set reasonable and clear expectations for him, and to grant him practical autonomy to step out and contribute directly to his work (1982, 239).

Current management approaches have been broadened to include several workplace issues and concerns. Today the application of any management system must include techniques and methods to support diversity, quality, ethics, and internationalism. Managers must be trained to handle issues of harassment, affirmative action, ethnocentrism, gender roles, workplace safety, and disabilities accommodations. These issues have caused the manager's role to become more complex and to require continuous training and development of knowledge and management skills. Managers of media centers must understand these issues and develop rules, procedures, and policies specific to their environment. These management workplace procedures and policies should generally focus on five themes:

Provide personal and organizational awareness.

Acknowledge biases or limitations of the specific work environment.

Focus on work performance and job quality.

Provide for the avoidance of assumptions.

Cause the appropriate development and modifications of manuals and operational procedures.

THE ORGANIZATIONAL STRUCTURE

In any situation where people have been brought together to provide a service, to produce something, or for other purposes, an organizational structure is necessary if the objectives for which they have been brought together are to be achieved. This poses no problem if only a few people are involved; the structure will be simple and easily understood. The structure of larger organizations is more complex and must be presented to those involved in a way that can be easily understood. Generally, how an organization operates is best depicted through an organizational chart showing, in a simple but formal form, who is in charge and how authority flows. An organizational chart presents an extremely complex meshing of many variables that interact with each other as people in an organization work together. Most charts are set up according to positions or functions so that all within the unit can see their places in the scheme of things.

Basic Considerations

A number of factors must be taken into account as an organizational chart is developed. Some of the important elements requiring consideration are vertical and horizontal dimensions, chain of command, line and staff, authority levels, responsibility and accountability, power, and departmentalization. Definitions and a short discussion of each of these elements follows.

Vertical and Horizontal Dimensions

The vertical and horizontal dimensions on an organizational chart provide an indication of where a department and/or manager fits into the host organization's power structure. The vertical dimensions indicate the chain of command, and the horizontal dimensions generally identify staff and service department locations. The importance of location on these dimensions varies from organization to organization.

Chain of Command

A good way of setting up an organizational chart is to identify who reports to whom. When charted, this chain of command depicts the flow of authority within an organization in vertical format leading from top to bottom. The chart depicts each authority level and position within the organization down to the position carrying the least decision-making authority. There are other kinds of positions within an organization, but only decision-making positions are found in the chain of command.

Line and Staff

The line-and-staff concept was originally developed by the military but has since been adapted for use in other organizations. Essentially, *line* identifies those positions carrying command authority. In military use, the line-and-staff organization is rigid because positive knowledge of who commands, who takes orders, and who supports whom is very important. Line positions are represented vertically in an organizational chart. Thus the private reports to the corporal, who reports to the sergeant, who reports to the lieutenant, who reports to the captain, and so on up the line to the commanding general. Orders come down from the top, along the same line. In a line-and-staff organizational pattern, a line person or officer has the authority and responsibility within his or her prescribed location in the scheme of things to make decisions and take action. Orders can flow only from above, and requests for changes and so on must go through channels.

Staff identifies those positions or functions in an organization that do not carry command or decision-making authority. Staff positions are support positions providing the services, advice, and counsel required by people in the chain of command. Examples of staff positions in a media center might be secretary or receptionist. Another might be an artist who prepares pasteups, posters, overhead transparencies, and other creative materials and artwork. Sometimes staff positions are identified on an organizational chart by colored or broken lines. More typically, staff positions are located along horizontal planes in an organizational chart (figure 4.2, page 64). The line-and-staff concept is described here only to provide a base from which to depart. Over the years, the line-and-staff concept has been modified and applied in a wide variety of organizations. Certainly a purely military type of organizational plan does not square very well with the kinds of activities found in most media centers, where the work calls for initiative and creativity from all employees, attributes much sought after by media managers. In its pure form, a line-and-staff arrangement does not work well with the more open management styles in use today. Thus, while concepts drawn from the line-and-staff concept may be used when mapping how an organization or unit within an organization works, there is plenty of room for variation on this basic theme.

One precaution must be observed regardless of the organizational plan adopted. It is best stated in the old axiom, "No man can serve two masters." The line of authority or unit of command must never be split so that anyone has to report to or take direction from more than one person. Misunderstandings and conflicts will surely arise, for no two people give orders the same way and hold the same expectations of their subordinates. Figure 4.3, page 64, illustrates how such a split

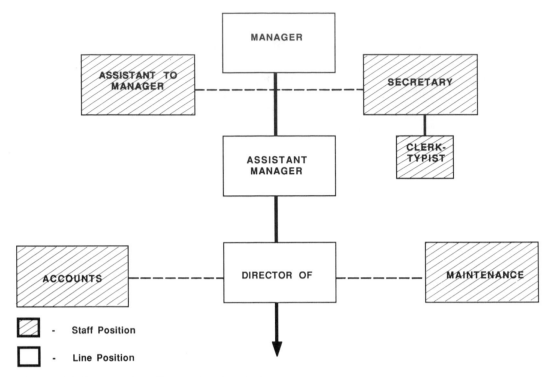

Figure 4.2. Line-and-staff organizational chart.

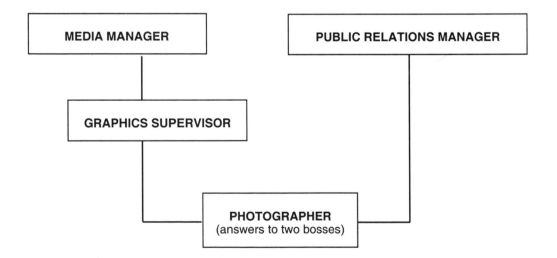

Figure 4.3. Violation of unity of command rule.

in the chain of command might look. In a strict line-and-staff organization, violating the unity of command principle could create problems. In organizations having less rigid patterns, conditions may exist where one person answers to two bosses because both need work done but neither has enough work for a full-time position. An example might be that of a photographer working part-time for the graphics department and part-time for the public relations department. There is, however, enough work of a similar nature for one person to serve both areas. In such cases, the parameters for both jobs must be clearly defined so that the photographer is not asked to do more than would be required when working for only one boss.

Authority and Authority Levels

In any successful organization, the authority or right to make decisions and take action is delegated to selected persons located in a chain of command. The amount of authority that a person can exercise depends upon the level that the person has achieved. An organizational chart indicates who has authority and what are the limits to the authority. The higher the placement on a chart, the more authority that can be exercised over a larger area of endeavor.

Responsibility and Accountability

These two concepts are hierarchical in organizational planning. Basically *responsibility* refers to what you have to do in your position and *accountability* refers to how well assigned tasks were performed. Responsibility and accountability are closely interrelated. One cannot delegate responsibility alone to someone to get something done without also making the person accountable. However, the ultimate accountability resides with the manager: Realistically, the person a manager reports to is going to hold that manager accountable for the performance of the entire unit or department. Thus it is imperative that tasks subordinates cannot handle are not assigned to them.

Power

Authority and power are not synonymous, therefore power was not included in the discussion on authority. In any reorganization, one will find people who have the authority to get things done but do not have the power to lead or to influence the attitudes and performance of those whose activities they direct. Power may reside with persons in authority, but often it will be found in persons outside of the command structure, the informal leaders. The power structure in an organization may not always appear on an organizational chart. An informal organization seems to arise within a unit without any conscious planning and exists whether or not the manager wants it. An alert manager will make it a point to be aware of this informal organization and, where possible, use it to the advantage of all. In units where the management philosophy and style of operation is open and sharing, this is comparatively easy to do. Under more restrictive types of management, the informal organization may go underground and can cripple or destroy the formal structure or even the unit itself.

Departmentalization

Departmentalization is the division of an organization or unit within an organization into smaller units or groups. This is usually accomplished along lines of location, function, process, or product and depicted on an organizational chart in the horizontal dimension. Departments within a media center might include television and video production, graphic production, circulation, maintenance and repair, photography, audio production, and printing. There might even be an accounting and billing department in a large media center if there is a charge-back system for services and products. A manager might also have to take into account physically dispersed service locations, as well as duplication of production facilities not housed under the media center roof.

Modifying Line and Staff

Few, if any, organizational patterns will turn out to be pure line-and-staff arrangements as the organization evolves. There may be times and situations in which so-called staff positions may also exert direction and authority on others. This will depend in part upon the management style of the manager and how he or she delegates authority and responsibility (figure 4.4). Many managers like to locate decision-making authority as close as possible to the point where the action takes place on the assumption that better decisions can be made by those most closely involved. For example, an artist who normally is in charge of no more than his or her own desk may be put in charge of a project and direct not only his or her own work but the work of others assigned to the project. In practice, certain positions may serve both line and staff functions.

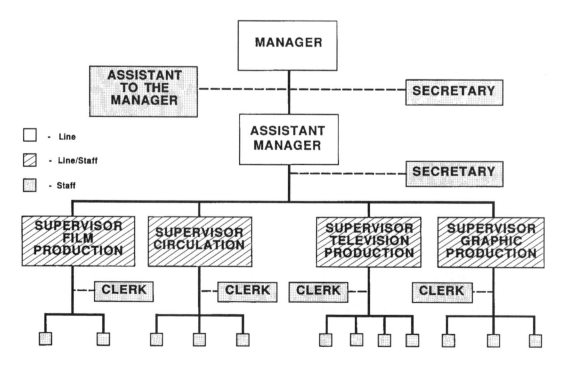

Figure 4.4. Typical modified line-and-staff organization.

Organizational charts are most useful for showing relationships within an entity; the flow (theoretically) of authority; and communications containing orders, suggestions, advice, ideas, and concerns that are essential to the overall operation. This does not mean, however, that such charts should be cast in bronze and displayed for all to see; rather they should serve as guides. Management attitudes regarding organizational charts need to be open and flexible enough to allow for change as needs dictate. It has been said that once a chart has been developed, and those concerned know who is who and what goes where, the chart can be put away. Once people working within an organization know the directions and flow of decision making, they usually do not have to be reminded of how things work. For a more extensive review of organizational patterns in media programs, see appendix 2 and *Learning Resources Programs That Make a Difference* (Schmidt 1987).

The Private Sector

The private sector has found it essential that the various media functions connected with education and training activities be carefully organized and operated in an efficient and cost-effective manner; otherwise unexpected problems may be created. Some time ago a heavy equipment manufacturer with factories located throughout the United States established media development facilities to produce materials keyed to its training and sales requirements. Media development units were set up at the local level without receiving any direction from the home office. Eventually it was discovered that the various units were often engaged in producing materials designed to meet the same need. Expensive productions had been duplicated several times while other critical media needs had not been addressed at all. Coordination from an upper management level would have resulted in a considerable savings of time, money, and effort. Certainly well-trained employees are essential in today's highly competitive and complex world if a company is to secure a fair share of the market.

Medium-Size Company

This section describes the education and training division of a well-known, medium-size American company that has a home office and numerous branch offices across the country. The company will not be named, as it prefers to remain anonymous. Figure 4.5, page 68, illustrates the organization of the company's education and training division. It shows where the various components of the division are located and to some extent how they relate to each other, but it does not show the actual working organization within each component. The actual organization of the media services center is shown in figure 4.6, page 69. The media services center works on a horizontal rather than a vertical plane; with the exception of the audiovisual clerk, the positions within the media services center are equivalent professional positions. The production facilities include fully equipped studios for video and audio recording plus complete graphic production and multi-image and slide programming services. The media service center's most common products include overhead transparencies, slides, audiotapes, multi-image presentations, films, and videotapes. Thus within the several areas of the media service center are found the requisite photographic, graphic design, technical equipment, and staging skills to support the products.

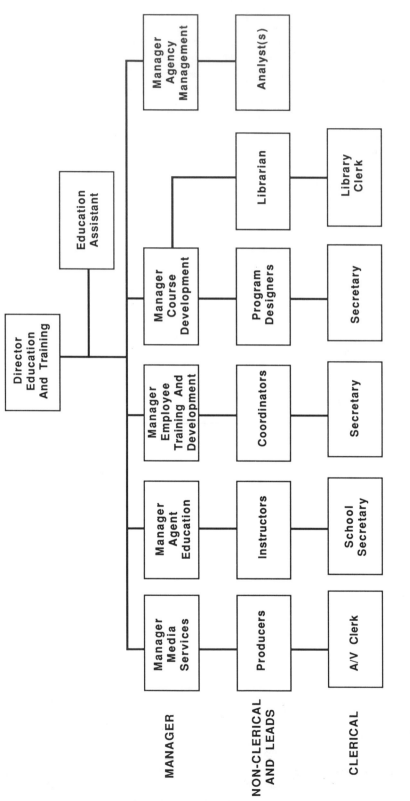

Figure 4.5. Organizational chart for the education and training division of a medium-size company.

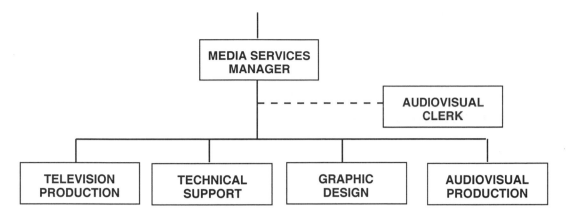

Figure 4.6. Media services organizational chart (medium-size company).

Objectives

No unit functions well without objectives to guide its activities. In this media service center, the objectives fall into two categories: Basic Responsibilities and Areas of Performance. Objectives are reviewed yearly and change somewhat from year to year as new objectives replace ones that have been achieved or in response to changes in direction or focus on the part of upper management. The first category, Basic Responsibilities, lists overall unit objectives. Note that the list is not long and the objectives are in one manner or another measurable, though not necessarily in dollars and cents or in numbers.

Basic Responsibilities
- Provide professional, creative, and cost-effective video and audiovisual support to the company and its subsidiaries.
- Provide guidance to all departments in the effective use of video and audiovisual programming and presentation techniques.
- Produce, stage, and present programs using media, including primarily video, slides, multi-image, multimedia, audiotape, and overhead transparencies.
- Coordinate technical service for and scheduling of all corporate video and audiovisual equipment and facilities, including distribution and delivery systems.
- Promote long-range planning and expense management for corporate video and audiovisual communications development, including staff, facilities, equipment, and materials.

The next set of objectives relate to the Areas of Performance, with the first category in this area being customer satisfaction. Even though the "customers" come from within the company, the objectives show that participation is not assured. In the case of the second item, one can see some center policy evolving.

Areas of Performance

Customer Satisfaction

- Provide cost estimates showing direct and indirect costs, signed by the appropriate department head for all projects (a) over $1,000 for Home Office and (b) $300 for regions or branches. Customers should not be shocked at the time of billing.
- Serve media clients in the following priorities:
  1. the company's related programs
  2. subsidiary programs
  3. revenue-producing projects
  4. outside community relations programs
- Develop a plan of workshops for clients to help both neophyte and experienced AV users, and strengthen importance of lead time and targeted deadlines.
- Improve communication with field offices to assist with equipment compatibility and use.

Last are objectives related to the unit's productivity. Here again, some are measurable but others are not.

Productivity

- Account for at least 65 percent of work time to client projects.
- Continue use of freelance help for technical and staging assistance.
- Add emphasis on use of creative freelance help (writing, videography, production, etc.) when needed to serve clients in priority areas 1 or 2 (company-related programs and subsidiary programs).
- Continue efforts to reduce requirements for overtime work by production staff and eliminate all clerical overtime.
- Research a plan to create video labels within the company, using PC-based program, to lower the cost of labeling internal videotapes.
- Research possible additional uses for the computer for purposes beyond creating slides and overheads (e.g., video and/or PC graphics interfacing potential).
- Develop a video master indexing system to improve the usability of raw footage and existing video materials.
- Identify new technical equipment and methods of production that may reduce costs and build effectiveness to encourage the use of media in the future.

Obviously, careful evaluation practices must be pursued in any assessment as to whether objectives have been realized.

It appears there is not a great deal of difference between the objectives of public and corporate media centers; all in all the similarities are much stronger than the differences. In essence, the reasons for which such centers exist reflect the needs of the parent organization; thus one center might focus upon sales training while another concentrates upon safety procedures. One center might focus upon the production of a single type of media while another's production might be more comprehensive and produce all types of media. The approach of a given media center will depend upon its mission and the leadership of its manager.

Large Company

The preceding material came from a company relatively small as compared to some of the industrial giants, such as International Business Machines (IBM). IBM obviously takes the education and training of its employees very seriously, as noted in a Carnegie Foundation report: "At IBM, for example, each division handles its own education and is responsible for its curricular materials. The overall goal, however, is to create a worldwide educational system for its 103,000 technology professionals" (Eurich 1985, 50). Other major corporations that have invested heavily in the education and training of their employees are AT&T, Wang, Polaroid, Dow Chemical, Hewlett Packard, Texas Industries, Boeing, and National Cash Register. Education and training have a high priority in such leading enterprises. People involved in training in the corporate world have established professional associations; one of the best known is the American Society for Training and Development.

A chart of the organization of a media development unit or units in a large company might resemble figure 4.7. The various media development units (one, two, three, and four) receive the benefits of overall coordination as well as the services of a unit that houses and circulates the growing collection of in-house productions and media acquired from outside sources. Any other services to be provided by this particular unit would depend upon needs.

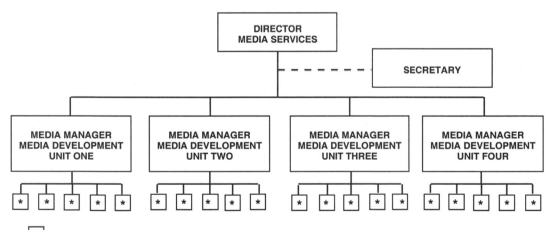

Figure 4.7. Organizational chart for a company with multiple media development units.

A basic organizational pattern for a smaller company might take the form of just one of the media development units found in a larger enterprise (see figure 4.8, page 72). Functions found in larger units are still represented but on a smaller scale (or not at all if they are not needed). In a small company or unit, the coordinators might well be practicing artists, writers, or producers who coordinate or supervise others part-time and produce part-time. It is essential to emphasize that organizational patterns develop with regard for the needs of a particular firm and with a view as to how the people work together. Thus patterns, job titles, and job responsibilities vary somewhat from company to company.

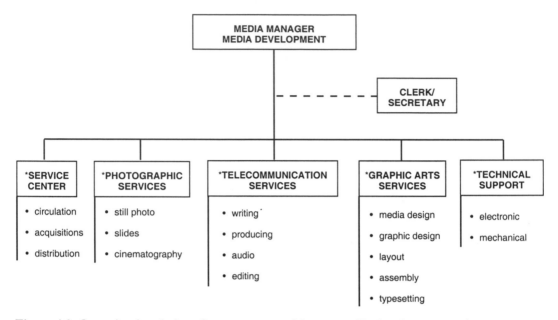

Figure 4.8. Organizational chart for a company with one media development unit.

RULES, PROCEDURES, AND POLICIES

Just as an entity must have an organizational structure, so must it also have controls to guide directions, operations, and activities if the entity is to achieve anything. Here again we find the need for a hierarchy. This time, instead of creating a hierarchy of authority levels, a hierarchy of rules, procedures, and policies must be constructed to govern the activities of those working in the organization. The purpose of these policies, procedures, and rules is to direct, restrain, and channel activities along acceptable courses of action.

In the management of today's service organizations, such as media centers, there exists a wide array of issues and evolving concerns that require continuous adaptation of rules, procedures, and policies. Media managers must develop a personal awareness, create organizational knowledge, and provide operational methods to administer and accommodate the needs of the center in its relationship to the following issues:

Ethics and social responsibility. Corporate social responsibility and business ethics are managerial obligations. Managers should take action to benefit society while furthering the interests of the organization. Media center managers must develop and implement such activities as codes of ethics, ethical business practices, and social audits.

Diversity in the workplace. Managers and their media organizations must operate within a global arena and international environment. They need to accommodate personnel, information, and technologies across multicultural and multinational themes. Diversity must be valued and integrated into the workforce and attitudes of the media centers.

Affirmative action. Managers need to define and provide for appropriate use of all available human resources. Issues of equal opportunity, reverse discrimination, and underutilized employment groups are elements of this management issue. If affirmative action laws are to be effective, managers must be accountable for their implementation.

Wellness and personal health concerns. Organizations need to provide healthy and safe environments for employees. The provision of wellness programs and facilities, drug abuse enforcement, and occupational safety are parts of this function of management.

Harassment and personnel interaction issues. Personnel issues ranging from sexual harassment to age discrimination must be dealt with through education and training programs coordinated by management. Policies and procedures for effectively and fairly dealing with these personnel relationships are required.

Disability accommodations and ADA requirements. Managers need to deal with access concerns of both workers and their clients. Compliance requirements for facilities, visual and audio standards, and handicapped accommodations are part of the requirements of the legal issues surrounding the Americans with Disabilities Act (ADA) and other governmental actions.

Crime prevention and organizational security. Violence in the workplace, corporate theft, and improper use of organizational facilities and materials are issues to be considered. Managers need to provide appropriate security and crime-prevention programs and deal with individual cases of office crime.

Legal requirements in hiring and other practices. Managers must continuously update organizational practices and compliance with appropriate employment methods. Proper position advertising, interview techniques, and local processing are all part of this activity. Compliance and the provision of correct information flow regarding copyright, work agreements, grant contracts, and other similar daily operations are part of this legal arena.

Copyright compliance. One of the issues that pervades both the service and development sides of media center management is the concern surrounding copyright and intellectual property compliance. Media managers are frequently challenged with questions and decisions regarding copyright law, fair use applications, identifying infringements, obtaining releases or permissions, and the application of guidelines to emerging technologies. The issues surrounding copyright compliance are dynamic and in flux due to the constant rate of technological change. Media managers and faculty clients must work continuously to update their knowledge and operational understanding of copyright law and its policy requirements. Following changes in copyright legislation and legal interpretations are best accomplished through attending appropriate media conferences, reviewing current references and media materials, and monitoring copyright Web sites. An excellent Web site that can direct users to sources where they can find guidance on copyright issues is at the Stanford University library: http://fairuse.stanford.edu/internet/. The federal government's explanation of the law is at http://www.loc.gov/copyright. Finally, the media manager might want to designate a staff member to be the point person to field copyright questions.

These issues and others require ongoing internal and external information and training programs for managers and their organizations. From this activity evolve specific rules, procedures, and policies for the organization or media center. The reference materials and sources at the end of this chapter, as well as local training and development organizations, state and national professional groups, and governmental agencies, should be utilized by managers to keep abreast with these evolving and demanding management topics.

Rules

Rules are short, explicit statements that tell what to do, or not to do, in specific situations. They are most often applied to human behavior but can cover many specific problems that are not complicated. At the behavioral level, rules might deal with the length of coffee breaks, where people may and may not smoke, or how the telephone should be answered. At the operational level, a rule might tell when to order an item and when to call for competitive bids. An example might be, "Items costing more than $1,000 must be secured through multiple competitive bids."

Rules should be as simple and direct as possible, leaving little or no room for interpretation. Typically, rules are established to provide guidance for employees working at lower levels in an organization, thus saving time and effort by eliminating the constant checking back and forth that would be necessary otherwise. Rules may also prescribe penalties for infractions. They should be considered to be relatively short term and open to change as needs dictate.

When establishing rules, managers must be aware of how rules affect people. Rules should emphasize positive rather than negative aspects. For instance, a rule proclaiming: "All injuries must be reported immediately," is positive and implies that management is concerned about the well-being of employees. A corollary to this is that management can also determine how the injury happened and take steps to see that the cause or causes are eliminated. Rules with a positive slant will reinforce positive attitudes and actions and at the same time reduce or eliminate negative ones. It might be said that positive rules seldom carry penalties. This is not meant to imply that penalties should not be imposed when infractions might create a critical situation. In many construction activities, for instance, hard hats are required, and workers who persist in not wearing them will be fired. Managers would be derelict in their duties if they did not make the rule known to all and proceed to enforce the penalty when the rule was not observed.

When applying the "keep it simple" philosophy to rules, managers should remember that too many rules may actually create control problems rather than reduce them. The more rules there are to be remembered, the more likely they will be forgotten because there is too much else to keep in mind.

Procedures

Procedures detail how something should be done. They usually involve a sequence of steps designed to facilitate an operation or task. Checking out a video from a video library involves a specific procedure. The details vary from library to library, but the basics are essentially the same because similar kinds of information are required. Procedures are usually designed and put in place by managers, though in some instances, where technical expertise is required, an expert may be called in to formulate the required procedures.

Perhaps the best way to differentiate between rules and procedures is to note that rules can be made regarding procedures but that procedures are seldom if ever developed regarding the rules themselves. One may, however, have to follow certain procedures if a rule is broken. For instance, there would probably be a required procedure for discharging workers who broke the "wear your safety hat" rule.

A procedure must be laid out clearly and precisely, step by step, and in this respect might be viewed as a set of rules detailing how something is to be accomplished. Like rules, procedures are precise and leave little room for deviation. In contrast to rules, however, procedures may in some instances be long and involved. An example here might be procedures detailing how to troubleshoot problems in electronic equipment. Other procedures, however, may involve only three or four steps to complete.

Policies

In general, rules deal with behaviors and procedures detail tasks. Policies, on the other hand, deal with goals. Policies are concerned with *what* should be done rather than *how*, as is the case with rules and procedures. Thus policies are less specific than rules and procedures and thereby require a measure of thought, judgment, and interpretation in their application. The basic purpose of policies is to provide an ongoing guidance system for an organization or unit within an organization. Policy can be developed at any level within an organization, though major policy usually comes down from the top. Policy developed within a unit in an organization must be in tune with those policies promulgated by upper management.

Policies are long-term, broad, generalized statements that provide guidelines, establish parameters, set directions, and identify goals. They are designed to determine organizational behavior and thus are the genesis of the rules and procedures that serve to implement policy. In this way all three are interrelated to some extent, and the lines between them are not always clearly defined.

Policies are not always written. In most organizations a small body of unwritten policy exists. Broad, general policy statements are often difficult to implement and as a result, informal unwritten policies often arise to assist in the interpretation of a written policy.

Unwritten policies are usually more specific than the written policy to which they apply. As conditions change, so might unwritten policy, even though the written policy does not. An example of written and unwritten policy might involve rewarding good performance. The written policy might state, "Outstanding contributions by employees will be rewarded." What is to be considered outstanding, and what form should the rewards take? Thus, in some cases the rewards might be monetary, while others might involve praise and recognition. Giving an appropriately engraved watch to a retiring employee has a long tradition and in essence was an unwritten policy.

MAKING DECISIONS

Managers at any level are basically concerned with four management activities: planning, organizing, leading, and controlling. All four functions require the application of decision-making knowledge and skills. Decision making is part and parcel of the manager's job, for problems come in all sizes and shapes and arrive at most inopportune times. Still, most managers are in their jobs because they like making decisions.

Basically, decisions fall into two categories that are commonly identified in management literature as (1) programmed decisions and (2) nonprogrammed decisions.

Programmed Decisions

Programmed decisions are the type that demand most of a manager's time and attention, for they are of a routine and repetitive nature. They have been made frequently in the past and will continue to be made in the future. The problems leading to programmed decisions are usually well structured and have well-defined parameters. Quite often the solution to the problem or problems can be found in existing policies, procedures, or rules. An example of a recurring problem and its programmed solution might relate to the purchase of costly items for the media center. In this example, the rules have come down from above and the decision has been entirely routinized, so it does not take much time or thought. The rules that apply might resemble the following:

Items listed at more than $1,000 must be purchased through competitive bids.

Three or more competitive bids are required unless three bidders cannot be found.

The most difficult decision that a manager might have to make in this case might be when to stop looking for more bidders when only one or two can be located.

In other situations, programmed decisions may have grown out of custom or precedent, and the manager follows what other managers have done in the past. For instance, a manager might send a note of apology where a mistake has inconvenienced a client. If something had been inadvertently lost or damaged, custom may call for the manager to replace the item, again with apologies to the client. This is not to imply that all programmed decisions are that cut-and-dried or that no analysis or judgment is involved. A policy might state that the customer is always right, which is intended to provide guidance, but the interpretation of *always* and *right* lies within the province of the individual manager.

Nonprogrammed Decisions

Nonprogrammed decisions are another matter entirely. Typically, nonprogrammed decisions will be made by upper management, for these decisions may be critical to the welfare of the entire entity. A manager may well become involved as upper management seeks information, statistics, educated guesses, and advice.

Nonprogrammed decisions arise from problems that usually cannot be anticipated, are of a nature where existing guidelines may not apply, are new and unique, and do not fit the familiar patterns used in solving previous problems. Looking to the concept of not buying trouble where it does not exist, remember that it is not always easy to identify nonprogrammed problems or to get a good hold on them. Once the fact that a problem exists has been established, it is in a manager's interest to "borrow a little trouble" and look beyond where the problem seems to lie. The following steps will facilitate decision making in the search for viable problem solutions:

1. *Identify the problem.* As noted earlier, most nonprogrammed decisions arise from relative nonstructured problems. For this reason, the parameters of the problem may be fuzzy and unclear. Be sure that all of the problem elements, not just some, have been perceived.

2. *Analyze the problem.* Look at it from all sides and investigate all angles with a view to developing alternative solutions. At this stage no decisions are being made; the task is to develop as many rational alternative solutions as possible. The more choices that are outlined at this point, the better.

3. *Review the alternatives previously developed.* Select the best course of action based upon criteria set up during problem analysis. One must assume that in determining viable alternatives, all possible ramifications of a particular proposal have been considered. In decision making, as in science, any action will create reactions, and not all reactions will produce positive results.

4. *Implement the decision.* This phase starts by informing all concerned about the decision. How one goes about this will be discussed later, but if everyone knows what is going on, implementation has a better chance of working. Put the machinery into place and start things going. Note here that depending upon the nature of the problem, a number of supporting decisions may be required to get things moving.

5. *Evaluate.* Just because a decision has been made and implementation is under way does not mean that the problem has been solved. Things may not work at all, or there may be bugs that must be worked out of the scheme. It is essential that the manager monitor the operation carefully to determine if and how much progress is being made. Thus when problems are noted, changes can be made.

The following example may not appear to be very complicated, but it represents at least one aspect of nonprogrammed decision making:

> Because of financial problems, the center manager has been instructed to reduce expenses by reducing personnel. The accepted policy for accomplishing this task is the "last on–first off" concept, and other managers in the organization follow it. Following the policy would offer an easy way out for the media manager, but to do so would mean discharging a new staff artist with talents critical to center services. The manager had searched for just such a person for several years.

No matter what happens, it is a tough situation, and here is where viable alternative solutions may have to be proposed. There may be more than one answer to the problem, if one does not consider this to be a "programmed" decision.

It is immediately apparent that there is not one right decision for any given problem. There are too many variables for a manager to be certain which is the best way to jump. Realistically, managers hope that the majority of their decisions will fall into the *right* category, but they recognize the fact that they will make some bad decisions too. In most organizations the unwritten policies make allowances for mistakes (as long as one does not make too many). Careful attention to the basics of decision making will assure a more positive average.

It stands to reason that problems requiring thoughtful decisions on the part of managers do not come in neat packages. Some will be structured and easy to handle, while others will almost defy analysis. Most fall somewhere in between. Thus, a decision may call for a manager to consult available rules, procedures, and policies on one hand and follow the five steps outlined earlier on the other. The ultimate evaluation centers upon how well the decisions made have worked.

TYPES OF DECISION MAKERS

Just as there seem to be two categories for decisions (programmed and non-programmed), so there seem to be two basic types of decision makers. Some prefer to employ a structured approach to decision making; others are intuitive decision makers. Decision makers taking the structured approach gather all available pertinent information relating to the problem at hand. The information is then organized, charted, graphed, and summarized for use in analyzing and structuring a problem when developing possible solutions. These managers try to consider every aspect bearing upon the problem, and no detail is too small for concern. They enjoy getting into a problem and researching its every aspect as they search for solutions.

On the other side are those managers preferring to deal with open-ended problems using an intuitive rather than structured approach. Intuitive decision makers appear to absorb information from a variety of sources as they get a "feel" for the problem and possible solutions. Charts, graphs, projections, and formulas do not play as big a role in their deliberations. Information is gathered in a nonsystematic manner, and intuitive decision makers usually cannot tell exactly how they arrived at decisions. The bits and pieces of available information are somehow gathered, assimilated, internalized, and arranged into a gestalt that leads to a decision. This certainly is not a very scientific approach to problem solving; but according to research, when creative, novel solutions to problems are needed, intuitive decision makers perform well. It appears that there are times when the structured approach works best and times when an intuitive approach is most effective. How one approaches problem solving and decision making may be so integral that it would be impossible to completely change one's approach to decision making. On the other hand, it may be possible to train oneself to do a little of both. All decisions have a certain amount of trial and error involved, and in the final analysis it is what works that counts, not the process employed to find the solution.

EFFECTIVE DECISION MAKING

One may well ask what qualities effective decision makers seem to have in common that are not found in less able managers. Perhaps there are too many inter-related factors to pinpoint everything, but a number of elements do seem to con-tribute to the process—judgment, experience, analytic ability, invention, insight, and creativity. Some contribute more than others to the overall process and some are most useful at different stages in the process. This depends in part upon the de-cision maker's style, and the makeup of the problem to be solved has a lot to do with how the above elements interact. Judgment and experience are critical elements in decision making.

Good judgment may be another name for what is often called common sense. Basically, good judgment calls for reasoning ability, the wise evaluation and applica-tion of pertinent data, and, of course, the effective use of lessons gleaned from past experience.

Experience contributes both breadth and depth to decision making, based in large part upon what has transpired and what has and what has not worked previ-ously. The value of experience depends in part upon how it was acquired: It is possi-ble to have had a single year's experience many times or to have grown with each experience so that experience is cumulative. Experience can interfere in the sense that old solutions may be inappropriate in new circumstances. Past experiences may color or block one's clear perceptions of certain problems. Less experienced man-agers may see the problem clearly and, therefore, come up with more effective solu-tions. Experience, then, may prove to be a two-edged sword. Managers must be careful in applying experience when assessing current problems and solutions.

Creativity relates to the ability to view problems from new or different perspec-tives and to come up with novel solutions. Creativity calls for a certain amount of invention, thus these two elements pair well together. A creative, inventive solution is often so simple, uncomplicated, and out in the open that others often wonder why they did not think of it. Perhaps being creative and inventive is something man-agers can train themselves to become as they develop problem-solving skills, but not much is known about this aspect presently. One technique that fosters creative thinking is to brainstorm a vexing problem with several other people. Collective thinking and discussion often result in finding creative solutions.

Analytic skills involve the knowledge and ability to pull together from various sources hard information, such as cost analysis, probability studies, and past opera-tions, that might have a bearing on the present problem or problems. Analytic skills enable decision makers to dissect, classify, and structure information in ways that facilitate interpretation in a search for appropriate solutions.

Insight refers to what is probably an innate ability to see to the heart of a prob-lem and make intuitive judgments that are not necessarily based upon hard facts. Managers who prefer dealing with nonprogrammed, unstructured, messy, open-ended problems often tend to make intuitive decisions.

Outside input is the ability to solicit and use the input from others, such as fellow managers and unit employees. Sharing problems with staff members is an excellent way of keeping them informed and at the same time getting the benefit of their thinking. Sometimes the best solutions to problems come from the employees who will be most affected by decisions made. Implementation of decisions is certainly facilitated if employees have been kept well informed and have been involved in working out solutions. In difficult situations, a constant flow of information will go a long way toward reducing negative stress for both employees and manager, thus resulting in a more effective working climate.

The manner in which the above factors, and many more not mentioned, interface with each other in a manager's mind precludes any effort to predict which style or method one should employ in decision making. Perhaps it is sufficient to suggest that whatever is most comfortable for the individual is the best method to employ— as long as he or she keeps coming up with good solutions.

SUGGESTED ACTIVITIES

1. Develop an organizational chart for a hypothetical media service center with four divisions. Add position titles/job functions as needed.

2. Review and evaluate the organizational charts and mission statements of several media or technology support centers on their Web pages. Compare and contrast their structure to determine their organizational management philosophy.

3. Write a rules, procedures, and policies manual for one division in the organizational chart already developed.

4. Given the following problem, apply the first five steps stated earlier in the chapter to arrive at a recommended solution. Explain each task you would employ and defend each position taken to arrive at your decision. Explain how you would implement the decision and evaluate the results.

    Problem: You are the media manager of a large media service program. One of your departments, Media Collection Services, is faced with a problem. The program has in the past purchased and circulated nonprint materials to your university faculty and students. But owing to a shrinking budget, you must now decide whether you should continue to purchase videocassettes at an average cost of $200 per title or switch to CD-ROM or some other server storage and distribution technology.

5. Develop a copyright compliance plan for a major multimedia production. Demonstrate how individual visuals, text, music, and other materials can be legally utilized through citation, licensing, and fair use compliance.

REFERENCES

Certo, Samuel C. 1997. *Modern Management.* 7th ed. Upper Saddle River, N.J.: Prentice Hall.

Eurich, Nell P. 1985. "Corporate Classrooms." *The Carnegie Foundation for the Advancement of Teaching.* (A Carnegie Foundation Special Report). Lawrenceville, N.J.: Princeton University Press.

Lemler, Ford L., ed. 1951. *Audio-Visual Programs in Action.* Ann Arbor, Mich.: Michigan Audio-Visual Association.

Peters, Thomas J., and Robert H. Waterman, Jr. 1982. *In Search of Excellence: Lessons from America's Best-Run Companies.* New York: Warner Books.

Schmidt, William D. *Learning Resources Programs That Make a Difference.* Washington, D.C.: Association for Educational Communications and Technology, 1987.

MEDIA RESOURCES

Abilene Paradox. CRM Productions, 28 minutes. Carlsbad, Calif.: CRM Productions, 1991. Videocassette.

CNN/Prentice Hall Video Program for Certo/Modern Management: Diversity, Quality, Ethics, and the Global Environment. (Series of 22 programs). Cable News Network, 4–14 minutes. Upper Saddle River, N.J.: Prentice Hall, 1994. Videocassettes.

Copyright: The Internet, Multimedia and the Law. Chip Taylor Communications, 40 minutes. Derry, N.H.: Chip Taylor Communications, 1996. Videocassette.

Fair Use Guidelines for Educational Multimedia: The Final Document and Its Implementation. Consortium of College and University Media Centers, 120 minutes. Ames, Iowa: CCUMC, Iowa State University, 1997. Videocassette.

Health and the Workplace. Films for the Humanities & Sciences, 19 minutes. Princeton, N.J.: Films for the Humanities & Sciences, 1990. Videocassette.

In Search of Excellence: Lessons from America's Best-Run Companies. PBS Video, 88 minutes. Alexandria, Va.: Public Broadcasting Service, 1985. Videocassette.

Introduction to Legal Issues. RMI Media Productions, 30 minutes. Kansas City, Mo.: RMI Media Productions, 1997. Videocassette.

Legal Issues for Managers. American Media Incorporated, 23 minutes. West Des Moines, Iowa: American Media Incorporated, 1997. Videocassette.

Managing Diversity in Business. Films for the Humanities & Sciences, 59 minutes. Princeton, N.J.: Films for the Humanities & Sciences, 1993. Videocassette.

The Mosaic Workplace (Series of ten programs). Films for the Humanities & Sciences, 14–30 minutes. Princeton, N.J.: Films for the Humanities & Sciences, 1991. Videocassettes.

New Issues: Copyright. Association for Information Media and Equipment (AIME), 18 minutes. Clarksdale, Miss.: AIME, 1994. Videocassette.

Quality: The Big Picture. Salenger Videos, 17 minutes. Santa Monica, Calif.: Salenger, 1990. Videocassette.

Sexual Harassment from 9 to 5. Films for the Humanities & Sciences, 26 minutes. Princeton, N.J.: Films for the Humanities & Sciences, 1991. Videocassette.

Sexual Politics at Work. Alvin H. Perlmutter, 57 minutes. Alexandria, Va.: Public Broadcasting Service, 1993. Videocassette.

Teaching the Elephant to Dance . . . Today: Empowering Change in Your Organization. CRM Productions, 40 minutes. Carlsbad, Calif.: CRM Productions, 1997. Videocassette.

Theory X and Theory Y: Two Sets of Assumptions. Salenger Videos, 11 minutes. Santa Monica, Calif.: Salenger, 1974. Videocassette.

Understanding the Americans with Disabilities Act. Eastern Paralyzed Veterans Association, 30 minutes. Edison, N.J.: Video Management Services, 1994. Videocassette.

Values and Ethics: Situations for Discussion. American Media Incorporated, 30 minutes. West Des Moines, Iowa: American Media Incorporated, 1993. Videocassette.

Workplace Violence: Recognizing and Defusing Aggressive Behavior. American Media Incorporated, 26 minutes. West Des Moines, Iowa: American Media Incorporated, 1997. Videocassette.

SELECTED BIBLIOGRAPHY

Adams, M., L. A. Bell, and P. Griffin, eds. *Teaching for Diversity and Social Justice, A Sourcebook.* New York: Routledge Press, 1997.

Bigelow, John D., ed. *Managerial Skills: Explorations in Practical Knowledge.* Newbury Park, Calif.: Sage Publications, 1991.

Bruwelheide, Janis H. *The Copyright Primer for Librarians and Educators.* 2d ed. Chicago: American Library Association, 1995.

California State University. *Fair Use of Copyrighted Works: A Crucial Element in Educating America* (pamphlet). Seal Beach, Calif.: Consortium for Educational Technology for University Systems, 1995.

Chaleff, Ira. *The Courageous Follower: Standing Up, To and For Our Leaders.* San Francisco, Calif.: Barrett-Koehler, 1998.

"Digital Copyright Guidelines Still in Flux." *School Library Journal,* 43, no. 3 (1997): 17–18.

Holoviak, Stephen J. *Golden Rule Management.* Reading, Mass.: Addison-Wesley, 1993.

Marlow, Eugene. *Managing Corporate Media.* Rev. ed. White Plains, N.Y.: Knowledge Industry Publications, 1989.

Marsteller, William A. *Creative Management: A Classic on Successful Management, Leadership, Creativity and Motivation.* Chicago: NTC Business Books, 1992.

Ritchie, Mark. "Organizing for Quality Service: Improve Internal Service First." *Tech Trends,* 39, no. 5 (1994): 15–18.

———. *Quality Management for Educational Technology Services.* Washington, D.C.: Association for Educational Communications and Technology, 1994.

Rosner, Bob. *Working Wounded: Advice That Adds Insight to Injury.* New York: Warner Books, 1998.

Schmid, William T. *Media Center Management: A Practical Guide.* New York: Hastings House, 1980.

Sinofsky, Esther R. *A Copyright Primer for Educational and Industrial Media Producers.* 2d ed. Washington, D.C.: Association for Educational Communications and Technology, 1994.

Software Publishers Association. "Software Piracy: Is It Happening in Your School or University? *T.H.E. Journal,* 25, no. 9 (1998): 66–67.

Van Orden, Phyllis J. *The Collection Program in Schools: Concepts, Practices, and Information Sources.* 2d ed. Englewood, Colo.: Libraries Unlimited, 1995.

Vlcek, Charles W. *Adoptable Copyright Policy: Copyright Policy and Manuals Designed for Adoption by Schools, Colleges, and Universities.* Washington, D.C.: Association for Educational Communications and Technology, 1992.

5

MANAGING MEDIA MATERIALS SERVICES

The media professional serves as an information broker; that is, the link between a user's expressed information need and the information which will fill that need. . . . In serving as an information broker, the media professional must provide access to resources. Access is probably the key word for the media professional. People who have studied information users have discovered that most individuals use information which is most readily at hand. The more difficult information is to obtain, the less likely it is that the person will seek it and use it.

Margaret E. Chisholm and Donald P. Ely,
Media Personnel in Education: A Competency Approach, 1976

OBJECTIVES

At the conclusion of this chapter you should be able to

1. List and discuss factors to be considered before determining media materials collection needs.

2. Describe the purpose and content of a materials selection policy.

3. List reference sources for locating nonprint instructional and training materials.

4. State the purposes and effective procedures that should be employed when evaluating instructional and training materials.

5. List the basic tasks involved in the technical processing of media materials.

6. Illustrate how each of the following materials should be prepared and labeled for circulation: videocassettes, CD-ROMs, videodiscs, and computer software.

7. Illustrate and discuss how materials should be cataloged.

8. List, diagram, and describe the major tasks and procedures involved in circulating materials.

9. Describe how a collection can be maintained in good physical condition.

10. List the basic criteria that should be included in a media collection weeding policy.

INTRODUCTION

Chapters 5 and 6 deal with ordering, processing, and circulating of materials and equipment. While there is a very strong trend toward automating these processes, there are numerous programs that have not become fully automated. For that reason information will be provided that deals with manual techniques for procuring and handling materials and equipment. Chapter 8 is devoted to the use of computers to automate these processes.

No two media material service programs are identical. While they may appear to be similar in terms of the names of the organization and its departments, the services will have many differences. As mentioned in chapter 1, there are a wide variety of names for media service programs. Departmental programs and organizational structures within a media program show the same diversity. Regardless of what each department of a media center is named, most provide a variety of services to their patrons, such as furnishing materials and equipment and delivering instructional development, production, and maintenance services. This chapter will discuss the center's materials collection.

As outlined in previous chapters, the media materials collection within a media service center may include a wide variety of materials or may be limited to a few types, depending upon client needs. During the last five years there has been a strong trend to standardize on the use of fewer media formats. Film, reel-to-reel audiotapes, phonograph records, and filmstrips have all experienced rapidly declining use, while videocassettes, videodiscs, computer software, and CD-ROMs have rapidly become the mediums of choice. Overhead transparencies, 35mm slides, and audiocassettes (or compact discs) are still used fairly frequently. Print materials are still heavily used, but, even here, there is a marked trend toward using more and more of these materials in CD-ROM and Internet format. The following are some typical materials found in media collections:

Materials showing motion
- 16mm films
- videocassettes
- CD-ROMs
- videodiscs
- computer software

Audio materials
- tape recordings
- phonograph records
- compact discs

Still projection materials
- 35mm slides
- transparencies
- filmstrips
- CD-ROMs
- videodiscs
- computer software

Sound and projected still images
- sound-slide programs
- sound filmstrips
- instructional kits
- CD-ROMs
- videodiscs
- computer software

Other materials
- maps/globes
- study prints
- specimen collections
- drawings
- models and mock-ups
- exhibits and displays
- realia

Print materials
- books
- media reference materials
- periodicals
- programmed instructional materials
- media materials catalogs

In addition to storing such materials, the media center must establish policies and procedures to facilitate their selection, processing, circulation, and maintenance. A collection is of little value if materials cannot be located quickly, circulated when needed, and maintained in excellent condition. To accomplish that objective, the following specific tasks need to be performed:

1. Determine collection needs.

2. Select appropriate materials.

3. Develop appropriate technical processing procedures.

4. Develop effective and efficient circulation procedures.

5. Develop materials maintenance procedures.

Each of the above tasks will be discussed in this chapter. The value of employing a computerized management system to semiautomate the logistical tasks involved cannot be overemphasized. Computers save valuable staff time that can be better used performing other necessary tasks. Data normally collected on forms can be input directly into a computer, thereby eliminating the cost and handling of many forms. Information usually repeated on a form each time a patron requests a service can be automatically programmed by the computer, decreasing the time it takes to complete requests for services. Daily schedules, due-out and due-in lists, shipping labels, and a multitude of other logistical activities can be preprogrammed and printed daily by the computer. These computer applications and others will be discussed in chapter 8. While the use of the computer will be stressed in this chapter, manual methods of performing these tasks will also be outlined, for there are still programs that must rely on these methods.

DETERMINING COLLECTION NEEDS

The first task in developing a collection is to determine the clients' needs. These expressed needs provide the basis upon which a collection is built. For this reason it is important to involve clients in the search and selection process. In K-12 schools, teachers and administrators must participate; in colleges and universities, faculty must provide input; and in corporate media centers, clients in engineering, sales, training, and other areas must become involved.

Client advice should not be limited to identifying the content of the materials to be purchased, but should also relate to the type of media. Should the collection be limited to videocassettes, computer software, CD-ROMs, or other media, or does it make any difference?

A factor that may dictate media format is cost. Some media formats, like film, are very expensive, while others, like CD-ROM, tend to be quite inexpensive. However, media materials costs are not the only cost consideration; the cost of the equipment used to display the materials must also be considered. While the cost of the CD-ROM might be quite low, be sure to consider the cost of the equipment needed to play it properly. Finally, there are valid reasons to use some of the older media formats (e.g., unique content or an only source of a subject).

Other factors to be considered include large image versus small image, equipment operational simplicity, user familiarity with equipment, reliability, and cost of maintenance. Consider these questions: Is the equipment easy to use or will complexity curtail use of instructional materials? Will users switch to an unfamiliar medium? Will a change to another format increase maintenance costs? After answers or best guesses are determined for the above concerns, the manager is in a position to balance all the factors and decide upon which media format to include in the media collection. In some cases a client will request specific titles in a particular format, and wherever possible the manager should accommodate the client.

SELECTING APPROPRIATE MATERIALS

Step one in selecting appropriate instructional/training materials is to develop criteria to facilitate the selection process. The rationale for such a policy is quite evident. It is to serve as a guide in selecting instructional/training materials. Most media professionals will agree that a written selection policy should exist, but in practice some prefer to have the freedom to operate without the limitations of a guiding policy. While this "no policy" policy may work in some institutions, the present movement toward more accountability mandates, at least in the public education sector, that a carefully developed selection policy be followed.

Developing a Selection Policy

The selection policy serves as the cornerstone of a media collection. It provides the guidelines that prevent haphazard collection growth, thereby creating consistency in the collection's development. The selection policy should reflect the institution's and the media center's clients' needs. User input should be obtained, considered, and integrated into the policy if it is to reflect those needs.

Before a policy can be developed, a number of questions must be answered. Answers based upon the needs of the users make each selection policy and the resulting collections different. The following are some typical questions to be addressed prior to developing a selection policy:

What content areas should the collection cover?

What media format(s) will be included?

How will materials be evaluated prior to purchasing?

What criteria will be used to evaluate quality?

Will professional review sources be used in the evaluation process?

Does potential use of the material justify the cost?

Are multiple copies needed?

Are similar materials already available in the existing collection?

Betty J. Morris, John T. Gillespie, and Diana L. Spirt, in *Administering the School Library Media Center* (1992, 264–65), have summarized the elements that should be addressed in a materials selection policy. It should include:

1. A statement of the school district and individual school philosophy, particularly in relation to educational materials and intellectual freedom.

2. A similar statement summarizing the aims and objectives of the library media center in relation to this overall philosophy.

3. A list of those who participate in selection and of the specific objectives of the selection function.

4. An indication of delegated as well as final responsibility for selection, including a definition of the position of the media center personnel in this operation.

5. A list of the types of media found in the center and of the criteria applied to the selection of each.

6. An enumeration of the selection aids most frequently consulted.

7. A description of the procedures, forms, and practices used in selection.

8. An indication of areas of the collection that will be either stressed or de-emphasized.

9. Additional or modifying criteria for the various clientele served. For example, a different set of standards might apply when buying professional materials for teachers than for purchasing high-interest material for slow or reluctant readers.

10. Statements concerning the media center's policies toward gifts, sponsored material, weeding, duplication, and replacement.

11. Information concerning any cooperative acquisition projects in which the center is involved with other schools and libraries.

12. A description of the procedures for handling complaints and a copy of any forms used when a request is made to reevaluate a particular piece of material.

An examination of the above guidelines discloses the fact that they address how the materials will relate to the institution's mission, goals, procedures, and who will be responsible. The guidelines do not deal with the specific selection criteria that should be used to evaluate materials for purchase. Van Orden, in *The Collection Program in Schools* (1995, 128–29), lists and discusses specific criteria that should guide the selection process. Only the list follows, for her discussion of the elements is quite thorough:

> How can one evaluate the idea of intellectual content of a work? Criteria can include (1) authority; (2) appropriateness of content to users; (3) scope; (4) accuracy; (5) treatment; (6) arrangement and organization; (7) literary quality; (8) materials available on the subject; (9) durability of information; (10) reputation of author, artist, or producer; (11) special features; and (12) value to the collection.

To the above list one might also add two more criteria—dated content and technical quality. Some media soon becomes dated because of the style of clothes worn or the vintage of automobiles or airplanes shown. Viewers can become so involved in those differences that they may miss the message of the material. Thus materials older than five to seven years should be carefully examined prior to purchase. For obvious reasons the technical quality of materials related to production techniques and visual and audio elements should also exhibit excellent quality. Examples of materials selection policies can be found in appendix 3.

Once a selection policy has been developed, it must be diligently applied if the policy is to be of any value. The temptation to purchase a few titles on impulse because of a sale or flashy advertising must be carefully controlled. If the policy has been carefully developed, it will reflect the *true* needs of the institution. It is doubtful that buying materials not scrutinized using the policy criteria would result in a high-quality and needed collection. The media executive must insist that all who are involved in the selection process apply the policy criteria when making their recommendations.

Locating Sources for
Instructional/Training Materials

Locating materials to purchase is not difficult, but finding materials that meet specific user requests is. Advertisements from media producers are readily available once they discover that you may be a potential purchaser. Catalogs and brochures are indeed valuable as sources of materials and should be retained and filed for future reference. Individual brochures and copies of specific titles from catalogs can be distributed to potential users.

Another source for materials are professional journals and periodicals. Most professional publications in all fields usually contain advertisements and/or reviews of available instructional or training materials. Clients also encounter materials at professional or technical conferences and workshops. Encourage your clients to inform you of materials from such sources if they are interested in considering them for purchase. The following is a selected list of publications for use when searching for instructional or training materials. Each publication lists titles that are available and, in most cases, provides short content descriptions. Most are published annually; always be sure to select the most current issue.

Available from R. R. Bowker, c/o Reed Reference Publishing, P.O. Box 31, New Providence, NJ 07974.

AV Market Place™
Directory of over 7,660 companies that create, apply, or distribute a wide range of AV equipment and services for business, education, science, and government.

Microcomputer Software Guide Online
Information on more than 17,000 software programs from over 4,000 producers, with search capability. Updated monthly.

Software Encyclopedia™
A list of computer software for business, industry, manufacturing, scientific research, education, and the home. Some 23,000 software programs from thousands of producers are indexed and fully described, including required memory, language, and systems on which each program is designed to run.

Available from the National Information Center for Educational Media (NICEM), P.O. Box 8640, Albuquerque, NM 87198-8640. NICEM develops several reference sources based on its extensive database of all types of software available from vendors for use in education and training.

NICEM NET, Web address: http://www.nicem.com. E-mail address:
nicem@nicem.com
Information on the complete NICEM database and other products.

NICEM Producer and Distributor Index Online
Contains over 25,000 producers and distributors of AV materials of all types. Also available as a CD-ROM.

NICEM MARC CD-ROM

For use in cataloging media collections, this CD-ROM provides access to individual MARC (machine-readable cataloging) records representing over 423,000 titles in all AV formats. Also available online.

NICEM Reference Online

Contains over 440,000 bibliographic records of nonprint educational materials which are searchable by title, date, age level, subject area, and media types. Also available on CD-ROM.

NICEM THESAURUS

This print version contains the 4,300 indexing terms that NICEM editors use when creating the bibliographic entries for their database. Useful for conducting searches and cataloging media collections. Also available online.

Available from other sources:

AV Online CD-ROM on SilverPlatter. SilverPlatter Information, 100 River Ridge Drive, Norwood, MA 02062.

A database of over 423,000 entries for users to identify materials on any subject or to look up known materials by title or distribution source.

Educators Progress Service, Inc. Box 497, Randolph, WI 53959.

Guides to free instructional and training materials in various subject fields. The individual guides include annotations and technical information.

Multimedia Compendium, Emerging Technology Consultants, Inc., 2819 Hamline Avenue North, St. Paul, MN 55113.

An annual guide to over 4,800 multimedia resources for education and training. Included are laser discs, CDs, multimedia software, and Internet courseware.

The Multimedia Source Book, Infinity Interactive, Inc., 274 Raritan Center Parkway, Edison, NJ 08837.

A guide to over 6,000 multimedia productions. Available as a book or on CD-ROM.

National Audiovisual Center, c/o National Technical Information Center, Technology Administration, U.S. Department of Commerce, Springfield, VA 22161.

The Natural Audiovisual Center provides central access to federally developed training and education materials. Over 9,000 audiovisual and media productions, grouped into more than 600 individual subject headings, are available.

Online Computer Library Center, Inc. (OCLC), 6565 Frantz Road, Dublin, OH 43017-3395.

OCLC is a nonprofit, membership, nationwide library computer and research organization whose network and services link more than 30,000 libraries in 65 countries and territories. OCLC services help libraries locate, acquire, catalog, access, and lend library materials.

Media reference materials and reviews should be made easily accessible to all clients. A convenient and effective method to do this is to establish a *media reference library* housed in a secure but accessible location. Catalogs, brochures, reviews, and any other books or material relating to the selection and use of media should be located here. The books and large reference indexes in the library should be cataloged and labeled for inventory and circulation purposes. If possible, create a friendly atmosphere with lounge chairs and tables to make the reference area comfortable and attractive.

Evaluating Materials

There are many existing procedures for evaluating materials for purchase. They range from simple to complex and some are effective while others are questionable. The following procedures are employed in many media service centers:

The "do-it-yourself plan," where only the media manager or the staff evaluate materials.

Materials are purchased as requested without evaluation.

All requests for materials from clients are obtained for preview.

Only materials most often rented are purchased.

Only materials highly recommended by professional review sources are ordered for preview or purchased.

A review committee (or committees) is used.

It is our opinion that a combination of most of the above options makes the best material evaluation program. Obviously the do-it-yourself plan is fraught with problems. While the manager and staff may think that they know client needs, it is doubtful that they truly do, especially in a large institution. To purchase materials without previewing and evaluating is equally bad. There are a lot of poor-quality materials that are made to look good in advertising brochures, but advertising does not improve a poor production. How can one know that the content fits needs or that the technical quality meets standards unless the material is evaluated? While evaluating and previewing materials is time-consuming, it is time well spent. Most materials are too costly not to evaluate; even less expensive materials, such as some CD-ROMs, should be previewed. Most distributors have "on approval" plans available to enable the purchaser to order materials and return them if they do not meet client content needs and technical or quality standards.

Materials requested for purchase by clients need not be bought unless the media service program budget is adequate. It is often more economical to rent films or other expensive materials from outside sources if the materials will have limited use within an institution. Generally, if the frequency of use at a given rental rate will not pay for the materials within five years, it is more economical to rent. This same rule can be applied in reverse to items that are rented. Even though the client has not requested that a title be purchased, once its frequency of use meets the established criteria, it should be purchased. Frequently, rented materials prove useful and make a strong argument for purchase.

Professional reviews of materials should be considered, but only as another evaluation source. While a particular title may be given a poor professional review, it may be the only material available or the material that best meets a client's need. It is the client who is going to use the material, and his or her evaluation should be given more weight than that of the professional reviewer. However, if favorably reviewed materials can be found that meet the client's needs, then they should be given higher priority for purchase consideration.

Finally, and probably most important, is the issue of evaluation committees. If evaluation committees are used, the media manager must be willing to accept and purchase materials based upon their recommendations. Busy people soon lose interest if their work and subsequent recommendations are not used. The committee should consist of people representative of clients, otherwise they cannot know the collection needs. While committee recommendations should be considered as advisory, a media manager is ill advised if materials that the committee recommends are not purchased, unless there are valid reasons for the decision. An expansion of the evaluation committee option is to appoint subcommittees, a group for each content area or related content areas. This method assures that content specialists evaluate materials before purchase recommendations are made.

Evaluation committees need some training. They must be familiar with the selection policy and understand the evaluation criteria. Training sessions should include the viewing of both good and poor productions with committee members, applying evaluation criteria, and completing evaluation forms. This activity should be followed by a critique and discussion session. Well-trained committee members are valuable to a media manager. Not only do they make valid evaluations, but through their own individual involvement within the institution's power structure they often can provide budgetary support for the media services program.

All materials should be stored in a humidity-controlled and dust-free environment, at a temperature comfortable for people. The temperature should be 60°–72° F, except for film archives. The recommended temperature for film archives is 40° F, with humidity maintained at 40–50 percent. This will prevent fungus from forming on materials (a problem in more humid areas). In order to prevent the deposit of oily oxides and dust on surfaces, personnel should not be allowed to eat, drink, or smoke in the materials storage or maintenance areas.

Professional Review Sources

Various review sources provide evaluations of instructional/training materials. Professional review sources select media professionals to individually preview materials and make critical reviews. The reviews are then published and made available to media managers usually by subscription or by membership in the parent organization.

The following major professional evaluation services are available:

Booklist, American Library Association, 50 E. Huron Street, Chicago, IL 60611

Educational Software Preview Guide, International Society for Technology in Education, 1787 Agate Street, Eugene, OR 97403

Landers Film and Video Reviews, Landers Associates, P.O. Box 27309, Escondido, CA 92027

Media and Methods (journal), American Society of Educators, 1511 Walnut Street, Philadelphia, PA 19102

> *Only the Best: The Annual Guide to Highest-Rated Educational Software and Multimedia,* Association for Supervision and Curriculum Development, 1250 N. Pitt Street, Alexandria, VA 22314

> *Science Books and Films,* American Association for the Advancement of Science, 1200 New York Avenue NW, Washington, DC 20005

There are other professional review sources. The California Instructional Technology Clearinghouse is on the Internet. This is an excellent source for reviews of K-12 materials. Many professional journals also provide reviews of media materials. *Tech Trends* and *Multimedia Schools* are two journals that have that regular feature. These sources provide technical data and a critical review of materials, which are useful to media managers seriously interested in purchasing quality materials.

Evaluation Forms

Many excellent forms have been developed to record media materials evaluations. Whatever form is used, it must reflect the individual media service center's selection criteria. A form should be simple to use but complete enough to include all the necessary evaluator data if it is to be effective. A review of the forms in figures 5.1 to 5.3, pages 95–99, should be helpful in selecting one for use or to provide ideas for modifying and/or developing one's own. However, remember the philosophical statement: Keep it simple.

DEVELOPING APPROPRIATE TECHNICAL PROCESSES FOR MEDIA MATERIALS

The technical processing of media materials has many similarities with routine processing of conventional library materials. Media materials also require the standard library processing tasks of acquisitioning, processing, cataloging, and shelving. However, some unique modifications of those standard tasks must be implemented. These modifications will be discussed as each processing task is described.

Acquisitions

Acquisitions is the name given to the process of ordering library and media instructional materials. It involves the placing of an order with appropriate accounting numbers, tracking it until the title(s) arrive, and authorizing payment. The procedure for ordering media materials is slightly different from the process for ordering print materials. A media materials order may be in the form of a contract which dictates the use and conditions under which the material will be used. Media producers and distributors normally restrict material use to specific uses, that is, nonprofit instructional uses, use by the agency purchasing the material only, and/or no distribution by television. If the purchaser has broader needs, then the purchase order must be in the form of a contract and the additional conditions specified, i.e., material will be rented to other nonprofit (or profit-making) agencies, copies will be made to meet peak demands, or material will be transmitted electronically to classrooms. Whenever possible, purchase requests should be held until a number

(Text continues on page 100.)

CD-ROM EVALUATION FORM
Puget Sound Educational Service District MultiMedia Services

Evaluator Information:

Grade level: _____ Subject: _____ Years taught: _____ Date: _____

Name: _____ School: _____ District: _____

CD-ROM Information:

CD Title:_____ Operating System: ____ Interface: _____

System Requirements: _____ RAM: ____ Visual: _____ Sound: _____ Multimedia: _____

Audience: _____ Producer: _____ Copyright: ____ Licensing: _____

Quality Analysis

5 = Outstanding   4 = Great   3 = Good   2 = Fair   1 = Poor   0 = Unacceptable

Design	Stimulates critical thinking. Presentation design appropriate for grade level.	5 4 3 2 1 0
Content	Accurate, current, thorough, relevant. Can be used across disciplinary boundaries.	5 4 3 2 1 0
Documentation	Instructions and information are clear and easy to read?	5 4 3 2 1 0
Interest	Motivating. Intellectually stimulating. Actively engages the students.	5 4 3 2 1 0
Navigation	Movement through the program is easy and pathways are diverse.	5 4 3 2 1 0
Technical	Visual and audio reproduction are of high quality. Software operates efficiently with minimum delays.	5 4 3 2 1 0
Bias	Meets state legal compliance guidelines (women's roles, ethnic balance, aged, etc.)	5 4 3 2 1 0
Violence/Sex	Includes no gratuitious sex or violence.	5 4 3 2 1 0

Total Points [　]

General Questions: (Use the reverse of this form for additional space to complete your answers.)

1. Would you recommend this CD to another teacher?   ❑ Yes ❑ No   Why or Why not?

2. How would you use this CD in a classroom or library?_____
   ❑ Teacher presentation ❑ Individual student   ❑ Small group exploration ❑ Other _____

3. How does the CD stimulate further exploration of the topic? _____

4. Where did you find out about this CD?
   ❑ Magazine ❑ Another teacher ❑ Presentation ❑ Catalog ❑ Workshop   ❑ Other _____

General Comments:

Figure 5.1. CD-ROM evaluation form. (Puget Sound Educational Service District Multimedia Services. Reprinted with permission.)

FILM OR VIDEO EVALUATION REPORT

FOR E.M. DEPT. USE

Order:
Yes . . . .
No . . . .
Deferred . . . .

Title . . . .

Series Title . . . .

Type of Material: 16MM . . . . Video . . . . Copyright Date . . . .

B & W . . . . Color . . . . Length . . . . Sound . . . . Silent . . . . Cost . . . .

Producer . . . . Distributor . . . .

▇ ABOVE FOR EDUCATIONAL MEDIA DEPARTMENT USE ONLY

A. By marking appropriate space(s) indicate principal use(s) by numeral 1 and lesser uses by either the numerals 2 or 3. Leave space blank if item not applicable. Any numeral may be used more than once.

. . . . Provides factual information   . . . . Skill building

. . . . Introduces topic or problem   . . . . Develops desirable attitudes and appreciation

. . . . Culminating activity   . . . . Other . . . .

. . . . Useful for individual study

B. Suggest, if possible, specific areas or units for which this material could be useful.

C. Circle grade-levels at which this material is appropriate: K 1 2 3 4 5 6 7 8 9 10 11 12 Col. Teacher Ed

D. Will this material become dated in near future?   Yes . . . .   No . . . .

E. Is this material free of cultural or sexual bias?   Yes . . . .   No . . . .

F. Rank material according to indicated scale: Please circle the number which best describes, in your judgment, the appropriate rating for this material.

1. Correlation to Curriculum

	1	2	3	4	5	6
	Little relation					Directly related

(See Reverse)

2. Content organization

	1	2	3	4	5	6
	Poor					Excellent

3. Content scope

	1	2	3	4	5	6
	Too limited or too great					Well selected

4. Potential for pupil interest and involvement

	1	2	3	4	5	6
	Low					High

5. Pupil comprehension

	1	2	3	4	5	6
	Low					Excellent

G. Technical quality:

Sound	1	2	3	4	5	6	Photography	1	2	3	4	5	6
	Poor					Excellent			Poor				Excellent

H. Overall rating: Poor.......... Fair.......... Good.......... Very Good.......... Excellent......

I. Utilization:

1. If you were teaching the subject at the grade-level indicated, would you use this? Yes..... No......

2. Do you think other teachers would use this material? Yes..... No.....

3. Do you recommend purchase? Yes..... No..... Urgent.....

J. Comments:

Name of Evaluator.. School..

Date of Evaluation.. Position..

Audiovisual Section--Educational Media Dept.   Portland Public Schools--Portland, Oregon

Figure 5.2. Film/video evaluation form. (Portland Public Schools, Media Services, Portland, Oregon. Reprinted with permission.)

MONTGOMERY COLLEGE
READING & WRITING CENTER
TAKOMA PARK CAMPUS
Software Evaluation Form

Title _____

Author(s) _____

Publisher _____ Date _____

Cost _____ Site license _____ Backup Policy _____

Disks: Size _____ Number _____ Length _____

Hardware Required _____ Memory Required _____

Grade Level ___ Group size: Individual__, Small group __, Class ___

Type of Program (Check one or more)
  Simulation _____   Drill & Practice _____   Remediation _____
  Tutorial _____   Enrichment _____   Educational games _____
  Testing ___   Problem Solving _____   Other _____

Other Notes

Program Objectives

Objective	Is it stated clearly?	Is it achieved?
1. _____	____	____
_____		
2. _____	____	____
_____		
3. _____	____	____
_____		

Comments:

Software Evaluation Form   Page 2

Educational Content	Yes	No	NA
1. Is the program content accurate?	___	___	___
2. Is the content appropriate for the intended users?	___	___	___
3. Is the difficulty level consistent?	___	___	___
4. Is there a variety of types of questions?	___	___	___

5. What types of questions? Recall___ Inference ___ Synthesis ___
   Interpretation ___ Analysis ___ Evaluation ___
   Comments:

Presentation	Yes	No	NA
1. Is the program free of technical problems?	___	___	___
2. Are the instructions clear and consistent?	___	___	___
3. Is the material logically presented and well organized?	___	___	___
4. Is the frame display clear and easy to read?	___	___	___
5. Do graphics, sound, and color enhance the instruction?	___	___	___

Comments:

Interaction	Yes	No	NA
1. Is record keeping possible with the program?	___	___	___
2. Do cues and prompts help students answer correctly?	___	___	___
3. Can students access menu for help or change activities?	___	___	___
4. Can students control the pace and sequence of program?	___	___	___

Comments:

Teacher Use	Yes	No	NA
1. Is record keeping possible with the program?	___	___	___
2. Does a teacher have to monitor student use?	___	___	___
3. Can a teacher modify the program?	___	___	___
4. Is the documentation clear and comprehensive?	___	___	___

Comments:

Overall Evaluation

__Excellent--recommend   __Good--   __Fair--Wait   __Not
   without hesitation   Purchase   for better   Useful

Reviewer's Name_____ **Date** _____

Figure 5.3. Software evaluation form. (Montgomery College, Takoma Park, Maryland. Reprinted with permission.)

of titles from an individual distributor have been collected. As with most commodities, the larger the order the larger the discount one can expect to obtain. Large volume discounts of 25 to 33⅓ percent are not unusual when purchasing media materials.

Technical Processing

Once materials have arrived, they must be viewed to assure that they are of expected technical quality. Materials with defects should be returned to the distributor. If approved, materials must then be prepared for circulation. Each media format requires a different treatment when preparing them for shelving and circulation.

Videocassettes

Videocassettes must be viewed when received to assure that the technical quality of the recording is acceptable. Here one checks that good-quality tape was used, a good duplicate was made, and the program is free of "glitches" or "wipe-outs." Both the videocassette and its storage box must be labeled. Following the same procedures as with other materials, each tape or videocassette should be given a location number affixed where it will be seen when stored (figure 5.4). Video materials are stored like books: on edge, on shelving, without dividers, and in an area free of magnetic fields.

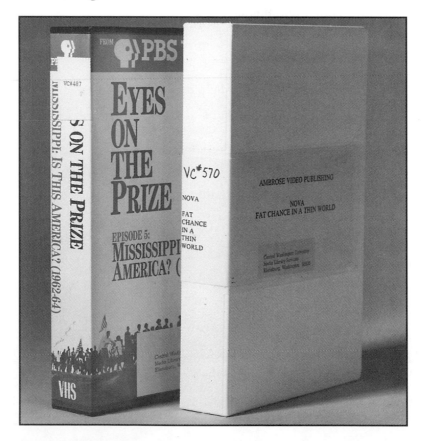

Figure 5.4. Labeling video materials. (Central Washington University, Ellensburg, WA. Reprinted with permission.)

CD-ROMs

CD-ROMs can be checked out as individual items or they can be networked in CD-ROM towers. If checked out to patrons, a packet like the one in figure 5.5 provides a handy way to circulate the disc, a user's guide, and any other materials that accompany the disc. A label like the one in figure 5.6, page 102, should be attached to the packet or included inside. This is useful information that helps protect the discs. Most CD-ROMs require preliminary installation on a computer's hard drive. For nonnetworked situations, the CD-ROM may be installed on a specified computer. Once this is accomplished, users can check-out the materials and take them to the appropriate computer.

CD-ROMs can also be placed on CD-ROM drives in devices called towers and accessed from computers networked to the tower (see figure 5.7, page 103). This arrangement reduces the technical processing tasks of labeling and provides for longer life of discs because they are not in physical contact with users. It also makes for more convenient use. Once the CD-ROM software is installed on the server, the disc can be accessed from any workstation on the network.

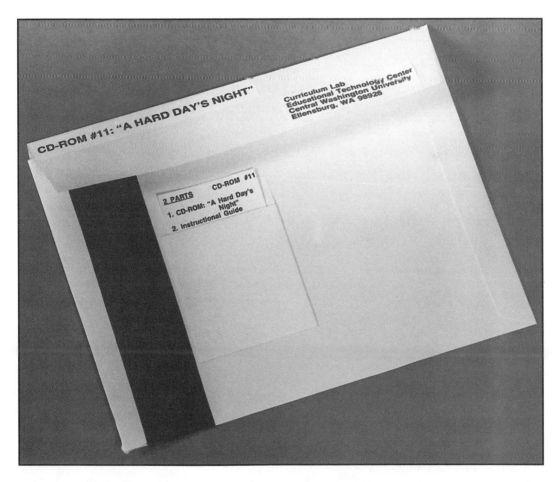

Figure 5.5. CD-ROM packet. (Central Washington University, Ellensburg, WA. Reprinted with permission.)

Keep these important safety instructions in mind as you use CD-ROM discs:

- Hold a disc by the edges or by one edge and the center hole. Do not touch the disc surface.

- To clean discs, wipe the shiny surface with a soft damp cloth, working in straight lines from center to edge. Do not use any form of cleaning agent.

- To avoid damage to your discs, keep these points in mind:

Do not expose discs to direct sunlight.

Do not write on discs.

Do not spill liquids on discs.

Do not put tape on discs.

Do not scratch discs.

Do not get dust on discs.

- Keep these instructions handy for reference.
- Follow all instructions and warnings dealing with your system.

Figure 5.6. CD-ROM care. Copyright © 1997 Apple Computer, Inc. All rights reserved.

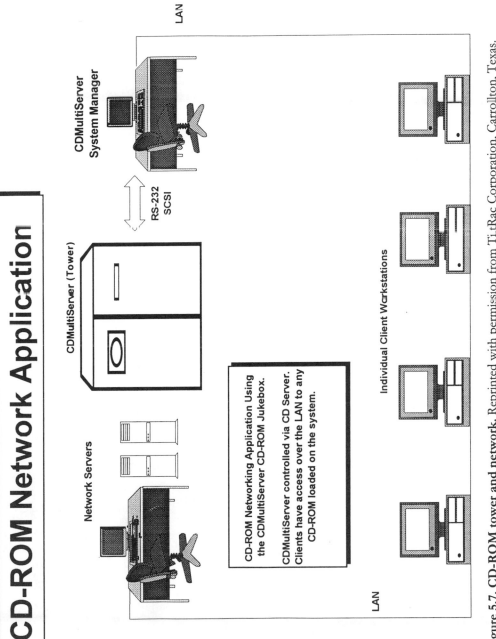

Figure 5.7. CD-ROM tower and network. Reprinted with permission from Ti:tRac Corporation, Carrollton, Texas.

Videodiscs

Videodiscs should be checked to make sure that all designed features operate properly. Check to make sure a printed guide to frame numbers on the disc are included. Make sure that numerical and barcode search features work.

List all contents (videodisc, separate discs if more than one, and an instructional guide) individually on the packet or box in which the materials are circulated. This will help assure that all appropriate elements are present at check-out and return. Finally, make sure a location number is clearly shown on the disc container (see figure 5.8). Videodiscs should be cared for and handled in the same ways as CD-ROM discs.

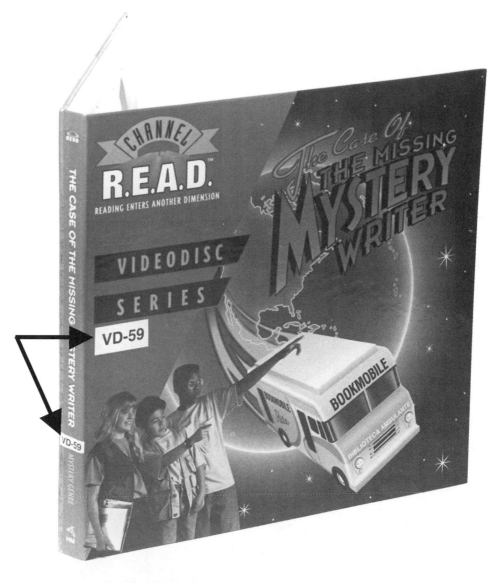

Figure 5.8. Videodisc with location number. (Central Washington University, Ellensburg, WA. Reprinted with permission.)
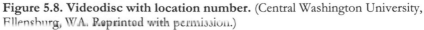

Computer Software

Computer software can be labeled and user manuals can also be put in individual packets like that shown in figure 5.5. The software itself is usually installed on the hard drive of a specific computer or it can be placed on a network server for easy access (see figure 5.7). Computer software placed on a server can be accessed by individual client workstations.

Films, Slide Sets, Filmstrips, and Instructional Kits

Today, most of these materials are used infrequently in instruction. If you are acquiring any of these materials, the first edition of *Managing Media Services* covers these media in detail. Please consult Vlcek and Wiman (1989).

Cataloging

The authors will not describe cataloging procedures in detail, as many texts already exist on this subject. Two issues require some discussion, however: (1) materials must be cataloged and included within the institution's library catalog and (2) media materials do not necessarily need to be classified using conventional standardized classification systems. That is not to say that they need not be cataloged. It must be emphasized that a consistent cataloging system must be used if materials are to be located for use. That will be discussed later; first, two terms should be defined:

> *Classification* is the systematic arrangement of materials into meaningful and related groups following some established criteria and coding system. The two most common classification systems used for classifying print materials are the Dewey Decimal System (DDS) and the Library of Congress system (LC).

> The *catalog* is the index to the total collection. It is the reference source that is organized to identify the location of the materials within the collection and provides an abbreviated description of each title.

As stated earlier, all collections must be cataloged if patrons are to learn what is available. The catalog is usually in the form of a card catalog or computer catalog, but smaller collections can be provided in a printed catalog. The format for each catalog entry should be standardized for easy use and simplicity. Catalog cards can be created by local staff or purchased commercially. Most catalog cards are available commercially, and it is more economical to purchase them when possible than to develop one's own. Commercially produced cards usually contain the following information:

> *Location device.* Usually the call number, consisting of the Dewey Decimal or Library of Congress number and either a Cutter number or the first several letters of the main entry. The call number can also be an accession number. Figure 5.9, page 106, has an accession number (in the upper left corner): VT-5901.

```
VT-5901
Videocassette      Alternatives [video recording] / M & S Productions;
Media Circ            producer and director, Bob Bronson. – New
                      York : Educational Media, Inc., 1999.
                      1 videocassette (15 min.) : sd., col. ; one
                   half inch + 1 guide.
                      Title from data sheet.
                      Credits: Camera, Reed Smith ; editor,
                   Marshall Henricks ; music, David Schultz.
                      Summary: Presents alternative configurations
                   to the typical elementary school classroom
                   arrangement.
                      1. Short video recordings. I. M & S Productions.
                   II. Educational Media, Inc.


WAE1C      18 May 99         38873414      EUNsl
```

Figure. 5.9. Media catalog card.

Main entry. The person or corporate body chiefly responsible for the intellectual content of the work. For audiovisual and computer media, the main entry is most often the title. Figure 5.9 has the title (Alternatives) as the main entry.

Title, general materials designation, and statement of responsibility. The title of the item is followed by the type of media in brackets and ends with the persons or corporate bodies that had principal responsibility for the intellectual content of the item. In figure 5.9, the title is followed by "video recording" as the general materials designation and finally the company and the producer, Bob Bronson, are given credit for the intellectual content of the work.

Publication, distribution, and other information. The place of publication or production, the name of the publisher, and the date of release or publication are recorded. Figure 5.9 shows that the video recording was released in New York by Educational Media, Inc. in 1999.

Physical description. The details of the format are given here, including the number of pieces, the type of media, size, color, and accompanying materials. Figure 5.9 lists one video recording having both sound and color, lists VHS (one half inch) as the format, and indicates there is an accompanying teacher's guide.

Series. If the item belongs to a series, the series title is listed after the physical description. The example in figure 5.9 does not belong to a series.

Note. Any information needed by the patron, including a short contents description, can be added as needed. In figure 5.9, credits are given to the camera person, the editor, and the composer of the music.

Standard number. If there is an ISBN (International Standard Book Number) or ISSN (International Standard Serial Number) given to the item, that fact is recorded. Figure 5.9 does not list an ISBN number. The numbers and information at the bottom of the card are the institution's reference information.

Other access points. A list of subject headings and other entries are given, providing the master list of every access point to the item in the catalog. In figure 5.9, there is an entry for the subject of short video recordings, and entries for the production company and the release company are provided. This means that a person could find this item in a card catalog, book catalog, or computer catalog in five different ways: by call number, title, subject, company who created the content (M & S Productions), and distributing company (Educational Media, Inc.).

The usual library practice of placing cards in the card catalog under title, author, and subject is also recommended for media with minor modifications. These materials can generally be used in several subject areas and/or for several purposes. For that reason, one should be generous in assigning multiple subject headings to media titles. After all, it is through the subject headings that clients will find materials. In addition, many media centers add a card naming the producer.

Previously it was stated that media materials do not necessarily need to be classified. In fact, most higher education media collections do not use Library of Congress or Dewey numbers. Let us now explain. Because media materials require some form of equipment to view or hear their content, it is difficult, if not impossible, to "browse" as one often does with books. Therefore, shelving these materials within the book collection is not very practical except in small centers. While some large library/media centers do intershelve books and media materials, they must also locate equipment for displaying the contents of the materials nearby. The intershelving arrangement also compounds security problems; it is difficult to monitor the media collection to know that filmstrips remain in their cans, slides have not been removed from trays, and related print materials for each title have not been removed. In centers where the print and nonprint collections are relatively small and the entire collection can be placed within one area easily visible to media center staff, this arrangement can work satisfactorily. It is in these intershelved facilities that the media collection must be classified using the same classification system that is used for the print collection. In such systems, books, films, videotapes, and other media related to a specific topic would be all located together.

However, if the collection is located in multiple locations or floors, the problems will outweigh the advantages. In such facilities, it is better to place the media collection in a separate but convenient location for patrons. The patrons are referred to this location by placing a specific notation on each media title catalog card. In figure 5.9, under the accession number, "Media Circ" indicates the video recording is in the Media Circulation department. This arrangement facilitates both access to and the security of the media collection. Here the standard classification system employed for books would serve no purpose. The materials can be labeled with a media prefix and location number. Managers can generate or devise their own prefixes to meet local or institutional requirements. If possible, the prefixes should bring to mind the name of the media, thus the use of the designation MP as the prefix for a motion picture or CP for a computer program. The following prefixes for materials are typical of those used in centers throughout the United States:

PR	Phonograph disc (Record)	OT	Overhead transparency
CD	Compact disc	S	Slide
MP	Motion picture	SFS	Sound filmstrip
VD	Videodisc	SS	Sound slide set
RVD	Recordable videodisc	AT	Audiotape
VT	Videorecording	CP-MAC	Computer program (Macintosh)
FS	Filmstrip	CP-DOS	Computer program (DOS)
KIT	Kit	CP-WIN	Computer program (Windows)
CD-ROM	Compact disc–read only memory		

If so desired, a Dewey or Library of Congress number can be given to the media, but one must remember that the classification numbers give no hint as to whether the materials are print or nonprint or *where* the materials are located unless they are intershelved with books. Each type of media requires specially designed spaces, and prefixes provide a simple method for identification and location. Beware, however, that the prefixes presented above conflict with Library of Congress classifications. For example, PR means phonograph disc in the above system, but English literature in the Library of Congress scheme.

Keeping It All Straight

The technical processing of materials before they are made available to patrons is an involved process. Considering the fact that fifty to several hundred materials might be in the process at a given time, it is a good idea to maintain some method of tracking the process from receipt of the materials to their being made available for circulation. The form shown in figure 5.10 may prove helpful in keeping track of materials being processed for circulation.

CIRCULATION PROCEDURES

The only justification for the development of a collection of instructional materials is the subsequent utilization by the organization's patrons. The best collection is of no value if it is not needed or used. Therefore, simple but effective circulation procedures must be developed to facilitate that use. Figure 5.11, page 110, illustrates the basic functions within a materials circulation process. Although it looks involved, it actually is not, as the procedure is routinized so well that it becomes a standard operating procedure.

Reference and Retrieval

The first step in any circulation system is finding the desired materials. This requires a two-part process: (1) discovering that a specific title exists and (2) finding its physical location so that it can be retrieved for use. The card catalog, in conventional card form, printed in book form, or by computer terminal, provides this information. Other information reference vehicles (e.g., specific-subject brochures)

MATERIAL PROCESSING RECORD

Type of Material: Shelf # _____
                                                          Deposit _____
16mm _____ VC _____ Other _____   Purchase _____

Title: _____

_____min _____sd _____slt _____B&W _____col _____ P I J S C

Producer_____   Copyright Date _____

Distributor_____   Cost _____

Date Received _____   Loan Rate _____

LC Number _____   Ordered _____

Condition _____

Authorize Payment _____ Date _____

TECHNICAL PROCESSING

_____ Obtain LC Records

_____ Printers Cards

Shelf List Cards
_____Shelf List
_____Subject
_____Series

Temporary Catalog Cards
_____Title
_____Subject(s) List: _____

_____ LC Order/Sample to Cataloging

_____ Booking Card

_____ Duplicate Study Guide, File Original

_____ Add Title to Depositors List (if applicable)

_____ Label Materials and Container

_____ File Cards and Place Material in Circulation

PHYSICAL CHECKS

	Initial	Date
First Check: (flaws, splices, verify title, producer, running time, grade level, description, copyright date)	_____	_____
Second Check: (leader, trailer, labeling, packaging)	_____	_____

Figure 5.10. Material processing record.

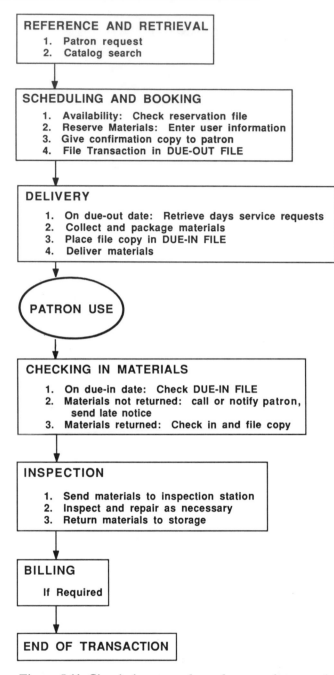

REFERENCE AND RETRIEVAL
1. Patron request
2. Catalog search

SCHEDULING AND BOOKING
1. Availability: Check reservation file
2. Reserve Materials: Enter user information
3. Give confirmation copy to patron
4. File Transaction in DUE-OUT FILE

DELIVERY
1. On due-out date: Retrieve days service requests
2. Collect and package materials
3. Place file copy in DUE-IN FILE
4. Deliver materials

PATRON USE

CHECKING IN MATERIALS
1. On due-in date: Check DUE-IN FILE
2. Materials not returned: call or notify patron, send late notice
3. Materials returned: Check in and file copy

INSPECTION
1. Send materials to inspection station
2. Inspect and repair as necessary
3. Return materials to storage

BILLING
If Required

END OF TRANSACTION

Figure 5.11. Circulation procedures for nonprint materials.

may be used, but the catalog provides the base for searching for desired materials in the center's collections.

After the reference to the material has been located, the reference should provide information for locating it for retrieval. This referral should be in the form of a standard classification system previously discussed when audiovisual materials are shelved with print materials, or a location referral or shelf number if the materials are shelved in another location.

Scheduling and Booking

Once the patron has located a specific title for use, a booking system must be available to schedule the material. The booking process must allow a patron to reserve materials for future use, schedule the necessary period of time, clear the transaction upon its return, implement billing if required, and provide all the necessary data required for an annual report. The scheduling and booking process can be computerized or managed manually. Many effective manual systems have evolved over the years; nearly all media center managers have tailored systems to meet their individual needs. Given the availability of computerized circulation systems available today, it would be foolish to implement a manual system unless funds for a computer system cannot be found. Details on computerized circulation systems are covered in chapter 8.

The process of checking out media materials is generally called *booking*. The booking record must provide all the required information to maintain control over the materials. In essence, it should be considered as a contract between the media center and the patron. It should provide the who, what, where, when, and conditions under which the material is to be used. With an automated system, this information is put into the computer at terminals located in the booking area. When a manual system is used, the form should contain all the necessary copies in order to eliminate entering the information more than once. Keep the booking process as simple and free of red tape as possible; both patrons and staff will appreciate it.

The form in figure 5.12, page 112, illustrates an effective booking form for materials when a manual system is employed. The form has five different-colored pages using self-carboning backs. Pages are labeled as delivery copy, confirmation copy, two late return notices, and file copy. The file copy is printed on card stock to enable it to stand vertically in the file. The form is numbered sequentially for easy reference. Each copy has a purpose. The confirmation copy is provided to the patron at the time of booking, the delivery copy is attached to the material to be delivered or picked up by the patron, the late return notices eliminate the need of completing a notice(s) if the materials are not returned, and the file copy is the center's permanent record of the transaction. In a computerized system, these records are stored in the computer and the information provided by printouts as needed.

If materials are to be shipped away from the institution and rental charges are to be assessed, a different form may be helpful. Again, a computerized system will simplify the process but a manual system will work. Figure 5.13, page 113, illustrates a form being used for that purpose in a manual system. This off-campus booking form is used in a film/video rental program. It has six pages with built-in carbon inserts. Carbon inserts are necessary when the pages exceed approximately four copies. Again, the form has a sequential number for easy referral, the last copy is of card stock, the pages are different colors, and the carbon pages are not identical. Each carbon page has been designed to meet a specific need but arranged to eliminate multiple typing. The pages are labeled as follows: confirmation of booking, packing slip, shipping labels both to customer and return, business office copy, invoice, and office file copy. The confirmation copy is given or mailed to the patron and the packing slip is shipped with the materials for the patron's use. The purpose of the shipping label is obvious, the invoice is sent with the monthly billing, and the card is retained as a permanent record.

MEDIA LIBRARY SERVICES

ON-CAMPUS BOOKING FORM

DUE OUT		☐ PATRON PICK UP	☐ PATRON RETURN	DUE IN
OUT		BY	IN	BY
INSTRUCTOR		DEPARTMENT	DELIVER TO	BOOKER
NOTES				TIME

NUMBER	MEDIA	TITLE
		DELIVERY COPY

I HEREBY ACCEPT THE RESPONSIBILITY FOR THE ABOVE LISTED EQUIPMENT AND/OR MATERIALS WHICH I AM BORROWING.
(WAC 106 168-051)

RECEIVER'S SIGNATURE	STUDENT I.D. NUMBER

☐ FACULTY	☐ ADJUNCT FACULTY	☐ STAFF	☐ STUDENT

STUDENT ADDRESS

Figure. 5.12. On-campus booking form. (Central Washington University, Ellensburg, WA. Reprinted with permission.)

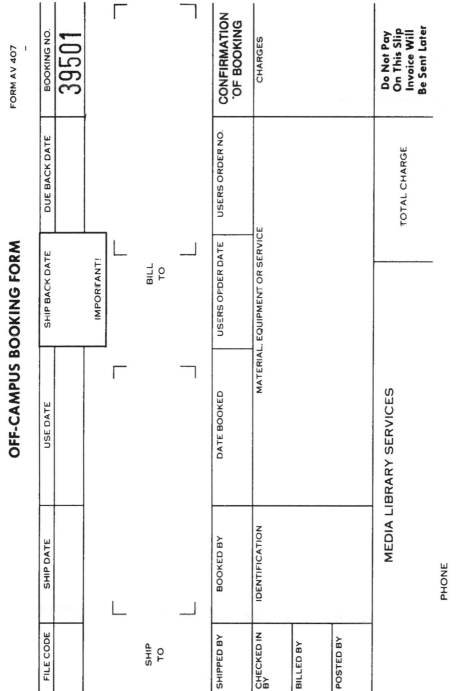

Figure 5.13. Form used when shipping and billing are required. (Central Washington University, Ellensburg, WA. Reprinted with permission.)

The booking forms are completed by trained staff. A simpler form can be used by patrons when they mail in requests for materials (figure 5.14). The requests on this form can be transferred by staff to the computer or to a regular booking form after the title's availability has been checked.

lmc ORDER FORM   Date Ordered _____

MEDIA LIBRARY SERVICES

To avoid delay in filling your order, please check each title ordered to be certain it is available from the Center to which this form is being sent.

NOTES AND SPECIAL BOOKING INSTRUCTIONS, VACATIONS AND DATES TO BE AVOIDED, ETC.:

_____

_____

_____

SHIP TO: _____

_____

_____

BILL TO: _____

_____

PURCHASE ORDER NUMBER

_____

SIGNATURE OF PERSON MAKING THE ORDER:

_____

PLEASE LIST TITLES IN CHRONOLOGICAL ORDER BY DESIRED DATES. INFORMATION REQUESTED IN COLUMN (2) AND IN COLUMN (4) IS FOR USE WHEN FILMS ARE NOT AVAILABLE ON THE EXACT DATE YOU WANT THEM

PLEASE LEAVE THESE COLUMNS BLANK		(1) FILM TITLES	PLEASE LEAVE BLANK	(2) EARLIEST USABLE DATE	(3) DESIRED DATE	(4) LATEST USABLE DATE

Figure 5.14. Mail-order booking form. (Central Washington University, Ellensburg, WA. Reprinted with permission.)

In all of the above-referenced records it is important to note that two dates are always requested: shipping date and return date. To arrive at these dates, the use date or allowable booking period as determined by policy and the delivery method and time must be considered by the person booking the materials. Some organizations allow patrons to use material for one, three, five, or any other number of days as stated by policy. Shipping or delivery methods also vary. All of these factors must be considered when determining the shipping and return dates. When a computer is used, these factors can be programmed for each customer and the computer will use those factors when booking a request.

Before materials are booked, their availability must be determined. A method of reserving material must be established. The computer can display a three-month calendar showing available dates based upon the allowable booking time and shipping parameters. The booking clerk can then select the booking date that best satisfies the request. An efficient manual method to reserve media materials can be established using cards like those shown in figure 5.15. A year's calendar with holidays indicated can be printed on each side of the card and one card assigned to each title within the collection. The title, catalog description, location number, card filing location, and any other desired information can be placed on the card. The date, shipping or delivery time, and client name is noted on the appropriate dates as requested. At a glance, available and booked times can be observed. The cards are filed alphabetically by titles and given a filing number for easy filing. The disadvantage of the manual booking system is obvious when one considers the time required to prepare these cards for use.

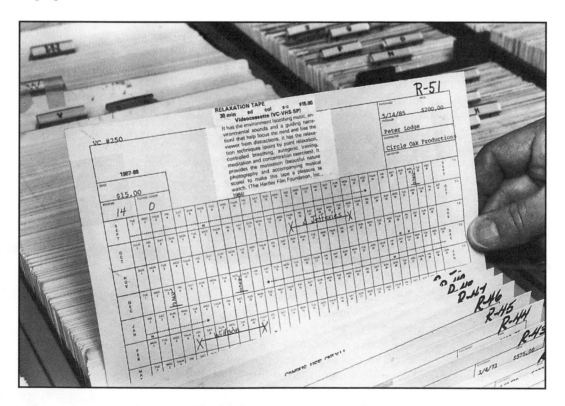

Figure 5.15. Reservation card. (Central Washington University, Ellensburg, WA. Reprinted with permission.)

Delivery

There are many ways to deliver materials to patrons. Patrons can be required to pick up materials, or a delivery vehicle on an established daily or weekly schedule can be used. Local deliveries are usually made to departmental offices with receiving signatures required. Commercial delivery services like United Parcel Service and the U.S. Postal Service can be used when distances are great. The delivery system or systems should be selected on the basis of which can provide the best service to patrons at an affordable cost.

Patron Use

The next logical step after delivery of the materials is their use by the patron. Some media centers expect patrons to operate their own equipment for displaying materials, some provide and schedule operators, while others provide operators for some display equipment and none for other types. The ideal is to provide operators to deliver and operate the equipment; however, budget constraints may not allow this. If patrons do have to operate their own equipment, they will need to know how, or materials will be damaged and the patrons will lose interest. If approached properly, most people are amenable to being shown how to run the equipment. If operators are provided, they too must be trained and be proficient not only in operating equipment but on the proper procedures for setting up equipment for projection or playback.

Checking In Materials

When materials are returned, the check-in procedure is simply the reverse of checking out. A printout of materials due in each day may be provided by the computer. Each title returned is entered into the computer by keyboard or by an automatic wand or scan system. This will be covered in chapter 8. When a manual system is employed, all materials to be returned each day are identified by the file copy in the due-in file. When they have been returned, the file copy is marked returned, and the material is sent to inspection. The file copy is then stored.

Inspection

After each use, materials must be inspected for damage. To ensure that all elements are accounted for, all components of an instructional kit should be matched against an inventory of contents fastened inside the box. If the contents are not complete, the previous user should be contacted immediately and missing items noted on the retrieved booking file copy. Slide trays should be checked for missing slides and sprockets examined for damage on filmstrips. It is difficult to inspect videocassettes unless they are placed in a VCR on fast forward and reverse to check for damage, or unless a commercial videocassette inspection machine is available. With the use of commercial film inspection equipment, 16mm film should be inspected, and damages repaired. After inspection, the film leader should be taped down to keep it from unwinding, and an "Inspected" label placed over the film reel spindle hole prior to returning the film to its container and thence to its shelf location.

Billing

If charges are assessed, an accounting system must be developed. Most organizations and institutions have established accounting procedures that must be followed, and therefore no one system will meet everyone's needs. However, a few points are common in all.

A numbered invoice must be available upon which to bill. The booking form presented earlier provided such an invoice. A monthly statement must be developed for each patron showing payments credited to the account, new charges, and the current balance. An "aged" report will be needed which lists all account balances by present status (amount overdue thirty days, sixty days, ninety days, etc.). Again, the computer can semiautomatically perform most of the accounting tasks.

MAINTAINING THE COLLECTION

Media collections are like living organisms. They will not last forever, and they require constant care. Maintenance can be divided into two parts: (1) keeping the collection in good physical condition and (2) keeping the collection current and up-to-date.

Keeping the Collection in Good Physical Condition

The best way to maintain a collection in good physical condition is to start with good materials. The stock or base of the materials should be of the best quality available. Videocassette programs should be recorded on high-quality tape in durable cassettes. Films should be on a Estar base and "Photoguarded" to reduce scratching during use. In humid climates, a fungus retardant should be applied to other film materials. As the film materials are used, they must be maintained by periodic cleaning with film cleaners on a soft cleaning cloth.

Videocassette inspection equipment is available. Serious consideration should be given to purchasing and using this equipment if numerous videocassettes are circulated. Videodiscs, CD-ROMs, and CDs should be periodically cleaned by wiping the shiny surface with a soft, damp cloth. Work in straight lines from the center to the edge. Do not use any form of chemicals or cleansers. See figure 5.6 for additional information on disc care.

Keeping the Collection Current: Weeding

Media collections age and become outdated if new titles are not purchased and old ones removed. Worn materials should also be removed and replaced. The process of removing materials from a collection is called *weeding*. A good rule is to replace 10 percent of the collection each year with new titles while removing worn-out or obsolete titles as needed.

Weeding is a time-consuming task that must be done carefully, as some materials may not be replaceable. The weeding process must be governed by a policy that sets forth the criteria by which materials will be considered for removal. The final decision should be made by a professional who knows the collection holdings, patron needs, and availability of up-to-date replacement materials. The following basic criteria should be considered in a weeding policy:

Age of the material. The media manager must determine how current the collection should be. Should materials older than five, ten, fifteen, or twenty years be considered for removal?

Circulation statistics. How many times has the material been used during the past two years? If a title has been used only once or twice, should it become a candidate for removal?

Physical condition of the material. Is it worn out, or in good enough condition for continued use? (Here the booking and maintenance records will prove helpful.)

Patron and collection needs. Are other titles available covering the same content, or are available titles very limited?

Answers to these questions need to be determined and criteria established prior to beginning the weeding process. No one criterion should be considered alone; all must be considered together before removing titles from the collection. A final step is often advisable: Ask some of the users of the material if it should be retained or weeded.

SUGGESTED ACTIVITIES

1. Visit a media materials collection service program and observe and discuss the tasks and procedures used. Write a brief description for each task performed.

2. Develop a materials selection policy for a real or hypothetical media materials collection service.

3. Review twelve media reference sources and describe the contents and organization of each.

4. Preview ten media titles in various formats and complete an evaluation form for each.

5. Develop a media materials evaluation plan.

6. Develop a technical processing policy and procedures manual for a media materials collection program, including cataloging and labeling details.

7. Develop a procedures manual for circulating materials.

8. Develop a weeding policy for a media collection.

REFERENCES

Chisholm, Margaret E., and Donald P. Ely. 1976. *Media Personnel in Education: A Competency Approach.* Englewood Cliffs, N.J.: Prentice-Hall.

Morris, Betty J., John T. Gillespie, and Diana L. Spirt. 1992. *Administering the School Library Media Center.* 3d ed. New Providence, N.J.: R. R. Bowker.

Van Orden, Phyllis J. 1995. *The Collection Program in Schools: Concepts, Practices, and Information Sources.* Englewood, Colo.: Libraries Unlimited.

Vlcek, Charles W., and Raymond V. Wiman. 1989. *Managing Media Services: Theory and Practice.* Englewood, Colo.: Libraries Unlimited.

MEDIA RESOURCES

Inside the Internet. Seattle Public Schools Instructional Broadcast Center, Producer. 28 minutes. Santa Monica, Calif.: Pyramid Media/Pyramid Film and Video, 1996. Videocassette.

Introduction to CD-ROM. RMI Media, Producer. 30 minutes. Washington, D.C.: Association for Educational Communications and Technology, 1995. Videocassette.

SELECTED BIBLIOGRAPHY

Byrne, Deborah J. *MARC Manual: Understanding and Using MARC Records.* 2d ed. Englewood, Colo.: Libraries Unlimited, 1998.

Davidson-Arnott, Francis. *Policies and Guidelines Developed for Community and Technical College Libraries.* Ottawa, Ont.: Canadian Library Association, 1983.

Ellison, John W., and Patricia Ann Coty, eds. *Nonbook Media: Collection Management and User Services.* Chicago: American Library Association, 1987.

Fecko, Mary Beth. *Cataloging Nonbook Resources.* New York: Neal-Schuman, 1993.

Ferguson, Bobby. *Cataloging Nonprint Materials.* Blitz Cataloging Workbooks series. Englewood, Colo.: Libraries Unlimited, 1998.

———. *MARC/AACR2/Authority Control Tagging.* Blitz Cataloging Workbooks series. Englewood, Colo.: Libraries Unlimited, 1998.

Fleischer, Eugene, and Helen Goodman. *Cataloguing Audiovisual Materials: A Manual Based on the Anglo-American Cataloguing Rules II.* New York: Neal-Schuman, 1980.

Frost, Carolyn O. *Media Access and Organization: A Cataloging and Reference Sources Guide for Nonbook Materials.* Englewood, Colo.: Libraries Unlimited, 1989.

Helmer, Dona J. *Selecting Materials for School Library Media Centers.* 2d ed. Chicago: American Association of School Librarians, 1993.

Imhoff, Kathleen R. T. *Making the Most of New Technology: A How-to-Do-It Manual for Librarians.* New York: Neal-Schuman, 1996.

Intner, Sheila S., Jean Weihs, and associates. *Special Libraries: A Cataloging Guide*. Englewood, Colo.: Libraries Unlimited, 1998.

Jones, F. F., G. Valdez, J. Nowakowski, C. Rasmussen, T. Balson, and R. Bas. *Plugging In: Choosing and Using Educational Technology*. Elmhurst, Ill.: North Central Regional Educational Laboratory, 1995.

McCroskey, Marilyn. *Cataloging Nonbook Materials with AACR2R and MARC: A Guide for the School Library Media Specialist*. Chicago: American Association of School Librarians, 1994.

Meghabghab, Dania B. *Automating Media Centers and Small Libraries: A Microcomputer-Based Approach*. Englewood, Colo.: Libraries Unlimited, 1997.

Rogers, JoAnn V., with Jerry D. Saye. *Nonprint Cataloging for Multimedia Collections: A Guide Based on AACR2*. 2d ed. Littleton, Colo.: Libraries Unlimited, 1987.

Thomas, Elizabeth. *Reference and Collection Development on the Internet: A How-to-Do-It Manual for Librarians*. New York: Neal-Schuman, 1996.

Valauskas, Edward J., and Monica Ertel, eds. *The Internet for Teachers and School Library Media Specialists: Today's Application, Tomorrow's Prospects*. New York: Neal-Schuman, 1996.

Van Orden, Phyllis J. *Library Services to Children: A Guide to the Research, Planning, and Policy Literature*. Chicago: American Library Association, 1992.

Yesner, Bernice L., and Hilda L. Jay. *Operating and Evaluating School Library Media Programs: A Handbook for Administrators and Librarians*. New York: Neal-Schuman, 1998.

6

MANAGING MEDIA EQUIPMENT SERVICES

The most fundamental element of effective media use is simply keeping the equipment . . . running and being able to cope with the snags that always seem to occur at the most inopportune times.

Robert Heinich, Michael Molenda, and
James D. Russell, *Instructional Media and
the New Technologies of Instruction,* 1989

OBJECTIVES

At the conclusion of this chapter you should be able to

1. Provide a rationale for centralizing equipment services administratively in the media service organization.

2. List and discuss the guidelines and criteria that a manager should consider when selecting media equipment.

3. Develop equipment evaluation procedures and instruments for making intelligent equipment selection decisions.

4. Prepare functional and technical purchasing specifications for equipment.

5. Develop and discuss appropriate technical processing procedures for preparing media equipment for circulation.

6. Describe and discuss the advantages and disadvantages of equipment delivery placement strategies.

7. Discuss the three elements necessary in a good equipment circulation system and develop procedures for implementation.

8. Describe two methods of facilitating the maintenance of equipment and discuss when each should be employed.

9. Name, describe, and distinguish between the two levels of equipment maintenance.

The largest and best media collection can serve no purpose unless appropriate equipment is available to allow patrons to "read" those materials. Most materials require equipment, visual or audio or both, to display their content. Projectors, tape recorders, disc players, video playback units, and computers are all delivery systems for media materials. Not only must the right equipment be available to display materials but it must also be in the right location at the right time. The purpose of this chapter is to outline some ideas and guidelines that will help to accomplish those tasks. As in the previous chapter, the computer must be considered a basic management tool but a manual system will also be described. A full discussion of computers as media management tools will be treated in chapter 8.

CENTRALIZE MEDIA EQUIPMENT SERVICES

Experience has shown that audiovisual equipment is best administered from a single equipment service center in order to provide the most efficient and effective service. This does not mean, however, that all equipment is housed in one place, since, for a number of reasons that will be discussed later in this chapter, other arrangements may be necessary to meet instructional needs. The media center should be assigned the responsibility for evaluating equipment prior to purchase, selecting the best equipment available, and, once it has been acquired, assigning and distributing audiovisual equipment to departments from the equipment pool.

When individual departments are responsible for buying their own audiovisual equipment, a hodgepodge of equipment collections composed of many different makes and models will result. Such lack of standardization compounds problems of stocking replacement parts and lamps and requires more extensive training for the maintenance and repair technicians. Further, departments become very possessive about their equipment and are loathe to allow it to be used in other areas or departments. Centralization, on the other hand, allows better inventory control and ensures that when equipment is not being used in one location it can be assigned elsewhere as needed. Thus a smaller total equipment inventory will be required to meet instructional needs. It also means that a certain amount of standardization of brands and models is possible, thereby reducing the need for stocking a wide variety of repair parts and lamps. Further, specifications can be developed before purchases are made, defining what the institution will accept, thus ensuring that well-designed, high-quality equipment will be purchased and anything that does not meet the specifications will be rejected. If specifications are not noted in the purchase order or bid, vendors will tend to bid low and supply cheaper, less well designed and constructed equipment than desired, resulting in the concomitant problems of durability, reliability, and so on. All orders for media equipment purchased for the institution should be processed through the media center for approval prior to purchase.

Centralization also improves maintenance efficiency through the development of appropriate use and maintenance records. Make no mistake about it, centralized administration of equipment will facilitate service for all concerned. The only reason centralized service may be challenged is when that centralized service no longer is sensitive to the needs of the various units in the organization. This can happen.

SELECTING APPROPRIATE EQUIPMENT

Selecting media equipment is not a simple process; there are many manufacturers offering many brands and models from which to choose, some good and some not. The problem is further complicated by the variety of instructional settings, teaching strategies, client biases, and various other constraints. The teaching/training setting may be in a conventional classroom, auditorium, seminar room, or individual study carrels. Teaching strategies may involve lecture, group discussion, or laboratory work, in situations ranging from large-group presentations to individually programmed instruction. Media center clients may have personal preferences (right or wrong) regarding the brand or model of equipment that they want to use, and these must be considered. Finally, the ever-present fiscal limitations must be taken into account.

Guidelines for Selecting Equipment

How does a media manager make intelligent equipment selection decisions? There are no universal answers, however there are guidelines that may help one to make those decisions.

First, *equipment must relate to the collection requirements.* Equipment to be purchased must be compatible with materials in the collection. It would be foolish for the center to own sound-slide projectors if no sound-slide materials were in the collection. Purchase only equipment for displaying and listening to materials presently owned by the center. Equipment for other media formats can be acquired when, or before, a new media format is selected.

Second, *equipment that is selected must meet client needs.* If a client needs media equipment for displaying small images only within individual carrels or for individual work in a laboratory, the purchase of large-image projection equipment would be unwise. If the setting is in a large hall, one should not send a projector with a small sound amplifier. Always keep in mind the client's and the student's teaching/training/learning requirements when selecting equipment.

Third, *standardize on equipment whenever possible.* Standardization simplifies client use of equipment and reduces maintenance problems. Clients prefer to use equipment with which they are familiar. Maintenance technicians become familiar with the idiosyncrasies of particular makes and models and learn where problem areas exist. It is also easier to stock parts for a standardized equipment collection, which saves money in the long run. However, as models change and as manufacturers' quality control changes, do not be afraid to change makes or models when change is justifiable. When new or unfamiliar equipment is added to the collection, inservice training sessions must be initiated for all concerned.

Fourth, *purchase high-quality and reliable media equipment.* Purchases should not be based upon price only. Select equipment that, according to one's own judgment and that of one's staff, will be dependable and will give years of trouble-free service.

Fifth, *develop and follow a long-range media equipment selection and purchasing plan.* The smart manager plans ahead in order to budget ahead. Develop a replacement schedule for media equipment designed to keep the collection current and reliable. Generally it is easier to "sell" an equipment replacement program to administrators than it is to obtain support for new equipment. Administrators are accustomed to amortizing equipment over an estimated expected life and the manager should develop the same approach. Based upon early Educational Products Information Exchange

(EPIE) reports and our own experience, projected life expectations for the various media equipment are summarized in figure 6.1. Note that life expectancy of micro-computers should be considerably less today due to rapid upgrading cycles (EPIE various dates).

In addition to planning for replacement of equipment on a scheduled basis, the purchase of additional equipment to meet increased volume of use or equipment required for new programs must also be planned. Projections should be made on five-year modules so that budget requests can be developed according to these projected needs.

EQUIPMENT	EXPECTED LIFE
Slide projector	10 years
Sound-slide projector	8 years
Sound-filmstrip projector	8 years
Overhead projector	10 years
Opaque projector	12 years
Record player	8 years
Tape player	8 years
Audiocassette player	5 years
Videocassette player	8 years
Television monitor/receiver	10 years
Video cameras	8 years
Computer terminals	8 years
Microcomputer	8 years

Figure 6.1. Life expectancy of media equipment.

Criteria for Selecting Equipment

While no one set of criteria will meet everyone's needs, a general set may serve as a guide for the media manager when developing criteria specific to an institution and to specific application needs. The following are adapted from criteria developed many years ago (Brown, Norberg, and Srygley 1972, 231–33). They will serve as a base upon which to build a working set of criteria for your particular needs.

Usefulness. Is there a need for the equipment and enough anticipated use to justify the cost? Does the media service center presently use something else that performs the same function equally well? Will patrons accept it? Will it become obsolete prior to expected wear-out?

Performance. Will the equipment meet performance standards: size of amplifier, light levels, sharpness of images, frequency response, signal-to-noise ratio, and dual purposes?

Compatibility. Does the equipment work well with other existing equipment? Will it require special equipment to service? Are some frequently replaced parts interchangeable with stocked parts within the institution?

Portability. If portability is required, is the equipment light enough to allow expected users to move it easily? Is its size conductive to easy movement?

Operation. Is the equipment operation facilitated with clear and visible directions printed on the equipment? Is the equipment simple to set up? Is it semiautomatic for easy use?

Reliability. Does the equipment appear to be designed and constructed for long service? Does the manufacturer have a history of building good equipment? Do other users recommend it? Do repair technicians recommend it? Is the equipment sturdy enough to operate within the environment for which it is being purchased?

Safety. Does the equipment meet appropriate national, state, and local codes? Is the equipment well balanced to eliminate toppling? Are power cords of sufficient length? Are remote-control fittings designed to eliminate incorrect connections?

Cost. Does the expected usefulness of the equipment justify the cost, or is other similar equipment available at a more reasonable cost? Does the expected life of the equipment justify the cost? If costs must be covered, can the patrons afford the amortized cost? Would leasing be a better option?

Repairability and service. Does the equipment appear to be easy to repair? Are parts readily available at reasonable cost? Is repair service easily and quickly available and at reasonable cost? Are service manuals available? Will the dealer install the equipment?

Reputation and warranty. Does the equipment manufacturer and dealer have a good reputation for selling and servicing quality equipment? Does a warranty exist, and does it provide free service and parts for a period of time? Is the warranty equivalent or better than warranties available on similar equipment?

Establish Equipment Specifications

The first step is to identify equipment that appears to meet needs by reviewing catalogs, brochures, and advertisements. It is advisable to maintain a carefully organized, current file of equipment brochures and catalogs. An extremely helpful directory that lists and provides specifications for hundreds of media equipment items, *The Directory of Video, Multimedia and Audio-Visual Products,* is published annually by the International Communications Industries Association (ICIA 1998–99). By reviewing the specifications in the catalogs, brochures, and various directories, one can develop a list of equipment that appears to meet the institution's requirements. Most major manufacturers maintain Web sites with current technical information about their equipment. This is an effective means to keep current and to download up-to-date specifications.

EVALUATING EQUIPMENT

Evaluate equipment carefully before purchasing. Media equipment purchased today will be with you for a long period, therefore evaluation time is time well spent, as poorly selected equipment can be a continuing embarrassment. After one has determined the type of equipment that is needed based upon collection and client needs, standardization, quality and reliability factors, and long-range plans as discussed earlier, a manager is ready to evaluate the various makes and models available.

Test the Equipment

After the list of equipment has been developed and refined, obtain the equipment from prospective vendors for testing and evaluation. Determine through operation if it will meet functional or performance needs. It is wise to have clients evaluate the ease-of-use of the equipment too. If a media service center has technicians who repair equipment, they should test the equipment to be sure it meets the technical requirements of sound fidelity, light levels, resolution, and so on. In addition, one should obtain permission from the vendor to allow technicians to remove the equipment from its case for further inspection to evaluate the dependability of the equipment for belt sizes, reinforced stress points, gear and bearing construction, and so on. Careful records of all evaluations should be kept for later review and comparison. In fairness to vendors, identical tests should be performed on all brands of equipment. Test all brands under the same conditions and using the same materials. An evaluation instrument should be used when collecting data and when performing the tests.

Evaluation Instruments

Evaluation instruments are helpful in standardizing the evaluation of equipment and for obtaining evaluation data. The instruments should be complete but simple to use. The value of recording evaluation data cannot be overemphasized. Unwritten evaluation data become lost and confused with other evaluations. The manager may also need the data later to support a selection decision. Figure 6.2, pages 128–29, and figure 6.3, page 130, provide examples that may prove helpful in developing appropriate instruments.

(Text continues on page 131.)

GENERAL INFORMATION

Make_____ Model_____

Sales Agency_____ Address_____

Service Facilities:

    Repair facilities located at _____
    Spare parts available at _____
    Service calls to building available   Yes _____   No _____
    Minimum service call charge _____
    Reputation of manufacturer _____

LIST OF FEATURES

Check list rating: (high)   3   2   1   (low)   NA

   I. Portability

      _____Light weight
      _____Requires special preparation to transport
      _____Possible to bolt machine to cart if desired

   II. Formats Accepted

      _____Videodiscs, 12 inch (yes, no)
      _____Videodiscs, 8 inch (yes, no)
      _____Compact disc, 3 inch (yes, no)
      _____Compact disc, 5 inch (yes, no)
      _____Compact disc, video
            Sizes & formats -
                _____ (yes, no)
                _____ (yes, no)
                _____ (yes, no)

III. Durability

_____Connections, joints fastened securely
_____Construction material of adequate strength
_____Machine operates without vibration

IV. Sound Quality and Control

_____Machine is free of noise
_____Two stereo outputs (yes, no)
_____Audio channels - 2 digital, 2 analog (yes, no)

V. Ease of Maintenance

_____Service manual available
_____Easy access to internal mechanisms
_____Lubrication
_____Overhaul

VI. Ease of Operation

_____Controls well marked
_____Switches operate smoothly and effortlessly
_____Scan control on unit
_____Skip control on unit
_____Two-sided play
_____Remote control ease of use

VII. Electrical System

_____Meets federal, state, and OSHA codes
_____Plug is grounded
_____Power cord length (list)

VIII. Adaptability

_____Serial interface connection to computer
_____Accepts both CAV and CLV discs
_____Accepts barcode reader

Figure 6.2. Videodisc player evaluation form.

BRAND _____ MODEL _____ PRICE _____

OK	POOR		
_____	_____	1.	Meets federal, state, and OSHA requirements
_____	_____	2.	Power cord three wire grounded, permanently attached
_____	_____	3.	Power cord length acceptable (10 ft.)
_____	_____	4.	Thermostatically activated fan
_____	_____	5.	Overload protection with fuse or circuit breaker
_____	_____	6.	Cord storage adequate
_____	_____	7.	Quiet running with no vibration*
_____	_____	8.	Rack and pinion focusing mechanism? Other _____
_____	_____	9.	Easy to focus*
_____	_____	10.	Adequate distance allowed between lens post and stage
_____	_____	11.	Projection lamp easily changed*
_____	_____	12.	Built in storage space for spare lamp
_____	_____	13.	Glare from lighted stage acceptable*
_____	_____	14.	Even light distribution over screen (check with meter)
_____	_____	15.	Objective head installation discourages removal
_____	_____	16.	Sturdy construction, no sharp edges or corners
_____	_____	17.	Weight is acceptable*
_____	_____	18.	Acetate roll is easy to change*
_____	_____	19.	Dimensions acceptable
_____	_____	20.	Service manual available
_____	_____	21.	Carries service warranty for _____
_____	_____	22.	Service and parts readily available. Where _____
_____	_____	23.	Projector maintenance not complicated
_____	_____	24.	Switches and controls permanently identified

*Should be evaluated by equipment users

Evaluator: _____ Date: _____

Please use the rest of this sheet and the back for pertinent comments regarding any aspect of your evaluation, with particular attention given to items receiving a poor rating.

Figure 6.3. Overhead projector evaluation form.

WRITING PURCHASING SPECIFICATIONS

Specifications for purchasing are basic communication tools that media managers must learn to develop. They establish very succinctly what is to be purchased. The purchase specification document communicates not only with vendors but also with institutional business personnel and administrators. The purchase specification establishes the ground rules and assures that all sellers or bidders are competing fairly.

Two types of specifications should be developed prior to ordering media equipment: functional and technical. A *functional specification* states and describes how a particular piece of equipment is to be used and in what type of environment. It should describe to a bidder or seller how one intends to use the equipment to better prepare that vendor to recommend or to bid the appropriate equipment. As its name implies, a functional specification states all the functional details of the equipment to be used (figure 6.4).

1.1   The Video Presentation System will be used to view VHS tapes.

1.2   The unit must have a VHS videocassette playback unit built into a single chasis with a 20″ color TV screen.

1.3   The unit must be easy to operate without consulting a manual, with operating instructions clearly marked on the unit.

1.4   The sound level must be adequate to be easily understood in close proximity to the unit (up to fifteen feet).

1.5   The speaker must be built into the unit.

1.6   The unit must have a still or pause control.

Figure 6.4. Functional specification, Video Presentation System—VHS.

The second part of a media equipment specification is the *technical specification*. When writing technical specifications, review the evaluation forms (figures 6.2 and 6.3) to be sure that all relevant factors are covered. This specification provides the physical, mechanical, and electrical or electronic details that are desired. Technical specifications are very precise and tend to be quantifiable with numerical data. They inform the bidder or seller precisely, in technical terms, what is expected. An example of a media equipment technical specification is provided in figure 6.5, page 132.

Ordering Equipment

After the equipment has been selected and specifications written, it can be ordered using the institution's purchasing procedures. If the institution does not require bidding, the task is simplified. A purchase order is issued directly to the vendor selected. In public institutions and in large businesses and industries, bidding is usually mandatory. The specifications are transferred from a requisition to a

The Video Presentation System must have the following features and must meet or exceed the specification listed.

1. <u>Features</u>

   1.1 Tuner: 181 channel cable-ready FS tuner
   1.2 Menu: on screen display (English and Spanish)
   1.3 Remote control: 35 button TV/VCR remote control
   1.4 Captioning: closed captioning capability

2. <u>Specifications</u>

   2.1 Forward/reverse: 27x forward/reverse latching
       search (SLP)
   2.2 Heads: 4-head system
   2.3 Sound: stereo, bass/treble/balance control, with
       headphone jack
   2.4 Head cleaner: built-in
   2.5 Listings: U.L.

3. <u>Options</u> (to be available but not included in a bid)

   3.1 Wireless remote control

4. <u>Manual</u>

   4.1 Operation, service, and parts manual included in
       price

   NOTE:

   1. The Video Presentation System will be a
      Magnavox CCR202AT or acceptable
      alternate.
   2. Detailed technical specifications must be
      provided with bids that substitute
      equipment.

Figure 6.5. Technical specification, Video Presentation System—VHS.

purchase order and prepared by a central purchasing office for bidding and subsequent ordering. When bidding is required, it is important that the institutional procedures allow the media manager to review low bids in which bidders substitute equipment. While equipment that is substituted in a bid by a vendor may meet specifications, in many cases it does not. In those cases the media manager should examine the substitute and, if it does not meet the specifications, state so in writing and deny the low bid. However, a word of caution: Be sure that the reasons stated in writing for denying the low bid are for substantial reasons that can be defended in court. A good practice is to emphasize this point to your technicians or technical consultants who write and review specifications. Be sure they understand and are confident that they can defend the reasons listed on an evaluation when the low bid does not meet specifications. To simplify defense of your choice of bids, you may want to use the terminology "must meet or exceed the performance and specifications of" the make and model that you know will fulfill your need.

TECHNICAL PROCESSING

When the equipment arrives, it must be processed. Shipping cartons should be inspected immediately and opened so that problems are fully covered under shipping insurance or equipment warranty. The equipment must be tested to be sure it is operable and checked to be sure all the accessories are included. It can then be placed on the inventory and marked with the appropriate ownership logo and inventory number. It is advisable to affix a media center number that can be seen from a short distance. This procedure speeds up the inventory and circulation processes, as equipment does not have to be viewed closely for identification. Another recommended practice is to affix an ownership logo or initials to the equipment to deter theft. Stenciling is an effective and inexpensive way to label equipment. Hand labeling is not recommended unless the person doing the labeling possesses lettering and art skills.

After checking the equipment and labeling it with inventory number(s) and an ownership logo, the maintenance and booking cards can be prepared. As with a film circulation system, equipment booking and maintenance records can be computerized. If a manual system must be used, a booking card will have to be made for each item of equipment. The equipment description, prefix code, and media center inventory number are placed on this card, and the card can then be placed in an availability booking bin. A maintenance card is also prepared with full information. This would include the equipment description, prefix code, media center inventory number, institution number, serial number, date purchased, vendor, and price. The balance of the card is used to list repairs made and parts installed during the life of the equipment (figure 6.6, page 134). Additional cards can be added as needed.

CIRCULATING MEDIA EQUIPMENT

Like materials, equipment used to display these materials must be made available to the media center's patrons. As was noted earlier, departments could be required to purchase and circulate their own equipment, which under most circumstances is inefficient. The institution loses any leverage of quantity purchasing, standardization, or inventory control, and the practice does not allow the reassignment of equipment to other areas when it is not needed in a specific area.

Media Equipment Services
MAINTENANCE REPORT

Requisitioned: 5/20/94

Purchase Order: 79023

Date Purchased: _7/16/94_ Cost: _$1192.36_ Model _16-AL_

Manufacturer: _____ Elmo_   Dealer: _Troxel, Seattle, WA_

Date:	Action
11/10/94	Take up erratic. Cleaned, polished take up drive mechanism, lubed, checked. RVM
3/4/95	Preventative maintenance. Complete maint. Replaced take up arm assembly (314-4100). Used lube chart. WLH/vj
2/26/96	Preventative maintenance. Replaced spare lamp, replaced drive belt (part 12-1567). Installed new motor (part 45-23491). AF/kas
4/1/97	Preventative maintenance. Replaced drive belt (part 345-9801). Cleaned. AF/kas

Location IMC pool   Equipment: 16mm Projector   CWU#: 59691

Serial #: EL 14501   Prefix and center #: MP16

Figure 6.6. Equipment maintenance report.

A more efficient choice is to control all media equipment from one central agency, the media center. This is highly recommended for reasons previously established. A circulation procedure must be simple, thorough, and efficient if it is to be effective. Equipment must be easy for patrons to obtain if they are to use it. Several options will be presented for consideration.

Provide Full Operator Service

This service provides an operator for the center's clients. The client simply schedules the materials and equipment for the desired time and place, and media center staff members make the delivery and operate the equipment. This is probably the most convenient to users, though very labor intensive.

Use Telecommunication Delivery Systems

Telecommunication delivery involves placing a teaching console and all required media display equipment in each classroom. Each classroom has a television distribution system that originates in the media service center (figure 6.7). Films are transferred to video (by licensing agreement) or are distributed by television film chain, again with appropriate licenses. Videotape playback facilities must be available to allow direct dialing or a prearranged appointment to start playbacks of film, video, or videodisc to the classrooms. Display equipment in the classroom will include television monitor(s) or a projector and a teaching console with lectern and overhead projector. All equipment will be fastened permanently in the classroom for security reasons. Teachers/trainers will not need to deliver equipment or materials to the classroom. They will only need to schedule them so that they can be programmed for playback within a specified period of time. During this time they can start, stop, rewind, and replay programs or segments of programs by intercom or by using in-classroom controls. This is a high-cost option.

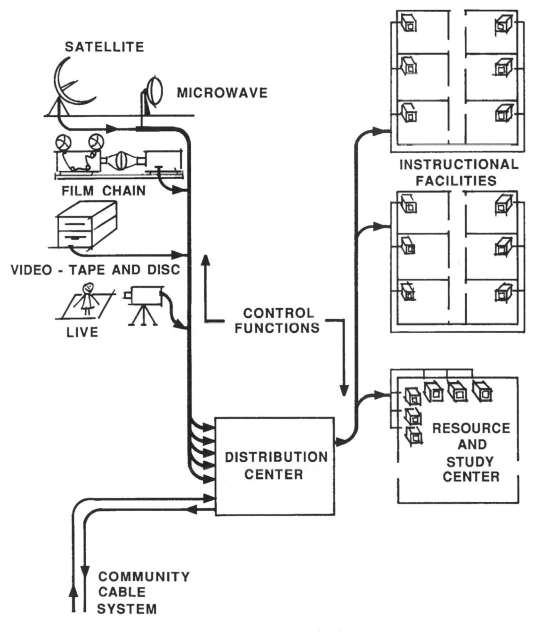

Figure 6.7. Circulation of materials using telecommunication system.

Keep All Equipment in Classrooms

This option involves the permanent placement of a teaching console and all media display equipment needed by patrons in all classrooms. The teacher/trainer would need to obtain the desired materials and bring them to the instructional environment. Obviously, for security purposes, all display equipment would need to be locked or bolted in place, but the practice makes good use of instructor time and provides maximum control of media equipment to the individual. The cost of this plan is moderate.

Equipment can be operated with each component's controls or, at considerable extra expense, have a more user-friendly system in which all equipment is linked to a push-button or touchpad control unit at the teacher's main presentation location. If a computer is stationed in the classroom, control of equipment can also be accomplished from the computer's monitor.

Establish Equipment Pools

A relatively inexpensive option involves the placement of equipment in a secure equipment pool—a large closet or small room—in each building with classrooms. This equipment pool should be as close to a concentration of classrooms as possible. When a large number of classrooms are involved, several equipment pools may be desirable. In this option a teaching console with a permanently mounted lectern and overhead projector should be provided for each classroom. Each instructor must have a key to the equipment pool and assume responsibility for scheduling equipment as needed on a weekly schedule board. Each instructor must also assume the responsibility to transport the equipment to the classroom and return it after each use. If the desired equipment is not available or is already scheduled, the instructor must schedule additional equipment from the media center for delivery to the equipment pool on the day needed. Under this option, the user schedules and transports all instructional materials and equipment to the classroom and returns the same after use. This option uses the most instructor time, but it is the least expensive of the plans presented for the media center. Less equipment is required because it can be shared among many classrooms, and fewer employees are needed to transport equipment around.

Another option is to require all instructors to obtain all display equipment directly from the media center each time it is needed. This practice is not recommended because most equipment is difficult to carry very far, and transporting the equipment shortens its life measurably.

Establish a Media Satellite

It is sometimes feasible to station a member of the central media services program in buildings or areas of extremely high media equipment use. If this is done, and adequate space is allocated within the building or area, circulating media equipment by one or a combination of the previous four methods can be coordinated by this staff member.

Which Plan Should Be Used?

Obviously, any option that delivers or permanently places equipment in the classroom would be most convenient for clients. All display equipment is in place and controlled by the instructor/trainer from the classroom. However, budget constraints may not allow these options. Therefore, an analysis of the costs for all four options or combinations of the options should be completed before a media manager can implement a plan for equipment location and use.

Circulation Procedures

Regardless of the circulation option or combinations of options that are selected and implemented, the equipment must be booked and controlled. A good equipment circulation procedure consists of the following four elements:

a system for *reserving* equipment,

a system for *booking* the equipment for varying amounts of time,

a system to *assign delivery and return* responsibilities, and

a system for *inspecting* returned equipment before reshelving.

A reservation system includes a method to assign equipment for future use. A computer booking system or a manual card method can be used for this purpose. Clients should be able to book equipment for any period of time from one hour to several weeks if they have defensible daily needs. For reporting consistency, it is convenient to divide bookings into three classifications: short-term (one week or less), long-term (between one week and four weeks), and semipermanent booking for longer periods of time (quarters or one year). The time limits should be established to meet individual as well as institutional needs.

When a computer booking system is used, daily "due-out" and "due-in" printouts will assure that the equipment is prepared for delivery and return. In a manual system, a booking form must be completed, filed, and retrieved each day. The booking form should have as much information as possible preprinted on it to save completion time (figure 6.8, page 138), as well as an adequate number of copies to satisfy the logistical requirements, that is, confirmation, pick up or delivery, and file copy. A copy is usually attached to the equipment and another is placed in the due-out file, which is organized by months and days. Each day the due-out requests are processed and the file copy is placed in a due-in file by the return date. Patrons are called if equipment is not returned as scheduled. After the transaction is completed, the file copy goes to the "completed transaction" file.

MAINTAINING EQUIPMENT

The value of maintaining media equipment cannot be overstated. Users soon lose interest in materials if the display equipment consistently fails. An excellent equipment program involves more than making repairs after breakdowns occur; it involves preventive maintenance.

IMC / MEDIA CIRCULATION
REQUEST FORM
LIBRARY 103

Name _____

Department/ID_____

Faculty ☐   Adj. Faculty ☐   Adm. ☐   Staff ☐   Student ☐   Other ☐

Date Requested _____   Time _____

Phone _____

DELIVERY INFORMATION

Building _____   Room # _____

Deliver _____   Pickup _____

User Will: Pick-up ☐   Return ☐

EQUIPMENT

☐ TV #	☐ OVERHEAD PROJ #
☐ VHS #	☐ 16 MM #
☐ 3/4" VCR #	☐ MICROPHONE #
☐ 1/2" VCR #	☐ PA SYSTEM #
☐ CAMCORDER #	☐ CART #
☐ TRIPOD #	☐ REEL TAPE #
☐ BATTERIES #	☐ CASSETTE TR #
☐ VIDEODISC #	☐ SCREEN #
☐ VIDEO PROJ #	☐ SLIDE PROJ #
☐ CARREL #	☐ REC PLAYER #
☐ CABLE #	☐ LCD DISPLAY #
☐ MISC. _____	☐ MISC. _____

I HEREBY ACCEPT THE RESPONSIBILITY FOR THE ABOVE LISTED EQUIPMENT MATERIALS WHICH I AM BORROWING (WAC 106-120-027).

Signature: _____

Student Initial: Check Out _____   Check In _____

DESCRIPTION _____

_____

_____

_____

Figure 6.8. Equipment/booking card. (Central Washington University, Ellensburg, WA. Reprinted with permission.)

Commercial Versus
Institutional Maintenance

One of the problems facing a media manager is to determine who should maintain the media equipment. Should it be sent to a commercial repair facility, or should personnel be employed to make the repairs within the media center? A myriad of variables complicate this issue. Are repair facilities with trained technicians located within a reasonable delivery distance of the media center? Does the yearly volume of breakdowns justify the development of a repair facility? Is a preventive maintenance program desirable to decrease breakdowns? Do other services requiring the use of an electronic technician exist? Is space available for a repair facility? Is a repair facility affordable? Is administrative support required and obtainable?

If a repair facility is not available within your community, thereby requiring shipping equipment to a distant facility, then the volume of repairs needed per year to justify the development of a repair facility will logically be smaller than when the services are easy to obtain. Shipping costs can be expensive, and shipping can cause damage and misalignment after repairs have been made. Even so, a small program with very few yearly repairs may never justify the development of a repair facility. The same may be true for a large media center with a large volume of breakdowns, if a commercial facility is readily available at a reasonable cost. The case for a repair facility is strengthened when an electronic technician is also needed for other purposes within the media center. If space cannot be made available, a repair facility cannot be considered. Finally, the need for administrative support is obvious.

Where does one begin when considering the development of a maintenance program? The first step is to determine the present commercial cost of repairs being made. When it exceeds the cost of employing your own electronic technician(s), then the development of a repair facility should be investigated. Other costs exist and must be considered: space, utilities, test equipment, tools, and an inventory of parts. However, these costs may be offset by the extra benefits that may be obtained, such as no shipping costs, addition of a preventive maintenance program, other needs for technicians, and faster turnaround on repairs. Each case is different and each manager must weigh the factors carefully before making a decision.

Levels of
Maintenance

Basically, there are two levels to an effective equipment maintenance program: preventive maintenance and breakdown maintenance. The purpose of a preventive maintenance program is to service the equipment and make repairs before a breakdown occurs. Equipment service manuals outline and list recommended inspections, cleaning, and points to lubricate. During preventive maintenance, equipment is cleaned and lubricated as recommended, parts are inspected or tested, and worn parts, gears, bushings, belts, and other items are replaced. In this program, equipment is scheduled to be recalled on an established schedule based upon experience, the manufacturer's recommendation, and availability of technicians. It is not practical to monitor the hours of operation of all equipment, so estimates are made based upon the manager's knowledge and/or consultation with clients within departments regarding the volume of use equipment receives. With this estimate, a schedule can be established for preventive maintenance. The schedule should be faithfully followed if the program is to succeed. The program tends to lower the frequency of major breakdowns and can extend the life of equipment by several years.

A *breakdown maintenance program* waits until the equipment fails, and then repairs are made. While this program may seem less expensive to operate, it is not when the resultant shorter life of the equipment and the inconvenience to users are considered. However, well-maintained equipment can break down, and the center must be prepared. It may be necessary to maintain a small inventory of redundant or backup equipment in order to keep the service operating when emergencies occur.

Record Keeping

It is important to keep records of all maintenance completed. The records should be examined each time a piece of equipment fails. Consistent breakdowns can be an indication of misalignments or other problems that cause continuous failures. Without the records, a technician may not recognize a recurring problem on a specific machine. Maintenance records also can indicate when equipment should be replaced. When repair costs increase drastically, the piece of equipment should be replaced even if the problem is not caused by heavy use and/or age; sometimes one does get a lemon! Maintenance records can be maintained in a computer. When a computer is not available, the manual system and form previously described can be used.

SUGGESTED ACTIVITIES

1. Develop a rationale and case for centralizing media equipment services administratively within a media service unit.

2. Using established equipment evaluation instruments, evaluate several different pieces of equipment.

3. Develop evaluation instruments and evaluate the same equipment again using these instruments.

4. Write functional and technical specifications for several pieces of media equipment.

5. Develop a policy and procedure manual to guide the technical processing and circulation of media equipment within an institution.

6. Determine at what volume of maintenance it becomes cost-effective to implement an in-house media maintenance repair facility, and develop a case to support such a proposal.

REFERENCES

Brown, James W., Kenneth D. Norberg, and Sara K. Srygley. 1972. *Administering Educational Media: Instructional Technology and Library Services.* New York: McGraw-Hill.

Educational Products Information Exchange (EPIE). Various years and issues of *EPIEgram.* 103-3 West Montauk Highway, Hampton Bays, NY 11946.

Heinich, Robert, Michael Molenda, and James D. Russell. 1989. *Instructional Media and the New Technologies of Instruction.* 3d ed. New York: Macmillan.

International Communications Industries Association. 1998–99. *Directory of Video, Multimedia, and Audio Visual Products.* Fairfax, Va.: International Communications Industries Association.

SELECTED BIBLIOGRAPHY

Davidson-Arnott, Francis. *Policies and Guidelines Developed for Community and Technical College Libraries.* Ottawa, Ont.: Canadian Library Association, 1983.

Heinich, Robert, Michael Molenda, and James D. Russell. *Instructional Media and the New Technologies for Learning.* 6th ed. Upper Saddle River, N.J.: Merrill, 1999.

Post, Richard. "Longevity and Depreciation of Audiovisual Equipment." *TechTrends,* 21, no. 2 (1987): 109–18.

Schmid, William T. *Media Center Management: A Practical Guide.* New York: Hastings House, 1980.

Volker, Roger, and Michael Simonson. *Technology for Teachers.* 6th ed. Dubuque, Iowa: Kendall/Hunt, 1995.

MANAGING MEDIA DEVELOPMENT SERVICES

With a versatile production capability, the instructional materials center becomes a complete instrument for the facilitation of communication because it can supply not only a broad selection of ready-made instructional materials of all kinds but also can create new materials carefully designed to help a specific group of students to grasp a given concept or idea.

David V. Guerin, "Media's Influence on Design," in *Audiovisual Instruction,* 1965

OBJECTIVES

At the conclusion of this chapter you should be able to

1. Distinguish between these terms: *information*, *design*, *production*, *media development*, and *instructional development*.

2. Describe the types of services that can be provided by a media development unit of a media center.

3. State and discuss five statements that can serve as guiding principles for a media development unit.

4. Describe the basic steps involved in the graphic development process.

5. Describe the basic steps involved in the video development process.

6. Describe the nature and promise of multimedia development.

7. Discuss the value of integrating media development services.

8. Provide an overview of different charge-back practices of various media service programs.

9. Discuss the advantages and disadvantages of providing media development projects with and without charges to the patrons.

10. Describe and contrast the differences between desktop publishing and computer-generated graphics.

Most media centers have facilities for the design and production, or development, of media. Invariably, users of the center will ask the center to develop items as simple as overhead transparencies or as complex as a twenty-minute video production. Before considering the ramifications of media development, however, there is a need to clarify some terms. The words *design* and *development* have many meanings. This is even true within the instructional media and technology field. In order to guide his thinking, many years ago one of the writers of this book developed a distinction between development, design, and production from dictionary definitions. The dictionary definition of development is to "bring into being." Design is "to form a plan for, to draw a sketch of, or it's a visual composition or pattern." Production means to "manufacture, to bring forth, or to create" (Morris 1973).

INFORMATION, DESIGN, PRODUCTION, EVALUATION – MEDIA DEVELOPMENT

The process of media development includes information gathering, design, production, and evaluation stages. At the information gathering stage, the client describes the project and its intended use. This information and other vital elements are entered onto a form (date needed, phone number, etc.). The media design process (sometimes referred to as message design) is the making of a plan or pattern for a production. At the simple level, this may be nothing more than taking handwritten copy and deciding on type style and font size to be included on an overhead transparency. On a complex project like a video production, this would include the preparation of a treatment and a script. The media production process involves the creation or manufacturing of a design and its specifications. This would result in, for example, a completed overhead transparency or video production. The evaluation process involves the assessment of the materials designed and produced according to specified criteria. In the case of an overhead transparency, this would involve little more than preliminary rehearsal and/or use before an audience. The content could then be revised as necessary. With a videotape, evaluation may range from an informal tryout with an audience to more elaborate testing to determine the effect of the content on the target audience. The final evaluation step would be to revise the materials and possibly conduct further tryout and testing.

Media development is not to be confused with instructional development. This latter term refers to the systematic procedure used to develop courses or training programs (or segments of courses or training). On the other hand, there are connections between media development and instructional development. Media development is often used as part of an overall instructional development project to design and produce individual materials, such as a video, to be used in a resulting course or training program.

For purposes of discussion, media development services addressed in this chapter will be graphic services, photographic services, reprographic services, video services, and multimedia services. Other media development services, discussed briefly, are a media production laboratory, a television laboratory, and a community access television facility. While all the services may not be provided by all media service organizations, the major components most often provided are outlined. The reader can then pick and choose which media development components will best serve a given institution and which are likely to be affordable. Regardless of its simplicity or comprehensiveness, a media development facility's purpose should be to design and produce media for clients for use in instruction, training, public relations, publications, sales, and/or research. Its goal should be to provide high-quality media development services at the lowest possible cost to the institution. The organization and the cost accounting procedures to accomplish that task are the responsibility of the manager.

ESTABLISHING MEDIA DEVELOPMENT POLICY

As was discussed in chapter 4, all organizations must have a set of policies to govern the activities that take place within the organization. The policies that guide the media development service should be included in the parent media center's policies. They should describe *what* and *to whom* services are to be provided. If fees are required, the policy should identify who is to be charged and who is not. If all requests cannot be served and priorities are to be established, the priorities and their definitions should be included. The policy also must agree with the institution's and parent media center's policies. The following is an example of a media development service policy:

Graphic, photographic, reprographic, video, and multimedia services will be provided.

Clients to be provided media development services include the institution's faculty, staff, administrators, and students.

Fees for services will not be charged for media development projects requested by the faculty or trainers if the products will be used in the institution's instructional or training programs.

Fees will be assessed for all media development projects made for clients outside of the institution.

ESTABLISHING MEDIA DEVELOPMENT PROCEDURES

As in any service organization, and as was discussed in chapter 4, procedures must be established to provide order to the many tasks involved in developing media materials. Decisions must be made regarding the appropriate media to be used, who will do the work, when the work will be done, who will make cost estimates, and the defining and monitoring of quality control. Procedures provide consistency of operation within a media development facility and provide guidelines for how things are to be accomplished. Without carefully developed procedures, monitoring job requests and meeting deadlines would be very difficult, if not impossible, to accomplish.

In the early days of media development, Brown, Norberg, and Srygley (1972), in *Administering Educational Media: Instructional Technology and Library Services,* stated the following five reasons for monitoring media development services:

- to monitor quality products,
- to avoid waste of supplies and time,
- to ensure proper budgeting for these activities,
- to meet time schedules and deadlines imposed by those using the services, and
- to abide by existing copyright and privacy regulations.

Those five statements have withstood the passage of time and can serve as guiding principles for a media development unit. Let us look at each of the activities separately.

Quality

The manager of a media development service who does not insist that all materials produced must be of high quality will soon lose clients and "go out of business." A standard of quality must be established and employees informed that poor quality will not be acceptable. Clients expect and are entitled to first-class products. In fact, high quality should become a part of the media development unit's philosophy. It is not enough to have high standards, products must be monitored to assure that the desired quality is produced consistently. To accomplish this task, each completed production must be reviewed and approved by a staff member. This person should be the media development unit manager or his or her designee. Remember, good products bring clients back, and satisfied clients become the media center's best advertisers. Product tryout with target audiences and other forms of evaluation are invaluable if time and funding permit. This more formal approach is discussed in later sections about the design of graphics and video materials.

Avoid Waste

Waste of materials and time transposes into higher costs per product. A manager wants staff members to use their time productively but not to work so fast that they are careless. Procedures should be developed and monitored to ensure that the media development staff is efficient. Employees who work too slowly or waste time in other ways should be counseled and terminated if necessary.

Budgeting for Activities

For high-quality productions, adequate operational and personnel budgets are essential. Media development requires many workers doing a variety of jobs, and this fact is sometimes difficult to communicate to higher management. Detailed explanations must be developed, with documentation of personnel costs, when preparing production budgets. It may be helpful to demonstrate production products, along with a breakdown of personnel used to create productions, to the formal and informal leaders discussed in chapter 3. This selling activity is a continuous process and takes place at any opportune time.

When budgets are not adequate, three options exist for the media manager if quality is to be maintained. They are: (1) develop a priority system defining who gets served first, second, and third; (2) eliminate some clients; or (3) eliminate some types of projects. Such decisions, while not easy, must be made, for the primary concern is to serve the institution's greatest needs. A matrix or form will help to explain the priority system and help to determine which projects will be accepted.

Time Schedules and Deadlines

Failure to meet accepted deadlines will cause the center to lose clients. One must monitor workloads so that realistic and accurate time estimates can be given. It is imperative that a client be told at the outset that a request cannot be completed when desired rather than to make commitments that cannot be met. The client will then have the option to take the request elsewhere or, if possible, adjust the projected use date.

Copyright Laws and Privacy Regulations

An ounce of prevention here can save much grief later. Since the implementation of the revised U.S. Copyright Law, PL 94-553, in 1978, publishers and producers have increased their educational awareness programs and policing of the copyright law. Copyright clearances must be obtained before using copyrighted materials. It is important to assign this responsibility to someone within the media service center to ensure compliance. In addition, when photographs are used, the privacy of individuals and groups must be respected by getting clearances to use photographs when individuals are identifiable. A verbal agreement is not sufficient; signed releases must be obtained.

GRAPHIC AND REPROGRAPHIC SERVICES

The major components of a graphics development program are graphics, photography, and reprography (typesetting and duplicating). Any one service and various levels of each can be provided, or, in a comprehensive graphics development program, all may be available. Typical services provided by each of the three areas are as follows:

Graphics
- Do conceptual design consulting
- Design, layout, and produce instructional, training, public relations, and sales materials
- Design and create signs, posters, and charts
- Construct mock-ups, models, and displays
- Dry mount and laminate materials
- Produce duplicating masters
- Paste up copy
- Produce computer presentations
- Provide instructional design and development for major instructional and publicity events, i.e., trade shows, farm shows, state fairs, etc.

Photography

- Provide photographers for institution photographic assignments
- Produce slides and transparencies
- Produce photographic prints
- Photograph masters for video productions
- Produce line and halftone negatives for offset printing
- Produce masters for reproduction
- Provide photo searching
- Provide slide scanning and printing of slides and transparencies from presentation software, such as Microsoft PowerPoint
- Produce digital images with cameras and other devices
- Provide archiving and image retrieval services

Reprography

- Prepare copy for instructional, training, and public relations materials
- Provide quick copy service to clients
- Provide offset and laser printing services

Graphic Development Process

Regardless of the simplicity or complexity of the institution's services program, some form of centralized control should be present. Otherwise cost estimates, scheduling, and product quality will be difficult if not impossible to achieve. To implement control, a production work flow or production process with procedures must be established. The established work flow and procedures that govern "who does what and how" must be followed by the entire media development staff.

Figure 7.1, page 150, outlines an effective graphics development work flow process. It is conveniently divided into four stages: (1) information gathering, (2) design, (3) production, and (4) evaluation.

Information Gathering Stage

At this stage of the media development process the client requests and describes the requested project. A request form is completed which documents the information required for the transaction, who is making the request, that person's department, the type of product desired, and general job specifications. A job number should be assigned for future reference and for collating control data as the work progresses. With this information, a decision based upon established criteria is made regarding whether the job is routine or more complex, requiring special handling. The criteria may be the following:

Routine requests involve only one production process without any design consultation. Examples would be photocopying, slide duplication, transparencies run from an established master, or a simple poster.

Complex requests require more than one production process and design consultation. Examples would be graphics, photography, typesetting, and duplication.

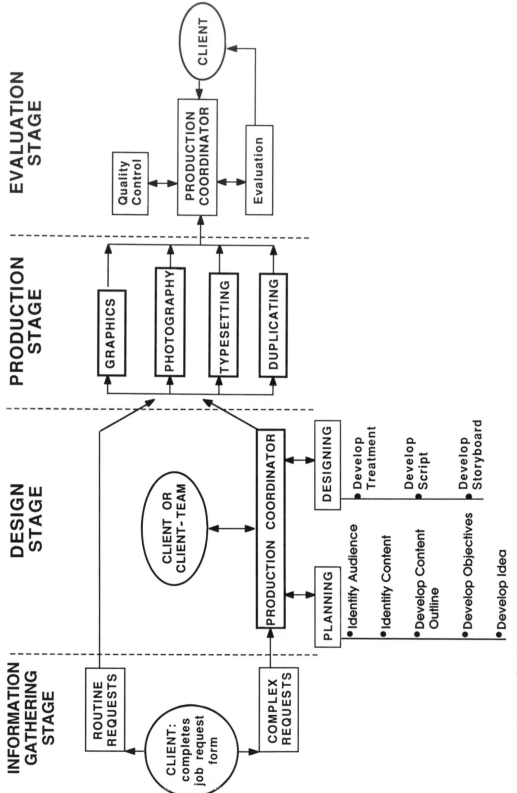

Figure 7.1. Graphics development process.

Given adequate criteria, a secretary or clerk can decide where to route a job and forward the request accordingly. If the request is determined to be routine, it bypasses the design stage and is routed directly to the appropriate area for completion.

Design Stage

Requests determined to be complex are routed to design. Here, a production coordinator who is a professional media designer should analyze each request to decide if what is being requested—a slide series, a pamphlet, a set of transparencies, a videotape, or a Web page—is appropriate. The designer should work directly with the client to help specify the objectives for the project. The production of materials is expensive, and the smart media manager wants to be assured that products will be effective. Effectiveness cannot be measured unless purposes are specifically defined by objectives before production begins. After the objectives have been developed, then the appropriate medium can be selected and product planning can begin. At this stage the media development coordinator may involve other staff members (i.e., artist, photographer, and desktop publishing and printing personnel) to help develop the design parameters and to advise on specific production problems and limitations. The project is then assigned and routed to the appropriate team of staff members as needed to complete the work. Involve instructional development specialists as required by the projects.

Production Stage

The request then flows among the artist, photographer, and desktop publishing and printing personnel, with all working on various parts of the project separately and simultaneously. The media development coordinator should develop appropriate timelines to assure that each task is completed and routed to others as needed.

Because many people may work on a project, some control and documentation must be implemented, usually in a form like the master job ticket shown in figure 7.2. It provides a job identification for each production request and gathers the "who" information. It also identifies the job priority that the media development coordinator has given to the request, and when the job is needed. The product objectives are stated on a separate sheet and attached to the request. Material and labor costs are recorded for customers who by policy are to be billed. The customers not billed still get a copy of the request when finished so that they are made aware of the production's cost. The form can be made with multiple copies for convenience.

During the production stage further interaction may take place among various members of the production unit, the media development coordinator, and the client. The client should be given an opportunity to react to the work being completed at various stages in its development. To avoid costly revisions, the client should review the work before every step in the process where a major cost is to occur.

Evaluation Stage

After the production is complete, the media development coordinator should review it to be sure that it meets the media center's quality standard and the client's objectives. If not, problems should be corrected. If a project requires duplicating, the quality control check should be completed prior to duplication. The production

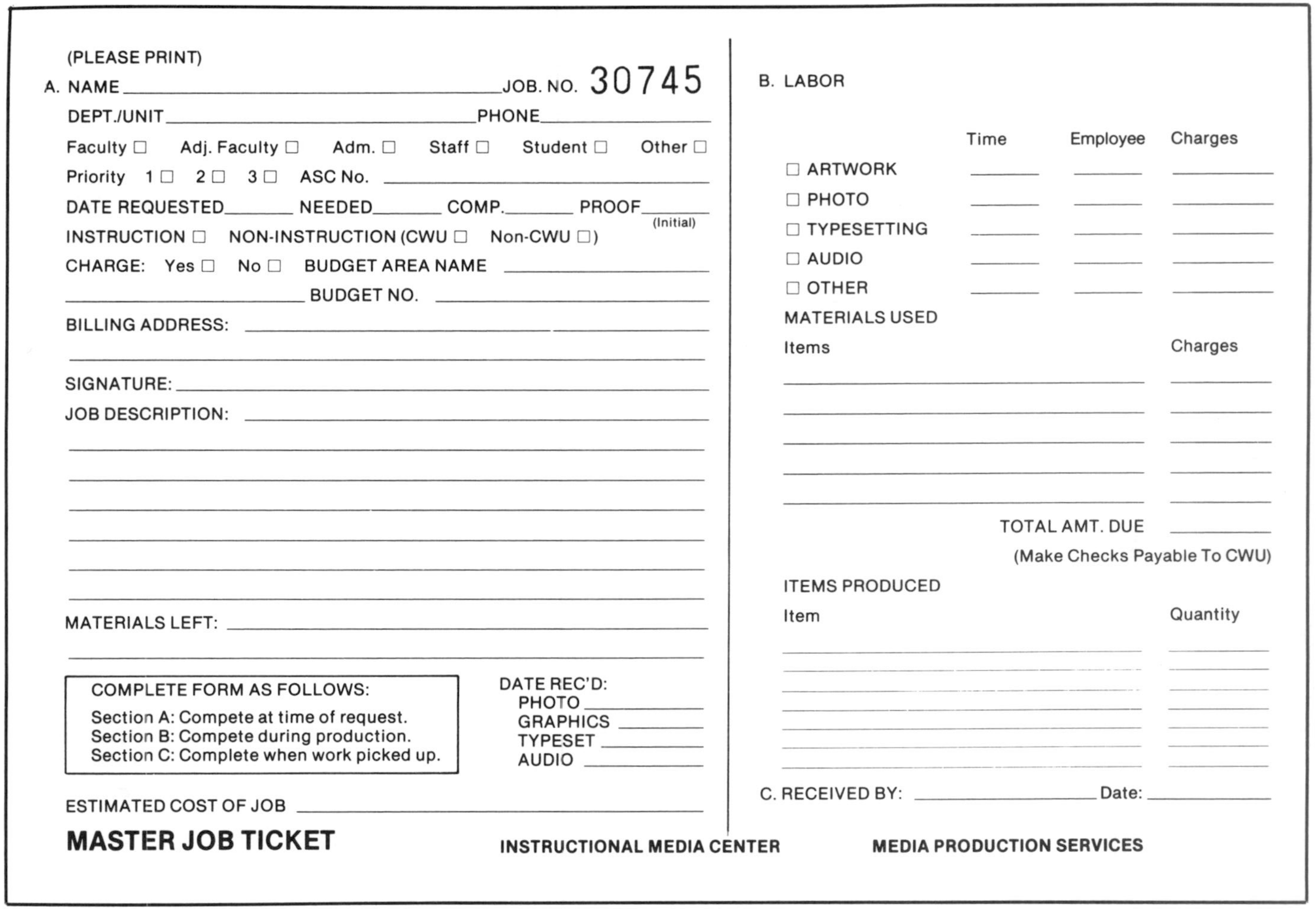

(PLEASE PRINT)

A. NAME ________ JOB. NO. 30745

DEPT./UNIT ________ PHONE ________

Faculty ☐ Adj. Faculty ☐ Adm. ☐ Staff ☐ Student ☐ Other ☐

Priority 1 ☐ 2 ☐ 3 ☐ ASC No. ________

DATE REQUESTED ________ NEEDED ________ COMP. ________ PROOF ________ (Initial)

INSTRUCTION ☐ NON-INSTRUCTION (CWU ☐ Non-CWU ☐)

CHARGE: Yes ☐ No ☐ BUDGET AREA NAME ________

________ BUDGET NO. ________

BILLING ADDRESS: ________

SIGNATURE: ________

JOB DESCRIPTION: ________

MATERIALS LEFT: ________

COMPLETE FORM AS FOLLOWS:
Section A: Compete at time of request.
Section B: Compete during production.
Section C: Complete when work picked up.

DATE REC'D:
PHOTO ________
GRAPHICS ________
TYPESET ________
AUDIO ________

ESTIMATED COST OF JOB ________

MASTER JOB TICKET

B. LABOR

	Time	Employee	Charges
☐ ARTWORK			
☐ PHOTO			
☐ TYPESETTING			
☐ AUDIO			
☐ OTHER			

MATERIALS USED

Items	Charges

TOTAL AMT. DUE ________
(Make Checks Payable To CWU)

ITEMS PRODUCED

Item	Quantity

C. RECEIVED BY: ________ Date: ________

INSTRUCTIONAL MEDIA CENTER **MEDIA PRODUCTION SERVICES**

Figure 7.2. Production job ticket. (Central Washington University, Ellensburg, WA. Reprinted with permission.)

should then be evaluated in use to determine if it meets the specified objectives developed prior to development. When possible, provide for some form of evaluation and tryout of materials with a target audience. Instructional and training applications, as well as cognitive, motor, and effective knowledges and skills, should then be measured in the classroom or laboratory. Based upon the results, segments of the production can be reviewed as needed prior to future use.

Computer Systems

Beginning in the 1980s, great strides have been made in the development of computer-generated graphics. This capability began early in the television field with the evolution of electronic special effects, as stations searched for ways to generate new eye-catchers in order to capture a larger part of the television audience. Simple switchers evolved into more intricate and complicated switchers that, when eventually coupled with the memory capabilities of a modern computer, became endowed with a myriad of artistic capabilities when directed by creative people. Such developments soon found their way into the commercial art world and were adopted to generate and develop all types of graphics. As equipment costs have decreased and programs for creating computer graphics evolved, systems capable of producing very sophisticated graphics have become commonplace.

Graphics Systems

A number of computer graphics systems are available that put some graphics capability into the grasp of most computer owners. With such systems, artists, executives, secretaries, and others who know how to use them can quickly prepare charts, graphs, and a wide variety of other business, sales, or instructional graphics. An almost unlimited array of colors can be added as desired, and revisions can be made at any time without spending time redrawing the work. One can create original illustrations, move symbols around freely, and enlarge or reduce images to meet aesthetic and visual objectives. A large selection of type fonts and sizes is available, along with a variety of shading and shadow effects. The high-resolution output of today's equipment makes it difficult to separate computer-generated work from original hand and typeset creations. Production costs are reduced, making computer-generated graphics very cost-effective. The output from the computer can be rendered in various formats, such as paper printouts, slides, and transparencies, to meet many graphic needs. Quality, however, depends upon the capabilities of the equipment and software being used and the person using them.

In large media development centers where many artists may be employed or in institutions where personnel in other locations need sophisticated computer graphics capabilities, systems are available for networking. In this application, high-quality processing and output equipment is located in a central location and accessed by artists from their computers.

Desktop Publishing

The rapid developments in computer graphics systems soon found their way into software designed for the creation of publications using low-cost microcomputers. This application, called *desktop publishing*, involves, as its name implies, the creation of copy using a microcomputer with appropriate software and printer to integrate words and simple graphics into low-cost publications. Desktop publishing programs are available for all microcomputer systems. They can reproduce a number of type fonts, type sizes, and some commonly used symbols, and have the capacity for the creation of simple artwork (or, more commonly, importing of quite sophisticated graphics). The operator can move elements around a page, set type up in full-page or column format, and output the information to a printer. When a laser printer is used, the resulting copy can be nearly as sharp and precise as typeset copy. Typeset quality is also available as an end product at an increased cost per page by using advanced equipment. This book was created using desktop publishing.

Implications for Media Centers

Both computer graphics systems and desktop publishing have a place in media center service programs. As previously noted, comprehensive computer graphics systems can perform electronically a wide variety of tasks previously performed manually by an artist. We must emphasize, however, that artists are still necessary, for it is the artist who can use the equipment creatively to produce the desired materials. The computerized equipment may increase the speed, complexity, and scope of a center's production output, but only with a capable, creative operator. When the workload increases to justify the employment of an additional artist, perhaps the purchase and implementation of a computer graphics system should be considered with the idea of making better use of existing staff.

In some production centers, desktop publishing software available for existing microcomputers and printing equipment will be sufficient to meet client needs, thus a comprehensive computer graphics system will not be necessary. How can a media manager know when to purchase one or the other? The deciding factor should be the level of quality that the administration and the center have established. In most institutions, desktop publishing systems should be adequate for in-house publications and perhaps for some publications with limited outside distribution. When top quality is desired, better quality, larger, more comprehensive systems should be used.

In summary, computer graphics systems are available to expand the creative abilities of an existing graphics staff. Both expensive comprehensive systems and relatively inexpensive desktop publishing systems are available. Media managers in consultation with the production staff should select appropriate systems to meet their clients' needs.

A final note of caution is in order. The wide availability and user-friendliness of computer graphics and desktop publishing systems is tempting to many to create their own products. Not everyone has design skills and a sense of aesthetics. Institutions should develop some type of control of how created materials are disseminated, particularly outside of the institution. An institution's image is precious and to develop effective graphic and printed products requires skilled designers.

VIDEO/TELEVISION SERVICES

A broad range of video/television services can be found in corporate and educational institutions. They range from inexpensive programs with a capital investment under $25,000 to complex video production facilities that cost several million dollars. Understandably, the range of services provided by these facilities also are diverse. However, the most common types of services provided are as follows.

Playback of Purchased Video Products

Thousands of programs are presently available for purchase and use in instruction and training. The simplest service is to collect and provide playback units for users of these materials. This can be facilitated inexpensively via a videocassette player, monitor, and mobile cart made available to the user or via a relatively expensive closed-circuit video/television distribution system. However, the growing opinion is that these materials might better be circulated from the media center's materials circulation unit, where they can be selected, acquired, cataloged, and circulated following established procedures for the media materials.

Off-Air or Off-Cable Recording

An inexpensive source of programs for nonprofit educational use is recorded video programs transmitted directly by television stations (off-air) or programs delivered by cable transmission (off-cable). This is a popular practice that brings a wide variety of excellent material to classrooms. The videorecorder is connected directly to the antenna or cable or through a timer that will automatically start the recorder when the program is to be transmitted.

The copyright law allows most programs to be retained and used in the classroom within ten school days of the recording date. The law further allows that the program may be retained for a total of forty-five days for review purposes before it must be erased.

Single-Camera Productions

Single-camera video production equipment is relatively inexpensive and can provide surprisingly good technical quality, and the quality continues to improve. The following are examples of possible single-camera production uses:

- Record and playback presentations made by salespeople, teachers, trainers, students, and trainees for critiquing purposes
- Record testimony for trials when an individual cannot attend
- Record and playback assembly tasks at reduced speed for time-and-motion study or problem analysis
- Produce programs demonstrating equipment operations
- Produce simple instructional programs
- Produce programs that new employees follow to learn complex production tasks
- Record faculty for observation and review of teaching skills/methods
- Develop a video training facility for teaching video/television production skills
- Use as an observation tool in dangerous environments
- Use as an observation tool in high-theft areas

Complex Productions

When extensive multiple-camera video/television production facilities and staff are available, excellent instructional/training or sales materials can be created. These services are only recommended when the number of students/trainers or clients that will use the materials is high enough to amortize the production cost at a reasonable level.

Because video/television production is expensive, it is important that finished productions meet the needs of the requesting clients and are effective when used. Planning must be very thorough if this objective is to be met, therefore the prudent media manager will insist upon adequate preproduction planning. Remember, what works well locally may not market or function nationally because of a variety of factors.

Video Development Process

To implement this phase, information must be collected before any decision to accept a design and production request can be made. Therefore, as in any other media service request, a form is necessary to collect the appropriate information. The form in figure 7.3 can serve that function. Once a production request has been accepted, a production work flow must be established and followed. An effective video development work flow process is illustrated in figure 7.4, page 158. As with graphic services, four basic stages exist: information gathering, design, production, and evaluation.

Information Gathering Stage

As with graphics and reprographics, at the information gathering stage the client describes the requested production. A request form is completed in order to gather all the pertinent preliminary information needed. The manager must insist that the "shoot now and assemble later" method is not allowed. Careful planning will greatly curtail costly postproduction work and is time well spent. Planning involves identifying and specifying *what* information is to be transmitted and *who* is going to receive that information.

Design Stage

After the *what* and *who* have been identified, the design can be developed. The design specifies *how* the content will be presented and involves many tasks:

- *Develop the idea from a need.* A need should be evident before a production is considered; the need then becomes an idea for a production. Several ideas for a production may surface because of a single need. At this point, an idea for a production is simply a thought that a specific topic (based upon the evident need) would make a good subject for a production. Research is necessary at this point to develop ideas, refine ideas, eliminate ideas, and select an idea for development. The final idea(s) must be very carefully researched and developed. Ideas generally require an incubation period if they are to be fully and properly developed.
- *Identify the content.* From both the need and idea for a production, the content should become quite evident. The content must be refined and delineated

(Text continues on page 159.)

VIDEO PRODUCTION REQUEST

Name _____ Date _____

Dept./Course _____ Requested Completion Date _____

Telephone Number _____

Estimated Number of Productions _____

Estimated Uses Per Year _____

Content:

Target Audience:

Objectives:

Desired Reaction of Audience After Viewing Program:

Conference Dates (with Production Coordinator): _____

Estimated Production Cost: (to be completed by Coordinator)

     Labor: _____ Cost _____ Date _____

     Materials: _____Cost _____ Date _____

Request Approved:

Client: _____ Date _____

Dept. Head: _____ Date _____
(if charged back)

Production Coordinator: _____ Date _____

IMC Director: _____ Date _____

Figure 7.3. Video/television production request form. (Central Washington University, Ellensburg, WA. Reprinted with permission.)

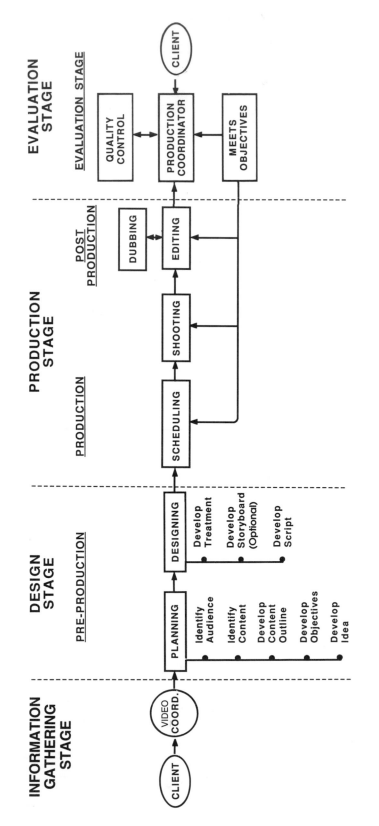

Figure 7.4. Video development process.

so it is of a manageable size for a production. Further research is usually required before the specific content to be presented is fully identified, refined, and delineated.

- *Develop the content outline.* The content must be arranged in a logical presentation order. The old rule applies: "First things first." Break the content into logical topics and subtopics.

- *Identify the audience.* The first step in any planning stage is to identify the expected viewers. Their age, grade level, skills, training, background, and knowledge or experience within the content area will determine the vocabulary level used, pacing, examples used, and other production factors. The learning entry level of the expected viewers must be considered if the production is to be successful.

- *Develop the objectives.* After the content outline and the audience have been identified, specific objectives can be developed. They should be written simultaneously with content evaluation questions. The effectiveness of a production cannot be measured unless realistic evaluation questions or activities are developed. The best time to determine the evaluation procedures is when the objectives are being developed. Do not allow too many content objectives to be written. If the content has been carefully selected and limited, this will not be a problem.

- *Develop a treatment.* The treatment serves as a summary of the proposed production. It should briefly and succinctly inform a client what content will be presented and how it will be presented (figure 7.5, page 160). It states objectives, briefly describes the idea, and summarizes the content. The treatment should provide the reader with a visual mental image of the finished product. It should describe the presentation format (e.g., documentary, dramatization, live, animated). As the treatment is developed, the writer must think visually. The treatment should present the case or sell the proposal, and it must communicate exactly. Several treatments may be proposed for the same content for a client.

- *Develop a storyboard.* The development of a storyboard (figure 7.6, page 161) is an optional but highly recommended step. It is essential for animated, highly technical productions and is often necessary for multimedia productions. A storyboard fully describes each shot individually with both a visual description and audio statement. Each shot is placed on separate four-by-six-inch or larger cards so their sequence can be easily reordered. Individual frames can then be changed, resequenced, dropped, or added. After the writer and reviewers are satisfied with each shot and sequence, then, working from the storyboard, they write the script.

- *Transpose the storyboard into a script.* Once the storyboard has been developed, it is transposed into script form (figure 7.7, page 162). The two-column script provides a brief narrative description of each visual in one column and the narration/audio that is to occur with each visual in a second column. Another type of script is the single-column format (see figure 7.8, page 163). The advantage of this format is that it is easier to read. You don't have to jump back and forth between columns. The script is used by the director to orchestrate the obtaining and assembling of the visual and audio materials while shooting and/or editing.

(Text continues on page 164.)

TREATMENT

Title:_____The Building_____ Medium:__Super 8mm, Sound_____

Running Time:_5 minutes__ Color or B&W:___B&W_____ Approximate Cost:__$50.00____

Sound:_Music background throughout._ Narration: Use only several key questions to____

provoke imagination. Sound to be on tape cassette on non-synch equipment._ Very___

_loose synch required for several scenes which have accompanying narrative._____

Shooting Location:_New State Historical Building in Columbus, Ohio_____

Intended Audience:_This film will be instructional in nature._ It is to be used at___

_the upper elementary level in a creative writing situation._____

Objectives:__ To present a situation which is mysterious and intriguing and which___

leaves many things unanswered. After viewing the film, the student will write a___

_200-word story based on what he has seen, and using his imagination, to try to____

_surmise the purpose of the building._____

Summary:

   Open with a boy and girl who are viewing a massive and intriguing building from a
distance._ The boy points in a sweeping fashion to show the girl that a ramp leads to
the second level of the structure._ The two get on their bicycles and ride up the ramp.
When they reach the second level, they are attracted by what appear to be large steel
mounds._ They proceed to the mounds, they hurriedly run to look into one of the huge
windows nearby._ After peering in, the boy makes a shrugging gesture to indicate that
he saw nothing revealing; the windows are dirty and it is dark inside.

   Next they run up a flight of stairs that takes them to the top of the tallest
steel mound._ They discover that this one is actually an observation platform presenting a good view of the surroundings._ They descend the steps and wheel their bikes
toward the side railing._ Here they pause and peer over the side at the building
structure below._ As they begin to wheel their bikes once again, they notice some
small openings high above them on the side wall._ They pause and ponder what they
might be.

   Finally, they get on their bikes and ride rapidly down the ramp and away from
the building._ They stop momentarily and gaze back at the massive structure._ They
are still puzzled about what is housed in the strange building, but they have some
ideas._ They continue bicycling and ride out of sight.

Figure 7.5. Example of a treatment. From William D. Schmidt, *Designing the Film* (Pullman, Wash.: Information Futures/Community Computer Centers, 1978), 27. Reprinted with permission.

SKETCH OR PHOTO:

PRODUCTION NOTES AND DISCRIPTION OF VISUALS:

3

LS with boy and girl on bikes arriving on site of large and intriguing building.

SUGGESTED NARRATION:

A boy and a girl were out for a ride in a new area one day and they noticed a massive and intriguing building.

ADDITIONAL AUDIO:

Music Down

SKETCH OR PHOTO:

PRODUCTION NOTES AND DISCRIPTION OF VISUALS:

4

MS of boy and girl. Look at building and at each other as if to ask if they dare go closer.

SUGGESTED NARRATION:

None

ADDITIONAL AUDIO:

Music Up

Figure 7.6. Example of storyboard form. From William D. Schmidt, *Designing the Film* (Pullman, Wash.: Information Futures/Community Computer Centers, 1978), 31. Reprinted with permission.

SCRIPT	
<u>Visual</u>	<u>Narration/Audio</u>
1. Title:	1. <u>Music</u>
"The Building"	
2. Credit Title:	2. <u>Music</u>
by	
Gene Anderson	
and	
Greg Jones	
<u>Fade-out - Fade-in</u>	
3. <u>LS</u> of building with boy and girl in fore-ground viewing a massive and intriguing building. Boy points in a sweeping fashion to show girl that a ramp leads to the second level of the structure.	3. <u>Music down</u> Narrator: "A boy and a girl were out for a ride in a new area one day and they noticed a massive and very intriguing building."
4. <u>MS</u> of boy and girl. Curious, intrigued look. They look at each other as if to ask if they dared go closer. Deciding affirmatively, they mount their bicycles and start up the ramp.	4. <u>Music</u>
5. <u>MS</u> as they begin to move away.	5. <u>Music</u>
6. <u>MS</u> of them riding by camera as they reach midpoint of ramp.	6. <u>Music</u>
7. <u>MS</u> as they reach top of ramp. They proceed to ride but at a slower and more cautious pace. They glance at the "steel mounds" ringing the building.	7. <u>Music</u>
8. <u>MS</u> as they approach camera and round corner and then move away from camera on way to mounds.	8. <u>Music</u>
9. <u>MS</u> as they dismount and cautiously approach a mound.	9. <u>Music</u>
10. <u>CU</u> of their faces to show caution.	10. <u>Music</u>
11. <u>MS</u> of boy crawling up side of mound and attempting to look inside.	11. <u>Music</u>
12. <u>CU</u> of boy looking back at girl. His expression indicates he is beginning to understand but is worried.	12. <u>Music</u>
13. <u>MS</u> as boy scrambles down from mound and the two run toward one of the huge windows and attempt to peer inside.	13. <u>Music</u>

Figure 7.7. Example of a script. From William D. Schmidt, *Designing the Film* (Pullman, Wash.: Information Futures/Community Computer Centers, 1978), 33. Reprinted with permission.

Production: "The Magic of Business Week"

1. CU of students listening to general session speech.

> SOUND: Sound of speaker up momentarily, then under as narrator begins.

2. General session presentation: Pan from students to teacher to business employee to   business executive (who is speaking).

> NARRATOR: (Voice Over)
> IT WOULD BE A WEEK UNLIKE ANY THEY HAD EVER EXPERIENCED. HIGH SCHOOL STUDENTS . . . TEACHERS . . . BUSINESS EMPLOYEES . . . AND . . . BUSINESS EXECUTIVES FROM THROUGHOUT THE STATE OF WASHINGTON

> SOUND: Up full to hear speaker momentarily, then under as narrator continues.

3. CU of students listening.

> NARRATOR: (Voice Over)
> THEY CAME TOGETHER TO SHARE A UNIQUE EXPERIENCE; SOMETHING AT WEEK'S END THEY WILL CALL THE MAGIC OF BUSINESS WEEK.

4. Shots of Business Week activities with emphasis on sharing--caring--communicating, shown with music of Business Week Song.

> SOUND: (Vocal Song) "It's magic . . . Business Week. No fantasy, but reality. It's magic . . . giving, caring, sharing, growing as one! Magic . . . Business Week. It's in the air, just take a look . . . . Magic . . . changing, working, striving, giving it all! Business Week! . . . Telling the Private Enterprise Story!"

 Super title: THE MAGIC OF BUSINESS WEEK

5. Close up on interviewee before beginning to talk.

> NARRATOR: (Voice Over)

Figure 7.8. Example of a one-column script.

A case study of the design of a video production is presented in appendix 6. Every step in the design process is identified and explained, from idea generation through script preparation.

Production Stage

Once production planning has been completed, production can be scheduled and work begun. The script provides the opportunity to break down the shooting and optimize the work schedule. Production work involves two specific but related components: the actual shooting, which may be in the studio or in remote locations, and the postproduction work of editing and dubbing.

The production stage is expensive, as it usually requires many people, especially for studio productions when multiple cameras are used. Therefore, it is important that all activities be planned and scheduled carefully to avoid wasteful delays. Then previously taped segments from various locations are selected and edited into the program. Voice-over audio and sound effects are added as required. Again, careful planning can decrease costly editing time.

Evaluation Stage

The evaluation stage is not unlike the graphics evaluation stage. The media development coordinator and the client review the program to be sure that it meets the established objectives. It may involve field testing with a representative audience in the classroom or laboratory (students used in a formative evaluation step) to determine if the affective, cognitive, and psychomotor skills have been achieved. If not, problems should be corrected prior to duplicating for wider use. The media development coordinator must also make sure that the production meets established quality standards.

MULTIMEDIA DEVELOPMENT SERVICES

One of the writers of this book attended a session on multimedia production at the 1996 Association for Educational Communications and Technology convention. At the conclusion, Dr. Jerry Kemp, longtime author of a leading textbook on media development, also in the audience, said to that writer something to the effect of, "If only we had some of these powerful computer tools when we were struggling with Leroy and Wrico lettering sets and other now largely discarded production devices." Computers are revolutionizing the processes of media development. During the design stages, you can use software to automate the format for scripts and storyboards. There are some programs that will even help you write through the use of a prompting process. During the production process, software is available to make signs, posters, slides, and overhead transparencies, as well as more complex productions, such as slide shows, videos, and other forms of multimedia productions.

The term *multimedia* is used somewhat reluctantly here to describe the "use of a computer to present and combine text, graphics, audio, and video with links and tools that let the user navigate, interact, create, and communicate" (Hofstetter 1997, 2). *Multimedia* is a term that has been used in the instructional media field for decades to describe an approach to instructional presentation that involved the use of more than one medium at a time. The computer field has adopted this term as if it were a new discovery. In any case, it is widely used to describe what Hofstetter has defined and for that reason we will use it in this text.

Among the multimedia products that make the task of production easier are presentation software, such as Corel Presentations and Microsoft Power-Point. These programs allow you to generate slides or overhead transparencies that can be used on conventional projectors, or the images created can be shown as a slide show on the computer monitor or projected by a data projection device.

For more sophisticated multimedia productions, Roger Wagner Publishing's HyperStudio or Pierian Spring's Digital Chisel are available. These allow for some program branching, video, sound, animation, and numerous special effects. These are very user-friendly and ideal for instructor/trainer use. For the media professional, there are more powerful authoring programs for creating interactive computer or CD-ROM multimedia presentations. Macromedia's two programs, Authorware and Director, and mFactory's mTropolis are powerful programs but have a steeper learning curve.

The model for video development (see figure 7.4) can be used to develop multimedia productions. However, after a script is developed, some additional steps, such as flowcharting, are required because of the complexity of designing branching programs. Planning the navigation through a multimedia program is complex enough that it needs to be flowcharted. Figure 7.9, page 166, illustrates a flowchart for a short HyperCard program on the three basic parts of a script (the beginning, the middle, and the end). Each number represents a different card or visual. In the case of figure 7.9, the user has multiple branching choices at steps 4 and 5. These choices lead to different subject content and visuals. At steps 14 and 15, the user can select a specially made videodisc that will show (on demand) examples of good beginnings and endings to media productions.

In spite of the great power and promise of multimedia, it is not as simple to create and use as one would believe from reading or viewing the hype of advertisements. Production is certainly easier once one assembles all the needed equipment and software, but good design is still necessary. One still needs to go through all the steps until you have a script. That was summed up succinctly by one observer:

> Multimedia and interactive video computer software can build and play presentations but it can't design them. It takes human beings to do that, and designing good presentations is a unique challenge (Victor 1993, 75).

Furthermore, the design and development can be very time-consuming and, in that sense, a very expensive form of media development. Figure 7.10, pages 167, shows the type and configuration of equipment that is needed to develop complex multimedia productions. Simple productions can be developed with a much simpler system.

NAVIGATION FLOWCHART

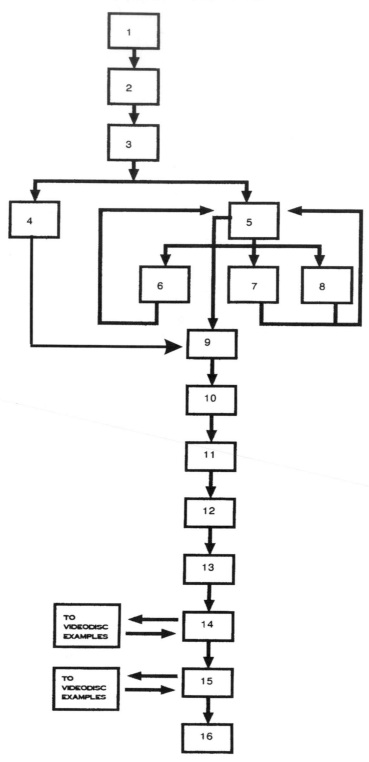

Figure 7.9. Flowcharting a multimedia production.

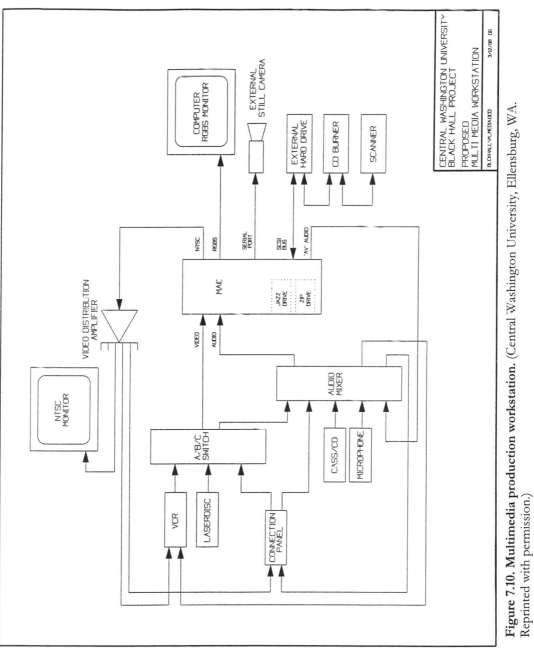

Figure 7.10. Multimedia production workstation. (Central Washington University, Ellensburg, WA. Reprinted with permission.)

SHOULD MEDIA DEVELOPMENT SERVICES BE INTEGRATED?

We have previously discussed the value and economics of integrating the various media services within an institution: Integration usually results in less duplication of personnel and equipment. Therefore, a strong argument can be developed to support the concept of combining graphic and video development services into one media development unit. Video development does require some graphics work, either mechanically or electronically. With an increase in the use of computers to create graphics materials, savings can be realized in both equipment and personnel if only one graphics unit within the media center serves video as well as other needs. Photographers, artists, and other technicians within the graphics unit can be used as television operators when a large production crew is needed, thereby eliminating some television operator positions that may not be needed on a full-time basis. Integration allows for flexibility in scheduling production personnel for more efficient use of the staff. However, when the workload can be documented to justify separate personnel, then separate employees for each function should be employed to allow specialization.

CHARGE BACKS FOR SERVICE

In chapter 3, there was a general discussion of whether or not to charge for services, with the general advice to not charge clients if an adequate budget can be established to provide services. In the area of media development, this issue usually looms large. Some design and production services tend to get expensive, and even a generally adequate budget can be overwhelmed by video or multimedia productions.

Learning Resources Programs That Make a Difference (Schmidt 1987, 107) provides one way of looking at how different institutions handle the use of charge backs. What follows is no answer to whether or not to charge for services. It is only a survey of some of the practices in the field. Of the institutions studied, if the program used charge backs to recover costs, it was almost always for the design and production of materials. These costs can grow very rapidly, and charge backs appeared to be used as a way to meet requests without rapidly depleting a program's budget. For instances in which charges were made for labor, the practice varied from attempting to recover all personnel costs to the practice of charging a nominal fee to partially cover labor costs. This latter practice was viewed as a way to control the making of requests of questionable value which might result if the service were without charge.

At the four-year university and college level (doctorate-granting universities and comprehensive universities and colleges), of the eleven programs studied, slightly more than half charged for supplies and labor for instructional requests. Almost without exception, all the universities charged for supplies and labor for producing materials for research, public relations, and nonuniversity work.

At the two-year college and institute level, one college charged for supplies but not for labor for materials produced for instruction, research, and public relations. Three of the other four did not charge for either supplies or labor. All charged full costs when they did noninstitutional work. About five years ago, one college, Kirkwood Community College (Cedar Rapids, Iowa), changed from a charge-back system to appropriated budgets. Budgets are based on trends and the ability to supply the needs of the college.

Of the public school districts, three charged for supplies only for production jobs for instruction. The other two districts provided these types of production services without charges. None of the districts charged for labor on instructional requests, but one charged for both supplies and labor for research and public relations jobs. All five of the districts reported charging for both supplies and labor for non-institutional requests.

Regional media centers were funded differently in the four states visited. The two Iowa programs received funds from taxes and charged only for the supplies used in all production requests. One of the two Oregon programs studied charged for graphic production requests on a contractual basis.

COST ACCOUNTING

Because media development is an expensive undertaking, it must be treated like a business, and good cost accounting procedures must be implemented regardless of whether fees are assessed for the services rendered. As was stated earlier, media development must be performed at a speed that patrons or the institution can afford but still maintain an acceptable level of quality. Four cost areas must be monitored in media development: labor, material, equipment, and overhead. Each must be reflected in the total cost of a production job.

Many educational institutions consider media development as a service to the institution and therefore provide a budget, eliminating the need for charging patrons. The services are limited to the institution's employees for official purposes. This practice is highly recommended. First, the practice eliminates the fact that charges tend to inhibit use; second, it eliminates accounting and billing costs, freeing dollars which can be better used for production; and third, it eliminates a good deal of resentment by clients who are not provided with services unless their budget will allow it.

OTHER TYPES OF MEDIA DEVELOPMENT SERVICES

A *media laboratory* is another type of media development service that an institution and its media center may find helpful to patrons. This provides a place where teachers, trainers, students, trainees, salespeople, and others can produce their own materials. This type of laboratory has proven extremely popular in college and university media centers, where students can produce materials for class activities and reports. Teachers can use a media laboratory to produce their own instructional materials. A media laboratory should provide a comfortable work environment with basic production equipment, tables, dry mounting presses, laminators, drawing equipment, computers with word processing software, duplicating equipment, transparency makers, old magazines, commercial transparency masters, cameras (video, digital, and photographic), computers with graphics and desktop publishing capabilities, scanners, CD-ROM recorders, and other equipment. Employees must be available to demonstrate, assist, and sell production supplies. Some media laboratories provide a photographic darkroom, audio laboratory, and slide duplicating facilities.

A *video laboratory,* where patrons can learn how to set up and operate video equipment and produce simple programs, is another service that can be provided. Again, an employee must be available to instruct and assist.

Community access television is another production service that many schools and universities find needed within a community. The program can obtain some funding support through cable service franchise agreement fees. Such facilities provide a useful training laboratory for students. Usually the laboratory must be available for community residents who desire to learn how to produce television programs of community interest. Again, staff must be provided to instruct and assist.

Computer laboratories are also becoming popular, where patrons, including students and trainees, can learn and practice computer skills and develop computer instructional/training programs. A wide selection of computer programs, including graphics, desktop publishing, presentation, and multimedia production software, should be available within a computer laboratory. Staff must be available to supervise.

SUGGESTED ACTIVITIES

1. Develop a policy to guide the production activities of a media development unit of a media center.

2. Prepare a media development staff procedures manual that will assist staff in delivering services.

3. Develop a rationale or case to present to the institution's appropriate body or administrator to eliminate media development charges.

4. Develop a proposal justifying the purchase of a desktop publishing system for a media development center.

REFERENCES

Brown, James W., Kenneth D. Norberg, and Sara K. Srygley. 1972. *Administering Educational Media: Instructional Technology and Library Services.* New York: McGraw-Hill.

Guerin, David V. 1965. "Media's Influence on Design." *Audiovisual Instruction,* 10, no. 2: 95–97.

Hofstetter, Fred T. 1997. *Multimedia Literacy.* 2d ed. New York: McGraw-Hill.

Morris, William, ed. 1973. *The American Heritage Dictionary of the English Language.* Boston: Houghton Mifflin.

Schmidt, William D. 1987. *Learning Resources Programs That Make a Difference: A Source of Ideas and Models from the Field.* Washington, D.C.: Association for Educational Communications and Technology.

Victor, Tim. 1993. "It's All in the Mix: A Guide to Multimedia Presentation Software." *CD-ROM Today,* 1, no. 2: 71–75.

MEDIA RESOURCES

Introduction to HyperCard. RMI Media Productions, 30 minutes. Washington, D.C.: Association for Educational Communications and Technology, 1995. Videocassette.

Introduction to HyperStudio. RMI Media Productions, 30 minutes. Washington, D.C.: Association for Educational Communications and Technology, 1995. Videocassette.

The Multimedia Revolution—Today and Tomorrow. RMI Media Productions, 30 minutes. Washington, D.C.: Association for Educational Communications and Technology, 1995. Videocassette.

Multiple Options with Multi-media. Seattle Public Schools Instructional Broadcast Center, 28 minutes. Santa Monica, Calif.: Pyramid Media, 1996. Videocassette.

Orientation to Multimedia. RMI Media Productions, 30 minutes. Washington, D.C.: Association for Educational Communications and Technology, 1995. Videocassette.

SELECTED BIBLIOGRAPHY

Appleman, Robert. *Video Editing the Pictorial Sequence*. Washington, D.C.: Association for Educational Communications and Technology, 1996.

Barron, Ann E., and Gary W. Orwig. *Multimedia Technologies for Training: An Introduction*. Englewood, Colo.: Libraries Unlimited, 1995.

Briggs, Leslie J., Kent L. Gustafson, and Murray H. Tillman. *Instructional Design: Principles and Applications*. 2d ed. Englewood Cliffs, N.J.: Educational Technology Publications, 1991.

Curchy, Christopher, and Keith Kyker. *Educator's Survival Guide to TV Production Equipment and Setup*. Englewood, Colo.: Libraries Unlimited, 1997.

Garrand, Timothy. "Scripting Narrative for Interactive Multimedia." *Journal of Film and Video*, 49, nos. 1–2 (1997): 66–79.

Gayeski, Diane M., ed. *Multimedia for Learning: Development, Application, Evaluation*. Englewood Cliffs, N.J.: Educational Technology Publications, 1993.

Green, Lee. *Creative Slide/Tape Programs*. Englewood, Colo.: Libraries Unlimited, 1986.

Hartwig, Robert L. *Basic TV Technology*. 2d ed. Boston: Focal Press, 1995.

Heid, Jim. "Multimedia Options Multiply." *Macworld*, 113, no. 5 (August 1996): 100–105.

Hodge, Winston W. *Interactive Television: A Comprehensive Guide for Multimedia Technologists*. New York: McGraw-Hill, 1995.

Ivers, Karen S., and Ann E. Barron. *Multimedia Projects in Education: Designing, Producing, and Assessing*. Englewood, Colo.: Libraries Unlimited, 1997.

Kemp, Jerrold E., and Don C. Smellie. *Planning, Producing, and Using Instructional Technologies*. 7th ed. New York: HarperCollins College Publishers, 1994.

Kyker, Keith, and Christopher Curchy. *Television Production: A Classroom Approach*. Englewood, Colo.: Libraries Unlimited, 1993.

———. *Television Production for Elementary and Middle Schools*. Englewood, Colo.: Libraries Unlimited, 1994.

Marlow, Eugene. *Managing Corporate Media*. Rev. ed. White Plains, N.Y.: Knowledge Industry Publications, 1989.

Mayeux, Peter E. *Writing for the Electronic Media*. Dubuque, Iowa: WCB Brown & Benchmark, 1994.

Rieber, Lloyd P. *Computers, Graphics, and Learning*. Dubuque, Iowa: WCB Brown & Benchmark, 1994.

Sammons, Martha C. *Multimedia Presentations on the Go: An Introduction and Buyer's Guide*. Englewood, Colo.: Libraries Unlimited, 1995.

Schmid, William T. *Media Center Management: A Practical Guide*. New York: Hastings House, 1980.

Schwier, Richard, and Earl R. Misanchuk. *Interactive Multimedia Instruction*. Englewood Cliffs, N.J.: Educational Technology Publications, 1993.

Sherman, Mendel. *Videographing the Pictorial Sequence*. Washington, D.C.: Association for Educational Communications and Technology, 1991.

Swain, Dwight V., and Joye R. Swain. *Scripting for the New AV Technolgies*. 2d ed. Boston: Focal Press, 1991.

Willis, Edgar E., and Camille D'Arienzo. *Writing Scripts for Television, Radio, and Film*. 3d ed. Fort Worth, Tex.: Harcourt Brace Jovanovich College Publishers, 1993.

COMPUTERS AND THE MEDIA CENTER

Technology never sits still. . . . I see several developments. First, it is reasonable to expect that programming for teaching machines will move from the verbal Socratic-Skinner type to the audiovisual-branching type. That is, the machine will present, based upon student pre-tests, conceptual content using films, slides, filmstrips, tapes, and/ or videotape as the medium. The presentation sequences will be longer and the student will be given an opportunity to select additional sequences for further exploration if the machine, through testing, informs him that he needs it. Records, of course, will be maintained instantaneously. . . .

James Finn, "Technology and the
Instructional Process," in *Audio-Visual
Communication Review,* Winter 1960

OBJECTIVES

At the conclusion of this chapter you should be able to

1. Understand the differences between the Internet, an intranet, a LAN, and a WAN.

2. List and describe six media center management tasks that can be performed using the computer.

3. Describe how the computer can be used to perform the logistical tasks of the following common media service functions:
   a. selecting and acquiring supplies, media equipment, and instructional materials
   b. cataloging
   c. circulating the center's collections
   d. generating catalog copy
   e. maintaining current inventory
   f. maintaining electronic maintenance records
   g. maintaining and tracking production schedules

4. List and describe two modes of instructional computer services.

5. Explain why many instructional computer services may be assigned to the media center.

6. Describe two strategies for curtailing illegal copying of computer programs within an institution.

7. List and discuss the attributes that should be considered before purchasing a computer system.

8. List and discuss steps that a manager should follow in collecting information necessary to make a computer system purchase decision.

Computers were once considered to be the mysterious and expensive tools of industry and government. Today there is little doubt that the human race has entered the age of the computer. They are used everywhere in industry, government, schools, and homes. Our very rapidly changing computer technology has reduced the size, lowered the price, increased the capacity, and made them portable. In a media center, computers that can perform a number of logistical tasks, quickly and effectively, are a valuable management tool. With them, many aspects of media service programs can be improved and streamlined.

THE BASICS

Computers cannot think but they do have good memories. They are not smarter than people, but the people who write the programs must be intelligent. Computers cannot think or solve problems; they can only manipulate data and report data based upon the parameters established by managers and programmed into their memory. Basically computers perform the following tasks:

1. *Accept information.* A *computer workstation* allows one to *input* information through a keyboard similar to a typewriter, or information can be fed in directly from other computers.

2. *Store information.* The storage device, called a *memory,* holds information on a magnetic tape or disk until it is needed. Depending upon the quantity of information required, the extent or size of a computer's memory may determine how useful a particular computer will be.

3. *Process information.* This is done through a unit called the central processing unit (CPU) of the computer. The CPU manipulates information according to directions contained in a *program* that tells it what to do with the information stored in the memory.

4. *Display information.* The *display* unit is similar to a television monitor. It displays both input and output information as directed in monochrome or color. The visual display unit can present information in the form of graphics such as charts, graphs, maps, and animations which can also be printed by a *printer* that produces *hard copy* (see figure 8.1, page 176).

COMPUTER PROGRAMS

All computers—mainframe, mini, or micro—must have instructions to tell them what to do. A set of such instructions is called a *program*. A program might instruct a computer to calculate a bank account balance, project the effect on income by raising the price of a product a few cents, or print out a list of media materials due for distribution on a specific date. Computer programs are called *software,* and the computers themselves are called *hardware.* Software costs vary from a few dollars for a computer game to several thousand dollars for a complicated management program. Thousands of educational computer programs have been prepared on almost any subject one can name. Computer programs are generally supplied on diskette, tape, or CD-ROM. Programs may also be created by the user, but program development is generally a difficult and time-consuming task.

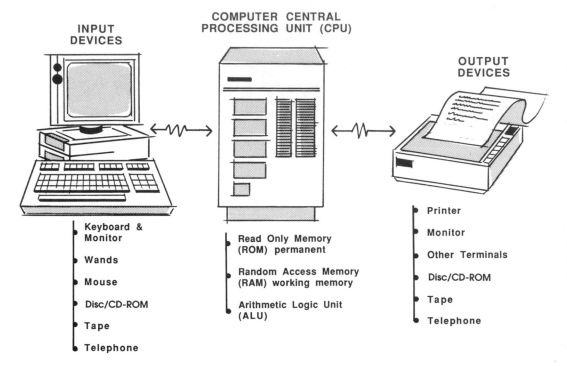

Figure 8.1. Basic components of a computer system.

NETWORKS

The Internet

Connecting computers, whether thousands of miles apart or in close proximity, is the essence of networking. Discussed here are the Internet, intranets, and local area networks (LANs).

One would have to have been living in a cave or on a remote island during the past few years to miss observing the phenomenal growth and development of the Internet. The Internet is a worldwide linking of networks. Millions of computers in more than 100 countries are connected. Through the Internet, the media director has access to information on the latest developments in many, if not most, of the topics in this book. It is an incredible source of information. This can best be illustrated with an example. One of the authors is chair of the building committee for a new university teacher education building. One of the areas of the Educational Technology Center in that building will be a curriculum lab. He submitted searches on the Internet for "curriculum labs." In less than two hours, he had located and had printed documents on nearly two dozen curriculum labs at various universities across the nation. In pre-Internet days, it would have taken days or weeks to assemble the same volume of materials. The Internet will help the media director to gather information rapidly for writing reports and publications, for conducting research, for obtaining specifications on equipment, and for designing media service facilities. In addition, it will greatly facilitate communication with colleagues in the media field via electronic mail.

Intranets

A more recently coined term, an *intranet*, refers to a Web site or a group of Web sites belonging to an organization. It is accessible only to the organization's authorized users.

Local Area Networks (LANs and WANs)

A LAN connects computers over a relatively small area, within a building or among a group of buildings. One LAN, however, can be connected to other LANs by telephone lines or other means. Such a configuration of LANs is called a wide area network (WAN).

Each individual computer on a LAN can access data or devices anywhere else on the LAN. After the operator obtains a network license for a software application package, all computers on the LAN may access this software. In addition, a high-quality laser printer could be used by all LAN computers. Graphic files can be sent over a LAN to a film recorder, to be converted into color slides and transparencies, or to a color printer for creation of color paper prints.

Definitions

New computer terms are being created daily or weekly. A good source for definitions of the latest "computer talk" is the PC Webopaedia. This can be found on the Internet at http://pcwebopaedia.com.

USING COMPUTERS
IN THE MEDIA CENTER

Computers have revolutionized activities in school library media centers. Circulation and cataloging software make the processing of new materials so easy that student help can do a lot of the tedious tasks involved in that job. Companies such as Winnebago, Follett, Nicholas Advanced Technologies, and COMPanion all market circulation and cataloging software designed for the school library media center. These software programs automate the process of entering catalog data in a system and manage the circulation process (search, check-out, fines, and check-in). Most of these systems have or will soon have Internet accessibility to the program. These systems are all adequate for school library media programs.

Other uses of computers in the school library media center include student word processing, running CD-ROM and diskette-based instructional programs, creating spreadsheets, accessing databases, doing inventory, and preparing reports and presentations.

School district central media service centers, as well as higher education and corporate media centers using automation software, sometimes require more sophisticated products. Such computer-based media management systems are an affordable way for media centers to modernize operations, reduce workloads, and minimize errors. Because of a computer's ability to store and manipulate a large volume of information quickly, it can decrease the time it takes to book media service requests for patrons, keep up-to-date records, reduce material turnaround time, and reduce labor costs. The scheduling of media equipment and software, rooms, services, and people has been a cumbersome task when paper forms, card systems, blackboard schedules, magnetic boards, and work schedule calendars were used. Such tasks can now be modernized with a computer management system (figure 8.2). Computers can be programmed to assist in the following conventional media center management tasks:

- select and acquire media resources,
- catalog materials,
- circulate the media center collections,
- generate copy for a catalog,
- maintain accurate and current inventories of the collections,
- monitor electronic maintenance records,
- monitor or track production schedules,
- maintain and make reports regarding media center activities, and
- perform accounting and billing.

Selection and Acquisition Functions

Supplies

The computer can be used to order, monitor, or track an acquisition transaction through all of the steps involved in purchasing and clearing transactions for payment. Programs can be established to tell the computer to alert a media manager when the inventory of certain supply items falls below a preestablished minimal level (e.g., electronic repair parts, photo and graphic production supplies, and projection lamps). Specifications for purchase orders or bid documents listing vendors can also be generated by the computer. Upon receipt of supplies, the information can be input into the computer which then generates payment procedures, thus completing the cycle.

Media Equipment

The task of constantly evaluating media equipment and the typing of detailed specifications is a time-consuming process. Equipment evaluation reports and detailed specifications can be stored within a computer and the specifications made available at any time for review and/or comparison. Appropriate specifications can be readily recalled and printed after a purchase decision has been made. Technical aspects of the transaction can be monitored using the same computer procedures as for the purchase of supplies.

Instructional Materials

As was discussed in a previous chapter, extensive procedures are employed in the selection of instructional materials because of their high cost. Again the computer can save time performing the tasks required in selection. Information about media material under consideration for purchase, such as films, videotapes, CD-ROMs, videodiscs, computer software, audiotapes, filmstrips, and slide sets, can be input into the computer. Such information should include title, applicable curriculum areas,

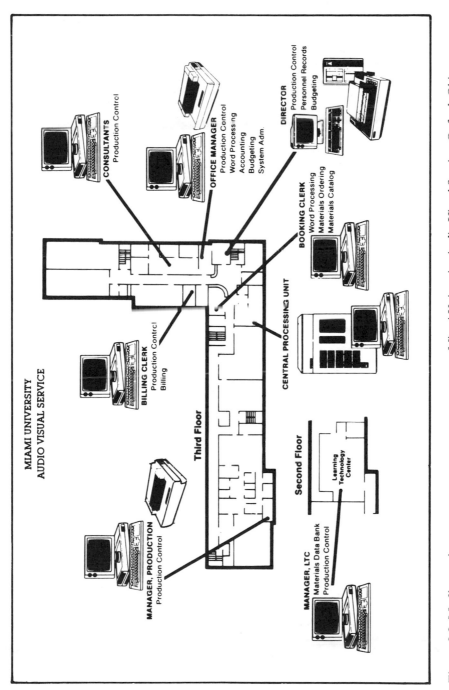

Figure 8.2. Media services computer management system. Miami University Audio Visual Service, Oxford, Ohio. Reprinted with permission.

producer, copyright date, awards, price, annotation of its content, and the distributor. After materials have been previewed and evaluated by clients and staff, evaluation reviews can be added. Any published reviews can also be included. When final decisions for purchase are being made, information to help the media manager decide which materials to purchase can be easily obtained from the computer by asking for specific data. An example of such data follows:

1. List all materials recommended

    a. with five or more uses estimated per year

    b. with a 1995 or later copyright date

    c. strongly recommended by two or more reviewers

2. Arrange in alphabetical order by distributor all materials listed in number 1 above.

3. Arrange all materials listed in number 1 above by applicable curriculum area.

4. Rank in order by preview evaluations materials reviewed during the last six months.

Similar information can be obtained from the computer prior to ordering materials for preview. Such information will enable a manager to identify quickly current materials that are needed. If the manager and clients are attempting to strengthen the materials collection in a specific curriculum area, the manager can use the computer to obtain lists of materials for that particular area. If the manager is attempting to obtain a discount by delaying an order to a distributor until the order is large enough to qualify for a price break, the information gained from number 2 above will be helpful. As with ordering supplies or equipment, the computer can then be used to prepare purchase orders and monitor the purchasing transactions.

Cataloging

After media materials have been purchased, they must be cataloged if clients are to know they are available. Cataloging takes time and several options exist to speed the process. Catalog cards can be ordered from various sources at the same time the materials are ordered. Some distributors will provide catalog cards with the materials; others have them available for purchase separately. Catalog cards are also available from the Library of Congress (LC) in either Dewey Decimal or Library of Congress classifications. Cards are also available from Online Computer Library Center, Inc. (OCLC), Dublin, Ohio, with LC classifications. They should be purchased from one of these sources when available. Another option is to obtain the catalog card information from an online library network like OCLC electronically with the computer. The cards can then be made and the information is available to patrons immediately. Finally, many publishers will supply electronic versions of catalog material on disc or diskette for easy entry on your computerized cataloging and circulation system.

Circulation

Perhaps the function where computers can be of the most assistance in a media center is in the management of the large variety of tasks involved in circulating materials and equipment. Media centers receive orders for the use of materials and equipment by telephone, in person at the counter, and by mail, e-mail, and fax. Requests may be for single items or for many items, for the same date or for multiple dates. Some requests are for the materials requested to be picked up, shipped, or delivered. When the volume of such requests numbers in the thousands each year, it is easy to see how time-consuming circulation tasks become. Circulation tasks that a computer program may perform follow. Many of the examples that follow were created on Medianet, one of several automated systems currently available.

Reserve media. A computer reservation or "booking" program can reserve media materials and equipment for any period of time requested or preprogrammed. The program can allow for single- or multiple-day bookings, allow for different length of booking periods for different customers, and provide priority service to some groups of clients by not allowing others to reserve materials more than a specified time in advance. Reservations can be made online, with an attendant booking the requested materials using a keyboard. If first choice or alternate items or dates are available, the computer makes the booking and prints confirmation sheets.

Provide alternate title options. When an item cannot be booked on the requested date or dates, the computer can provide a display of alternate titles on the same subject matter and level. This can be accomplished by listing titles with a limited number of identical words in the title or by actually selecting materials with similar content and listing their titles as alternates. The latter procedure requires a great deal of time in the initial program preparation, but is extremely valuable to clients searching for appropriate materials (see figure 8.3). Another option is to call up the appropriate subject index that has all of the related titles listed. From this index the client can select alternate titles for consideration.

```
     TITLE #                              TITLE              PRODUCER   YR   TY

032544   CHILDREN IN AUTUMN                                    EBEC 58   C PI   11  M  MB  O
    1        019700    MB  PI  AUTUMN OF THE FARM
    2        060884    MB  P   FARM FAMILY IN AUTUMN
    3        271325    SF  PI  CHANGING SEASONS - AUTUMN IN MY NEIGHBORHOOD

032704   CHILDREN OF SWITZERLAND                               EBEC 40   B IJ   11  M  MA  O
    1        032720    MB  IJ  CHILDREN OF THE ALPS
    1        271969    MB  PI  FLURINA

032720   CHILDREN OF THE ALPS                                  EBEC 50   B IJ   13  M  MB  O
    1        032704    MA  IJ  CHILDREN OF SWITZERLAND
    2        271969    MB  PI  FLURINA

032736   CHILDREN OF THE COLONIAL FRONTIER                     MGHT 62   C IJ   20  M  MB  O
    1        035104    MA  IJ  COLONIAL CHILDREN
    2        050364    MA  I   EARLY SETTLERS OF NEW ENGLAND
    3        272202    MB  IH  LIVING IN THE NEW ENGLAND STATES - BIRTHPLACE OF

032752   CHILDREN   THE FORT                           HT  67     IJ  19      MB  O
```

Figure 8.3. Alternate title report.

Display annotated descriptions. The computer can also serve the same purpose as a card catalog or a printed catalog by displaying the full annotated description and other information listed on a conventional catalog card. Given this electronic card catalog, clients call up a subject index, view the titles and select those for which an annotated description is desired, and then select specific titles for booking. If linked by network to other areas of an institution, clients can use their connected computers to search for appropriate materials. Bookings can then be made online by the client or by telephone, e-mail, or fax with media center staff, thus saving considerable time for all concerned. Many centers now maintain catalog Web sites for ease of access by their clients.

Create and display calendar showing available dates and holidays. The computer can be programmed to display a calendar covering the time material is being requested (see figure 8.4). All dates not deleted with a pair of xx's are available. Thus the client can be assured that the materials will be available when needed. If a request conflicts with another booking, alternate available dates are displayed on the screen for use by the attendant and client in deciding when to book.

```
45018 How Do You Buy a Business?
16     Prints:  1  Rent:   24.70
Jan    Su Mo Tu We Th Fr Sa     Feb   Su Mo Tu We Th Fr Sa     Mar   Su Mo Tu We Th Fr Sa
98                 xx xx xx      98    .. 2  3  4  5  6  ..     98    .. 2  3  4  5  6  ..
       xx xx xx xx xx xx xx            .. 9 10 11 12 13  ..           .. 9 xx xx xx 13  ..
       xx xx xx xx xx xx xx            .. 16 17 18 19 20 ..           .. 16 17 18 19 20 ..
       xx xx xx xx 15 16 17            .. 23 24 25 26 27 ..           .. 23 24 25 26 27 ..
       .. .. 20 21 22 23 ..                                           .. 30 31
       .. 26 27 28 29 30 ..

Apr    Su Mo Tu We Th Fr Sa     May   Su Mo Tu We Th Fr Sa     Jun   Su Mo Tu We Th Fr Sa
98                 1  2  3  ..   98                   1  ..     98          1  2  3  4  5  ..
       .. 6  7  8  9 10  ..            .. 4  5  6  7  8  ..           .. 8  9 10 11 12  ..
       .. 13 14 15 16 17 ..            .. 11 12 13 14 15 ..          .. 15 16 17 18 19 ..
       .. 20 21 22 23 24 ..            .. 18 19 20 21 22 ..          .. 22 23 24 25 26 ..
       .. 27 28 29 30                  .. .. 26 27 28 29 ..          .. 29 30 31
                                       ..

Exit, + next <E>?
```

Figure 8.4. Computer booking calendar display. Reprinted with permission of Iowa State University (created on Medianet software).

Reservations

Confirm reservations. Most clients require a written confirmation for their use in planning. Confirmations can be printed by the computer immediately after booking (see figure 8.5). Computer-generated confirmations can release clerks to perform service tasks that require more sophisticated human skills.

```
                                        Iowa State University
                                        Instructional Technology Ctr.
                                        121 Pearson Hall
                                        Ames  IA 50011-2203
                                        (800)447-0060


            Department Chair
            Iowa State University
            Journalism & Mass Communication
            109 Hamilton Hall
            Ames IA  50011-1180


Type: Rental  Your client#: 54321  Course: JLM461 1  Date: 30-Dec-97

Do not pay from this confirmation notice.  For changes or corrections please
notify us immediately.   Please refer to your client number and order number
in all correspondence or phone calls.

To be shipped and returned via Will Call:

Ship Date  Use Date   Last Use                       Attention   Bld/room
   Order#  Title#     Title                                       Charge

29-Dec-97  29-Dec-97  05-Jan-98                       Preview
   164185  47802, VH  The Road to Rock Bottom                       26.40
                                                 100% Discount    -26.40

   164185  67036, VH  Tet, 1968 (Episode 7)                         28.65
                                                 100% Discount    -28.65
```

```
ISU Media Equipment Services -   **CONFIRMATION**  Notice


The following are reserved for date(s) indicated; contact 294-8022 with change


                                     Client: 65432
                                     Date:   05-Jan-98
      George M. Brown
      ISU
      Agronomy
      2101 Agronomy
      Ames IA  50011-1010



Show       Return     Order # Print #   Title                              A

03-Feb-98  06-Feb     158724            AC2, EQ   Marantz Cassette         A
03-Feb-98  06-Feb     158724            AC2, EQ   Marantz Cassette         A
03-Feb-98  06-Feb     158724            MM1, EQ   Mic Mixer, 4 Channel     A
03-Feb-98  06-Feb     158724            MP4, EQ   PZM Microphone           A
```

Figure 8.5. Media confirmations. Reprinted with permission of Iowa State University (created on Medianet software).

Computer shipping times. Shipping or delivery times may vary for different clients owing to distance or available transportation. These variances can be preprogrammed for each client, thus eliminating wasted time because the same time need not be allocated for shipping to all clients. Local delivery schedules may involve only one day for shipping and one day for return, while the time required to ship to distant clients may be several days each way. When programmed to provide such information, the computer allows a media manager to specify the required shipping time for each client. The resultant saving in time allows the materials to be available to more users or for longer periods of time.

Print due-out and due-in lists. Each day media center materials and equipment that are to be circulated or returned must be identified. A computer can print daily due-out and due-in lists for staff use.

Print shipping labels. Shipping labels can also be generated and printed by computer, thereby eliminating hours of typing time by clerks. Once the customer's name and shipping address have been placed in the computer memory, retyping is not necessary for future transactions; the computer program will assure that the correct labels are printed as needed (figure 8.6).

Bar code wand. The use of a "bar code wand sensor" simplifies the checking out and in of materials and equipment. Automated data reading with bar codes is a valuable tool within library and media service centers. This technology has made retrieval of information through optical scanning devices possible. One such system becoming popular in public academic and industrial libraries and media service centers is known as the bar code system. The bar code can be used for inventory control and in automatic circulation of media materials. It is a series of printed lines and spaces of varying widths which represent numbers, symbols, or letters. Various formats have been developed, but two types—"Code-A-Bar," developed by the Monarch Division of Pitney Bowes Corporation, and "Code 39," developed by Interface Mechanisms, Inc.—have become the most popular in library and media centers. Another code, the Universal Produce Code (UPC), commonly used in grocery stores, is used to speed check-out and maintain inventory information. In a media center the printed bar codes are purchased and affixed to materials (figure 8.7). The code is then read by a bar code wand sensor as it is passed over the code or by passing the material over a scanner within a table. The wand informs the computer that a transaction is being made, the code identifies the material, and the computer records the transaction.

Generate overdue list and print notices. Notifying clients of overdue materials involves considerable staff time. The computer can be programmed to generate a daily overdue list and to prepare and print overdue notices for mailing to the clients (see figure 8.6).

Generate invoices and maintain a general ledger. Computers simplify accounting procedures. If charges to users are mandated by policy, billing can be built in as an integral part of the computer program. In such cases, after materials have been booked and returned, the rental fee is added to the client's bill. Credit for payments to the account can also be input; thus the account is always current and invoices with the correct address are computer-generated quickly for mailing statements.

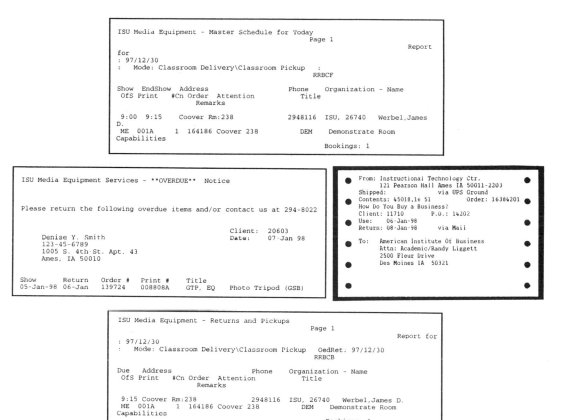

```
ISU Media Equipment - Master Schedule for Today
                                        Page 1
                                                             Report
for
: 97/12/30
:    Mode: Classroom Delivery\Classroom Pickup    :
                                         RRBCF

Show  EndShow  Address               Phone    Organization - Name
 OfS Print     #Cn Order  Attention            Title
                         Remarks

 9:00  9:15    Coover Rm:238         2948116  ISU, 26740   Werbel,James
D.
 ME  001A     1  164186 Coover 238       DEM    Demonstrate Room
Capabilities
                                              Bookings: 1
```

```
ISU Media Equipment Services - **OVERDUE**  Notice


Please return the following overdue items and/or contact us at 294-8022


    Denise Y. Smith               Client:    20603
    123-45-6789                   Date:      07-Jan 98
    1005 S. 4th St. Apt. 43
    Ames, IA 50010


Show      Return   Order #   Print #    Title
05-Jan-98 06-Jan   139724    008808A    GTP, EQ   Photo Tripod (GSB)
```

```
From: Instructional Technology Ctr.
      121 Pearson Hall Ames IA 50011-2203
Shipped:              via UPS Ground
Contents: 45018,16 51        Order: 16384201
How Do You Buy a Business?
Client: 11710         P.O.: 14202
Use:    06-Jan-98
Return: 08-Jan-98     via Mail

To:    American Institute Of Business
       Attn: Academic/Randy Liggett
       2500 Fleur Drive
       Des Moines IA  50321
```

```
ISU Media Equipment - Returns and Pickups
                                        Page 1
                                                      Report for
: 97/12/30
:    Mode: Classroom Delivery\Classroom Pickup   OedRet. 97/12/30
                                         RRBCB
Due   Address                 Phone    Organization - Name
 OfS Print     #Cn Order  Attention             Title
                         Remarks

 9:15 Coover Rm:238           2948116  ISU, 26740   Werbel,James D.
 ME  001A     1  164186 Coover 238       DEM    Demonstrate Room
Capabilities
                                              Bookings: 1
                 --
Tr mode:      1
                                              Bookings: 1
```

Figure 8.6. Computer generated lists and labels. Reprinted with permission of Iowa State University (created on Medianet software).

VOLCANOES (FS-CASS)

CODE:MM0361 COPY:00 REEL 1 of 1

WHATEVER HAPPENED TO LINDA (FS-CASS)

CODE:MM0366 COPY:00 REEL 1 of 1

WHEN LEGENDS DIE (FS-CASS)

CODE:MM0372 COPY:00 REEL 1 of 1

Figure 8.7. Bar codes.

Generate statistical reports. If the computer has any specific area where it provides a higher level of service than other areas, it may be in generating statistical reports from information in the computer's memory. Weeks and even months of statistics collected during daily business can be recalled and manipulated by a computer in a matter of minutes. User information, collection data, costs to client summaries, frequency of turndowns, age of inventory information, or other data that are needed and have been programmed for retrieval can be "called up" for review as needed (see figure 8.8).

```
Iowa State - Student Equipment Usage Data - FY 97 - [dymax.184003]SHIPFY97.YTD
Page 1    06-Nov-97
:    :     Subsort:,,,
Select: !\Bk-Olocshp\=2% AND \Bk-CAudtyp\=102%::!                        RRBKSN


TITLE                        FCODE        Tot#    E-Delv    E-Chrg    E-Dis    Total$

8mm Film Projector           8MM             4                75        75
Marantz Cassette             AC2             3               138       123        15
Audio Cassette Recorder/Playe AC4            2                25        25
Audio Patch Cord             APC           277             3,079     3,079
Audio Adapter                APT             4                45         4         5
PH Audio Cassette Recorder   CAS            22               275       275
Powerbook Video Adapter Cable CC2            2                50        50
Mac II Cable for Sharp LCD   CC3             4               110       110
Cassette/PA, Apollo and Sharp CPA            3               135       135
Demonstrate Room Capabilities DEM            6
Easel                        EAS            12               240       240
Endless Loop Cassette        ELC             2                23        23
Multiple Outlet Strip        EX1            29               430       430
100' AC Extension Cord       EX2             1                11        11
50' Triple Head Extension Cor EX3           15               169       169
```

```
Iowa State Client Summary Report
  Page 1    10-Feb-97


:    :     Select: !\CNEWDAT\<=7487% AND (\CLASTDAT\>=7122% AND \CLASTDAT\<=7487%)
!          RRCSUM


AUDTYP              # ShpNyrShpYtdShpLyr Ref  Ref  Lat  Lat  Lat  Npk  Npk
                                        Ytd  Lyr  Now  Ytd  Lyr  Ytd  Lyr

Consortium Member   7            13                          1
Extension Member   20            34                          5
Faculty           369    10    2910       52           1   128       130
General Public    242    96     413   2   10       2    9         6
Other Universities  6             8                          3
Staff             281    22    1319       27              49        26
Student          1614    17    6553   3  190       4  542    3   427
Student Organizatio 3             5
```

Figure 8.8. Media statistics. Reprinted with permission of Iowa State University (created on Medianet software).

Generation of Copy for Catalog

Copy for a printed catalog can be computer-generated after all data have been transmitted into the memory. Materials can be easily added to or deleted from the computer catalog database. Titles can also be manipulated from the total information base to develop catalog copy for special collections. The catalog can be printed by the computer directly when a few copies are required, or the output can be transmitted to a typesetter for the creation of a printed catalog when many copies are required. In some cases the computer tape or disc containing the catalog can be delivered to the printer for printing. It is wise in this circumstance, however, to maintain a backup copy of the program, in case the other is lost or destroyed.

Maintaining Current Inventory

Inventory records are easy to maintain with a computer. As materials and equipment are purchased, the appropriate data (cost, date, identification numbers, etc.) for each item can be recorded in the computer's memory. Thus the current inventory can be printed or called up on the display whenever needed. Maintaining an adequate inventory of spare parts for an equipment repair facility poses another difficult inventory problem. When several hundred different parts must be kept on hand, it is difficult to keep track of how many of each exist. As repairs are made, information on the number of parts used can be input as the maintenance record is completed. The computer can then subtract the parts from the inventory and print or display a list of parts needed whenever the inventory falls below a desired level. The same procedure can be used for other inventories such as projection lamps.

Electronic Maintenance Records

It is advisable to keep repair records on media equipment. The computer facilitates the upkeep of complete and current records. Typical record information for an item includes the date of purchase, price, identification numbers, and repairs made by dates listing parts and labor. Such information is useful when reviewing equipment for replacement, as the repair history will show when equipment is beyond economical repair.

Maintaining Production Schedules

Computers can be used to track production activities. At any given time a report of each production project can be retrieved and reviewed. All activities involved within a production can be input into the computer and reported—major steps involved, timelines, progress to date, materials used, labor in time and dollars, and total cost to date.

PROVIDING INSTRUCTIONAL COMPUTER SERVICES

As the capacity of computers has increased and costs decreased, experimenters soon discovered the value of computers as instructional tools. With its capacity to store and route nearly unlimited numbers of alternatives, the computer has opened the door to truly individualizing instruction. The computer makes the programmed instruction envisioned by B. F. Skinner and other learning pioneers actually possible.

As the use of computers increased, it soon became apparent that some organization within an institution would be needed to coordinate the logistical tasks involved in making both computers and computer programs available. Traditionally, administrative records have been kept on separate computers and networks due to concerns about security, but there appears to be some interest in having just one system for both administrative and instructional applications. The reason for this consideration is cost-effectiveness. This type of arrangement is especially feasible when building new buildings and networks (Business Publishers 1996). Of institutions that chose to keep them separate, some have decided to place the coordination of instructional computing activities within the purview of the media center. Their use is for instruction and training, as is the case with other media materials. The selection and control of computer programs and equipment is very similar to the tasks involved in handling other materials. They must be carefully selected, cataloged, circulated, and maintained, and it makes sense for the media center to oversee such activities. We will now explore some uses and discuss the logistics required to coordinate instructional computing activities within the media center.

Types of Services

For purposes of discussion, the types of computer services will be organized into three types of uses: classroom use, laboratory use, and check-out by patron. Each creates different sets of problems.

Classroom

When computers are to be used nearly daily during the course of instruction, microcomputers should be placed permanently in the classroom. This particularly helps classes in which instructors desire to demonstrate procedures followed directly by student applications and practice. Usually, a large-screen monitor or data projection device is provided for group viewing. When computer equipment is placed in the classroom, security can be a problem. Analyze your situation carefully. If theft is a problem, the equipment must be located in a lockable cabinet or secured to tables with fasteners that require special tools for installation and removal. Security systems are also available which trigger an alarm when equipment is cut off from its power source or when moved. Ownership labels should be clearly visible and neatly placed on all equipment. It is recommended that classrooms equipped with computer equipment be locked, requiring instructors or lab assistants to unlock them for every class session. Such rooms should be inventoried daily.

Maintaining the appropriate software and data files is a special problem for shared classroom computers. Also providing technical support on-site in classrooms is another challenge for media personnel in this usage approach. This is due to the limited time for technician access in heavily scheduled classrooms.

Laboratory

Many institutions have found it beneficial to establish and place computer laboratories in various locations for employee and/or student use. This practice is used largely in training facilities. Instruction and limited practice may take place in a classroom setting, but students/trainees are then required to complete assignments in laboratories. This practice is also valuable when employees need to use computers part-time but their individual use does not justify installing equipment in their workplace.

Laboratories can be established using a variety of computers or with each laboratory containing only one manufacturer's equipment. This practice allows laboratories to be established to meet special needs or a broad range of needs. A wide range of computer software should be available in each laboratory and be easily available to patrons.

In computer laboratories it is important that someone be employed in each laboratory to assist patrons to check-out computer software, troubleshoot equipment and software problems, monitor the security of the equipment, and curtail copyright infringement. Users of computer equipment in a laboratory setting will need assistance, especially in a training environment. If a laboratory is to meet maximum needs, it must be open for extended hours.

Check-Out

Another type of service found in some institutions is the development of a computer equipment pool from which patrons can check-out and use a wide variety of computer equipment. Computer "notebooks," "laptops," or "palm tops" are often placed in such pools. This practice is especially valuable when users are fully competent to use the equipment and when their need does not justify purchase of additional equipment. It is cost-effective and makes equipment and programs available to patrons who may not otherwise be able to obtain either. As with other media resources, the logistical procedures for facilitating this mode already exist within the center. It is in both the center's and the user's interest to determine that the user knows basic computer operation before checking the equipment out. Programs have been devised to teach the basics. Beginners can work through them in the center or computer lab before checking out the desired equipment and programs.

Software Selection

Procedures for selecting computer software are no different from those followed in selecting materials in other media formats. The policy that guides the selection of other materials can be followed for the selection of computer software. Software must be purchased according to user needs and users should be involved in the selection process. Previewing programs prior to purchase is again highly recommended. For a further discussion of the selection process see chapters 5 and 6.

Circulation Procedures

Procedures for circulating computer equipment and software are also similar. Computer equipment can be booked on a yearly, monthly, weekly, or daily basis depending on user needs. The same booking forms and records can be used as for other materials and equipment. When programs are circulated directly from the media collection, the existing booking procedure is also applicable. A similar booking procedure must be used in computer laboratories or the software located there may disappear or be copied.

In addition to the booking procedure, some form of copyright control must be implemented. Some computer programs can be easily copied on microcomputers, but others have controls inserted in the program that prevent copying. Computers located in areas where no supervision or limited supervision is provided should be labeled with the appropriate copyright warning notice to alert users that copying programs may be a violation of the copyright law. It is especially important that computers to be checked out directly to patrons are so labeled.

The responsibility for user-controlled copying should be transferred to the computer program user. This can be accomplished by placing such a statement at the bottom of the software booking form. The following notice should discourage illegal copying and transfer the responsibility to the user:

> Notice: [name of institution] does not allow its computer equipment to be used to make illegal computer program copies. The copyright law of the United States (Title 17, U.S. Code) governs the making of copies of copyrighted materials. The person using this equipment/material(s) is liable for any infringement.

Another effective method to discourage illegal copying and to transfer the responsibility to the user is to require the user to sign a statement recognizing that copying computer programs may be a violation of the copyright law and agreeing not to make illegal copies. This copy is then placed on file and checked before an individual can use computer equipment and software. The wording should be as follows:

> I, [name], recognize that copying computer software may be a violation of the copyright law of the United States (Title 17, U.S. Code) and hereby agree not to make illegal copies of computer programs I am borrowing, or to use the institution's computer equipment to make illegal copies.
>
> Signature: _____

Maintenance

Like other media equipment, computer equipment must be maintained in good condition if it is to meet user needs. Media center maintenance staff with appropriate training can fulfill most maintenance and repair needs.

PURCHASING COMPUTER SOFTWARE AND HARDWARE

Considering all of the different manufacturers and kinds of computers that are presently available and with the rapid change in the market, the matter of purchasing computer hardware and software can be fraught with difficulties. Computers are not equal; each brand or category of computer has certain drawbacks and attributes that should be assessed before computer equipment is purchased. How does a manager approach the problem? The following guidelines will prove useful for those beginning to research computers before making any purchase decisions.

Attributes to Consider Before Purchasing

Ease of use. The system must be easy for inexperienced operators to use. The program (software) must be simple and have a detailed table of contents, referred to as "menu driven." The program must lead the operator with prompts by asking the operator for each element of data required to complete a transaction. A menu or table of contents must be easily available for call-up to allow the operator to move from one functional program to another. The keyboard should be full typewriter size and have the same touch sense as a typewriter.

Readability. The screen size must be large enough to allow easy readability of required data. Brightness, color, and contrast must be adjustable to allow for comfortable viewing by operators. There does not seem to be any consensus on this issue, therefore each operator must decide which combination of color and contrast best suits that individual. For most applications no less than an 80-column screen (normal typewriter page width) should be considered. For graphics, the greatest pixels per image are recommended if the finished images are to be printed or transferred to a transparency and projected on a screen instead of a monitor. Each pixel is a tiny dot and the sum of the dots creates the image. A 240,000-pixel image would be created by 600 vertical lines and 400 horizontal lines: Each intersecting line would make a pixel (figure 8.9). Many of the microcomputers now support 832 by 624 pixel resolution or higher. Some reach as high as 1,600 by 1,200 pixels.

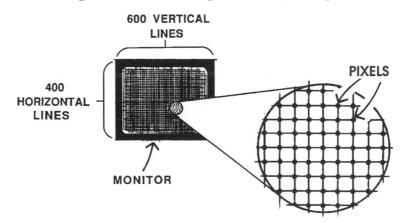

Figure 8.9. Computer images are created by pixels.

Flexibility. The system should meet specific programmatic needs as well as the needs for administrative data control. It should allow for future growth of the media center collections and patron lists. The programs must allow for changes, for the sorting of data in different ways, and for adding additional programs in the future.

Adaptability. A media management computer system should be adaptable for interfacing with mainframe or minicomputers presently located within the institution. This kind of networking enables the planned media center computer system to take advantage of these more powerful computers' memory capacity, greatly expands the capability of the system, and provides for additional uses of the media center computer.

Consider what peripheral equipment will be used with the computer. Are there adequate input and output sources? Is a video output needed?

Cost-effectiveness. The operational and maintenance costs of the system should be low. The system should be operable without additional staff and should save staff time that can be used elsewhere. Maintenance costs must be kept to a minimum if the system is to be cost-effective.

Dependability. An effective system must have dependable equipment. When a system malfunctions and shuts down for any reason, this puts a burden on the staff, as everything must stop or be done by hand. Suddenly key information is not readily available. Schedules cannot be checked. Information cannot be entered, nor can any of the other tasks that are computer-generated be completed. Further, computer downtime quickly dissatisfies clients, who may not return. A balky computer can give the entire center a bad name. Therefore, before computer equipment is purchased, both the equipment and the vendor should be thoroughly checked out. A reputable vendor will stand behind the product and will usually be prepared to provide repairs or replacement equipment while repairs are being made. Good computer equipment is amazingly dependable, but one should try to prepare for any eventuality.

Getting the Facts

A review of television and newspaper advertisements, computer supplier Web sites, professional journals, or a walk through trade shows or educational conventions quickly emphasizes the fact that many brands and types of computers are manufactured. Software available for these computers is almost unlimited. Each advertisement and each salesperson attempts to convince the prospective purchaser that they have the best computer. The selection of computer equipment or programs is not easy and there is no one best way. However, there are a few basic steps that managers should follow for collecting and organizing information needed to make their decisions.

Step 1. Educate yourself regarding the potential uses of computers as management tools. Read about computers and talk with people who use computers in their work. To really learn how to become a consumer of computer technology, learn how to operate one. In this way you will learn computer language well enough to communicate and understand vendors and computer users, and become familiar with the available software. Set aside some time daily to work at a computer within your institution to familiarize yourself with this tool. Next, visit media centers that are already using computers as management tools. Find out how the system is being used, what functions it performs, and what strengths, weaknesses, and problems have been discovered as the system has been used. The experience of others can be most helpful—use it. Visit computer stores and corporate and educational computer system companies. Listen to what they have to offer and suggest. However, a word of caution is necessary. You should enter computer stores with some degree of skepticism. Some dealers will try to convince you that their systems will meet your needs even if they cannot. They may try to divert your attention by demonstrating features of their equipment that are not required. In such cases, leave and go somewhere else! Reputable computer salespeople will first determine your needs, demonstrate what they have to offer, and then discuss price, or, if their equipment does not meet stated needs, will tell you so. When you start looking at equipment, let the vendors know that you are gathering information; most will be happy to help. Reputable firms must stay current and be able to demonstrate state-of-the-art equipment and systems. They can also refer you to customers who have applications similar to what you are considering. Do not be afraid to show your ignorance; ask for demonstrations and explanations. If you do not understand something, keep asking questions until you do understand. Sit down and operate the equipment to familiarize yourself with it. Do not be embarrassed about making mistakes; becoming computer competent takes time and effort. Make the sales representative assume the role of teacher as you learn. After you feel somewhat knowledgeable about how computers operate, how other media managers are using them, and have a broad exposure to what is available, then you are ready to begin comparing features, quality, prices, reliability, adaptability, and servicing.

Step 2. Analyze your computer needs. Now that you have an idea of what computers can do and how they are being used in other media centers, develop a list of functions that you think computers can perform within your center. Be comprehensive. Involve staff members, for they may have good ideas; remember that they are the people who will use the system. A convenient form for analyzing computer needs is presented in figure 8.10, page 194. List each identified function in the first column. Answer the questions in columns A, B, and C with a *yes*, *no*, or *maybe* for each function listed. Leave columns D and E blank at this time.

Ask each department head within your media center who might use the computer to answer the same questions. You may also want to involve appropriate staff members in this analysis. Collate the results and save them for future reference. Before staff are asked to work through the computer function analysis, they should know as much about computers and computer applications as possible. This can be accomplished by bringing computer experts into staff work sessions. These people can provide basic information, answer questions, and discuss possible computer applications. If computers are understood, more effective contributions to the analysis will be forthcoming.

Step 3. Determine what computer services and expertise are available within your institution. Some institutions have a centralized computer service center with equipment and/or resource persons to assist departments in determining appropriate computer services. If this service is available, the job of gathering information and making a purchase decision will be much easier. These experts can guide a manager through the process of identifying needs and selecting an appropriate computer

Possible Functions (List all you can think of)	A Will save staff time	B Will improve accuracy	C Will provide faster response time to clients	D Cost	E Decision: Is this function worth the cost?
	yes-no-maybe	yes-no-maybe	yes-no-maybe	yes-no-maybe	yes-no-maybe
PERFORM CIRCULATION FUNCTIONS OF MEDIA MATERIALS:					
1. Provide database maintenance of collections					
2. Provide database maintenance of borrowers' accounts					
3. Provide interactive booking and reservation system					
4. Specify holiday and variable shipping times					
5. Provide collection and circulation procedures					
6. Generate reports					
7. Provide back up procedures					
PERFORM PRODUCTION LOGISTICAL SUPPORT:					
1. ETC.					

Figure 8.10. Computer function analysis.

system to fill those needs. However, do not let them determine the center's needs; that is your job. Final decisions must be made by the media center management. The job of the computer experts should be to help define center requirements and to find or develop the appropriate computer system to meet those needs. If your institution does not have the necessary computer expertise available, then the full responsibility for gathering information prior to making decisions is yours.

Step 4. Obtain informal computer system proposals. Using the list of functions developed in step 2, ask vendors or your institutional computer experts to develop a proposal for the center listing in detail what system modules are necessary, what each will do, and the software costs. Ask them to group the list of functions as needed, but try to identify the costs for each group. When working with vendors at this stage, emphasize that you are requesting an informal proposal with estimated costs and that they should not interpret this as a bid. Inform them that the information they supply will help you decide what computer functions you can afford. Two types of requests are commonly used when seeking proposals. The first is "Request for Information" (RFI). This request should include the preliminary specifications for the system, indicating to a dealer that the requester is not ready for a formal proposal or bid but is still seeking information. The dealer may submit a full proposal, but at least he or she knows the purpose and makes the choice. The second type is called a "Request for Proposal" (RFP). This request indicates to the dealers that the manager has completed the needs analysis and is ready for proposals preparatory to asking for bids. This request should include detailed specifications. The preparation of a full proposal may cost the dealer several thousand dollars depending upon the complexity of the computer management system required.

Step 5. Decide on the functions that the management system will serve to accomplish this, and review carefully the proposals obtained from the institutional computer service center or from vendors. Transfer costs from the proposals to the computer function analysis form (figure 8.10) developed in step 2 (column D). Add any new functions suggested in the proposals in order to have all the current data required to make thoughtful decisions regarding functions the center really needs and can afford. The manager and staff can now ask another question for each computer function listed: Are the benefits worth the cost (column E)? When making these decisions, weigh the time-saving benefits carefully. It is doubtful that most single applications will save large dollar amounts, but the cumulative effect of savings in all applications may be significant, especially when computed over a long period of time. Dollar savings should not be the major consideration, however. Employee time saved can be utilized to provide additional services, and the elimination of errors in customer services should also be considered. Another factor is staff morale: The addition of computers may make some jobs dull and repetitious but create more interesting challenges for others. Weigh all factors carefully before deciding.

Step 6. Once the functions have been decided upon, the system specifications can be developed and written. Two types of specifications should be prepared: (1) functional specifications, what the system will do; and (2) technical specifications, detailed information about the desired equipment. Writing functional and technical specifications for computer systems will be discussed later in this chapter.

Step 7. Obtain firm quotations for the computer management system. Send your specifications to as many reputable dealers as you can identify for quotations or bids. Answer inquiries but be careful to provide the same information to all dealers. If something has been overlooked in the initial specifications, all potential bidders must be notified. It may be wise to arrange your quote or bid request into logical functional alternatives (i.e., basic package and then Options A, B, etc.). That procedure may save repeating the bidding process if the bids or options surpass your available budget.

Step 8. Review the quotations and bids very carefully, study the functions listed by each bidder, and compare them with your specifications. In some cases the bidders may provide functions that exceed your specifications. Some institutions may not consider the additional functions, as only the low bid meeting the specifications will be accepted. Before bids are considered and purchase orders let, arrange to have the detailed specifications of each bidder reviewed by a computer specialist. Although some systems may meet the required functional specifications, they may not meet certain detail specifications that the specialist considers important. Make the final decision to purchase only after making certain that all specifications have been met.

Step 9. Check with other customers regarding the dealer's reputation. Are customers satisfied with the assistance and service provided? It does not make much sense to purchase a system from a firm with a poor reputation; one that may not be there to help when problems arise. This can be a problem if the media manager is required to accept the lowest bid. However, to circumvent that problem, write into the specifications that the dealer must (1) provide evidence of having been in business for a period of five years, (2) provide consulting services and maintenance for one year, and (3) be able to provide a list of five comparable installations the dealer has made within the past three years. Consult with those purchasers to determine the dependability of the dealer.

WRITING SPECIFICATIONS

As was emphasized earlier, it is important to transpose information about what the computer system is to do for a service program into a written document. This document is usually called a *specification*. As stated earlier, two types of specifications should be developed: functional and technical.

Functional Specifications

The functional specifications should be very precise and specify in detail what tasks the computer management system must perform when installed. For each function accepted as necessary from your list in figure 8.10, write a paragraph or more describing exactly what the function is to accomplish. The following is an example of a functional specification:

Function 1: Database Maintenance of Collections

Function Description: The database will include a minimum of 8,000 media instructional materials consisting of videotapes, CD-ROMs, computer software, videodiscs, sound-slide sets, sound filmstrips, audiotapes, and instructional kits. Titles of items in the collection will be referenced by one- to six-character title codes. Title data will include title name, producer, grade level, media type code, running time, release date, color or black and white, number of parts, number of copies that may circulate, number of copies withdrawn or damaged, and circulation restrictions. A short annotation describing the content of each title and all catalog card information will be included.

Function 2: Database Maintenance of Borrowers' Accounts

Function Description: Information on accounts stored in data files in the computer may be added, changed, or deleted with simple, menu-driven procedures. Borrowers' accounts may be referenced by a three-part account number, each part corresponding to the levels in a typical school-district hierarchy. Each part of the account number contains from one to four digits. The first part denotes where billing and other accounting information may be sent. The second part denotes a school or destination within the main account to which requested items are to be shipped (and billed if applicable). The third part denotes a borrower who requests items from the media library. Names, addresses, shipping and scheduling specifications, and a variety of special-processing indicators must be included in the account files.

Technical Specifications

Technical specifications are more difficult to write; they must be written by a person knowledgeable in the computer field. Most managers will need to have the technical specifications written by someone else. If the institution has a computer services department, this department should be able to provide such assistance. Reputable computer sales corporations are also willing to provide this service. However, they must be cautioned that their specifications should be broad enough for another manufacturer to bid if other systems exist that can meet your functional specifications. Some institutions may not require bidding, but obtaining high-quality equipment depends upon the vendor having to meet a set of clearly written, precise specifications.

SUGGESTED ACTIVITIES

1. For those who have limited experience with computers: Work through some introductory computer literacy programs.

2. Visit several media centers in educational or corporate institutions that use a computerized media management system. Learn from the media managers and observe what functions the computer systems perform. List the hardware and software used, advantages, disadvantages, problems encountered, and costs.

3. Write for information from companies that sell media management computer programs and study and compare the programs. Visit users of these programs if you can. Again identify the advantages, disadvantages, problems encountered, and costs.

4. Make arrangements to spend a week as a volunteer worker or intern in a media center that employs a media management system, to gain experience and "learn by doing," performing a wide range of functions on the computer.

5. Visit an instructional computer laboratory or center where computers are available to users. Determine the procedures used to select and circulate computer programs within the laboratory. Compare the procedures used with those used to circulate other media materials from a media center and list the similarities.

6. Design a form for booking computer software and equipment.

7. Discuss the advantages of adding an instructional computer service unit to a media center.

8. Complete the computer function analysis illustrated in figure 8.10 and discussed in step 2 of the section called "Getting the Facts."

REFERENCES

Business Publishers. 1996. "Should Instructional, Administrative Technology Be Integrated?" *Educational Technology News,* December 3, 245–46.

Finn, James. 1960. "Technology and the Instructional Process." *Audio-Visual Communication Review,* 8, no. 1: 5–26.

SELECTED BIBLIOGRAPHY

Albright, Michael J. "Computer Networking and College Media Centers." *College and University Media Review*, 1, no. 1 (1994): 7–24.

Barron, Ann E., and Gary W. Orwig. *New Technologies for Education: A Beginner's Guide.* Englewood, Colo.: Libraries Unlimited, 1992.

Berge, Zane L., and Mauri P. Collins. *Wired Together: The Online Classroom in K-12.* Cresskill, N.J.: Hampton Press, 1998.

Caffarella, Edward P. "Planning for the Automation of School Library Media Centers." *TechTrends*, 41, no. 5 (1996): 33–37.

Dewey, Patrick R. *303 CD-ROMs to Use in Your Library: Descriptions, Evaluations, and Practical Advice*. Chicago: American Library Association, 1996.

Fischer, Charles, David C. Dwyer, and Keith Yocam, eds. *Education and Technology: Reflections on Computing in Classrooms*. San Francisco: Jossey-Bass Publishers, 1996.

Forcier, Richard C. *The Computer as an Educational Tool: Productivity and Problem Solving*. Columbus, Ohio: Merrill, 1999.

Jamsa, Kris. *Welcome to . . . Personal Computers*. 3d ed. New York: MIS Press, 1995.

Khan, Badrul H., ed. *Web-Based Instruction*. Englewood Cliffs, N.J.: Educational Technology Publications, 1997.

Levine, John R., Carol Baroudi, and Margy L. Young. *The Internet for Dummies*. 3d ed. Foster City, Calif.: IDG Books Worldwide, 1995.

Lockard, James, Peter D. Abrams, and Wesley A. Many. *Microcomputers for Twenty-first Century Educators*. 4th ed. New York: Longman, 1997.

Maurer, Matthew M., and George S. Davidson. *Leadership in Instructional Technology*. Columbus, Ohio: Merrill, 1998.

Merrill, Paul F., et. al. *Computers in Education*. Boston: Allyn & Bacon, 1996.

Molvar, Andrew R. "Computers in Education: A Brief History." *T.H.E. Journal*, 24, no. 6 (1997): 6–68.

Provenzo, Eugene F. *The Educators Brief Guide to Computers in the Schools*. Princeton, N.J.: Eye on Education, 1996.

Rieber, Lloyd P. *Computer, Graphics, and Learning*. Dubuque, Iowa: Brown & Benchmark, 1994.

Snyder, Ilana. *Page to Screen: Taking Literacy into the Electronic Era*. New York: Routledge, 1998.

MANAGING TECHNOLOGICAL CHANGE

Dr. Arthur Adams, president of the American Council on Education, once said, "To report on the use of television in teaching is like trying to catch a galloping horse." If this statement is true for educational television, think how much more true it is for general technology.

James S. Kinder, *Using Audio-Visual Materials in Education*, 1965

OBJECTIVES

At the conclusion of this chapter you should be able to

1. Describe the difference between making purchase decisions for experimentation and for adoption.

2. Describe some ways institutions are dealing with high costs of rapid technological changes in education.

3. Identify and list difficult technological change decisions that media managers face.

4. Describe and discuss a model that may help a manager in making difficult technological change decisions.

5. Define the role of a change agent.

Given the broad range of ever-changing media materials and equipment now available—videocassettes, videodiscs, computers, CD-ROMs, interactive video devices, recordable discs, talking computers, interfaces, and more yet to be invented—how does a media manager know when to change a format or adopt a new innovation? Changing formats or instructional tools may render a considerable inventory obsolete, which can be costly. Decisions to change should not be made without considerable study to determine time, efficiency, and financial trade-offs. Obviously, change should not be made for change's sake. It should be made to provide a purposeful and needed gain. Gains can be in the form of increased communications, or increased learning in less time, or the accomplishment of the same tasks faster or at less cost, or providing a higher level of patron service at equal or less cost. The bottom line is that a problem must exist that a new technology might solve *before* change is indicated.

That is not to say that the media manager should never purchase a newly invented or adapted item of equipment; that would stifle practical action and field research. If the heavy so-called portable videotape recorders had not been purchased by institutions for experimental applications in the 1960s, we probably would not have lightweight videocassette camcorders in use throughout the United States. If institutions had not purchased and experimented with early computer systems in the 1970s, we probably would not have such fine microcomputers in most schools today. This does not mean that media managers should purchase every new invention that becomes available. Before purchasing an item for experimentation, the manager should have a potential use for it. The equipment or system is then tried and, if it is effective, it can be considered for adoption.

The manager need not rely strictly upon his or her own experimentation. As others experiment, the manager can also draw upon their experience. Managers stay current and knowledgeable regarding new technologies by sharing with others, reading, and examining equipment and applications at conferences, exhibitions, by Internet searches, and by enrolling in listservs. Media managers cannot expect to have budgets that allow them to experiment with each new item as it is placed on the market, but they should allocate some funds for experimentation and exploration of emerging technologies. In this era of rapid technological change, media center managers may not be able to provide the latest model or version of each technology. It has been suggested that we may have to bypass some generations of some technologies in order to contain costs and operate within current budgets. This concept is similar to that of *not* buying a new car every year but only every third or fourth year.

There are two possible purposes for making media equipment purchase decisions. One is for research and experimentation and the other for adoption. We have already discussed the need to purchase for research and experimentation. The balance of this chapter will explore the issue of purchasing new technologies for adoption.

RAPID TECHNOLOGICAL CHANGE

Technological change used to evolve over decades or years; now it evolves in months or even weeks. In the face of such rapid technological change, media managers need new strategies to contend with the enormous costs of replacement of technologies. Institutions at the higher education level are dealing with this change in various ways by: (1) charging students a technology fee, (2) renting or leasing equipment to students with return privileges or credit for an option-to-buy, (3) requiring students to purchase some technologies, e.g., computers, and (4) requiring students to have e-mail and Internet access.

These trends may mean that we need to move from a position of being hardware suppliers to that of establishing connectivity and developing information centers. In these centers, students can expect to use their own equipment to connect to networks rich with resources and use abundant and readily available center resources (MacKnight 1995).

MAKING CHANGE DECISIONS

Deciding what new technologies to adopt, and what older technologies to downplay or abandon, is difficult. Before intelligent decisions can be made, information related to recognized problems must be systematically collected. The media manager who makes decisions with limited or poor information cannot expect to arrive at consistently sound decisions. Therefore, managers must develop and use a systematic strategy to collect and analyze information prior to making any decisions. An effective strategy is summarized in figure 9.1. If followed, the steps that should be completed before replacing one set of materials, equipment, or technologies with another should help one to make better decisions. Basically, the process starts with an expressed problem, then proceeds to identifying the problem, finding the solution, implementing the solution, and evaluating the results.

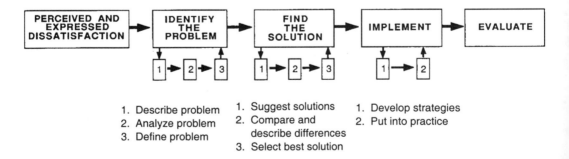

Figure 9.1. Managing technological change.

Perceived and Expressed Dissatisfaction

There is no need to make changes unless problems exist, and those problems must be more than just perceived. Instructors or trainers may express dissatisfaction with a training program, or management may state its displeasure with the cost of training, or learning results may not meet the institution's standards, or users of sales packages may state that materials are ineffective. Regardless of the reasons, a problem must be identified and defined before a solution can be found. The larger the client group(s) that perceive a problem, the better the chance that a change will be implemented. After dissatisfaction has been expressed, the process of problem identification can be undertaken.

Identify the Problem

Sometimes it is difficult to pinpoint problems after they have been expressed. While instructors may express dissatisfaction with a training program because they perceive it to be ineffective, one must determine what, specifically, the problem is. Are objectives not clear? Are materials used in the program inappropriate? Does the fault lie in the productions that have been created? Are the prerequisites for entry inadequate? Does the fault lie in the evaluation materials? Were inappropriate display or delivery devices used? Did the message reach the wrong audience? Clearly, a problem that may have seemed simple on the surface is not, and identifying more precisely the probable causes may be difficult.

At this point, three steps may help one to identify the problem: (1) describe the problem, (2) analyze the problem, and (3) define the problem. To describe the problem, each of the symptoms and possible causes should be identified and described. Information must be obtained pertaining to each possible cause. The information is then analyzed and possible causes not supported by the research are discarded. Through this process the probable cause(s) is identified and can now be precisely defined.

Find the Solution

The media manager may also find three steps helpful in determining the best solution to a defined problem: (1) identify possible solutions, (2) compare and describe their differences, and (3) select the best solution. All possible solutions should be considered, regardless of how simple or complex they may appear. They may include revision of objectives, materials and equipment used; redesign of productions; adding prerequisite training; modifying evaluation instruments, activities, and delivery vehicles; or making changes in the combinations of the technologies employed. In keeping with our participative management philosophy, all individuals and groups concerned with the problem should be involved in the search for solutions. Each possible solution must be defined, analyzed, gains identified, and costs estimated.

The next logical step is to compare the costs/benefits between the possible solutions in terms of gains and limitations. Such factors must be examined, as it would not make sense to select a solution that is too costly for the organization or require facilities or services that cannot be made available. The best solution should be selected according to its potential to solve the problem at the lowest affordable cost.

Implement

The next step in the model is to implement the best affordable solution. A plan or strategy will have to be developed to ensure that necessary details are identified and completed prior to implementation. A case may have to be developed to sell the change to the administration, instructor/trainers, or staff. Staff training may have to be developed and completed prior to implementing the change. Facilities may have to be remodeled or constructed. Equipment and/or materials may have to be selected and purchased. Productions may have to be designed and produced, evaluation tools changed or designed, and delivery vehicles selected. All these tasks must be completed before putting a change into operation.

Evaluate

As in all projects, evaluation is the final step. Without evaluation, one will not know if the change has had any negative or positive effect. If the previous steps in the model have been followed and the appropriate solution implemented, the results should be better products, increased sales, increased learning, more efficiency, increased speed, or less cost. If the results do not meet expected objectives, then a problem still exists and the manager must once again begin the search for a solution.

CHANGE AGENTS

Chapter 1 briefly retraced the history of media technology. The media field is not static—it is a continuously changing field and changes are thrust before us at an ever-increasing rate. Media managers are faced with deciding when, where, how, and if they should use these new potential tools. In this role, the media manager serves as a change agent who must design, oversee, and direct change within his or her organization and in programs provided by the media center.

The media manager serves as a catalyst in getting others to notice when a change may be necessary, as a solution searcher, and as a problem solver. The manager is a process assistant who guides others through the process of change and is a resource linker who brings together the people necessary to solve problems. The manager involves people from within the media center and external users to assist in the process before making decisions to delete, alter, or change media technologies. Through this process, media managers should be able to avoid making decisions that do not result in positive gains.

A final word of caution. Look for solutions to problems, but *do not be a solution salesperson.* In other words, avoid the trap of confronting a problem with an immediate technological solution without thoroughly analyzing the problem and looking at alternative solutions. If you become known as a solution salesperson, your credibility will become undermined.

As the availability of new materials, equipment, and interfaces between media devices increases, the media manager is faced with major decisions. For example: Should I discard the old for the new? When? How could we use this new device? How long will this new format be available? Managers should resist the temptation to change just because something is new! Decisions to change must be made only when change offers a good solution to a defined problem. There are five basic steps to follow before making a change decision.

1. A problem should exist and be expressed as a problem.

2. The problem must be defined.

3. Solutions should be identified and the best affordable solution selected.

4. The solution should be implemented after careful planning.

5. The results should be evaluated.

Media managers serve as change agents. In this role they serve as a catalyst for change, problem solver, process helper, and resource linker to bring people together to solve problems. By following the five steps for decision making, the media manager should make decisions that result in more effective use of media technologies.

SUGGESTED ACTIVITIES

1. Given complaints by media center patrons regarding their perception that the use of LCD projectors in classrooms is difficult, describe the steps you would follow to make a decision regarding a solution to the problem.

2. Describe the role of a media manager as a change agent.

REFERENCES

Kinder, James S. 1965. *Using Audio-Visual Materials in Education*. New York: American Book Company.

MacKnight, Carol B. 1995. "Managing Technological Change in Academe." *Cause/Effect Magazine*, 18, no. 1: 29–35.

MEDIA RESOURCES

David Thornburg on Managing Change with New Technologies. Technology in Today's Classroom Series. KOCE-TV (PBS Affiliate), 80 minutes. Santa Monica, Calif.: Canter and Associates, 1997. Videocassette.

The Dynamics of Change. John Linton and Blanch Linton, producers, 30 minutes. Sandy, Utah: Linton Professional Development Corporation, 1992. Videocassette.

Organization and Management for Technology Use. Seattle Public Schools Instructional Broadcast Center, 28 minutes. Santa Monica, Calif.: Pyramid Media, 1996. Videocassette.

Planning for Change. John Linton and Blanch Linton, producers, 30 minutes. Sandy, Utah: Linton Professional Development Corporation, 1992. Videocassette.

SELECTED BIBLIOGRAPHY

Anandam, Kamala, ed. *Integrating Technology on Campus*. San Francisco: Jossey-Bass, 1998.

Bowen, David. *Multimedia Now and Down the Line*. London: Bowerdean Publishing, 1994.

Havelock, Ronald G., with Steve Zlotow. *The Change Agents Guide*. 2d ed. Englewood Cliffs, N.J.: Educational Technology Publications, 1995.

Jenlink, Patrick M., Charles M. Reigeluth, and Alison A. Carr. "An Expedition for Change: Facilitating the Systemic Change Process in School Districts." *TechTrends*, 41, no. 1 (1996): 21–30.

Kemp, Jerrold E. *A School Changes*. Washington, D.C.: Association for Educational Communications and Technology, 1995.

Leggett, Wesley P., and Kay A. Persichitte. "Blood, Sweat, and TEARS: 50 Years of Technology Implementation Obstacles." *TechTrends* 43, no. 3 (1998): 33–36.

Means, Barbara, John Blando, Theresa Middleton, Catherine Coff Morrocco, Arlene R. Remz, and Judith Zorfass. *Using Technology to Support Education Reform*. Washington, D.C.: Association for Educational Communications and Technology, 1993.

Salisbury, David F. *Five Technologies for Educational Change: Systems Thinking, Systems Design, Quality Science, Change Management, Instructional Technology*. Englewood Cliffs, N.J.: Educational Technology Publications, 1996.

Scrogan, Len. *Tools for Change: Restructuring Technology in Our Schools*. Washington, D.C.: Association for Educational Communications and Technology, 1993.

Walker, Julie. "Managing Change in the School Library—Paddling Through White Water." *Multimedia Schools*, 3, no. 2 (1996): 6–7.

10

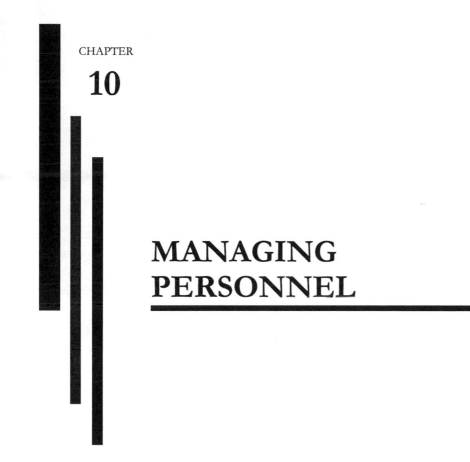

MANAGING PERSONNEL

This sense of visionary acceptance of change and permissiveness to try new approaches must be established by the director of the center and must pervade the entire staff.

Margaret E. Chisholm and Donald P. Ely,
Media Personnel in Education: A Competency Approach, 1976

OBJECTIVES

At the conclusion of this chapter you should be able to

1. Develop a series of statements outlining your personal philosophy regarding personnel management.

2. Develop and write good job specifications and explain why they are important.

3. Describe the importance of providing for staff development and list and explain the three areas of staff development that should be provided.

4. Identify and explain the function of each stage of a Personalized Employee Performance System of Evaluation (PEPSE).

5. Explain the value of delegating and list nine major tenets of successful delegating.

6. List seven points that a media manager should find helpful in maintaining a healthy problem-solving climate that will help control interpersonal conflicts.

7. Illustrate and explain a simple model that demonstrates the importance of helping employees balance the three major factors of their lives to enable them to achieve their maximum human potential.

8. List eleven factors that make the work life of employees more satisfying.

From their study of the ten best-run companies in the United States, Peters and Waterman found there was not a more pervasive theme than that of "respect for the individual" (1982, 238). They amplified the point by saying, "We are talking about tough-minded respect for the individual and the willingness to train him, to set reasonable and clear expectations for him, and to grant him practical autonomy to step out and contribute directly to his job" (239).

This could not be stated more clearly. The best media facilities in the world would be of limited value without a staff of well-trained individuals committed to what they do. Each individual is important, with each performing a series of tasks that he or she knows best and that add collectively to the mission of the media service center. Each individual must have a feeling of ownership in the program and share in the rewards and failures of endeavors. How can a manager handle personnel in such a way as to instill a feeling of pride in his or her employees and treat each as an important individual? This chapter discusses some concepts that will be useful in personnel management. The application and adaptation of these philosophical statements, suggestions, models, and techniques may produce better manager/employee relationships and employee appraisal/evaluation systems.

DEVELOPING A PHILOSOPHICAL BASE FOR MANAGING PERSONNEL

As discussed in chapter 2, one's philosophy is important. The development of a philosophy for managing personnel is no exception. Though job positions and classifications change as the media center's mission and work environments change, the manager's philosophical base must remain stable. That base may be modified by experience, but basically it will remain relatively stable.

Following is a list of statements that can form the base of a philosophy for managing personnel. The statements will not be applicable in an authoritarian management environment, but from our experience and recent research we believe that the concepts presented are important in today's more open working environments. Times have changed. "Like it or lump it" management is a style of the past. Employees today are more educated and sophisticated, and the nature of the media work environment is "people centered." Very few tasks within a media center do not require employees to interact with patrons. If employees are expected to treat patrons in a friendly and helpful manner, they will expect to be treated the same. Because every manager is an individual and all work environments are different, all of the statements may not work for all readers. However, they should provide thought-provoking help in the development of a personal philosophical base for managing personnel.

- Managers do not manage people, they manage the efforts of people. In this day and age of litigation an employee's race, dress, religion, and idiosyncrasies cannot be considered. The only important consideration for evaluation is job or task performance based upon carefully defined criteria.

- Each employee is an individual with special abilities, needs, and feelings. A good manager will continuously endeavor to match an individual's abilities to specific positions. The manager will recognize that if the individual employee's needs and feelings are not considered and met, the employee will not be able to function to full potential. In the book *First Things First*, the authors recognize the value of fully developing individuals:

> "Accomplishing tasks through people" is a different paradigm than "building people through the accomplishment of tasks." With one, you get things done. With the other, you get them done with far greater creativity, synergy, and effectiveness . . . and in the process, you build the capacity to do more in the future as well (Covey, Merrill, and Merrill 1994, 256).

- Each job is different. Within the same job classification, differences may be slight, but differences will exist. These differences need to be considered in employee appraisal and evaluation.

- Two-way communication is essential in personnel management. Employee input is important; the expert in any particular job is often the individual performing the tasks. Employees want to know what is happening and want to be involved.

- Personnel management must include a fair employee appraisal and evaluation system based upon mutually agreed upon and clearly defined job performance expectations. An employee cannot be held accountable for his or her performance unless the employee knows what is expected.

- Staff development opportunities must be available to employees which are dynamic enough to provide for the development and maintenance of day-to-day job skills as well as for opportunities for exploration, growth, and promotion. Staff development should be based upon needs that are both presently relevant and futuristically oriented.

- Employees who enjoy their work and work environment produce the best results. Employees who dislike their jobs and "hate" reporting to work are often counterproductive. The work environment should be made as pleasant as possible and the work tasks challenging to each employee.

- Employees must be given praise when praise is due. Everyone likes to know how they are doing and if what they are doing is right. Blanchard and Johnson in *The One Minute Manager* emphasize the value of giving praise to reward positive behavior and reprimands for reshaping negative behavior (1984).

- Effective managers manage by walking around and listening a lot. Managers who walk around the work environment demonstrate their interest in employees, become more informed about work tasks, and can gain much information by encouraging conversation and listening to employees.

- Effective managers follow the Golden Rule of personnel management: Treat employees the way you want to be treated. All of the preceding statements could be summarized in that one rule.

The media manager who employs these concepts as his or her base for managing personnel should be rewarded with a dedicated and faithful staff who will give their best effort to their work assignments. Employees should contribute ideas for task improvements, work well with patrons, work as if they shared ownership within the program, and become a close, cohesive unit. Ponder these statements, modify them, and add to them, but develop your own personalized philosophical base for managing personnel.

MAJOR TASKS OF PERSONNEL MANAGEMENT

After a philosophical base for managing personnel has been developed, the tasks involved in effective management of personnel can be presented and examined. For discussion purposes these tasks are separated into the following major headings:

Develop job specifications.

Select good employees.

Provide for staff development.

Evaluate employees.

Delegate responsibility.

Solve interpersonal conflicts.

Assist each employee to achieve maximum human potential.

Motivate employees.

While each item will be discussed separately, managing personnel involves all of the tasks being performed in concert. It is a continuous and ongoing activity, with many elements interacting simultaneously.

Develop Job Specifications

The first step is to prepare job specifications for each different position within the organization. This does not mean that if there are twenty-two employees within an organization there will be twenty-two separate job descriptions. There should be a job description for each specific type or class of position—secretary, receptionist, clerk, electronic technician, photographer, and so forth. Within these classifications, different levels may exist, such as Secretary I, II, III or Photographer I, II, and so on; in these cases the job specifications should delineate the differences. Salary scales must also reflect the differences in expected levels of performance.

How can job descriptions be developed? Many methods are used. One, which is not recommended, involves the manager who simply writes a specification based upon his or her perception of each position. The problem is obvious: The specification reflects only one person's view of a position. A second method requires that all employees who perform the same or similar tasks and the manager each write a job specification and then pool their efforts to develop the job specification. The second method is obviously more valid because all concerned have been involved. Finally, a third method is to perform a job and task activity analysis by observing employees performing their tasks over a period of time. All tasks are observed, recorded, collated, and summarized into a job specification.

While commonalties exist within job classifications, each position is unique. Job tasks within a classification are divided among employees simply to get the tasks completed. Each employee brings special and individual talents to a position, and the smart manager takes advantage of these individual differences. Job descriptions and specifications should be broad enough to allow a manager to take advantage of those unique talents. The job description system must allow the manager and the employee to understand both the attributes of the job and the employee in a holistic way.

Job specifications need to include many attributes of a position. Three major attributes usually exist in most positions: critical attributes, variable attributes, and indefinable attributes.

Critical attributes are the routine tasks performed daily, weekly, or monthly that are common to all employees within a classification. Examples include answering the telephone, doing word processing on a computer, and completing monthly reports.

Variable attributes are tasks that vary from position to position within the classification. Two accountants may be expected to complete two reports using the same data but with a different focus. One photographer may be assigned outside photographic tasks while another may be assigned copy work and large-format camera work. While each of the employees in these examples is classified as an accountant or photographer, the assignments are quite different and allowed within a job specification because they are considered as variable attributes.

Finally, *indefinable attributes* are those that cannot be defined as they are too numerous and different. In many job specifications these are covered by a simple statement, "perform other tasks as required."

After the first two categories have been specified for each position, then add the final inclusive statement and the job specification is complete. It should be as specific as possible. When very limited differences appear on the job specification for several positions, the positions should be combined into a single specification and the limited differences added as variable attributes. This procedure simplifies the personnel classification process and results in valid job specifications.

One consideration to include in the job specification is that of minimum qualifications necessary for personnel to perform the tasks listed. The qualifications may be limited to months or years of experience, attendance in technical schools, or even the requirement of a degree. A word of caution is offered here. Managers are tempted to specify higher qualifications than necessary in an attempt to obtain high-quality personnel. That is a noble practice; however, in most institutions the minimum qualifications must be defensible to the administration or unions. Remember, higher qualifications generally translate to higher salaries.

The last task left in preparing a job specification is to give the position a title and brief description. The title should be short and the position description should be limited to two or three sentences that list and describe the major performance tasks required.

Other headings sometimes found in job specifications include definition, typical work, and distinguishing characteristics. There may be others, but the job specification elements presented here will enable the manager to write precise, clear, descriptive, and defensible specifications. See figure 10.1 for an example of a job description.

Specification for Class

MEDIA SERVICES DISPATCHER

Definition: Direct the operation of a media services distribution center dispatching equipment and/or operators and materials.

Distinguishing Characteristics: Positions in this class are responsible for the operation of all activities for a small unit, or one or more specific activities of a larger unit. May direct the work of other media operators (full-time and/or part-time).

Typical Work:
A. Critical Attributes

Serve as dispatcher; confer with users; ascertain individual and/or program requirements, translate requests into instructions and assignments, and assure that these requirements are met;

Order supplies incidental to operator duties;

Operate public address systems in pavilions and stadiums as required;

Direct media operators in the setup and operation of film and slide projectors, record players, tape recorders, videotape playbacks, public address systems, and other media equipment;

Train others in the performance of simple maintenance to assigned equipment;

Provide initial training and supplementary refresher instructions to students, staff, and faculty; perform backup to maintenance for media maintenance technicians; review and evaluate performance of operators.

B. Variable Attributes

May maintain unit or department records, security, and inventory control of media equipment or circulation and pools;

May be responsible for the implementation and operation of a transportation service which includes pickup and delivery of film and equipment on and off campus;

May be expected to examine new audiovisual equipment to evaluate their technical specifications; prepare materials for circulation;

Perform related duties as required.

Minimum Qualifications: High school graduate or equivalent and three years full-time experience as a Media Services Operator or equivalent, OR two years of college coursework in education, radio, TV, or related field; and one year of full-time related work experience; OR three years related work experience and training.

Figure 10.1. Example of a job specification.

Select Good Employees

One of the most important tasks that a media manager performs is to hire good employees. Employees provide the backbone of a media service program; without them, a program is doomed to failure. In most corporate or educational institutions, hiring procedures are very precise and the manager must follow the prescribed procedures. However, this does not preclude employing excellent people. There are usually at least four steps in the hiring procedure where the manager has input and is given data to help select a potentially good employee: (1) the job specification, (2) job application and test if it is required, (3) interview, and (4) references.

A well-stated job description increases the probability of attracting applicants who may be genuinely interested in the position, while a very loose specification may invite a large number of applicants who do not really understand the functions of the position. The job position title, description, and part or all of the specification should be included in advertisements for the position. Do not underestimate the value of precise job specifications. Insist that the position be advertised adequately. Many institution personnel or human resources offices post positions only on internal institution bulletin boards. That practice is not adequate to attract a large number of applicants. Mail the job posting to fellow media managers and see that the posting is given wide distribution and advertised in the newspapers.

A job application form is the major source of information about candidates. Insist that the application form request from applicants information about previous and related experience, training, education, and job and character references. In some institutions some type of test is given to applicants, such as general objective, take home, subjective essay, and/or practical. If any of these are used in your institution, review the tests and match against the position classifications. Attempt to make appropriate changes if the tests are simplistic or unrelated. From the application data and test information, usually three to five candidates are selected for interview by the personnel office or by the media manager. To select the candidates for interview, it is helpful to establish and apply a point system when analyzing the data in relation to the job description. For each factor listed in the job description, points on a scale ranging from one to ten are awarded based upon the information from the job application and tests.

The next step is the interview. It is a good practice (and a requirement in some institutions) to write the interview questions so that the same questions are asked of all candidates. If the applicant is to be supervised by another person, that supervisor should also have an opportunity to interview. Notes are then shared and all who interview are involved in the selection decision.

Interviewing is serious business and the manager should prepare for it carefully. Interview questions should probe for skills that will be used on the job, clarify previous related experience, and expose character and reliability. Open-ended questions should be employed to force the candidate to respond in detail. Interviewing techniques are a subject of many books and media productions, and the interviewers are encouraged to read and view materials on this subject. Be especially careful to not ask questions that may be viewed as discriminatory, such as questions related to age, race, marital status, and other topics.

The final source of information about candidates should come from their references. *Follow up on references.* One author recalls an experience when a call to the writer of a job reference prevented a potentially disastrous hiring. An applicant appeared to be an excellent candidate until a person listed as a reference asked, "Have you met the candidate?" He would not elaborate on his comment. The candidate lived a considerable distance away, so based upon the data on the application form and take-home test results, the candidate was going to be interviewed by telephone. It was decided to invite the candidate for a face-to-face interview which proved to be a wise decision. The candidate was not hired.

With the information gathered from the application form, tests, interview, and references, the best (it is hoped, excellent) employees can be selected.

Provide for Staff Development

An integral function of personnel management is the development and implementation of a broad and continuous staff development program. Staff development should not be limited to specific job-related activities; professional growth and personal growth should be included as well (see figure 10.2).

Job-related staff development activities are specific to employee job tasks. These activities are targeted to improve job skills. New employees must be trained when they arrive on the job by fellow employees and by the supervisor. As new procedures, materials, tools, and equipment are employed, new job-related staff development activities should be scheduled.

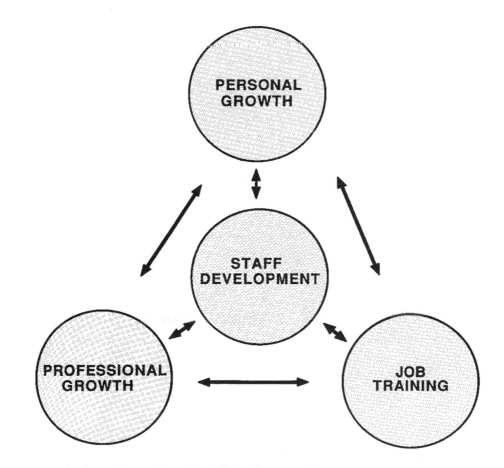

Figure 10.2. A balanced staff development model.

Also to be scheduled periodically are professional growth activities that provide the employee an opportunity to acquire information needed for advancement within the organization. The topics covered should include skills and knowledges required in a higher job classification, and the activities should be relevant for both the present and the future.

A third area of staff development activity is personal growth. These activities should benefit the employee intellectually, socially, and personally. They need not—and generally will not—be job related. They could include workshops on such subjects as family relationships, budgeting, investing, and communicating. These workshops may help the employee to have a more wholesome and happy life. The benefits should be obvious to the institution: Happy and content employees are productive. Personal growth activities are usually made available to the entire workforce of an institution and are not mandatory. Employees can pick and choose among offerings or not attend any. This contrasts with many job-related or professional growth activities that are usually planned and conducted within a department. There attendance may be required as a part of the job.

A staff development program should be based upon several principles:

The program should be founded upon current and future needs.

The program should be planned by the staff—not imposed upon employees by outsiders.

The program should be designed for all segments of the institution's staff.

The program should be comprehensive and continuous.

A comprehensive staff development program should not be limited to on-site workshops and conferences. Professional and technical associations and agencies offer many workshops and conferences. Employees should be given the opportunity to participate in such workshops and conferences when the activities are relevant.

Evaluate Employees

A rather difficult element of managing personnel is evaluating employee performance. While most employees generally know how they are performing, without a formal evaluation system, they may not know how their supervisor perceives their performance. Job performance evaluation should be considered by both management and the individual employee as a process or vehicle for improving performance and not for disciplinary purposes. It should be a process in which both the supervisor and employee discuss performance expectations so there are no surprises. Most employees will perform well if they know what is expected from them; that is the purpose of employee performance evaluation.

If an evaluation program is to accomplish that purpose, it cannot be completed by putting a few check marks on a simple form. It must be a process that is completed over a period of time and one that involves discussion between the individual employee and his or her supervisor. An effective Personalized Employee Performance System of Evaluation model, or PEPSE, is summarized in figure 10.3.

PEPSE helps supervisors and employees communicate about goals, objectives, and performance expectations. In the process, if properly handled, it helps to break down communication barriers. PEPSE provides a means for translating institutional goals and priorities into specific performance activities. It is a simple and

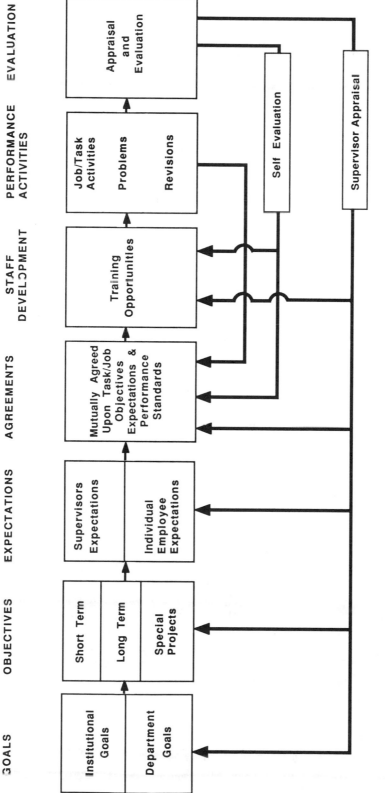

Figure 10.3. Personalized Employee Performance System of Evaluation model (PEPSE).

action-oriented method of attaining institutional goals and of getting individual employees and supervisors to mutually agree upon job and task performance expectations and then evaluate the outcomes based upon those agreements. PEPSE is divided into seven stages: (1) examination of goals, (2) development of objectives, (3) identification of job expectations, (4) job expectation agreements, (5) staff development, (6) performance, and (7) evaluation.

Examine Institutional Goals

At the base of PEPSE, institutional and media center goals must be made explicitly clear to all employees. All activities and outputs of an organization must relate to those goals. Managers and supervisors cannot establish and structure their efforts unless they know the goals of the institution and of the unit. This gives direction and purpose to their areas of responsibility.

Develop Task Objectives

Using as a basis the institutional goals and the goals of the individual employee's department, one can develop short- and long-term task objectives for each employee. Short-term objectives are the completion of routine tasks that the employee is expected to accomplish quite routinely within a relatively short period of time—hourly, daily, or weekly. Long-term objectives may be a combination of short-term tasks in a larger project that may require several weeks or months to complete. Both types of task objectives should be included in an individual employee job classification.

Occasionally, special projects may be required to meet an institutional goal, and tasks to complete the project may fall outside an individual's job classification. The tasks to complete the project may be experimental or new to the employee and department and may require a large amount of time on a one-time basis. In these cases, a supervisor may negotiate with the employee to work on the project which is outside of his or her normal job classification but is important to the institution.

Identify Employee and Supervisor Expectations

Both employers and employees have certain job expectations. The employer's representative (the employee's supervisor) will expect that tasks be completed meeting quality standards within resource and time allocations. Each individual employee brings to the job not only job expectations but promotional aspirations and a desire to enjoy family and social activities. Because employees who have family or social problems will not be as effective or helpful as those who are content, outside work environment factors should also be a concern to employers.

Employees also need to understand the role of the supervisor. What is the job description of the supervisor? What can the employee reasonably expect from the supervisor to make his or her job easier?

Develop Performance Agreements

In the PEPSE model, this agreement stage is central and crucial to the entire process. It is the stage at which the supervisor and the employee meet to discuss the organization's ends, the individual's needs, the tasks to be completed, and the criteria for measuring satisfactory job performance. Both the employee and supervisor should leave this meeting with a clear understanding of what needs to be done and how the tasks are to be accomplished and measured. Short- and long-term objectives and special projects should be delineated. This stage can be informal, but it should culminate with a written agreement of tasks to be performed by the employee and how they are to be measured. The agreement may be written on a standardized form, a standardized form with modifications, or in a formal contract. Examples of an employee performance evaluation form and the evaluation criteria are included in figure 10.4, pages 222–23 and figure 10.5, pages 224–25.

An agreement conference is not limited to a discussion of job and task activities. Other activities related to the individual employee's promotional and professional growth activities should also be explored. The employee should be encouraged to attend workshops or conferences which may not only improve his or her present job performance skills but expand individual horizons and skills for upward movement to other positions and for personal development. It may take several meetings to fully discuss and arrive at mutual agreements.

Identify Staff Development Needs

If employees are to be evaluated according to mutually agreed-upon task/job objectives with performance criteria, the employer is obligated to provide staff training for employees. Employees cannot be expected to meet performance criteria if they are not trained adequately. A staff development program aimed at improving employee craftsmanship performance and providing ways to expand the expertise and interest of employees will require significant effort by both the administration and staff. Staff development activities may include on-the-job training, workshops, conferences, and even advanced training in other facilities.

Performance of Job Tasks

Each employee must perform the agreed-upon job tasks as identified in their job specification. This is where the employee will spend 99 percent of his or her time. If unforeseen problems occur while the employee is performing the job tasks, solutions must be found and revisions made to the agreements. New agreements should not be difficult to reach in an open atmosphere.

Evaluate Employee Performance

All the previous parts of the PEPSE model culminate in this stage—a fair appraisal and evaluation of the individual employee's job performance. The formal evaluation can take place at the logical end of a project or be scheduled on a quarterly, semiannual, or annual basis. New employees are usually evaluated monthly or quarterly during the first year. Appraisal methods should be as comprehensive as possible and should include a review and evaluation of long- and short-term institutional and individual employee objectives, as well as the individual's growth activities. The appraisals need not be limited to the individual's supervisor; they may include others. The purpose of the evaluation process should be constructive and used to emphasize employee strengths as well as areas where improvements can be

(Text continues on page 226.)

EMPLOYEE PERFORMANCE EVALUATION

EMPLOYEE'S NAME	CLASSIFICATION TITLE	EVALUATION PERIOD	EVALUATION DATE
		FROM TO	

PERFORMANCE FACTORS	PERFORMANCE EXPECTATIONS: COMMENTS AND / OR EXAMPLES (ATTACH EXTRA SHEETS IF NEEDED)	RATING
1. QUALITY OF WORK COMPETENCE, ACCURACY, NEATNESS, THOROUGHNESS.		OUTSTANDING * EXCEEDS EXPECTATIONS MEETS EXPECTATIONS NEEDS IMPROVEMENT UNSATISFACTORY *
2. QUANTITY OF WORK USE OF TIME, VOLUME OF WORK ACCOMPLISHED, ABILITY TO MEET SCHEDULES, PRODUCTIVITY LEVELS.		OUTSTANDING * EXCEEDS EXPECTATIONS MEETS EXPECTATIONS NEEDS IMPROVEMENT UNSATISFACTORY *
3. JOB KNOWLEDGE DEGREE OF TECHNICAL KNOWLEDGE, UNDERSTANDING OF JOB PROCEDURES AND METHODS.		OUTSTANDING * EXCEEDS EXPECTATIONS MEETS EXPECTATIONS NEEDS IMPROVEMENT UNSATISFACTORY *
4. WORKING RELATIONSHIPS COOPERATION AND ABILITY TO WORK WITH SUPERVISOR, CO-WORKERS, STUDENTS, AND CLIENTS SERVED.		OUTSTANDING * EXCEEDS EXPECTATIONS MEETS EXPECTATIONS NEEDS IMPROVEMENT UNSATISFACTORY *
5. SUPERVISORY SKILLS TRAINING AND DIRECTING SUBORDINATES, DELEGATION, EVALUATING SUBORDINATES, PLANNING AND ORGANIZING WORK, PROBLEM SOLVING, DECISION MAKING ABILITY, ABILITY TO COMMUNICATE.		OUTSTANDING * EXCEEDS EXPECTATIONS MEETS EXPECTATIONS NEEDS IMPROVEMENT UNSATISFACTORY *
6. OPTIONAL FACTOR		OUTSTANDING * EXCEEDS EXPECTATIONS MEETS EXPECTATIONS NEEDS IMPROVEMENT UNSATISFACTORY *

DEPARTMENT

DEFINITIONS OF PERFORMANCE RATING CATEGORIES

OUTSTANDING * — The employee has exceeded all of the performance expectations for this factor and has made many significant contributions to the efficiency and economy of this organization through such performance.

EXCEEDS EXPECTATIONS — The employee regularly works beyond a majority of the performance expectations of this factor and has made significant contributions to the efficiency and economy of this organization through such performance.

MEETS EXPECTATIONS — The employee has met the performance expectations for this factor and has contributed to the efficiency and economy of this organization.

NEEDS IMPROVEMENT — The employee has failed to meet one or more of the significant performance expectations for this factor.

UNSATISFACTORY * — The employee has failed to meet the performance expectations for this factor.

* Give specific examples of this employee's performance.

7. SPECIFIC ACHIEVEMENTS (Attach additional sheets if necessary)

8. PERFORMANCE GOALS FOR THE NEXT EVALUATION PERIOD

9. TRAINING AND DEVELOPMENT SUGGESTIONS

10. ATTENDANCE (Supervisor's Comments)

RATER'S NAME (Print or type)	RATER'S TITLE	RATER'S SIGNATURE *	DATE RATED

EMPLOYEE'S COMMENTS

This performance evaluation was discussed with me on the date noted above. I understand that my signature attests only that a personal interview was held with me; it does not necessarily indicate that I agree with the evaluation.

	EMPLOYEE'S SIGNATURE	DATE SIGNED

REVIEWER'S COMMENTS

REVIEWER'S NAME (Print or type)	REVIEWER'S TITLE	REVIEWER'S SIGNATURE *	DATE REVIEWED

FORM HEP 029 (7/81) Reverse -238-   * A copy of the signed annual evaluation form will be provided to the employee upon request.

Figure 10.4. Employee performance evaluation. (Central Washington University, Ellensburg, W.A. Reprinted with permission.)

1.   Quality of work
     a.   Outstanding
          Meticulous in quality control and follow-up
          Comprehends and carries out instructions
               without direct supervision
     b.   Exceeds expectations
          Few errors
          Comprehends and carries out instructions with little
               direct supervision
     c.   Meets expectations
          Carries out assigned duties with reasonable care
     d.   Needs improvement
          Frequent errors
          Needs repeated instructions
     e.   Unsatisfactory
          Many errors
          Misinterprets instructions
          Requires continuous supervision

2.   Quantity of work
     a.   Outstanding
          Keeps ahead of fluctuating work flow
          Meets deadlines
          Schedules own time effectively
     b.   Exceeds expectations
          Seldom falls behind work flow
          Normally meets deadlines
          Willing to complete supplemental duties assigned
     c.   Meets expectations
          Usually keeps up with assigned tasks
     d.   Needs improvement
          Does just enough to get by, resulting in backlogs
     e.   Unsatisfactory
          Constantly behind schedule
          Fails to alert supervisor or seek assistance

3.   Job knowledge
     a.   Outstanding
          Is proficient in all areas of job
          Advises supervisor of changing or unusual situations
     b.   Exceeds expectations
          Is proficient in most areas of job
          Solicits assistance when necessary
     c.   Meets expectations
          Understands most duties
          Asks questions when necessary
     d.   Needs improvement
          Needs assistance with most duties
     e.   Unsatisfactory
          Cannot perform routine tasks without
               close supervision

4.   Working relationships
     a.   Outstanding
          Works as a team member contributing significantly
               to the department mission

                    Maintains self-control in tense situations
                    Demonstrates interest in assisting others
                    Objectively accepts ideas

    b.   Exceeds expectations
                    Responds tactfully in tense situations
                    Easily approached and responsive
                    If necessary, seeks help in assisting others
                    Receptive to new ideas

    c.   Meets expectations
                    Gets along with most people
                    Has a good relationship with others
                    Gives help willingly on request
                    Refers problems to others
                    Generally accepts new ideas

    d.   Needs improvement
                    Causes some tension within organization
                    Strained relations with fellow employees
                    Indifference apparent

    e.   Unsatisfactory
                    Cannot work with others
                    Arouses antagonism
                    Overreacts
                    Rude and resentful
                    Rejects new methods

5.   Supervisory skills
    a.   Outstanding
                    Always keeps work running smoothly
                    Is always impartial and firm
                    Always develops staff to highest potential
                    Always recognizes strengths and weaknesses
                        of subordinates

    b.   Exceeds expectations
                    Normally keeps work running smooth
                    Normally impartial and firm
                    Achieves progress with each individual
                    Normally judges strengths and weaknesses of
                        subordinates correctly

    c.   Meets expectations
                    Can plan and organize the work of others obtaining
                        adequate results
                    Most often is impartial
                    Develops good workers giving adequate instruction
                    Usually sees strength and weaknesses in subordinates

    d.   Needs improvement
                    Lack of perception and foresight hampers
                        accomplishment of mission
                    Tends to be partial
                    Rarely develops staff
                    Often misjudges obvious characteristics

    e.   Unsatisfactory
                    Loses control when problems arise
                    Plays favorites
                    Has little training ability
                    Poor judge

Figure 10.5. Performance rating criteria for Media Maintenance Technician I.

made. When improvements are needed, they should be listed with the required staff development activities identified in the performance agreement for the next evaluation period.

In summary, the Personalized Employee Performance System of Evaluation (PEPSE) considers the needs of the institution, the department, the position, and the employee. When PEPSE is used in an open, developmental, and constructive spirit it can result in an evaluation system superior to other employee evaluation systems.

Delegate Responsibility

Delegating responsibility to employees stretches a media manager's time. An effective manager cannot hope to accomplish all that needs to be done unless he or she delegates responsibility to others. Delegating is also the key that unlocks "people power" within an organization and increases productivity, efficiency, and employee morale. If done correctly, delegating will promote a healthy and well-functioning organization and will make best use of the organization's people power. Dale D. McConkey in *No Nonsense Delegation* states the importance of delegation in this way:

> The manager who refuses to delegate is not unlike the person who has considerable money but refuses to use it even to earn interest. The wise manager delegates as much as his people can handle. In doing so, he maximizes the return on the people investment with which his organization has entrusted him (1986, 22).

When delegating, both authority and responsibility must be transferred to be effective. The subordinate must be able to enforce his or her decisions and assume responsibility for them. Successful delegating can be summarized into the following major points:

- Know employees' performance potential, strengths, and weaknesses.
- Delegate tasks that stretch employees.
- Delegate tasks that others can learn and assume.
- Expect mistakes but be tolerant.
- Explain and demonstrate the tasks to be delegated.
- Provide for practice.
- Provide for critique and feedback.
- Follow up and reinforce.
- Give credit when credit is due.

Michael Hammer in *Beyond Reengineering* (1996) quotes some of the employees of a new but growing type of corporation:

> "Nothing we do is more important than creating the best value for our customers. No other work matters at all." "Serving and creating value for the customer means that each member of the firm must be treated as a professional who, whenever possible, is in charge of the whole job, not just pieces of it. Stop checking with

the boss. You know what's best and you have an obligation to serve your customer and not keep asking for permission. If you need assistance, ask for it." "To be effective, you must have both freedom and autonomy while at the same time acting professionally." "If we are successful at becoming truly focused on creating value for our customers, we shouldn't need bosses in the traditional sense at all. We will already know what to do. We will need only to be kept informed and coached so we can be even more effective at what we do" (167).

Some media managers may be uncomfortable in going this far in delegating authority. In truth, this type of work environment requires a good deal of preparation and employee training. If this approach appeals to you, experiment with it before launching it throughout your organization.

Solve Interpersonal Conflicts

In every organization interpersonal conflicts will occur. In our democracy people have grown up free to express themselves and gain broad experiences. When people bring these experiences and the broad cultural backgrounds together into an organization, conflicts are bound to happen. Not all conflict is bad. Research provides evidence that some conflict among people working together increases productivity and creativity. Studies indicate that some divergence and conflict can serve as a stimulus and remove people from their personal comfort zone, forcing them to change their viewpoints and assumptions.

While interpersonal conflicts within an organization cannot be eliminated, nor is it desirous to do so, they can be controlled and coped with. Conflict is the clash between wants and needs. It can occur among companies, departments, and individuals because they all have a desire to exist, grow, and prosper within an environment with limited resources.

The most serious type of conflict to deal with is interpersonal because it usually involves emotion and anger, and angry people become irrational. Therefore, the first step in dealing with interpersonal conflict is to defuse the anger. Many would agree with Carl Rogers's (1969, 222–37) recommended approach to dealing with the emotional aspect of these conflicts. He says to first, truly hear what the other parties feel in regard to the conflict or dispute in question. Second, after you truly hear what others say about the conflict in question, present your own views, needs, and feelings. It is only after listening and then stating your own views clearly and carefully that any progress can be made in searching for a solution to the problem.

Interpersonal problems can be controlled in an organization by establishing a healthy problem-solving climate where conflict is permissible and is considered as a resolvable difference of opinion. To develop that climate, a manager should insist that all supervisors

- listen,
- be highly supportive of individuals,
- encourage and practice teamwork,
- practice participatory decision making,
- employ two-way communication,

- have a concern for individual employee welfare, and
- make resources available to the best of their ability and explain why resources are not available when they cannot be made available.

Assist Each Employee to Achieve Maximum Human Potential

We all know a few people like Jack. Jack is thirty-four years old and has a reputation of being a fine manager. New managers in Jack's company are told that if they perform like Jack, they will go a long way in the organization. Jack is hardworking, aggressive, and knows how to get through the bureaucracy of the organization. He is the first to arrive and the last to leave, and is in the office many nights. He can be seen outwitting his peers and has been known to "get" some of his co-workers in his quest to climb to the top. Jack is divorced and has minimal social life and high blood pressure. His life is his job. Jack is a workaholic.

Now consider Paul. Paul is at the other end of the spectrum. He is self-indulgent. He puts all of his efforts and energy into his social life. He lives in a house with a swimming pool; plays volleyball, racquetball, and tennis; and jogs. He owns a large car and a sports car. He is single and is out every night involved in his sports activities, dining, or at parties. While he works as a computer specialist, he tolerates his job as a means to provide him with the financial resources to support his social life. Paul has many acquaintances but few close friends, and is not active in any volunteer organizations. He suffers from insomnia, has an ulcer, and is on the verge of becoming an alcoholic.

We all know both kinds of people. They represent extremes, but are real. Both Jack and Paul do not have balanced lives, and while they may appear happy on the surface, they may not be. They have not learned to fulfill their lives by balancing their social, personal, and professional lives. Eventually both Jack's and Paul's productivity will deteriorate. Jack will suffer burnout and will be less effective. Paul's fast life probably is already affecting his performance, as his insomnia and tendency toward alcoholism indicate.

It is for those reasons that employees should be encouraged to improve the quality of their lives by achieving a balance in their social, personal, and professional lives. Employees who fail in this will not reach their maximum human potential. When in balance, each aspect of our lives—professional, personal, and social—may consume about one-third of our time. When any of the three consumes more than its share, anxiety and stress result. Figure 10.6 illustrates the balancing of these factors.

Research and experience have identified some key factors that can make professional or work life more satisfying and challenging:

- job satisfaction
- an opportunity to influence the work situation
- support from one's organization for growth and development
- a close fit between the employees' skills and competencies and the organization's needs
- meaningful responsibility to do work that has personal significance
- support of peers
- support of one's supervisor

- growth opportunities in terms of learning and promotion
- equitable rewards in terms of pay and opportunities
- multiple career opportunities for a variety of one's interests
- challenging work

As one responsible for the professional or work life of others, it is important that the media manager lead a balanced life to maximize his or her human potential and also serve as a role model for others by guiding employees into activities that will enable them to find balance in their own lives. Employees who are self-fulfilled will be more effective and productive members of an organization.

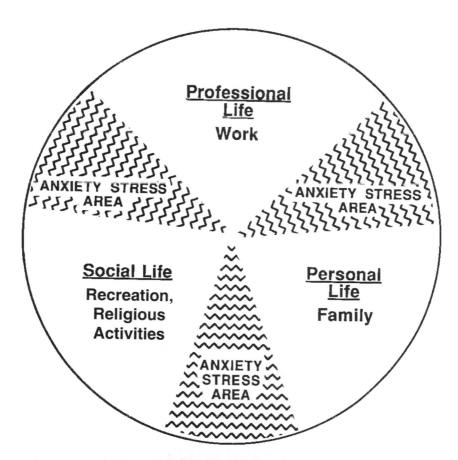

Figure 10.6. Balancing the major life factors.

Motivate Employees

If all the elements for managing personnel previously discussed in this chapter are implemented, then motivation may not be a problem and most employees should be motivated. While there will always be exceptions, when employees are treated justly as individuals, are involved as team members, are held responsible for their performance, are provided with promotional opportunities, and are fairly rewarded for their efforts, they will be self motivated.

SUGGESTED ACTIVITIES

1. Interview several program managers in any field and ask them to state their philosophies toward personnel management.

2. Select three jobs in the media field and write a job specification for each.

3. With another person, play the manager/employee roles in the PEPSE evaluation model and evaluate each other using the model.

4. With another person, stage an interpersonal conflict. Apply Carl Rogers's recommendations to defuse the emotional part of the conflict.

5. Analyze the relationship of your professional life, personal life, and social life on the Balancing the Major Life Factors model illustrated in figure 10.6. How balanced is your life? What can you do about it?

REFERENCES

Blanchard, Kenneth, and Spencer Johnson. 1984. *The One Minute Manager*. New York: Berkeley Publishing Group.

Chisholm, Margaret E., and Donald P. Ely. 1976. *Media Personnel in Education: A Competency Approach*. Englewood Cliffs, N.J.: Prentice Hall.

Covey, Stephen B., A. Roger Merrill, and Rebecca R. Merrill. 1994. *First Things First: To Live, to Love, to Learn, to Leave a Legacy*. New York: Simon & Schuster.

Hammer, Michael. 1996. *Beyond Reengineering: How the Process-Centered Organization Is Changing Our Work and Our Lives*. New York: HarperBusiness.

McConkey, Dale D. 1986. *No Nonsense Delegation*. New York: American Management Association.

Peters, Thomas J., and Robert H. Waterman, Jr. 1982. *In Search of Excellence: Lessons from America's Best-Run Companies*. New York: Warner Books.

Rogers, Carl R. 1969. *Freedom to Learn*. Columbus, Ohio: Merrill.

MEDIA RESOURCES

The Art of Resolving Conflicts in the Workplace. Peggy L. Scott, producer/director, 38 minutes. San Francisco: Kantola Productions, 1992. Videocassette.

In Search of Excellence. Nathan/Tyler Productions, 88 minutes. Waltham, Mass.: Nathan/Tyler Productions, 1985. Videocassette.

A Passion for Excellence. Lauren Hudson, director, 60 minutes. Des Plains, Ill.: Video Publishing House, 1985. Videocassette.

Winning Face to Face: The Art of Resolving Conflicts in the Workplace. Peggy L. Scott, producer/director, 90 minutes. San Ramon, Calif.: International Video Network, 1991. Videocassette.

SELECTED BIBLIOGRAPHY

Alesandrini, Kathryn. *Survive Information Overload: The Seven Best Ways to Manage Your Workload by Seeing the Big Picture.* Homewood, Ill.: Business One Irwin, 1992.

Bailey, Gerald D., and Gwen L. Bailey. *101 Activities for Creating Effective Technology Staff Development Programs: A Sourcebook of Games, Stories, Role-Playing and Learning Exercises for Administrators.* New York: Scholastic, 1994.

Belker, Loren B. *The First-Time Manager.* New York: American Management Association, 1993.

Bittel, Lester R. *Right on Time! The Complete Guide for Time Pressured Managers.* New York: McGraw-Hill, 1991.

Bradley, Howard. *Staff Development.* New York: Falmer Press, 1991.

Burton, John W. *Conflict: Resolution and Prevention.* New York: St. Martin's Press, 1990.

Drucker, Peter F. *Managing in a Time of Great Change.* New York: Truman Talley Books/Dutton, 1995.

Gatewood, Robert D., and Hubert S. Field. *Human Resource Selection.* Forth Worth, Tex.: Dryden Press, 1994.

Lieberman, Ann, and Lynne Miller, eds. *Staff Development for Education in the '90s: New Demands, New Realities, New Perspectives.* New York: Teachers College Press, 1991.

MacKenzie, R. Alec. *Teamwork Through Time Management: New Time Management Methods for Everyone in your Organization.* Chicago: Dartnell, 1990.

Marlow, Eugene. *Managing Corporate Media.* Rev. ed. White Plains, N.Y.: Knowledge Industry Publications, 1989.

Ravet, Serge, and Maureen Layte. *Technology-Based Training: A Comprehensive Guide to Choosing, Implementing, Managing, and Developing New Technologies in Training.* Houston, Tex.: Gulf Publications, 1998.

Rebore, Ronald W. *Personnel Management in Education: A Management Approach.* Englewood Cliffs, N.J.: Prentice Hall, 1991.

Rhodes, Susan R., and Richard Steers. *Managing Employee Absenteeism.* Reading, Mass.: Addison-Wesley, 1990.

Towers, Brian. *The Handbook of Human Resource Management.* Cambridge, Mass.: Blackwell, 1992.

Tracey, William R., ed. *Human Resources Management and Development Handbook.* New York: AMACOM, 1994.

Van Horn, Royal W. *Advanced Technology in Education: An Introduction to Videodiscs, Robotics, Optical Memory, Peripherals, New Software Tools, and High-Tech Staff Development.* Pacific Grove, Calif.: Brooks/Cole Publishing Co., 1991.

Weiss, Donald H. *Fair, Square, and Legal: Safe Hiring, Managing and Firing Practices to Keep You and Your Company Out of Court.* New York: AMACOM, 1991.

Whiteley, Alma M., ed. *The Teaching of Organizational Behavior Across Discipline and National Boundaries: A Role for Information Technology.* New York: International Business Press, 1996.

Yarbrough, Elaine A., and William Wilmot. *Artful Mediation: Constructive Conflict at Work.* Boulder, Colo.: Cairns Publishing, 1995.

CHAPTER

11

MANAGING
BUDGETS

The audio-visual program, being one important facet of the instruc-
tional program, must receive its share of financial support. The support
must be reflected in personnel, equipment, materials, and facilities
that will enable the audio-visual program to make its maximum
contribution.

K. C. Rugg, *Improving Instruction:*
Budgeting Your Audio-Visual Program, 1960

233

OBJECTIVES

At the conclusion of this chapter you should be able to

1. List three sources of funding for public schools, colleges, and universities.

2. Identify, describe, and state the advantages and disadvantages of seven types of budgeting systems.

3. Describe three systems of budget allocation.

4. Identify who should be involved in the budget process and how they should be involved.

5. List and discuss the steps involved in developing a budget.

6. Describe four strategies for justifying a budget.

John A. Tracy, in *Budgeting A'La Carte* (1996, 3), clearly defines the challenge facing any budget planner and administrator in a media program or any other public agency:

> Please don't confuse *business* budgeting with the budgeting done by individuals and households or with the budgeting done by government. Budgeting by individuals, households, and by government agencies is driven primarily by the need to allocate scarce resources among excessive demands and to stay within these allocated amounts once the budget is adopted.

While some businesses have ample resources to allocate, such is usually not the case in other sectors. Developing and managing a media service program budget is a critical function of a media manager. Facilities, program planning, and personnel cannot exist without a budget, but there is rarely adequate funds to meet all needs. Therefore, the media manager must learn to develop and apply budgeting skills if a service program is to be managed effectively.

The budget is the road map of the unit's programs. It is a written and numerical statement that tells the administration what the media service program is supposed to do, what it is doing, how much it costs and/or will cost, and how it is meeting its objectives in measurable terms. The budget should include planning not only for the present but also for the future, and should outline problems and solutions to those problems.

Developing and monitoring a budget is time-consuming because all the costs and benefits involved in providing media services to clients must be considered. The media manager must accept budgeting as an absolute necessity and a challenge. There are no shortcuts in the budgeting process. In order to receive a fair share of an institution's budget, it is crucially important that budget plans be completed properly within the host organization's budgeting procedures. Given the workload of most media managers, it is tempting to do superficial work when preparing a budget by considering the budget as just one more task to be completed. The manager who succumbs to that temptation is indeed foolish, since the entire success of the media service program depends upon an adequate budget. Therefore, budgeting deserves the most creative and thoughtful efforts that the media manager and staff can muster.

FUNDING SOURCES

A limited number of funding sources exists for institutions and consequently for media service programs. The major sources of funding for public organizations are local, regional, state, federal, or governmental funding; gifts; grants; and service/charges or fees. Not all of these funding sources are available to all media service centers. Corporate media centers must obtain their funds from the host organization. The wise manager must learn how various budgeting sources relate to the media service program. He or she must develop the perceptions, skills, and liaisons necessary to obtain funds from all available sources when purposes and guidelines allow them to be sought and used.

Funding Sources for Public Schools

Local Funds

Most school districts may ask taxpayers in their community to pass a local levy for specific purposes, e.g., maintenance, operations, special programs, remodeling, and new construction. When these specific needs and/or programs within a school district exceed the state allocation, local taxes may be the only source available. The amount that can be levied is regulated by the state.

State Funds

K-12 public schools obtain most of their funding through their state legislature. These legislatures appropriate allocations based upon a formula of cost per pupil enrolled. Some states base this figure upon an average daily enrollment while others may use the enrollment on one single day early during the fall term. The spending of the funds allocated usually must follow strict state guidelines. Limitations vary from state to state, and it is imperative that a manager be up-to-date on a state's funding formulas and procedures.

Regional Funds

In most states regional educational service districts have been established to assist local school districts. The purpose of the regional centers is to consolidate special services and specialists, that is, reading specialists, psychologists, testing specialists, media resource centers, and others that may not be cost-effective to duplicate in each school district. The regional media resource centers build media collections and employ production specialists to be shared by all the schools within their region. Regional centers obtain most of their funding from the state and/or by contracts directly with local school districts for services. Again, practice varies from state to state.

Federal Funds

In the past, federal funding has been a valuable source of funding for public schools; however, this source has been steadily decreasing. While most of the federal funds to education pass through the state educational hierarchy for distribution to local school districts, some funds do go directly to schools in the form of grants for specific purposes.

Grants

As available funds decrease or fail to grow, there has been a concerted effort to obtain grants from state and federal sources as well as from corporations and foundations. School districts successful in obtaining grants usually employ grant writers to prepare proposals for funds to meet special needs. Occasionally, highly motivated existing staff will take on this very time-intensive activity. Most of the grants are for research and demonstration projects.

Funding Sources for
Public Colleges and Universities

State Funds

Historically, the major source of funding for public colleges and universities has also been the state, but this appears to be changing. State legislatures authorize colleges and universities to collect tuition from students and to use these funds to cover part of their operating costs. In some states, the legislatures mandate that tuition cover a large percentage of costs. This percentage varies widely, with California requesting that tuition cover a very small percent of the educational costs while the state of Washington has mandated that tuition cover a significant share of the actual costs. The balance of costs is then allocated from the state's general revenue. Tuition must cover most of the costs in private colleges and universities.

Federal Funds

This has been a significant source for colleges and universities, with many large universities relying heavily on federal funds for their research efforts. Colleges and universities have considerably more freedom than public schools when applying for federal funds, with little or no state bureaucratic procedures involved. As in the case of the public schools, higher education is suffering from a decrease in federal funding.

Gifts

Gifts from graduates and friends are becoming a major source of funding for higher education, especially for larger universities. Most institutions have established an office with staff to actively promote gifts to the university. Gifts are received in many different forms—monetary, property, and present and future income generated from property. Some gifts are earmarked by the donor for specific purposes, while others can be used for whatever purposes the university desires. The income generated by these gifts is then available to augment the budget or to develop new programs.

Grants

As is true in the public schools, most colleges and universities have increased their efforts to raise funds for research and demonstration projects. These institutions seek funds from state, federal, corporate, and foundation sources.

Service Charges and Fees

Many colleges and universities have adopted a schedule of fees and service charges to increase their technology and media budgets. In most cases these service charges are used to supplement local and state budget sources. It is recommended this method of providing for budget revenues should be minimized and generally limited to the service support role for noninstructional clients.

Funding Sources for the Corporate Sector

In the corporate sector, funding for programs comes from generated income. While the firm may do business with states or the federal government, funds received are treated as income. Profit is the goal. All budgets must demonstrate that they generate income for profit or that they provide necessary services to income-generating programs.

BUDGETING SYSTEMS

Periodic economic downturns in the United States have exposed budgets, including library/media budgets, to considerable scrutiny by administrators. The traditional line-item budget has been replaced with other types of budgets in an attempt to derive better measures of cost-effectiveness. The days when requests for funds in a few simple categories or a lump sum with limited justification are over. As long as resources for education remain dependent upon the wealth of a state or community, the demand by the public for budget accountability will not go away—in fact, it will probably intensify. Because different budgeting systems are used in different institutions and because institutions are continually experimenting with budgeting systems, it is important that the media manager have some knowledge of the various budgeting systems used.

Lump-Sum Budgets

A lump-sum budget, as its name implies, is a single-figure budget. The service unit is simply allocated a sum of money to operate all the unit's functions during the budget time frame. The lump-sum budget is rarely used today and when it is, some type of line-item structure is usually developed for internal control—so much for materials, so much for equipment, and other items. The lump-sum budget's most defensible use is during the beginning of a new program or activity, when initial costs may be difficult to estimate. Once the initial costs have been established, another budget system is usually implemented.

Line-Item Budgets

In a line-item budget, all items to be purchased are simply listed on successive lines on the budget forms. While the system is cumbersome, it offers strict control of expenditures and is easy to prepare and review. However, line-item budgets tend to reinforce themselves by continuing year after year without any review of need or effectiveness. When items are cut from the budget by a reviewing officer, no information is available regarding the subsequent impact on programs. For instance, a piece of equipment may be comprised of two separate units which are listed on two separate lines of the budget. The reviewing officer may delete one unit on a line-item budget, not knowing that the two units must be connected for either to work. Usually the manager must wait until the next budget year to get the deleted item. Like the lump-sum budget, a line-item budget offers very little possibility for determining if program objectives are being achieved. Line-item budgets are still being used, however. Figure 11.1 is an excerpt from a line-item budget. Note that items are listed by object code, with items from various categories (equipment, supplies, subscriptions) intermingled.

Institution: Program Code:

Department: Year:

Object Code	Quantity Needed	Description	Current Inventory	Unit Price	Proposed Budget
101	4	Slide projectors	30	400	1,600
102	100 reams	Paper, white	10 reams	4	400
103	60 reams	Paper, colored	20 reams	4	240
104	1	Video player	5	800	800
105	25	Videocassettes	15	8	400
106	10 dozen	Pens	2 dozen	3	30
107	10 dozen	Pencils	1 dozen	2	20
108	1	TV receiver	10	800	800
109	1	Magazine rack	1	400	400
110	1	Microfiche reader	1	300	300
111	90	Desks	900	100	9,000
112-613		Library books 500 @ $30	50,000		15,000
		English books 60 @ $30			1,800
		History books 60 @ $30			1,800
616-666	50	Magazine subscriptions	50	50	2,500
667-767		Supplies, misc.			2,000
768	30	Computers	30	1,500	45,000
769	6	Projection screens	30	100	600
770-1070	300	Video rental		25	7,500
		Software			5,000
				TOTAL:	$95,190

Figure 11.1. Line-item budget (for illustration purposes).

Object-of-Expenditure Budgets

In this type of budget, the items listed in a line-item budget are grouped into preestablished categories, e.g., supplies, equipment, instructional materials, contractual expenses, furniture, and salaries. Each department, school, or unit submits a separate budget for each category. As one can see from a review of figure 11.2 (equipment) and figure 11.3 (supplies), there still is no provision for determining if the funds being spent are meeting program objectives. Therefore, the person responsible for the budget must submit a brief statement of justification which describes how the items requested will support the objectives. A separate form is submitted for each budget category.

Institution: Program:

Department:

Schedule 2: Equipment   Year:

Object Code	Quantity Needed	Description	Current Inventory	Unit Price	Proposed Budget
200-102	4	Slide projectors	30	400	1,600
200-103	1	Video player	5	800	800
200-104	1	TV receiver	10	800	800
200-105	1	Microfiche reader	1	300	300
200-106	30	Computers	30	1,500	45,000
200-107	6	Projection screens	30	100	600
200-108	6	Overhead projectors	24	200	1,200
				TOTAL:	$50,300

Justification:

102, 107, 108: Slide projectors and screens: The projectors and screens will replace projectors presently worn out and replaced under current district replacement schedule. (Projectors # MP-1, 4, 7 & 8)

103, 104: Video player and TV receivers: Will add another playback system to meet playback needs. Presently have a 10 percent turndown ratio.

105: Microfiche reader: Will add another unit to meet student needs. Presently have a 14 percent turndown ratio.

106: Computers: Will increase classroom inventory from one to two per classroom to meet student instructional needs.

Figure 11.2. Object-of-expenditure budget: Equipment.

Institution: Program:
Department:
Schedule 3: Supplies   Year:

Object Code	Quantity Needed	Description	Current Inventory	Proposed Budget
300-101	100 reams	Paper	10 reams	400
300-102	60 reams	Paper	20 reams	240
300-103	25	Videocassettes	15	800
300-104	10 dozen	Pens	2 dozen	30
300-105	10 dozen	Pencils	1 dozen	20
300-106-206		Supplies, misc.		2,000
			TOTAL:	$3,490

Justification:

101, 102, 104, 105,
    106-206:   Paper, pencil and miscellaneous supplies: Required to operate a media resource center program.

        103:    Videocassettes: Needed to meet teacher requests. Presently have a 15 percent turndown ratio.

Figure 11.3. Object-of-expenditure budget: Supplies.

Formula Budgets

Formula budgets are developed using a complex and time-consuming formula. They received a great deal of development effort between 1965 and 1975, and then interest diminished. Legislators and institutional administrators found the formulas too complex and difficult to understand.

Library resource formulas used factors such as inflation, collection size, number of faculty, number of students, and curriculum areas as budget "drivers." Most formulas further considered that some academic disciplines would require more materials than others and weighted them accordingly. The developers considered that upper-division students would use more books than lower-division students, and graduate students more than upper-division students. Most of the formulas did not consider nonprint media. The states of Washington and California developed nonprint formulas but never implemented them. The formulas were intended to generate a budget with other systems implemented for operational control. Formula budgets were effective in generating excellent library budgets during the years when student enrollments were growing, but they became disastrous when enrollments declined and they lost administrative support.

Program Budgets

Program budgeting requires the identification and division of the unit's programs into specific functional units or programs. In a media center, these program units may be media library, instructional computing, maintenance and repair, equipment distribution, and media development services. Coordinators of each of these program units develop a budget that includes all budget categories: salaries, equipment, supplies, and any others required to support their program. The result is a budget that reflects the cost of providing each of the center's programs (see figure 11.4).

Budget Category	Media Library	Instructional Computer Programs	Electronic Maintenance	Equipment Distribution	Production	Total
Salaries	$70,000	$35,000	$30,000	$17,000	$80,000	$232,000
Equipment	2,000	10,000	5,000	10,000	10,000	37,000
Supplies	6,000	2,000	10,000	5,000	10,000	33,000
Instructional materials	90,000	5,000	500	-0-	-0-	95,500
Contractual services	2,000	2,000	500	-0-	3,000	7,500
Furniture	1,000	500	500	500	500	3,000
Capital expenses	-0-	-0-	-0-	-0-	-0-	-0-
Communications	2,500	2,500	1,000	1,000	2,000	9,000
Maintenance and repair	-0-	1,000	500	-0-	500	2,000
Total	$173,500	$58,000	$48,000	$33,500	$106,000	$419,000

Figure 11.4. Summary of program budget.

Planning, Programming, Budgeting System (PPBS)

This system was developed for allocating resources and tracking program-related spending by the military and later by government agencies. It involves an analysis of an agency's program activities in terms of what they are supposed to do, who is to do it, how it is to be accomplished, and how much it will cost. This system of budgeting sometimes includes the word *evaluation* in the title (planning, programming, budgeting, evaluation system), as evaluation is an integral part of the process. The basic steps involved in PPBS budgeting include an identification of broad goals and a determination of how each department within an organization contributes to them. These goals are transposed into short- and long-term objectives with measurable outcomes and with alternate ways of reaching them. Probable costs for all alternatives are developed, and the alternative with the lowest cost and greatest effectiveness for each program is selected. The program is then implemented and evaluated objectively. If implemented and monitored properly, PPBS will ensure that through careful planning, analysis, and evaluation, resources are matched with objectives and tasks to be completed.

The major problem associated with PPBS budgeting is the large amount of work necessary before implementation. The work required for a changeover from other budgeting systems is often underestimated. Another problem is that data cannot be processed efficiently unless the institution's accounting and computing systems are redesigned. PPBS is a complex and time-consuming budgeting system.

Zero-Base Budgeting (ZBB)

This newest form of budgeting gained support in the late 1970s and early 1980s. In zero-base budgeting (ZBB), departments are identified and organized into decision units that develop decision packages which describe activities, goals and objectives, alternate means to reach the objectives, projected costs and benefits, and methods for quantifying performance evaluation. The decision units rank the decision packages and pass them up the ladder to upper management to make their decisions. Theoretically, ZBB should result in the allocation of available funds to high-priority programs within an institution.

ZBB is not too different from PPBS budgeting. Both budgeting systems require detailed preparation of goals, objectives, alternatives, costs, and quantitative performance evaluation methods. The major difference is the concept of separate numerically ranked decision packages from which upper management can make their selection for funding from available financial resources.

ALLOCATION SYSTEMS

Cost-allocating methods vary, but most systems allocate costs into at least three broad categories: direct, indirect, and capital. While not all of these are always allocated to a service unit, the costs do exist and must be considered by the institution. Direct costs are nearly always allocated to the service unit.

Direct Costs

Direct costs include the visible costs associated with operating a program. They include salaries, equipment, supplies, instructional materials, contractual service repairs to equipment, and communications. (In some institutions, however, very expensive equipment may be classified as a capital cost if its cost exceeds a preestablished dollar amount.)

Direct costs are usually divided into two cost categories, personnel and operational. The personnel budget covers the personnel costs of all employees. Instructional development and media development services require time and trained staff in addition to the staff serving clerical, delivery, and other functions. Thus, personnel costs may well constitute the highest budget item. The costs of such benefits as hospital insurance, vacation, sick leave, and profit sharing must not be neglected in the estimates. Benefits can easily add 20 percent or more to base salaries. In most cases the required benefits information is available from the personnel or human resources officer of the institution. Because media service programs are so people intensive, it is not uncommon for personnel costs to be 75 to 80 percent of the budget.

The operational budget covers costs for instructional materials, electronic equipment, production equipment, supplies, and other like items. Some of these are one-time costs, while others will come up again in subsequent years. The media manager will usually be expected to budget and monitor direct costs in the various programs.

Indirect Costs

Indirect costs are the hidden costs which may not be visible. They include the costs of space; maintaining the physical facilities; and the costs for utilities, including heat, air-conditioning, lights, and sometimes communication. Such costs are usually not allocated directly to a department or unit because of the difficulty of dividing and allocating them to separate departments. Heat and air-conditioning may be provided from a single central plant and piped to all units of the institution. Electricity and gas may be metered in one location for the entire facility. For these reasons, indirect costs are usually included in another budget area of the institution and not allocated to departments or units.

Capital Costs

Capital costs are large expenditure items with a relatively long life and are usually nonrecurring. Large equipment items, new buildings, and remodeling of buildings are examples of capital costs. The factor used by institutions to determine if equipment is classified as direct or capital cost expenditure is usually based upon its cost and its nature. Institutions or agencies arbitrarily establish a minimum monetary value or an expected life before an item is classified as a capital expenditure. While capital costs are not directly allocated to a specific unit or department, they are real and must be considered. Again, these practices vary from institution to institution.

ACCOUNTING SYSTEMS

The expanding demands of budgeting and accountability placed upon institutions require that exact and efficient budgetary controls be established. While these accounting practices within institutions vary widely, their purpose remains the same: to provide an accurate and efficient method to monitor income and expenditures within an organization so that meaningful analysis can occur.

To accomplish that purpose, an accounting system needs to record and monitor at least four items of information for each transaction.

- The *function,* which defines why the item was purchased. Examples include instruction, administration, research, and production.
- The *object,* which specifies what was purchased. Examples include salaries, supplies, and capital outlay.
- The *unit* or *program,* which identifies for whom the purchase is made. Examples include school department and program.
- The *fiscal year* to which the transaction is to be charged.

Each item of information is called a *dimension* within the institution's budget classifi cation system. In practice, more than the above four dimensions may exist within an institution's classification system. Others may include the name of a fund, an instructional organization, or a job classification activity.

Most public school districts employ an accounting system based upon the federal financial accounting handbook entitled *Financial Accounting for Local and State School Systems* (Fowler 1990). This accounting system provides a sophisticated finan cial managerial system for state and local educational agencies (LEAs) providing well-defined dimensions and codes for a wide range of activities. LEAs are encouraged to place all of their financial transactions into at least four dimensions specified in the handbook: program, function, object, and project/reporting (formerly called source of funds). A number of additional subdimensions are provided for use at the option of the LEAs. These include level of instruction, operational unit, subject matter, job classification, and special cost center. Each dimension and subdimension is defined in the handbook to help the user allocate income and expenditures consistently to the correct account. Each dimension has an alphanumeric code. The alphanumeric code system permits the institution's accounting office to keep like items together for ease of computerization. While the federal financial accounting handbook provides a complete accounting system, each state has the right and privilege to adapt the model to meet its specific needs. A brief summary of the list of expenditure classifications with numerical code sequences from about a dozen pages of the federal handbook is provided in figure 11.5, pages 246–47 (Fowler 1990, 19–32). In the handbook, each item is carefully defined.

The financial accounting system just described may not be employed in all institutions, but it can serve as a model. Most accounting systems in public schools, colleges, universities, and the corporate world are similar to it. The media manager must learn thoroughly the financial accounting system employed within his or her institution. The information should be available from the institution's business manager or finance officer. It is imperative to know the accounting system when preparing budget proposals and internal department budget accounting strategies.

FUND

Government Funds

1.	General Fund
2.	Special Revenue Fund
3.	Capital Projects Funds
4.	Debt Service Funds

Propriety Funds

5.	Enterprise Funds
6.	Internal Service Funds

Fiduciary Funds

7.	Trust and Agency Funds

Account Groups

8.	General Fixed Assets
9.	General Long-Term Debt

PROGRAM

100	Regular — Elementary/Secondary
200*	Special Programs
300*	Vocational Programs
400*	Other Instructional Programs — Elementary — Secondary
500	Nonpublic School Programs
600	Adult/Continuing Education Programs
700	Community/Junior College Education Programs
800*	Community Services Programs
900*	Enterprise Programs

FUNCTION

1000 Instruction
2000 Support Service

2100* Attendance and Social Work Service

2200 Support Services — Instructional Staff

2210 Improvement of Instructional Services

2211 Supervision of Improvement of Instruction Services
2212 Instruction and Curriculum Development
2213 Instructional Staff Training
2219 Other

---

*Subheadings eliminated for simplicity

2220   Educational Media Services

         2221   Supervision of Educational Media Services
         2222   School Library
         2223   Audiovisual
         2224   Educational Television
         2225   Computer-assisted Instruction
         2229   Other Educational Media Services

2290   Other Support Services — Instructional Staff

2300*   Support Services — General Administration
2400*   Support Services — School Administration
2500*   Support Services — Business
2600*   Operation and Maintenance of Plant Services
2700*   Student Transportation Services
2800*   Support Services — Central
2900*   Other Support Services

3000*   Operation of Non-Instructional Services

4000*   Facilities Acquisition and Construction Services

5000*   Other Uses (government funds only)

OBJECT

100*   Personal Services — Salaries
200*   Personal Services — Employee Benefits
300*   Purchased Professional and Technical Services
400*   Purchased Property Services
500*   Other Purchased Services
600*   Supplies
700*   Property (including furniture and equipment)
800*   Other Objects
900*   Other Uses of Funds (governmental funds only)

Figure 11.5. Summary of expenditure accounts.

DEVELOPING A BUDGET

Before a manager can develop a budget, the services that the unit is supposed to provide must be carefully analyzed. Decisions to consider are: Why should the services be provided, who is to provide them, how they are to be provided, and at what cost. To budget intelligently, the manager must know the program(s) and have answers to the above questions. Facts based upon inventories, records, statistics, and standards must be gathered, organized, and applied to help determine budget needs. The budget must then be prepared using the institution's budgeting system. Finally, because budgeting is also a political process, it must be precise, carefully justified, and defensible in terms of real need. The value of a consolidated media service program, with all media services integrated into one unit or division, as was discussed in chapter 3, becomes apparent in the budgeting process. The financial savings through the joint use of personnel, equipment, and service points become obvious.

Who Should Be Involved in Budget Development?

From the above statements, it should be apparent that department coordinators or supervisors must be involved in the budgeting process. They are closest to the service points and should know the most about their service and budget needs. They should be asked to submit budget requests to the media manager, whose task it is to analyze, screen, and consolidate their recommendations into a single media service budget request. The media manager must study all requests and justifications carefully to be sure that they represent real needs. Items that are selected for further consideration must be checked for accuracy and properly justified. To simplify the consolidation process, the department coordinators should submit their requests in the same format that the media manager will use for the consolidated budget. Conferences with each unit coordinator and all coordinators together are necessary to clarify and to help the manager decide which requests can be included. The manager should strive for consensus among all of the coordinators, if possible, to maintain maximum cooperation within and among the media service program units. Participatory management works only when employees are involved.

Procedures

In developing a budget, the following steps should be helpful.

Determine the needs for media services. With media service staff assistance, examine existing programs and the need for new programs. No program should be sacred just because it has met patron needs in the past. The only criteria for retention should be that it is still meeting patron needs. An analysis of past utilization records should demonstrate the value of the program. If it is not being used, it should be scaled back to match its use or deleted.

New programs may also be needed. Increasing requests for a service should be considered. In most cases, existing programs were developed owing to patron request and were small operations to begin with. As new instructional technologies develop, they need to be studied, tried, and implemented into programs when there is reasonable evidence that they will enhance services to the center's patrons. The institution's curriculum and programs must also be carefully monitored. As the curriculum changes or as new institutional programs are added, media services may have to add new services or collections to meet changing needs.

To become aware of the need for media service program changes, one must constantly study utilization records, keep abreast of new technologies, listen to patrons both informally and formally, and conduct questionnaires and surveys. Managers must also be involved with individuals and bodies that make policy that may affect program or curriculum—principals, deans, or new product councils—in order to learn about future changes or what might be needed to improve existing programs and facilities.

Transfer program needs into goal and objective statements. Whether or not the institution requires that budget goal and objective statements be formulated, it is still an important step in the process. Without such statements, one cannot evaluate the cost/benefit effectiveness of budget expenditures for specific services. Objectives, need, and measurement statements should be developed for each budget request in each category. An example of a complete budget objective statement is provided in figure 11.6, page 250.

Survey existing media services holdings. Based upon the needs identified in step 1 and stated in goal and objective statements in step 2, the manager should determine what holdings already exist within the media center that can be used to meet those needs through a reallocation of resources. Existing holdings that are surplus in one program because of the deletion or curtailment of that program should be reallocated to meet new needs, if possible. The difference between the resources that can be reallocated and those that are required to meet the new needs should be requested in the budget request. This ability to reallocate resources within the center to meet changing needs is another advantage of integrated media centers.

Tabulate budget request data and project costs. After existing resources that can be reallocated are identified, the costs of new required resources can be determined. These costs are not limited to materials, but may also include supplies, equipment, personnel, and indirect costs, if required by the budgeting and accounting procedures used by an institution.

Specify costs/benefits for each objective of the budget request. Costs/benefits for each budget objective should be determined and stated. The constraints, relative costs, and likely results or success of each budget request in relationship to its objectives must be analyzed. How many patrons will benefit? How many new patrons will be served? What and how many new services will occur? What increase in requests will likely occur? How much will production increase? How will the quality of the products improve?

Establish priorities. The next step in the budgeting procedure is to arrange the various program requests in order of priority. Most institutions cannot afford to fund all requests; therefore, prioritizing the segments of the media budget proposals provides the media manager and his or her coordinators an opportunity to inform the administration which programs are the most critical. Without this, the administration may inadvertently eliminate segments of a program without realizing that

Media Services

<u>Instructional Materials Request</u>   <u>Cost: $84,200</u>

Objective: To maintain an up-to-date collection of films,
                records, computer software, videodiscs, CD-
                ROMs, videocassettes, and filmstrips by
                 (a) withdrawing worn out and outdated materials
                from the collection; (b) purchasing new materials
                to replace the old; and (c) purchasing materials to
                meet new curricular needs.

Need: 1. *Replacement.* The media materials collection
                was increased by 301 software items during the past
                biennium while 200 items were withdrawn for
                obsolescence. Therefore, 101 new materials are
                necessary for replacement purposes.

                2. *To retain a current collection.* For the collection
                to remain current, 10 percent of the collection should
                be replaced each year. With a collection of 3,200
                items, 320 items should be purchased each biennium
                for currency purposes.

                Therefore, 421 software items should be purchased at
                an estimated cost per item of $200.

Measurement: At the conclusion of the biennium, 421 new software
                items will be purchased. Each purchase will meet the
                criteria of the media services materials selection policy
                and be previewed, evaluated, and recommended by
                the faculty.

Figure 11.6. Budget objective statement.

by doing so a program or programs will suffer more than if other, less critical items were eliminated. Establishing priorities among budget segments requires careful examination of the costs/benefits of each program.

Establish operational levels. There are three major levels of budget, commonly called a maintenance or continuity budget, an incremental budget, and an expansion budget.

A *continuity* budget is basically a status quo budget with the same level of expenditures as in the previous year, with an inflationary increase. It assumes that the programs are well established, are still meeting needs, and no major changes will occur. A continuity budget does not allow for improvements in the levels of services provided.

An *incremental* budget allows for a modest increase in the budget level over and above an inflationary adjustment. Its purpose is to cover the additional costs related to increased utilization of services or to improve the basic programs to meet additional goals advanced by the institution. An incremental budget expresses the recommended desirable level of funding.

When new programs are added or existing programs are greatly reorganized, an *expansion* budget is indicated. An expansion budget is used when a new media center is created or when a major new program is to be implemented. Budget goals and objectives, need statements, and costs/benefits are usually required in expansion budgets, even in institutions that do not require them in their normal budgeting procedures.

In addition to arranging the budget requests in order of priority, the media manager may be required, or may find it desirable, to submit each budget segment in both continuity or incremental levels. This strategy will provide the administration with additional information and data upon which to make decisions. It is a good strategy when the media manager has the support and confidence of the administration, but it can be detrimental when administrative support is weak.

Strategies for Justifying a Budget

An integral part of a budget proposal is a persuasive justification. When developing justifications, the budget writer should think as a lawyer presenting a legal case to a jury. The administration, like a jury, will decide for or against the budget, weighing the arguments presented. Therefore, accurate and persuasive justifications must be developed. Strategies for justifying a budget follow. The application of multiple strategies is recommended.

Cost-Per-Pupil Basis

This strategy is used quite commonly in educational institutions to explain where school funds are being spent—instruction, special education and other special programs, maintenance, and other programs. Because the expenditures for media services are small when compared to other programs within the educational institution, the cost-per-pupil basis for funding is a good argument. It is easy to calculate and transpose proposed expenditures into terms easily understood by others. One simply lists the items proposed to purchase and divides their total cost by the number of students in the total institution, individual schools, or program (see figures 11.7 and 11.8, page 252).

Media Equipment	Present Inventory	Continuity Level	Continuity Level Cost	Incremental Level	Incremental Level Cost
Computers	20	3	$ 4,500	4	$ 6,000
Videodisc players	10	1	700	2	1,400
Motion picture projectors	12	1	800	4	3,200
VCR playback units	7	1	1,400	3	4,200
Filmstrip projectors	25	3	900	4	1,200
Overhead projectors	40	6	1,200	8	1,600
Projection carts	75	8	800	14	1,400
Slide projectors	25	3	1,200	5	2,000
Screens	60	8	800	10	1,000
Microfiche reader	6	1	300	1	300
Total			$12,600.00		$22,300.00
Cost per pupil			$ 5.25		$ 9.29

Note: District with three schools, 2,400 students, and 70 classrooms.

Figure 11.7. Justifying a media equipment budget based upon cost per pupil.

Library/Media Materials	Present Inventory	Continuity Level	Continuity Level Cost	Incremental Level	Incremental Level Cost
Library books	50,000	600	$15,000	1,200	$ 30,000
Periodicals	50	50	2,500	60	3,000
Media materials	600	60	24,000	120	48,000
Films					
Videocassettes	600	60	6,000	120	12,000
CD-ROMs	50	5	250	10	500
Videodiscs	25	3	300	5	500
Other	1,000	100	10,000	0	10,000
Total			$58,050.00		$104,000.00
Cost per pupil			$ 24.18		$ 43.33

Note: District with three schools, 2,400 students, and 70 classrooms.

Figure 11.8. Justifying a media materials budget based upon cost per pupil.

Past Utilization

Justifying a budget based upon past utilization by patrons builds a strong case. How can one argue against success? This strategy requires that detailed records be kept regarding patron use. It is a time-consuming task, but through the use of well-designed booking forms, the necessary data can be collected, collated, and used effectively. The use of a computer to manage the logistical tasks within the media center simplifies the recording and collection of pertinent data. The data used must be sorted, selected, and summarized carefully so that only the most important factors are employed to demonstrate the value of the services rendered. If too much information is included, it may not be read by busy administrators. Remember the rule from chapter 2: "Keep it simple." We can add to that rule in budgeting: "Keep it simple but appropriate and precise" (see figure 11.9).

Department	Utilization					Percentage Change from Last Year
	93–94	94–95	95–96	96–97	97–98	
Media Library	11,000	11,645	12,056	12,602	13,119	+9.6
Media Production	15,101	15,721	16,252	16,780	17,351	+9.7
Media Equipment	11,760	12,205	12,620	13,341	13,892	+9.6
Television Services	6,063	6,321	6,894	7,540	8,162	+9.2
Computer Services	2,413	3,520	4,650	4,800	5,280	+9.0
Total Requests	46,337	49,412	52,472	55,063	57,804	+9.5

Figure 11.9. Justifying a media budget based upon past utilization.

Accepted Standards

Another strategy to build budget support is to compare existing resources with those recommended by state and national organizations and accrediting associations. This strategy is effective if the level of the resources in your media service program is below the minimum recommended by such groups. Obviously, the standards can work against you if you have resources that exceed the minimum. The media manager should determine the availability of recognized standards that are appropriate for his or her type of institution.

An influential document affecting K-12 schools is *Information Power: Guidelines for School Library Media Programs*. These guidelines were developed jointly by the American Association of School Librarians (AASL) and the Association for Educational Communications and Technology (AECT) (AASL and AECT 1988). While this document does not suggest specific quantity standards for collections, personnel, and facilities for library media programs, it does include recommendations for various levels of service based upon a national study of 4,500 K-12 public schools.

Information is divided into categories of elementary, middle, and high schools with enrollments of under 500 and enrollments over 500. There is an added category for high schools with enrollments of over 1,000. The guidelines emphasize planning, curriculum development, leadership, and promoting access to information. A recent version of *Information Power* (1998) changed the emphasis to standards for information literacy. Those administrators planning for individual public school buildings need to review this publication carefully to see how the new standards impact budgets.

AECT has published standards for resource centers in higher education. Their publication, *Standards for College and University Learning Resources Programs: Technology in Instruction*, provides standards rather than guidelines (AECT 1989).

The National Commission on Libraries and Information Science (NCLIS), an independent federal agency, developed a statement of priorities and policies entitled *Towards a National Program for Library and Information Services: Goals for Action* (NCLIS 1975). This document emphasized the need that library media centers be a part of a nationwide resource-sharing network. In 1978, the *Report of the Task Force on the Role of School Library Media Programs in Networking* (NCLIS 1978) was published, which presented the position of representatives from educational media associations and local and state agencies toward a resource-sharing network. Another noteworthy and helpful document is a summary of the proceedings and recommendations of the First White House Conference on Library and Information Science, held in 1980. The report is entitled *Information for the Eighties* (NCLIS 1980).

Most associations that accredit institutions of higher education include media standards within their evaluation criteria, and they should not be overlooked. Professional organizations at the state, regional, and national levels also sometimes develop standards.

The 1996 National Education Summit addressed how to infuse the public education system with new technologies and tools for improved teaching, learning, and school administration. One of the conference's policy statements was that technology is the equalizer in educational advancement (Lawton 1996). The Center for Children and Technology Education Development Center, Inc. (96 Morton Street, 7th Floor, New York, NY 10014) conducts research on educational technology and evaluates technology offerings for schools. In addition, the following organizations are promoting improved education standards, often including technology as a key component:

Council for Basic Education, 1319 F Street, NW, Suite 900, Washington, DC 20004-1154

Education Commission of the States, 707 17th Street, Denver, CO 80202-3427

National Educational Goals Panel, 1850 M Street, NW, Suite 270, Washington, DC 20036

New Standards, 700 11th Street, NW, Suite 750, Washington, DC 20001

Public Agenda, 6 East 39th Street, New York, NY 10016

Zero-Base or PPBS Budgeting System

The use of either ZBB or PPBS is an effective method of justifying a budget. These two systems are effective because they are all-inclusive. Both systems require detailed preparation of goals, objectives, alternatives, costs, and quantitative performance evaluation methods for meeting each budget objective. If each part of these budgeting systems is developed correctly, the justification is automatically an integral part of each objective.

BUDGETING TEMPTATIONS

After developing a budget, a media manager must avoid several temptations. Succumbing to them may mean losing both credibility with the administration and support for any budget—regardless of how good the justification. Therefore, develop *honest* budgets by avoiding the following pitfalls:

Never pad a budget request. For large projects, add a 5 or 10 percent contingency cost to cover unforeseen expenses, but label it as just that.

Do not try to hide costs. Do not try to obtain something by calling it something else or by padding the cost of some items to obtain funds to purchase something else.

Do not switch funds from one category to another after allocations are made. Making an occasional switch to cover unforeseen problems is acceptable, but the media manager who constantly switches funds is demonstrating poor planning.

The manager who follows the above advice will have greater budgeting success through the years.

MONITORING THE BUDGET

After the budget has been developed and funded, expenditures must be monitored. The allocation systems and accounting codes previously discussed must be implemented into a ledger system to allow easy monitoring of income and expenditures. While the ledger system can be handled manually as was done in the past, it is much easier to manage using a computer. Changes are easier to make, mathematical calculations can be programmed to be automatic, and printouts can be made at any time.

The practice of developing separate media center accounting procedures should be avoided if possible. It is inefficient to maintain duplicate sets of records. The media manager and the institution's accounting office should work cooperatively to develop accounting practices that will meet the needs of both the accounting and media services offices. Only when this is not possible should a media manager establish a duplicate set of accounting records.

SUGGESTED ACTIVITIES

1. Obtain and study the budgeting system used in an institution. Examine, illustrate, and define how the media service budget is placed within that system.

2. Select one media center department and develop a hypothetical budget, based upon figures supplied by your instructor. Write the budget in one of the seven budgeting system formats, applying the recommended procedures for developing a media service budget when the procedures are appropriate.

REFERENCES

American Association of School Librarians and Association for Educational Communications and Technology. 1998. *Information Power: Building Partnerships for Learning.* Chicago: American Library Association.

———. 1988. *Information Power: Guidelines for School Library Media Programs.* Chicago: American Library Association.

Association for Educational Communications and Technology. 1989. *Standards for College and University Learning Resources Programs: Technology in Instruction.* 2d ed. Washington, D.C.: Association for Educational Communications and Technology.

Fowler, William J. 1990. *Financial Accounting for Local and State School Systems.* Washington, D.C.: U.S. National Center for Educational Statistics.

Lawton, Millicent. 1996. "Summit Accord Calls for Focus on Standards." *Education Week,* 15, no. 28: 1-3.

National Commission on Libraries and Information Science. 1980. *Information for the Eighties.* Washington, D.C.: National Commission on Libraries and Information Science.

———. 1978. *Report of the Task Force on the Role of School Library Media Programs in Networking.* Washington, D.C.: National Commission on Libraries and Information Science.

———. 1975. *Towards a National Program for Library and Information Services: Goals for Action.* Washington, D.C.: National Commission on Libraries and Information Science.

Rugg, K. C. 1960. *Improving Instruction: Budgeting Your Audio-Visual Program.* Bloomington, Ind.: Audio-Visual Council on Public Information.

Tracy, John A. 1996. *Budgeting A'La Carte: Essential Tools for Harried Business Managers.* New York: John Wiley & Sons.

SELECTED BIBLIOGRAPHY

Kaganoff, Tessa. *Collaboration, Technology, and Outsourcing Initiatives in Higher Education: A Literature Review.* Santa Monica, Calif.: Rand, 1998.

Keltner, Brent, and Randy L. Ross. *The Cost of School-Based Educational Technology Programs.* Santa Monica, Calif.: Rand, 1996.

Marlow, Eugene. *Managing Corporate Media.* Rev. ed. White Plains, N.Y.: Knowledge Industry Publications, 1989.

Miner, Lynn E., Jeremy T. Miner, and Jerry Griffith. *Proposal Planning and Writing*. 2d ed. Phoenix, Ariz.: Oryx Press, 1998.

Morris, Betty J., John T. Gillespie, and Diana L. Spirt. *Administering the School Library Media Center*. 3d ed. New Providence, N.J.: R. R. Bowker, 1992.

Rubin, Irene S. *The Politics of Public Budgeting: Getting and Spending, Borrowing and Balancing*. Chatham, N.J.: Chatham Publishers, 1990.

Schmid, William T. *Media Center Management: A Practical Guide*. New York: Hastings House, 1980.

COMMUNICATING

Effective communication can no longer be considered possible with words alone. The very nature of language, coupled with limited experiences of most people, often makes it difficult to convey ideas and information efficiently without resources beyond words.

Jerrold E. Kemp, *Planning and Producing*
Audiovisual Materials, 1963

OBJECTIVES

At the conclusion of this chapter you should be able to

1. Describe five important communication lessons from America's best-run companies.

2. Describe the most important and best methods for communicating with employees and patrons.

3. List and describe three other communication vehicles that can be used to communicate with employees.

4. List and describe four communication vehicles that can be used to communicate with patrons.

5. Describe three types of inservice activities that can be used effectively by a media manager.

6. Describe the before, during, and after activities for conducting effective meetings.

The function of media service programs is to make materials available to teachers, trainers, salespersons, and administrators to enable them to communicate more effectively with students, trainees, employees, colleagues, potential customers, or the general public. Most media managers rise to these tasks and perform them well. They make appropriate instructional materials and display equipment available to patrons and develop media development facilities to produce in-house materials in photo, graphic, video, and multimedia formats. They also establish procedures for retrieving, circulating, and repairing materials. However, the tasks are not complete at that point. Successful managers must also be specialists in another type of communication—public relations. Their public includes the center's staff, patrons, their immediate supervisor, and the administrators of the institution. As was emphasized in chapter 10, staff members perform better when they know that they are integral to the service program. That requires communication. If patrons are to use the program services, they must know what is available and how to obtain the services. That also requires communication. Financial support is likely to be greater when administrators know what services the program provides and their value to the institution. That also does not happen by chance; rather, it comes about through a deliberate communication program. Before we present ideas on how to meet that challenge, some lessons on communication from American businesses may be helpful.

COMMUNICATION LESSONS FROM AMERICA'S BEST-RUN COMPANIES

Thomas J. Peters and Robert H. Waterman, Jr. (1982, 122–23), from their study of America's best-run companies, found that the excellent companies in the United States have "a vast network of informal, open communications." They call this the "technology of keeping in touch." They emphasize that "keeping in touch" means an extraordinary amount of communication throughout the institution. It means that people are working together in many kinds of settings, discussing problems, programs, and solutions. They further emphasize this usually means small groups of people, not large groups. The groups usually consist of a mix of people from the organization. Lunchrooms are designed to encourage communication between people. Peters and Waterman further state that the "intensity of communications is unmistakable in excellent companies." Using their findings, they list the following five attributes of communication systems that foster communication (Peters and Waterman 1982, 218–23):

1. *Communication systems are informal.* An attitude of openness must be prevalent so that everyone is free to discuss any problem. Barriers to conversation are removed. A policy of "open door" is practiced where employees are encouraged to talk with management. Managers are expected to get out of the office and manage while walking around.

2. *Communication intensity is extraordinary.* There is an attitude of openness, bluntness, and straightforwardness when discussing issues. No holds are barred and in meetings no one is afraid to challenge the chairman, president, or a board member. People are not afraid to talk because they talk together all the time.

3. *Communication is given physical supports.* An abundance of small conference rooms with chalkboards are available. Management encourages groups to have lunch together, and related departments are located physically close to each other to encourage "chance" informal communication.

4. *Forcing devices are created.* To spawn innovations, the best companies create and place a limited number of outstanding thinkers into special programs. Assignments may be made for a short period of time or several years. Programs are of a "think tank" nature, where the recipients are expected to dream, create, or shake up the system. Another forcing device is to expect managers to use a minimum of 20 percent of their time experimenting with new technologies. Regardless of the methodology used, the purpose is to spawn new ideas for the institution.

5. *Intense, informal communications systems act as a control system.* Because employees are observant and free to ask questions and make suggestions informally, projects that do not work are quickly identified before millions of dollars are expended.

Peters and Waterman, in quoting a 3M executive, related: "We just plain talk to each other without a lot of paper or formal rigmarole" (1982, 123). That effectively summarizes the authors' findings on the value of communication in the best-run companies. It would seem that a media manager should develop and apply communication practices being used effectively by the best-run companies in both the internal and external public relations efforts of the media center.

Try to remain aware of all of the factors that interfere with effective communication. Consider that each person (including yourself) hears messages that have passed through a number of filters which change or distort, to a certain extent, what was intended to be communicated, as is shown in figure 12.1. Good communication is thoughtful communication. Hearing what people are really saying is critical to being able to provide thoughtful answers.

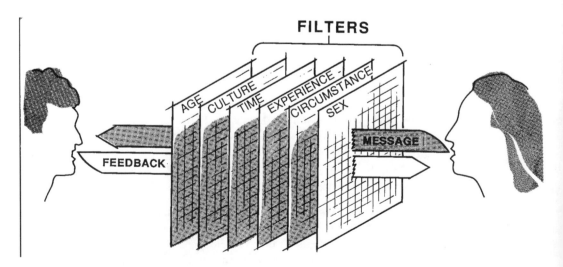

Figure 12. 1. Communication filters.

It might be good here to make at least one observation about the importance of listening. Listening to others is a cultivated skill; it usually does not just happen, though some people are better listeners than others. People usually have to train themselves in this most important task, for it is often difficult to concentrate upon what a speaker is saying without thinking about what you are going to say when the speaker stops talking. Take a few moments to compose your message based upon what the speaker has said. If you are not sure, summarize what you think you heard and let the speaker respond.

COMMUNICATION WITHIN THE MEDIA SERVICE ORGANIZATION

Personal Communication

It should be apparent from the previous discussion that personal and direct communication between employees and the media manager is the cornerstone of an internal communication program. Kenneth Blanchard and Spencer Johnson, in *The One Minute Manager* (1984, 100), further amplify that value. According to them, this manager does the following:

He sets One Minute Goals.

He gives One Minute Praisings.

He gives One Minute Reprimands.

He asks brief, important questions, speaks the truth, laughs, works, and enjoys.

And perhaps the most important of all, he encourages the people he works with to do the same.

All of these management tasks involve personal and direct communication. A smart media manager will employ personal communication daily or whenever possible.

While the ideal communication plan would be to personally interact with every employee daily, this is not always possible. Some information can best be communicated in other ways. Personal and written communication techniques should be used to their best advantage. Michael Hammer, in *Beyond Reengineering,* encourages looking at the whole process in a company (in manufacturing a product or completing a task) and has this view of the importance of communication:

> One particular skill is absolutely required in a process-centered world: communication. Despite the ever-increasing intrusion of technology into our world, human beings remain its key actors. Indeed, as machines take over more of the drone work, uniquely human abilities come to the fore. Process-centered work is interpersonal work. We no longer perform individual tasks in isolation; we perform processes in teams. Teams do not succeed unless they are based on solid mutual understanding. To that end, strong oral and written communication skills are essential (1996, 236).

Memos or Memorandums

Memos are short written statements. While the dictionary defines *memos* and *memorandums* as identical, we prefer to make a distinction. A memo should be used to provide information only. The information may be a brief summary of an agreement made among several people, or general information about a project, or just a reminder of an activity. A memorandum is a stronger document. It states what or how something is to be done. While we hesitate to use the term *order*, a memorandum might be considered as an order. It would be used in this context after the appropriate program coordinators and media manager and staff, when suitable, agree to a specific task or procedure. Memos and memorandums should be short and limited to one page. Again, keep it simple. Boil down what you have to say to what you really *want* to say. Remove the fluff to achieve better understanding. A recent advertisement said it succinctly: "One minute managers need ten second memos."

Reports

Reports are written or oral summaries of activities. A written report is used to present very detailed information. Examples of written reports are quarterly or annual reports, project status reports, and/or budget reports. Oral reports can be used to present a summary of meetings or workshops, but when detailed information is also to be presented, it should be summarized in written format for distribution. Written reports can be personalized by addressing the report to each employee or by distributing copies of the report to employees and discussing them during staff meetings. And once again, keep it simple.

Staff Meetings

Staff meetings are a good way of keeping employees informed, maintaining high morale, and keeping communication open. Establish and schedule a minimum of one meeting per month for the entire media center staff. Have a short agenda prepared and distributed before the meeting and provide an opportunity for the department coordinators or project heads to give a short summary of activities within their department. For the benefit of new employees, ask each employee on a rotating basis to explain his or her responsibilities to others during a staff meeting. Read appropriate thank-you or praise letters at staff meetings. Allow time for discussion, and have some meetings with no scheduled agenda to allow staff to just talk. Finally, have refreshments available, even if the cost is out of pocket; the human relations benefits that result are well worth the expense.

In addition to monthly media center staff meetings, a department coordinator's meeting should be scheduled weekly to discuss problems and solutions, and to brainstorm new programs or ideas. Such meetings should never last longer than two hours. Always work for consensus on all issues, but when this is impossible carefully weigh each department coordinator's input and do not be afraid to make the necessary decisions. Afterward, give the coordinators your rationale for the decision, to let them know that their input was considered.

Employees are usually the most alert early in their shift, so that is the best time to schedule productive meetings. Under no circumstances should meetings continue after hours.

Informal Activities

Many informal opportunities exist for communicating with others. They include break times, lunch in the lounge, or external activities like picnics, on the golf course, or in community or social organizations. During these activities, media managers and their employees can get to know each other as people. The key here, however, is to not talk shop. If something comes up, that is okay; otherwise talk about other things. Do not keep bringing up the job, or soon you will be avoided in informal social situations.

COMMUNICATING WITH PATRONS

The media manager must also communicate with patrons and potential patrons. Patrons will not use media services unless they know what is available. For that reason, one must maintain an effective public relations program. The manager, therefore, wears many communication hats: visualizer, writer, speaker, and advertiser. How can this challenge to communicate with patrons and potential patrons be met, and what communication vehicles are available to the media manager to present his or her messages to those patrons and potential patrons?

The first logical step is to identify the media service programs that are available to patrons and what messages are to be presented. The second step is to determine who the potential patrons are and where they are. Are they within the institution, in various distant locations, or completely outside of the institution? That may make a difference in how to reach your audience. After identifying these factors, appropriate communication vehicles for delivering messages can be selected.

Several communication delivery vehicles that can be used effectively for delivering public relations messages have already been discussed: short memos, reports, and informal activities. Memos can be sent to potential customers alerting them to available services, media collections, and procedures for obtaining them. Reports can be created and mailed to cover more detailed information about the value of the services, research findings that document that value, and existing utilization summaries. Finally, the informal and personal activities of having coffee and lunch with potential patrons and taking advantage of social contacts with them within the community cannot be overemphasized. Other communication vehicles that can also be used in a public relations program follow.

Publications

Publications include newsletters, brochures, and catalogs. Developments in desktop publishing have simplified the process and lowered the cost of creating and producing such publications.

Newsletters can cover a broad range of information in short, concise, capsule form. Enough information should be provided to stir the interest of the reader. Newsletters can include short progress reports of projects, summaries of appropriate research findings, listings of new holdings in the media collections, and notices of new equipment available to patrons. Newsletters normally are published on a regular basis, that is, bimonthly, monthly, or quarterly. The format of newsletters should be consistent from issue to issue and each given a date, volume number, and issue number for future reference.

Brochures are short pamphlets or booklets that can be used to advertise all the services or to describe the various programs of the center. The content of brochures should answer questions regarding what services are available, who can obtain them, where and how they can be obtained, and when. They can be as short as a single sheet of paper folded several times, or they can be several pages. However, apply the rule, "Keep it simple," with the brochures limited to four to six pages maximum (figure 12.2).

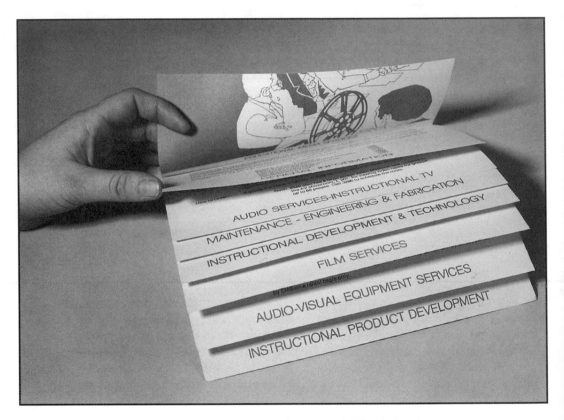

Figure 12.2. Information brochure. (Photograph by Benjamin Hambelton.)

Catalogs are most often used in media centers to provide listings of the center's instructional materials collection with a short content description of each title. Titles are also listed under extensive subject headings in the front of the catalog. All media formats can be included, including computer programs. As was discussed in chapter 8, because of the increasing availability of computers in institutions, most media managers are using computer catalogs in place of printed ones. Catalogs are convenient for patrons in either print or electronic formats because they can be available in their own workplace.

Displays and Media Presentations

Displays also can be used to advertise programs. Displays can graphically or visually describe media programs and can be placed in locations where display boards or space exist within buildings.

Media presentations can also be used for promotional purposes. A videotape or a computer-based multimedia program can be very effective in communicating the services available to patrons.

Electronic Communication

Within the past decade, electronic means have emerged which are potentially powerful ways to improve communication.

Voice mail is nothing more than providing a message to the incoming caller to leave a recorded message and phone number. This feature, while frustrating to some, can be much more effective than constantly playing "telephone tag." The incoming recorded message may provide all the information needed. Voice mail should be used by individual staff members while away from their office. The media center, however, should always have personnel answer all incoming calls during open hours. It is annoying to reach a voice mail message with no opportunity to immediately talk to a live person.

Electronic mail, or e-mail, is the sending of messages from your computer to other individuals with computers. Each party involved must have an e-mail address. The outstanding feature of e-mail is its great speed. E-mail can be used to rapidly solve or at least shed light on a subject without having numerous meetings. Another advantage is that it can greatly reduce the amount of paperwork flowing between participants. Electronic mail is evolving into a communication system whereby participants will be able to see each other and share graphic images as they communicate using their computers. This new system is often called desktop teleconferencing.

A Web site is another valuable means of communicating with patrons and colleagues. Your media program can create a Web site which can be easily accessed by interested parties. Your Web site can provide patrons with information on your hours, services, new acquisitions or procedures, and many other types of information. This information can be easily and constantly updated. Patrons and colleagues connected to the Internet and using a browser such as Netscape or Internet Explorer can easily connect to your site and retrieve information including text, graphics, sound, animation, and even video. A Web site can eliminate the need for newsletters and brochures *if* all of your patrons have Internet access. In any case, if some do not have access, the creation of a Web site will greatly reduce the quantity of newsletters you will have to reproduce. An example of a media center's home page promotion is shown in figure 12.3, page 268.

Thousands of Internet discussion groups, or listservs, exist. These groups can become a valuable method of communicating with colleagues in the media/technology field. You can subscribe to a discussion group in areas in which you want to receive and/or contribute input. For details on how to subscribe, consult one of the sources dealing with the Internet in the bibliography at the end of this chapter.

Figure 12.3. Media center home page. Reprinted with permission of Puget Sound Educational Service District Multimedia Services, Burien, Washington.

A word of caution: Electronic communication can depersonalize human inter-action. While electronic communication brings us powerful new tools, be careful to not lose the personal direct interaction with patrons and others. Electronic communication tools can make your operation very efficient, but without one-to-one interaction you may diminish or lose the camaraderie that translates into support for your program.

EVALUATION

Periodic evaluation of communication is important. Far too often our communication is one way, without adequate feedback from our patrons. Figure 12.4, page 270, is a good example of a brief instrument which can gather information about the quality of communication from the public being served.

INSERVICE ACTIVITIES

The many existing inservice activities should not be overlooked; these include tours of the media center, open houses, workshops, and faculty or staff meetings. Here one should seek out opportunities to make a short pitch regarding the center's activities and capabilities and how clients and students can make use of them.

Open House

An open house or tour of the media center provides patrons and potential patrons with an opportunity to see the media facilities and learn what services are available. Center tours also provide an opportunity for the media center staff to interact personally with potential clients. New acquisitions and materials produced by the center can be viewed. Every media center should schedule an open house with tours at least once a year. It is an effective information and public relations tool.

Workshops

Workshops are also useful public relations tools. Materials publicizing workshops should list specific objectives so that readers have an opportunity to determine whether the content is pertinent to them. Workshops are especially effective for presenting, demonstrating, and providing an opportunity for participants to learn and practice media application and presentation skills. If participants come to a workshop because of the objectives stated in the publicity and experience actual involvement with the content, they are apt to apply the skills learned and thereby make better use of the center's media services.

Faculty/Trainer Development

Some media service centers conduct a systematic faculty/trainer development program. Such programs include open house and workshop activities, but may also include various types of competitive grants aimed at improving teaching/training, consultation on improving teaching/training techniques and strategies, and various other strategies for making faculty or trainers more effective. In some institutions,

PUGET SOUND MULTIMEDIA SERVICES • COMMUNICATIONS EVALUATION FORM

Help us determine if our communication vehicles are working by filling out the form below. Please include the name of your school and district: _____

1. Are current forms of communication between MM Services and schools adequate?   ☐ Yes   ☐ No
   (Electronic Catalog-Medianet, *Multi/Media News*, Subject Flyers, School Presentations)
   If not, what else should we include? _____

2. Are you using the Medianet electronic catalog to locate media resources?   ☐ Yes   ☐ No
   If not, why?   ☐ lack of Internet access   ☐ unaware of services   ☐ need training   ☐ other _____

3. Is the information presented in the MultiMedia Newsletter relevant/helpful?   ☐ Yes   ☐ No
   If not, what should be included? _____

4. Are the Subject Flyers useful in selecting media for classroom use?   ☐ Yes   ☐ No   ☐ Didn't see
   (18 subjects were covered in 96-97. They were sent to school libraries and given to teachers during presentations.)
   What additional topics should be covered next year? _____

5. Would you find site visitation by our professional staff of benefit to your school?   ☐ Yes   ☐ No
   What information should be covered during the presentation? _____

Please return this form by **May 23, 1997** to Ann McLean, Director via:
1) weekly couriers 2) snail mail: Puget Sound ESD • 400 SW 152nd Street • Burien, WA 98166

Figure 12.4. Communication evaluation form. Reprinted with permission from Puget Sound Educational Service District Multimedia Services, Burien, Washington.

faculty/trainer development is a separate program. But, if one does not exist at your institution, consider starting one; it is a program that can give a media center some highly positive visibility.

Meetings

Media managers should not overlook the value of giving presentations during faculty or staff meetings. Such meetings sometimes provide a captive audience of potential patrons who may never have come to any optional invitational meetings when the choice was left to them. Presentations made at these meetings are usually limited to a very short period of time. They must, therefore, be planned carefully, and the media manager should use media skillfully to demonstrate their value as the message is presented. It is after such sessions that one gets the "Can you do this?" or "How did you do that?" or "Where can I get this?" types of questions.

CONDUCTING MEETINGS

All managers must conduct a variety of meetings within their institutions and may sometimes be asked to conduct meetings in regional and state organizations. While media managers grow accustomed to conducting meetings within the media center, they may be uneasy and uncomfortable when asked to do the same elsewhere. There is no need for anxiety if certain simple rules are followed. When rules are not established and followed, meetings can become a waste of time with no accomplishments. The following suggestions should help one to avoid that problem.

Before the Meeting

1. Establish the objectives. State precisely what it is you want to accomplish during the meeting. Identify the topics, problems, or issues that are to be discussed.

2. Estimate and establish time allotments for each objective or topic.

3. Gather appropriate materials and data for committee members.

4. Send the agenda and appropriate materials to the committee members.

5. Check the meeting room to be sure it is conducive to discussion and that needed media equipment is available.

During the Meeting

1. At the first meeting, get acquainted. Members should be introduced and asked to tell something about themselves. This might be the entire objective of the first meeting—to get acquainted. In subsequent meetings only guests or new members would be introduced.

2. State and clarify objectives, topics, problems, or issues to be discussed.

3. Add or delete topics from the agenda as necessary, based upon input from participants.

4. Revise and make time allotments for each topic.

5. Coordinate the meeting. Do not let any one person dominate the discussion, and encourage all to participate. Listen carefully and ask probing questions. Work toward consensus. Stick to time limits and come back to issues if possible.

6. Summarize agreements as the meeting progresses.

7. Make assignments if necessary.

8. Schedule the next meeting time and place.

At a media leadership conference many years ago, Dr. Maurice L. Pettit, then of Central Washington University, in speaking about making meetings more effective, advised the group to not only have a recorder but also an observer. The recorder records content; the observer observes the process used and gives feedback to the group by serving as a mirror. He went on to say that groups sometimes do not know when they have made a decision or solved a problem. Sometimes the group will talk right by an agreement until finally they are in disagreement. An observer can help the group avoid this and enable it to "pick up the winnings" when it is clear that a decision has been made (Anderson and Schmidt 1976).

After the Meeting

1. Summarize agreements and accomplishments. Write up only agreements, not a detailed description of the discussion. If a meeting secretary is used, give directions for writing the summary of agreements and review carefully.

2. Distribute the summary of agreements to members prior to the next meeting with a copy of the next meeting's agenda.

Following these suggestions, coordinating meetings will be easier, more effective, and productive. Communication is extremely important in meetings; it cannot be overstated that the coordinator must attempt to remove all barriers to communication. All must feel free to express themselves; an attitude of openness must exist.

SUGGESTED ACTIVITIES

1. List and describe five communication concepts employed by some of America's best-run companies.

2. State what you think is the most important method to communicate with employees and describe how you, as a media manager, can use that method.

3. List and describe four other vehicles that can be used to communicate with employees.

4. List and describe four communication vehicles that can be used to communicate with patrons.

5. Discuss the appropriate before, during, and after activities to perform when conducting meetings. Develop an agenda for a meeting demonstrating the above concepts.

REFERENCES

Anderson, Joyce, and William D. Schmidt, eds. 1976. Region IX of Association for Educational Communications and Technology Conference, Identifying and Utilizing Management Resources Effectively. Ellensburg, Wash.: Central Washington University.

Blanchard, Kenneth, and Spencer Johnson. 1984. *The One Minute Manager.* New York: Berkeley Publishing Group.

Hammer, Michael. 1996. *Beyond Reengineering: How the Process-Centered Organization Is Changing Our World and Our Lives.* New York: HarperBusiness.

Kemp, Jerrold E. 1963. *Planning and Producing Audiovisual Materials.* San Francisco: Chandler Publishing.

Peters, Thomas J., and Robert H. Waterman, Jr. 1982. *In Search of Excellence: Lessons from America's Best-Run Companies.* New York: Warner Books.

MEDIA RESOURCES

Be Prepared to Speak: The Step-by-Step Video Guide to Public Speaking. Katola-Skeie Productions, 22 minutes. San Diego, Calif.: Toastmasters International, 1985. Videocassette.

Educational Technology '97: Anything, Anytime, Anywhere, with Anyone. Dallas Teleconferences, 90 minutes. Dallas, Tex.: Dallas County Community College District, 1997. Videocassette.

I Have a Dream: The Nature of Great Speaking. John M. Davidson, 25 minutes. Davis, Calif.: Davidson Films, 1994. Videocassette.

In Search of Excellence: Lessons from America's Best-Run Companies. Nathan Tyler Productions, 88 minutes. Alexandria, Va.: Public Broadcasting Service, 1985. Videocassette.

Language of Leadership: The Churchill Method. Andrew B. Walworth, 70 minutes. Washington, D.C.: Blackwell Corporation, 1992. Videocassette.

SELECTED BIBLIOGRAPHY

Angell, David. *The Elements of E-mail Style: Communicate Effectively via Electronic Mail.* Reading, Mass.: Addison-Wesley, 1994.

Armstrong, Grady. "One Approach to Motivating Faculty to Use Multimedia." *Technological Horizons in Education Journal,* 23, no. 10 (1996): 67–71.

Barron, Ann E., and Karen S. Ivers. 2d ed. *The Internet and Instruction: Activities and Ideas.* Englewood, Colo.: Libraries Unlimited, 1998.

Eidgaby, S. Y., and John P. Shearman. "Training Partnerships Keiretsu Style." *TechTrends,* 40, no. 4 (1995): 12–17.

Lauro, Dennis R. "Five Approaches to Professional Development Compared." *Technological Horizons in Education Journal,* 22, no. 10 (1995): 61–65.

Marlow, Eugene. *Managing the Corporate Media Center.* Rev. ed. White Plains, N.Y.: Knowledge Industry Publications, 1989.

Morris, Betty J., John T. Gillespie, and Diana L. Spirt. *Administering the School Library Media Center.* 3d ed. Providence, N.J.: R. R. Bowker, 1992.

Williams, Constance D. *The Internet for Newbies: An Easy Access Guide.* Englewood, Colo.: Libraries Unlimited, 1996.

Zenor, Stanley, ed. "Creative Partnerships Bring Training Education Opportunities to Adult Learners." *TechTrends,* 40, no. 4 (1995): 10–11.

EVALUATING MEDIA SERVICE PROGRAMS

In our data banks we should document the causes and effects, the congruence of intent and accomplishment, and the panorama of judgments of those concerned. Such records should be kept to promote educational action, not obstruct it. The countenance of evaluation should be one of data gathering that leads to decision-making, not to trouble-making.

Robert E. Stake, "The Countenance of
Educational Evaluation," in *Classic Writings on
Instructional Technology*, 1996

OBJECTIVES

At the conclusion of this chapter you should be able to

1. State six reasons or purposes for evaluating media service programs.

2. List five questions that an effective evaluation program should answer.

3. Discuss the type of information that should be collected to find answers to the above five questions.

4. List who should be involved in a media center evaluation program, and describe their involvement and the type of information that can be obtained from each.

5. Describe the contents of several established media standards that should be considered for comparison purposes when evaluating a media center.

6. Name, describe, and explain how three types of data can be collected for an evaluation program.

7. List and describe four levels of evaluation programs.

8. List the logical steps in sequential order for implementing an evaluation program.

9. Describe how evaluation results can be used by a media manager.

In earlier chapters the media manager was advised to develop a philosophical base upon which to build media service programs as well as to develop service programs based upon needs. Further, one must develop and implement logistical procedures to make the services easily available to patrons, use the computer as a management tool, be sensitive to employee needs, and develop an effective budgeting system. The importance of developing effective communications with staff, patrons, and superiors has been emphasized. This chapter considers evaluating how well these tasks have been performed. Basically, an evaluation program must ask four questions: Why evaluate? What should be evaluated? Who should evaluate? and How should an evaluation program be accomplished? Systematic evaluation of media service programs is important to determine if the services, staff, and programs are meeting the needs of patrons.

WHY SHOULD MEDIA SERVICE PROGRAMS BE EVALUATED?

Evaluation is an important and difficult task. Parents or stockholders want to know how well their schools or businesses are doing. Administrators want to know how well the departments within an organization are performing. Business and production managers want to know how good the products (learners or goods) are and at what cost that quality is achieved. Program evaluation is inevitable, and that is as it should be. It is not a matter of whether the media service program will be subject to an evaluation, but rather whether the evaluation will be based upon valid, adequate, and accurate data. Wise managers will not wait for an evaluation to be thrust upon them; they will make evaluation an integral part of the overall service program. Accountability is the sole purpose of evaluation, and before embarking on an evaluation program some definition is in order. A careful perusal of several current expositions on evaluation reveals a relatively consistent agreement on what evaluation is. Michael Patton best summarizes the various definitions in his book *Practical Evaluation:*

> In the last fifteen years evaluation has emerged as a distinctive field of professional social science practice. The practice of evaluation involves the systematic collection of information about the activities, characteristics, and outcomes of programs, personnel, and products for use by specific people to reduce uncertainties, improve effectiveness, and make decisions with regard to what those programs, personnel, or products are doing and effecting (1982, 15).

Patton's definition makes it clear that to be systematic, an evaluation must be carefully planned. Activities to be assessed must be identified, outcomes of the program studied, and the people who serve programs and produce products evaluated. The results derived from an evaluation program must be studied and used to help personnel to improve their performance. Morris, Gillespie, and Spirt provide a definition that is more closely focused upon media services. They have defined evaluation as looking at all aspects of the functions of the school media center to determine the quality of each program component: the staff, the facilities, the collection, and the services provided. Because educational quality is an ever-changing phenomenon, the evaluation of the school library media center must be continuous. It must be done with the mission statement, goals, and objectives of a particular school media center in mind (1992, 499).

Several important concepts, implied within that short definition, should be emphasized. First, evaluation is a *continuous process*. It is not a task that is completed once or occasionally. If an evaluation program is to be useful it must be conducted yearly so that problems can be quickly identified. Second, both the *quality* and the *effectiveness* of the programs should be evaluated. There is a difference. Quality pertains to how well the services are provided, that is, logistical procedures work, services are provided on time, equipment is in good repair, and production standards are high. Effectiveness relates to whether or not the services produce the intended or expected results for recipients-learners, trainees, or viewers. Do the services enhance learning, increase interest, or motivate employees to perform better? Third, evaluation should involve the *users*. Users are the recipients of the services and, therefore, they can provide the best information about both the quality and effectiveness of the services provided. In order to accomplish effective evaluation, an organizational technology plan must be in place to provide the basis for this continuous, effective, and user-based approach. Finally, evaluation information is used *to make decisions* about the need for program modifications. Figure 13.1 graphs the evaluation process.

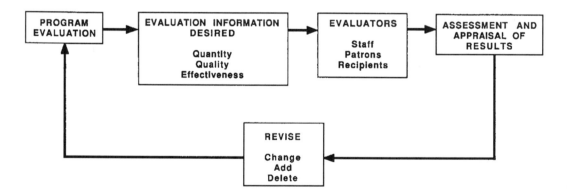

Figure 13.1. The evaluation process.

There are many reasons why an evaluation program should be an integral part of the media service program. Its design and implementation deserves the same detailed attention as any other service program provided by the unit.

Evaluation is a time-consuming endeavor; therefore, to assure that information gained will be worth the energy expended, careful planning must precede evaluation. The purposes or objectives of the evaluation must be clearly identified before the process can begin. There are many purposes for evaluating media service programs, including the following:

- As was stated in the preceding definition, one purpose of program evaluation is to gather information that can be used for making decisions. When evaluations are scheduled on an established schedule (yearly, biennially, etc.) they can provide useful comparison information. Increasing or decreasing utilization patterns may indicate that a program is healthy or that changes are needed. Media service programs must not be allowed to become static; they must change as needs change.

- An evaluation program can determine if existing logistical procedures are appropriate. Complaints may indicate that existing procedures are cumbersome or inefficient. As new automated equipment becomes available, the use of such equipment should be considered and, in most cases, implemented as soon as practicable.

- An evaluation program can identify small problems which can be corrected before they grow into large problems. Continuous equipment breakdowns and repeated scheduling errors, if allowed to continue, will soon be followed by a decline in patron use.

- A media service evaluation program can be used to improve staff performance. The evaluation methodology should include an appraisal of how well the staff members are providing the service for which they are responsible. Employees want to know how well they are delivering the services, as perceived by their patrons. If perceived positively, they will feel good about what they are doing and will continue to provide a high level of performance. If perceived negatively, most will seek to make corrections.

- Program evaluation can provide an opportunity for staff members to participate in program development. By reviewing a program evaluation report, staff members can see when changes are appropriate and will be willing to make those changes and adjust to revised work tasks and responsibilities. Strategic decisions on which services to add or increase and which to phase out or decrease can be appropriately made.

- Data collected by program evaluations can be used to justify the media budget and to defend the value of the program services. The worth of an evaluation program itself becomes evident when the manager is justifying budgets. Statistics proving that a program is effective are difficult to refute.

WHAT SHOULD BE EVALUATED?

After the discussion of the definition and purposes of evaluation it becomes apparent that the following questions should be answered by a media service evaluation program:

Are user needs identified?

Are services provided to meet those needs?

How well are those services being provided?

What should be changed to improve services?

Is quality leadership evident?

Are user needs identified? The most impressive and complete media service facility is of little value to an institution if it does not provide services that its patrons need. Media service programs do not exist to serve themselves, and media managers who think so will soon lose support. Programs must be built upon needs identified by the users; therefore, any evaluation program must seek information about how well the program has identified and is meeting those needs. Information must be sought to answer the following questions:

- Is there an active and positive relationship between those responsible for curriculum/learning improvement and media services?
- Are users actively involved in the development of media collections, services, policies, and procedures?
- Does a means exist to allow employees to provide input regarding the need for emerging service programs and technologies?

Are services being provided that meet user needs? Not only must user needs be identified, but, if a program is to be successful, services must be developed and implemented to serve those needs. The programs must be well defined, organized, and information on it disseminated so that all users and potential users will know what services are available. An effective evaluation program should seek to determine whether adequate programs have been developed and implemented. Answers to the following questions should be a part of the evaluation:

- What media service programs exist?
- Is instructional development an integral part of the media support program and services?
- Do utilization statistics indicate that the service programs are meeting user needs?
- Are classroom facilities and other learning spaces equipped for easy use of materials and technology?
- Are media development facilities adequate to produce quality materials for media service use?
- Do faculty and other employees of the institution know what services are available from the media center?

How well are the services being provided? As was noted in the definition of evaluation, two attributes, quality and effectiveness, must be examined when determining how well services are being provided. Several components of the quality attribute should be examined. The first is logistical procedures. Logistical procedures should be simple, accurate, and easy to follow and use. They should allow a user to locate and obtain what is needed quickly and with a minimum of effort, while still providing the media center with accurate user information and control.

The second component is the performance of the staff. The staff should be knowledgeable about the program policies and procedures and demonstrate the center's philosophy of helpfulness in a friendly manner. This staff evaluation should not be confused with the more detailed staff appraisal discussed in chapter 10. This evaluation should only ascertain how the employees relate to clients and deliver services; it does not evaluate the myriad of job tasks that each employee may be expected to perform.

A third component relates to in-house media development. The quality of any locally produced collection is determined by how well its content, instructional design, and technical production standards are met. While production quality—getting the best possible production—depends heavily upon the technology hardware being used, design and planning and the level of expertise of equipment operators are critical. Therefore, standards should be established and carefully monitored as an integral part of the center's evaluation program.

Another determinant of how well services are being provided is their effect on learners or recipients of the services. When instructional materials are employed in a teaching/learning environment, an evaluation program should attempt to assess how the materials facilitate learning. If materials from the collections or materials produced within the center are used for any other purpose (sales, demonstrations, etc.), the effect on the viewer should also be assessed. After all, a justifiable reason for using media resources is to bring about learning and improvement in the recipient. If the desired experience or change does not occur, the use may be a waste of time and money.

To help determine both the quality and effectiveness of media service programs, answers to the following questions should be helpful:

- Are media services provided to the clients with a minimum of inconvenience and operational service barriers?
- Are services available to the clients as needed?
- Are materials within the center's collection easy to locate and retrieve?
- Is the media center staff size adequate for meeting requests for service?
- Are the materials and equipment collections large enough to meet client needs?
- Do the resources used by clients actually enhance learning, provide experiences, or sell products?
- Are standards established and used in selecting quality instructional materials and for producing materials within the media center?

Is good leadership evident? Media center programs do not just happen. It takes a person or a team of individuals with insight and organizational and management abilities to develop and manage media service programs. Client needs must be identified, programs developed, reports prepared, policies and procedures established, and budgets justified. High-quality staff members must be employed and trained. Public relations and inservice training programs must be implemented. Without effective leadership, these activities will not occur and a program's success may be questionable. Therefore, program evaluation must include an evaluation of the media center's leadership.

The following questions should help determine the effectiveness of the center's leadership:

- Does the manager maintain a visible posture within the organization?
- Are clients and staff involved in program development?
- Does the management group delegate?
- Does the leadership possess personal and professional integrity?
- Are problems defined and analyzed and decisions made according to facts?

- Does the media service program have a well-organized public relations and inservice training program for the center's clients?
- Are staff development opportunities provided?
- Does the manager develop short-term and long-term program plans?
- Have appropriate policies and procedures been developed?
- Are the media center facilities adequate to meet client needs? Is there a plan for recommending continuous improvement of technology appropriate for learning spaces and hardware access?
- Is an adequate record system maintained and appropriate reports to management prepared regarding the services provided and needs of the media center?
- Has a continuous program evaluation plan been implemented to monitor the strengths and weaknesses of the media center?

What should be changed to improve the services? The final step in the evaluation program is to analyze the information collected to determine if changes need to be made, new programs added, or existing programs dropped or modified. Data must be carefully and objectively reviewed, comparisons should be made with previous evaluations, and trends questioned. Upward or downward trends may indicate a need for program change because of staffing problems or collection or production quality erosion. Problems need to be addressed and the indicated adjustments made. The evaluation should be shared and discussed with the entire staff. When credit or praise to staff members is due, it should be given with sincerity. Remember, many people have spent time and effort by the time an evaluation program has been completed; therefore, it is extremely important that time be taken to carefully review the collected information. Media center evaluations, when carefully used, can improve services provided to an institution's programs and provide data for justifying budgets or additional technology facilities.

WHO SHOULD EVALUATE MEDIA SERVICE PROGRAMS?

An oversimplified answer to the question, "Who should evaluate media service programs?" is "As many people as possible." However, implementing that concept would create many problems. More data may be collected than can be easily collated and interpreted. Everyone in an institution may not use the services of the media center, all may not take the time to complete an evaluation, and including too many could increase the evaluation costs dramatically. There are better ways!

Logically, three groups of people can be used effectively to evaluate a media service program: the media center staff, the clients or users of the services, and outside consultants. Each group offers both advantages and disadvantages.

Media Center Staff

Staff members are an important source of information regarding the strengths, weaknesses, and problems of the media center's programs. Staff members work daily with the center's clients and from that experience should be able to make contributions regarding the strengths, weaknesses, and problems in the center. Media managers should value the experience and knowledge of individual employees. Rene McPherson of Dana Corporation points out, "we believe that the expert in any particular job is most often the person performing it" (Peters and Waterman 1982, 249). By utilizing each staff member's expertise, much can be learned regarding the quality of the media programs provided. The use of staff in the evaluation program provides an opportunity to obtain information about the program without imposing additional work upon others outside the center.

There are a few disadvantages involved in using staff in an evaluation program. The information obtained from them reflects the opinions of staff members and how they perceive client opinions. Staff opinion may also be biased, as they may think that negative client opinions may be interpreted as reflections upon their own performance. For reasons of job security they may be hesitant to express an opinion that a program is no longer meeting client needs. However, if a climate of participative management and openness exists, then staff members are likely to participate and give honest opinions and suggestions.

Patrons

Probably the most important source for how well the media center programs meet client needs are the clients themselves. The center's programs exist only to serve clients; therefore, clients should have an opportunity to evaluate media services. The clients will remember both problems and good service. They should be asked if services meet their needs, are available when needed, are easy to obtain, and are reliable and of good quality. They should also be asked to provide input when they perceive new needs. Questionnaires and opinionnaires are good tools for collecting this type of data. Utilization records should also be an integral part of an evaluation program, as utilization provides a key measure of the importance that clients place upon media services. Clients will not use services that they do not think are valuable.

Outside Evaluators

Consultants are sometimes brought from outside the organization to evaluate internal programs. Most commonly, outside evaluators are used when a precise, formal evaluation is necessary to obtain or retain accreditation by an association such as the National Council for Accreditation of Teacher Education and Northwest (or other regional) Association of Schools and Colleges, and the National Association of Trade Technical Schools. Various other associations exist to accredit programs in specific fields (i.e., music, business, technology, and the various sciences). Accrediting evaluations are usually extensive and are preceded by an institution's self-study of its programs. Broad program standards are usually developed by the association; an institution must measure up to them to be accredited. The entire process may take a year. Outside evaluators are also helpful when major problems exist and no agreements or solutions can be found within the institution. Outsiders bring with them a degree of authority and can sometimes effect a solution because they come with no preestablished biases or alliances about the specific media center.

ADMINISTERING
AN EVALUATION PROGRAM

The media manager is ultimately responsible for the evaluation of the media center: The buck stops with the manager. However, that does not mean that the manager should necessarily be directly involved in an evaluation; it is better if someone outside the media center can be given this responsibility. Most large institutions have an office responsible for institutional research. This office may be under a variety of names, but it should be identified by the media manager and asked to administer such an evaluation program. An evaluation administered, tabulated, and summarized by an office completely independent of the media center is more credible because the chance of bias or data manipulation is eliminated. This strategy does not remove the manager from the task completely. The manager must initiate the request, explain what is to be evaluated, and review the evaluation instruments to ensure that they fully cover what is to be evaluated. That is where the media manager's interaction must end; he or she should have no further involvement until the evaluation report is completed.

Media Service Standards

Qualitative and quantitative standards for media service programs do exist for public schools, K-12. Some state departments of education have developed such standards, but most have not because the existence of state standards for media service programs would ultimately increase funding requests to implement those standards. The American Association of School Librarians (AASL) and Association for Educational Communications and Technology (AECT) jointly developed a set of guidelines for school library media programs in 1988 (AASL and AECT 1988). The guidelines are essentially qualitative and are intended to help centers strive for excellence. Based upon an extensive survey of 4,500 public schools and 1,700 private schools, quantitative descriptions of staff, collection, facilities, equipment, and budget of high-quality or state-of-the-art programs were identified. The survey results are found in appendix 4. Based on the findings of that survey, a set of quantitative national standards were developed. These standards are found in appendix 5. AASL and AECT (1998) developed new standards in a recent publication. Their new standards are based on information literacy for student learning. They do not give any media facility standards. For that reason, we are retaining the 1988 standards in the appendix.

Standards have also been developed by AECT for media centers in higher education (AECT 1989). The AECT standards are the result of many years of research within a wide spectrum of institutions of every conceivable size. In these standards each media service function is measured against (1) how well it can meet the needs and objectives of the institution; (2) the adequacy and appropriateness of personnel, equipment, and facilities for each function; and (3) the degree of interaction of all the media service functions. The levels of service of the functions are as follows:

    a.   Minimal—Defined as the lowest level of equipment, personnel, and facilities necessary to begin service in that area

b. Basic—Defined as a second stage of development which provides an acceptable service capacity for meeting day-to-day demands

c. Advanced—Defined as an expanded capacity necessary to support a sophisticated and comprehensive service (AECT 1989)

Unlike many other standards, the AECT document does not specify quantity of equipment based on faculty/classroom/student size. Instead, it suggests a general guideline. When the learning resources program cannot satisfy 95 percent of the requests for a service, it must grow to meet the needs. Such growth may be in personnel, facilities, equipment, or in any combination of these. A summary of the AECT standards for institutions of higher education is included in appendix 5. Readers are urged to obtain a copy of the complete standards document. We are not aware of any standards developed specifically for business and industry, but do believe that, because of their structure, the AECT standards are applicable to media centers in these areas.

When accepted and established standards for media services do exist, they can be used to help justify media service facilities, equipment, collections, and production budget requests. However, one must remember that some accepted standards may be the recommended minimum and if the media manager's resources exceed that minimum in any single part of his or her program, the use of the standards could have an adverse effect. The use of standards alone to justify facilities, resources, and staffing levels for a media center is not recommended. Standards should be considered as only one of many arguments for support.

Information Gathering Techniques

Information regarding the success or failure of a media center can be gathered from a wide range of sources and in many forms. Four basic types of informational data become apparent in the evaluation process: quantitative, subjective, normative, and empirical.

Quantitative data provide information about the utilization of the program services, a numerical accounting of what is used by whom and how often. Data are collected and summarized using the center's normal logistical reporting procedures. Although gathering and collating such information takes time, it does not involve an exorbitant amount of time nor complex bookkeeping tasks. Centers that use the computer can easily extract the necessary quantitative data and make them readily available in the desired format. Comparing your center's data to that of similar organizations may be helpful. Collect client materials, annual reports, and program reviews; then view the Web sites of similar media organizations to find parallels.

Evaluation information about the center's programs can also be collected in subjective form. Questionnaires and opinionnaires can be distributed to collect information about the center's programs, and interviews can be conducted. *Subjective data* provide information about opinions, attitudes, and perceptions that individuals hold toward the media center. Media center patrons, teachers, trainers, principals, coordinators, students, and trainees can all provide useful information regarding the state of the program and user attitudes. An example of a questionnaire used successfully to obtain client perceptions of a media service program is in appendix 6.

The center staff is another important source of subjective data. A self-study evaluation program can provide a wide range of information about staff perceptions of the media service programs. A self-study program asks media center program coordinators, supervisors, or the entire staff to evaluate media service programs. Self-assessment instruments can be prepared that require short essay or yes/no answers. Also used are simple rating (5, 4, 3, 2, 1) or Likert scale (strongly agree, agree, disagree, or strongly disagree) answers. Self-assessment instruments can be used to obtain staff perceptions of the adequacy of the logistical procedures and of the center's collections and facilities. Subjective information from all sources should be considered in concert with data collected from all other sources.

Normative data are a set of accepted norms that can be used for comparing one's media center services and facilities. While there are no established norms for media centers, there are standards developed by professional associations and some state departments of education that can be used in lieu of norms. The use of such standards was previously discussed in this chapter. Annual reports, informal and formal audits, trend analyses, and cost accounting techniques can assist in developing or amassing the quantitative data to be used in the comparison.

Another type of information that is useful and should be considered in a media center evaluation program is test results that indicate that the use of media increases learning, sells products, or changes attitudes. Verifiable information based on experiment or observation is called *empirical data*. Collecting empirical data to support the assumption that media use does make a difference is not easy. It is difficult to isolate the many factors that are present that may also effect change. Media are generally and correctly used in concert with other communication techniques, so pinning down the specific contributions made by media is difficult. While one should attempt to collect empirical data within the institution, it is also possible to cite research already completed in the professional field to support a contention that the materials do make a difference. For this reason, it is imperative that one keep informed about research in the field.

Another strategy for obtaining information to support the concept that media are effective as communication tools is to ask patrons about the effectiveness of the media that they use. For the lack of a better term, we will call this type of information *empirical opinion*. The following yes/no questions are representative of the type of questions to ask to obtain empirical opinion data:

The use of media in my application

	YES	NO
improved thinking skills		
developed new points of view		
stimulated discussion		
benefited students/trainees intellectually		

Questions that require the patron to make a more quantitative judgment about the value of media can also be developed. The same questions could be used with minor modification and require answers using the following scales:

1 = Strongly disagree	OR	1 = Unsatisfactory
2 = Disagree		2 = Marginal
3 = Neutral		3 = Satisfactory
4 = Agree		4 = Very good
5 = Strongly agree		5 = Outstanding
6 = Not applicable		6 = Not applicable

While empirical opinion is obviously not as powerful or valid as true empirical data resulting from test results, it does represent the opinion of media center clients based upon their experience. For that reason it can be used effectively and should be considered as another evaluation tool.

Levels of Evaluation

As was noted earlier, the evaluation of media service programs is a continuous process. Most media programs are also subject to other types of evaluations periodically, including institutional evaluation by accrediting associations and special specific school program evaluations. Evaluations of all kinds can be divided into four levels based on their level of detail and thoroughness.

Level 1. Level 1 evaluations can be considered the base or minimal level of evaluation. Level 1 evaluations are completed by the media manager annually using data submitted from media departmental coordinators. This culminates in an annual report which summarizes the activities of the center's programs during the year. It includes a summary of utilization statistics, collection development, media development activities, and other activities in which the media center has been involved. The report should also include a summary of staff activities.

Level 2. The manager completes the tasks stated in level 1 and, in addition, involves the media center staff in a self-study of the center's program. The manager also compares the center's facilities and programs against established recognized standards and preset criteria and objectives.

Level 3. This includes activities listed in levels 1 and 2. In addition, the manager seeks a person from the parent institution's research or evaluation office (outside the center organization) to administer an evaluation. The appraisal includes evaluation by media service patrons and includes qualitative and empirical data. Patrons are asked to make judgments regarding all components of the center's programs, including their perceptions of the quality of the services, quality of the holdings, and the performance of staff in providing services. At this level the media manager's involvement is limited to advisement.

Level 4. Levels 1, 2, and 3 will be completed. The media center, as a unit of the parent institution, is evaluated by an outside team of experts. Here the media manager cooperates in the evaluation by providing access to facilities and information as requested by the team. The manager will do well to have all information at hand, in case it is requested.

Levels of evaluations and recommended frequency of occurrence are summarized in figure 13.2, page 288.

Levels	Activities	Recommended Frequency
1	Media manager summarizes service activities into an annual report	Yearly
2	Level 1 activities Media center staff self-study Manager compares programs with established standards	Biennially
3	Level 1 and 2 activities Patron evaluation administered by someone outside the media center	Biennially
4	Levels 1, 2, and 3 activities Evaluation by outside evaluation team	Ten years

Figure 13.2. Levels of evaluation.

Types of Evaluation Information

Before beginning the planning for an evaluation program, the media manager should perform an assessment of the elements and documents available for use in the process. The manager should create a listing or file of all relevant materials and support information that may assist him or her in designing an appropriate evaluation plan at the desired level for the organization. Some of the support materials and activities that should be gathered and reviewed include:

- All previous evaluations and team reports on the center and organization
- Copies of all recent annual reports, data collection activities, and financial summaries
- Audit reports
- Student and teacher evaluations, assessments, and informal correspondence
- Documents that provide a historical perspective on the center
- Copies of all promotional materials, catalogs, and programs for public relations activities
- Staff information, vitas and background employment information
- A list of all staff member's publications and professional activities
- Data and plans on current facilities and their utilization
- Information on the services and activities of like agencies within the institution or organization
- Sample evaluation plans and reports from similar media centers and organizations
- Procedures and guidelines for evaluation planning recommended or required within the institution or organization

- References, checklists, or standards from professional organizations that apply to the center
- Background information on the center's environment, i.e., community resources, clients, and support climate

Proceeding with an Evaluation

All of the components of an evaluation have now been presented and discussed. The media manager is now faced with how to assemble these components into an effective evaluation program. There is no single correct procedure to be followed in implementing an evaluation program. The process is continuous, and procedures that work in one institution may not work in another. The manager needs to start somewhere, however, and then make changes as experience dictates. The following list of steps should be considered as a guide:

1. Identify the mission of the media center as stated by the administration of the institution.

2. List the goals and objectives (technology plan) of the media center.

3. Compare the goals and objectives of the media center with institution expectations of the center (as identified in step 1).

4. List all the service functions and programs of the media center.

5. List program service objectives of the media center for the current year.

6. Identify and categorize the patrons of the center.

7. Study the center's existing annual reports and other documentation to determine if the reports describe both services provided and patron utilization.

8. Determine the appropriate desired level of evaluation.

9. Develop an appropriate timeline and budget to conduct the evaluation.

10. Identify accepted media standards that might be used for purposes of comparison.

11. Compare the media center's collections and facilities with accepted standards or with other media centers.

12. Develop strategies to obtain empirical evidence.

13. Collect empirical evidence that documents media as effective.

14. Identify research that documents the value of services being provided by the media center.

15. Develop self-study instruments that can be used by center staff.

16. Obtain assistance from the institution's research or evaluation office or someone outside the media center to administer an evaluation of the services provided by the media center.

17. Develop or assist in developing questionnaires and opinionnaires that can be used to gather patron opinions toward media services that are provided.

18. Be sure that questions on all evaluation vehicles and instruments are fair and nondirective.

19. Participate and cooperate in an evaluation of the institution by an outside team of evaluators from an accrediting association where the media center is one of many programs to be evaluated.

20. If deemed necessary and financially feasible, seek an evaluation of media center services from an outside evaluator(s).

USING EVALUATION RESULTS

The efforts expended in completing an evaluation of a media service program can now be put to use. The data collected must be carefully collated, summarized, reported in written and graphic form, and studied carefully; change decisions must be made; recommendations must be formulated; and the report must be disseminated. An evaluation provides the media manager with both the information and opportunity for making changes. Problems should be solved, programs should be modified, and new programs implemented as the findings suggest. The development or revision of the center's strategic plan or technology plan should be a natural outcome of an effective evaluation of the center.

Evaluations provide an opportunity for effective staff improvement and growth, and sharing the results with staff may make them more receptive to change. Inservice training opportunities should be provided when the need for additional training is indicated. Unmotivated employees may understand the need to carry their share of the workload when they see that their behavior is observed by patrons.

Critical evaluations provide the media manager an opportunity to review and change procedures. Procedures should never be set in concrete. The manager and staff, cooperating as a team, should study problem procedures, making changes until the procedures work well. The goal should be to develop simple, efficient, and accurate procedures that require the least amount of effort from both patrons and staff.

Evaluations can provide support for new program proposals. When ideas for new programs are identified, proposals may need to be developed, justified, and forwarded to the administration. Patron support identified during an evaluation of the media program can be used to help justify proposals.

The media manager who does not analyze service evaluation results carefully and use them to improve what the center is doing is missing an opportunity and may soon lose the support of clients and upper management. The patrons and administration deserve and expect to see results. The media manager should not expect to fix all problems overnight; however, some problems take longer and some may not be fixable owing to budget or facility constraints. However, clients and superiors should be given explanations. Desirable follow-up activities should be planned and scheduled to eliminate possible inaction on recommendations.

The evaluation report should be disseminated to the administration, the center manager's immediate supervisor, and the center's patrons. That does not mean the entire report should be widely distributed; the total report should be directed to one's supervisor and a few specific administrators related to the media manager on the organizational chart. Other administrators and patrons should receive a summary of the most important findings, along with a statement of appreciation for their participation in the evaluation.

SUGGESTED ACTIVITIES

1. Select a media center with which you are acquainted, or consider a hypothetical center, and carry out the following evaluation activities.

    a. Develop a series of evaluation questions for each department of the media center.
    b. For each question, describe the type of information that will be necessary to obtain.
    c. For each question, list who can best provide the information needed.
    d. Develop appropriate instrument(s) to collect the information required.

2. Review several media standards instruments; make notes on their strengths and weaknesses.

3. Develop a list of steps with an appropriate timeline for preparing, implementing, and analyzing an evaluation program.

4. Develop a time sequence for implementing and using the four evaluation levels in an evaluation program.

REFERENCES

American Association of School Librarians and Association for Educational Communications and Technology. 1998. *Information Power: Building Partnerships for Learning.* Chicago: American Library Association.

———. 1988. *Information Power: Guidelines for School Library Media Programs.* Chicago: American Library Association.

Association for Educational Communications and Technology. 1989. *Standards for College and University Learning Resources Programs: Technology in Instruction.* Washington, D.C.: Association for Educational Communications and Technology.

Morris, Betty J., John T. Gillespie, and Diana L. Spirt. 1992. *Administering the School Library Media Center.* 3d ed. New Providence, N.J.: R. R. Bowker.

Patton, Michael Quinn. 1982. *Practical Evaluation.* Beverly Hills, Calif.: Sage Publications.

Peters, Thomas J., and Robert H. Waterman, Jr. 1982. *In Search of Excellence: Lessons from America's Best-Run Companies.* New York: Warner Books.

Stake, Robert E. 1996. "The Countenance of Educational Evaluation." In *Classic Writings on Instructional Technology*. Donald P. Ely and Tjeerd Plomp, eds. 143–59. Englewood, Colo.: Libraries Unlimited.

MEDIA RESOURCES

Creating Sound Classroom Assessments. Assessment Training Institute, 60 minutes. University Park, Pa.: Pennsylvania State University, 1994. Videocassette.

The Information Power Video. American Association of School Librarians and Association for Educational Communications and Technology, 19 minutes. Chicago: Encyclopaedia Britannica Educational Corporation, 1988. Videocassette.

New Tools: Teaching with Technology, No. 5, Organization and Management for Technology Use. Seattle Public Schools, Instructional Broadcast Center, 28 minutes. Santa Monica, Calif.: Pyramid Media, 1996. Videocassette.

New Tools: Teaching with Technology, No. 8, Standards and Assessments. Seattle Public Schools, Instructional Broadcast Center, 28 minutes. Santa Monica, Calif.: Pyramid Media, 1996. Videocassette.

SELECTED BIBLIOGRAPHY

American Association of School Librarians and Association for Educational Communications and Technology. *Information Literacy Standards for Student Learning.* Chicago: American Library Association, 1998.

Association for Educational Communications and Technology. *Guidelines for the Accreditation of Programs in Educational Communications and Information Technologies.* 3d ed. Washington, D.C.: Association for Educational Communications and Technology, 1996.

Brown, James W., Kenneth D. Norberg, and Sara K. Srygley. *Administering Educational Media: Instructional Technology and Library Services.* 2d ed. New York: McGraw-Hill, 1972.

Bryson, John. M., and Farnum K. Alston. *Creating and Implementing Your Strategic Plan: A Workbook for Public and Nonprofit Organizations.* San Francisco: Jossey-Bass, 1996.

Everhart, Nancy. *Evaluating the School Library Media Center: Analysis Techniques and Research Practices.* Englewood, Colo.: Libraries Unlimited, 1998.

Flagg, Barbara N. *Formative Evaluation for Educational Technologies.* Hillsdale, N.J.: Lawrence Erlbaum Associates, 1990.

Learning Resources Association of California Community Colleges. *Assessment System for the Evaluation of Learning Resources Programs in Community Colleges.* Suisun, Calif.: Learning Resources Association, 1985.

Marlow, Eugene. *Managing Corporate Media.* Rev. ed. White Plains, N.Y.: Knowledge Industry Publications, 1989.

North Carolina State Department of Public Instruction. *Media Programs Recommendations: Guidelines for School Media Programs at the Individual Schools and Administrative Unit Levels.* Rev. ed. Raleigh, N.C.: Division of Educational Media, June 1981. ERIC Document ED 208 878.

Scrogan, Len. *Tools for Change: Restructuring Technology in Our Schools.* Boulder, Colo.: Institute for Effective Educational Practice, 1995.

Woolls, Blanche. *The School Library Media Manager.* Englewood, Colo.: Libraries Unlimited, 1994.

Yesner, Bernice L., and Hilda L. Jay. *Operating and Evaluating School Library Media Programs: A Handbook for Administrators and Librarians.* New York: Neal-Schuman, 1998.

DESIGNING MEDIA SERVICE FACILITIES

. . . the physical environment of the classroom is a crucial factor which affects teacher and students in many ways. Fixed space and facilities, for example, coupled with the great expense of modern school equipment, are sometimes capable of "freezing" teaching methods and even curricular goals to those which were in effect at the time the building was erected—perhaps decades ago.

James W. Brown, Richard B. Lewis, and
Fred F. Harcleroad, *A-V Instruction
Materials and Methods*, 1959

OBJECTIVES

At the conclusion of this chapter you should be able to

1. Describe the role and responsibilities of the media manager in designing media service facilities.

2. Describe the design considerations for *user* media facilities.

3. Outline and describe the design considerations for *resource* facilities.

4. Describe the technical concerns, such as choice of lighting, cooling, ventilating, electricity, acoustics, carpeting, and communications, that must be addressed in a media facility design.

5. Outline the guidelines of the National Information Infrastructure.

6. List and describe several established media facility space standards that can be used to justify space needs.

7. State the purpose of and describe the activities that should be completed in the needs assessment phase of planning a facility.

8. Describe the activities, procedures, and steps that must be completed in the predesign phase of a facility design.

9. Describe the activities, procedures, and steps that must be completed in the design phase of a facility design.

The media manager who has the opportunity to be involved in designing or re-designing a media resource center is fortunate, for while the task is at times frustrating, it is also very rewarding. No other task that a media manager undertakes within his or her professional career is more critical. While working with patrons and performing the everyday tasks of media managers are important, the design of a facility will have a long-term effect, not only on the current generation of patrons but also on future generations. Once a facility is constructed it is difficult if not impossible to make major changes; therefore, facility design must be thorough—even small details must not be overlooked. The purpose of this chapter is to introduce procedures that have proven helpful in designing media facilities.

ROLE OF A MEDIA MANAGER IN FACILITY PLANNING

The media manager should be considered an important member of a facility design team. It is the manager as the professional expert, who by education and experience knows what is needed within a media facility, who can interpret and translate teaching, learning, communication, and production needs into functional facility requirements that will allow for expansion and change. The institution's administration can allocate the budget for a facility, and may know how to write the construction contracts, but the media manager is the expert who must be involved in the facility's design. Architects know how to draw plans, write specifications, and oversee a building's construction, but they are not experts on the facilities required to provide media services. The media manager, working with architects and building planners, can provide that expertise.

A building committee is the decision-making body that discusses all facets of a building's design. As a member of this committee, the media manager is the one best qualified to identify media needs and describe what kinds of spaces are required and how those spaces relate one to another. He or she is also in a position to determine the furnishings and equipment necessary to meet the various functional needs and how these needs may have an impact on the lighting, electrical, acoustics, or communications requirements. A small example might be useful to clarify this. In a photographic darkroom, what kind of switches should be used and where should they be placed? Chances are that neither the building committee nor the architect would know that such factors are important in the efficient operation of a darkroom.

A facility's design includes more than providing for spaces such as classrooms and laboratories; it includes the facilities for the preparation, maintenance, circulation, production, and storage of media resources which may include both print and nonprint formats. If media resources are to be available when requested, the facilities for their storage must be designed for efficient location and retrieval. The architect employed to design the building must consider the functional specifications, space relationships, and proposed facility layouts provided by the building committee and transpose them into a plan. These plans are reviewed and discussed with the architect and modified until a plan evolves that satisfies both the program's functional needs and the principles of building design. It is imperative that the media expert in an institution be included as a member of any building committee involved in the planning of instructional facilities or instructional support facilities. New buildings must be designed with a flexibility that allows for the implementation of new technologies as they are developed. This requires that the media manager be constantly alert for instructional applications of technological innovations. If the media manager is unaware of new technologies and their applications in the teaching, training, telling, and selling world, he or she is not and will not be seen as an expert in the media field.

This discussion makes clear that the media manager has a varied and important role to fulfill in designing media facilities and must make every effort to assure that the institution uses his or her knowledge when planning new buildings or remodeling projects where media resources are to be involved within the finished facility. In many cases it is up to the media manager to sell the idea of his or her participation on the building committee to upper management.

Using a Consultant

Even the most knowledgeable of media managers can no longer be an expert in all areas of educational technology. This was probably possible several decades ago, but all the new technologies are so complex and ever-changing that the media manager needs an outside consultant when involved in planning a new facility with technology applications.

The media manager should consider his or her own skills and the expertise of other media center staff members and then recommend a consultant in technological areas where outside expertise or a second opinion is needed.

Opinions of outside experts are often given more credence than local institutional individuals with comparable expertise. Because of this phenomenon, the use of an outside consultant can sometimes reinforce the recommendations of the media manager and his staff or interject new applications of educational technology that may have been overlooked.

Today, some architects have a technology consultant on their team. Scrutinize the background and experiences of these individuals to make sure they have the kind of expertise needed on your project. If you find their backgrounds do not relate adequately to the task at hand, do not hesitate to inquire whether a different or an additional technology consultant can be added to the project.

MEDIA SPACE CONSIDERATIONS

Many types of spaces need to be considered in the design of media facilities. All types of media spaces may not be appropriate for all institutions. The spaces to be included and designed into a building or facility depend entirely upon the immediate and future needs of the institution. Each facility must be individually designed to meet specific needs. A brief listing and discussion of the most common types of media spaces follows.

Media spaces can be placed into two general categories: user facilities and resource facilities. User facilities are, as the name implies, facilities that are used by the service consumers—such as teachers, trainers, students, trainees, salesmen—and they include classrooms, laboratories, carrel areas, and auditoriums. Resource facilities include those spaces that are necessary to provide media resources and include media collection, circulation, development, and maintenance facilities.

User Facilities

The usefulness of a wide variety of facilities can be enhanced with proper design. The first major consideration is to select user facilities that are needed. Care must be taken to determine real facility needs and not just individually perceived needs. Buildings are expensive and the manager who overdesigns by requesting unnecessary facilities will soon lose support. However, overdesigning should not be confused with requesting space for expected growth, which is good planning.

Teaching Auditoriums

Teaching auditoriums should be included in a plan only if presentations are presently made or planned for large groups. Auditoriums should be designed to include a full range of equipment mounted in appropriately placed cabinets or consoles. Slide projectors can be mounted on a shelf, cabinet, or booth in the rear of the room. 16mm film projectors are used so infrequently today that they can probably be brought into the classroom when needed or placed on a shelf or in a cabinet or booth. Computers with CD-ROM or DVD-ROM drives, a videodisc player, a video-cassette recorder/player, and an audio CD and cassette recorder/player need to be located in the front of the room where the instructor makes presentations. An overhead projector and possibly a document camera should also be located in the front of the room. All projection equipment should be placed in a presentation console (see figure 14.1) or in other cabinets nearby. All equipment, lights, volume control, and screen control should be controllable from the console location (see figure 14.2, page 300) and preferably in another location in the opposite front side of the room.

Figure 14.1. Presentation console. Reprinted with permission of VanSan Corporation, City of Industry, California.

Figure 14.2. Equipment control panel. Reprinted with permission of Crestron Electronics, Inc., Rockleigh, New Jersey.

A good-quality data and video projector should be ceiling mounted and focused on a properly located electrically operated screen. Often, it is desirable to have multiple screens in the facility. Audio from all sources, including a microphone from the presentation console, should be channeled through a central sound system. The auditorium lighting should be on dimmers or other satisfactory intensity control and should be controllable from the console and near student entrance doors. A writing surface should be available at each seat. A setup as described often requires the services of staff trained to prepare and troubleshoot the equipment. Many instructors will be wary of such an array of equipment, but to allay their fears, the control of equipment must be made as user-friendly as possible. Figure 14.3 shows some of the elements discussed above. Some of the equipment used in this room is housed in an AV rack in order to minimize the size of the presentation console, but all is controllable from the console.

Classrooms

Much of what was said about teaching auditoriums can also be applied to classrooms. There is a trend to permanently place as much equipment as is economically feasible in the classroom. Figure 14.4, page 302, illustrates such a classroom.

Classrooms of various sizes provide for flexibility. While the use of dividable walls was popular in the past, there were problems. They did not isolate sound effectively and were often not easy to operate. There are indications that the newer dividable walls are better designed, but they should be evaluated carefully for need and increased costs.

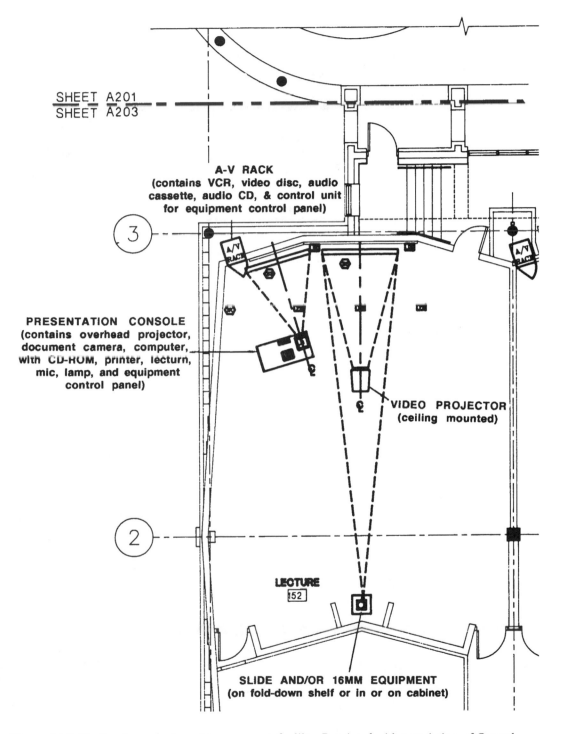

Figure 14.3. Technology-equipped large-group facility. Reprinted with permission of Central Washington University.

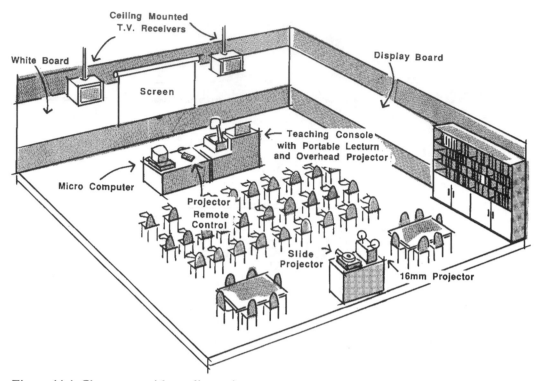

Figure 14.4. Classroom with media equipment.

Figure 14.5 shows another classroom with virtually all technologies in place. The presentation console is situated to project the overhead image on a corner screen. This accomplishes two important presentational advantages: The audience has a better view of the overhead projector images because the presenter is not standing directly in front of the screen, and the presenter can see images shown on the center screen (video, slide, document camera, computer, etc.) much easier than if he or she has to turn around and view a screen directly behind them.

Video Delivery Systems

The technology has long existed to deliver video to the classroom via various telecommunication systems from a central distribution point, but such systems are also very expensive and require technicians to maintain and monitor them. Many universities and other educational and corporate organizations have video delivery systems.

One of the most innovative systems exists at Indiana University–Purdue University Indianapolis (IUPUI). Video can be delivered from an automated video storage system over a fiber optics network to all Macintosh and PC workstations in the library and most campus classrooms. Television receivers throughout the campus can also retrieve about 400 video titles from this system's video jukebox nerve center (Jafari 1996).

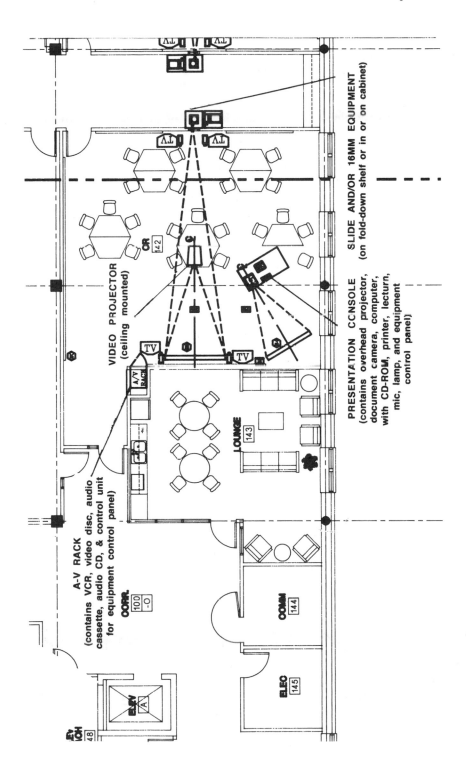

Figure 14.5. **A classroom design.** Reprinted with permission of Central Washington University.

Greenwood Middle School in Greenwood, Indiana, has an automated media retrieval and management system that links their school with the Greenwood Public Library and a local parochial school. These links effectively make the system accessible to the community as a whole. The media retrieval system takes all video equipment (VCRs, videodisc players, CD-Is) and other sources of media and rack-mounts them in a central location. Each classroom in the Greenwood Middle School, the public library, and the parochial school are equipped with a television monitor and a device (remote control or wall mounted) to control the media. Media programs for retrieval can be scheduled remotely at the locations throughout the system. Videoconferencing is another feature of the system. This system is a good example of a partnership. The AMX Corporation, Ameritech, and the public library all play key roles: AMX provides the hardware for the retrieval system, Ameritech provides the fiber-optic line services, and the public library provides public access to the network.

In September of 1992, the University of Notre Dame opened DeBartolo Hall, a new building designed to incorporate all the latest technologies that could support teaching. Included in the building is a computer-controlled, fiber-optic system for delivery of video programs to each of the building's 84 classrooms (Williams and Crowell 1993).

In late 1998, Central Washington University initiated a system whereby video sources (videocassettes and laserdiscs) can be scheduled through the Center for Learning Technologies (CLT) for a class period. In the CLT building these video sources are activated in playback units. Users can then take remote control of the video sources in two new buildings on campus. In the science and teacher education buildings, the videocassettes and laserdiscs can be remotely controlled in classrooms and seminar rooms by use of Crestron touch-pad panels built into teaching and learning stations.

Independent Study

Another facility that must be considered is independent study facilities. If clients are expected to use media resources independently, space and facilities must be planned. Small rooms are appropriate for viewing and listening by small groups, while learning carrels are appropriate for single users. Carrels can be arranged in many configurations (see figure 14.6).

Conference Rooms

Figure 14.7, page 306, shows the redesign of an existing conference room into a videoconferencing/boardroom. This was a project of a professional facility design firm. Note the use of rear projection. Rear projection has the advantage that it can tolerate more ambient room light falling on the screen. It does, however, require a room or space for the projector and a mirror system. This room also uses AV equipment racks and the new plasma-type flat monitor.

Computer Laboratories

Computer laboratories may be required to meet specific needs. They require extensive power outlets with power surge protection. Special computer furniture is required for placement of each terminal and its related components and wiring. A computer lab used for teaching may also require high-resolution television projection equipment or high-resolution monitors in multiple locations. Power and communication cable needs must be planned to eliminate surface wiring. A computer floor is often built to accommodate ease of routing and rerouting cables and wiring. These floors are usually built over existing floors with an elevation of about three inches.

Computer laboratories may also require extensive wiring to connect with the institution's mainframe or distributed computer system. Computer lab equipment is expensive and somewhat portable, thus requiring careful security measures.

Figure 14.6. Learning carrels arranged in space-efficient configurations.

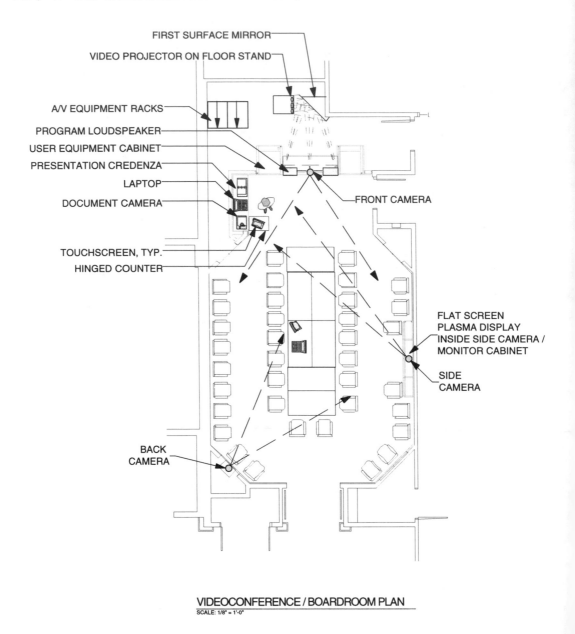

FIRST SURFACE MIRROR

VIDEO PROJECTOR ON FLOOR STAND

A/V EQUIPMENT RACKS

PROGRAM LOUDSPEAKER

USER EQUIPMENT CABINET

PRESENTATION CREDENZA

LAPTOP

DOCUMENT CAMERA

FRONT CAMERA

TOUCHSCREEN, TYP.

HINGED COUNTER

FLAT SCREEN
PLASMA DISPLAY
INSIDE SIDE CAMERA /
MONITOR CABINET

SIDE
CAMERA

BACK
CAMERA

VIDEOCONFERENCE / BOARDROOM PLAN
SCALE: 1/8" = 1'-0"

Figure 14.7. A technology-equipped conference room. Plan drawing courtesy of Waveguide Consulting, Inc., Decatur, Georgia.

Special Purpose Laboratories

Other laboratories that require extensive use of media resources may also be appropriate to meet user needs. Science and language laboratories are two examples where facilities are necessary for both independent and instructor or guided instruction. Therefore, it is necessary to work with individual departments to ensure that such laboratories are designed for the effective use of media and the selection of the best available equipment.

Graphics, Photo, Television, and Multimedia Production Laboratories

In some institutions, production facilities may be appropriate to enable students/ trainees or others to learn and use production skills. Such special purpose laboratories may include graphics, photography, television, or multimedia. Graphics laboratories require good lighting and appropriate power and communication access to meet requirements of computer, copy, and typesetting equipment. A sink should be provided for cleaning equipment. In photo laboratories, noncorrosive sinks and plumbing materials must be used to eliminate corrosion caused by photographic chemicals. Adequate ventilation to exhaust chemical fumes and to move air through small labs must also be provided. Adequate power must be available in the right places and of the appropriate voltage and current-carrying capacity for both the wet and dry photo production areas.

Television and multimedia laboratories require special furniture and adequate power, video, and data connections. In multimedia production, for example, many devices are needed to input and output signals to a computer. This requires the special design of counters, shelving, and routing of cables and wiring.

Television Facilities

Television facilities may also be desirable. Because television facilities are expensive, they usually must be used by students and trainees as well as for production purposes. In large universities when both student training and production needs of the institution are extensive, separate facilities may be appropriate. In small universities and colleges with limited production classes and production requirements, the budget most often dictates a single facility. Facilities in business and industry do not have a sharing problem unless they serve as a training lab.

Television facilities are most often divided into several specific functional spaces: (1) studio, (2) studio control, (3) master control, (4) library, (5) editing rooms, (6) staff planning, and (7) reception. The studio is used for multicamera productions when good acoustics, lighting, and audio are required. Switching, special effects, and audio controls are placed in a studio control room. Program directors create and mix multiple images into a single program in the studio control room. The master control room houses the technical components of a television production facility: camera controls, video recorders, video playbacks, special postproduction equipment, and distribution equipment. Editing equipment is often located in the master control room when separate editing rooms are not available. Television facilities require a library to store film, video, and audio materials used for production and finished productions. Editing rooms are recommended to give staff privacy to improve concentration during postproduction editing. Offices are required for program directors, producers, engineers, and for visiting personnel who may be serving as talent or subject-matter specialists for programs. Program talent need a private and secure place to gather and store materials and to plan programs. Finally, a television production facility needs a general reception area for meeting patrons, for scheduling activities, and for individuals or groups to congregate before moving into the studio to perform as talent. Multicamera production can also be accomplished outside of the studio with electronic field production (EFP) equipment. Field production takes longer because of the time required to transport and interconnect complex equipment and the postproduction assembly of the program.

The design of a television production facility is complex and the services of a television consultant are strongly advised. However, several television facility requirements warrant emphasizing. Television production activities are so interrelated that they must be contiguous to facilitate the flow of equipment, materials, and talent. While not mandatory, it is helpful for a program director to be able to see into the studio. Audio rooms must be acoustically isolated from all their surroundings. The easiest way to accomplish this is to select a location for the studio and audio rooms away from noisy areas. An effective way is to surround the studio with quiet buffer spaces, such as dressing rooms, offices, conference rooms, and limited-access hallways. The space both above and below the studio must also be considered. The selection and treatment of walls, windows, and doors must be considered to prevent noise from penetrating a studio (see figures 14.8–14.11). Walls must be well insulated. Double windows with an air space separating the glass helps prevent noise from being transmitted into the studio. Air locks using two doors are also effective to curtail noise at the studio entrances. Both high and low frequencies must be controlled. The use of double walls with offset studs is highly recommended. For maximum sound control, the use of a "floating studio" principle is advised. In floating room construction (figure 14.10) all surfaces are isolated or suspended from each other. The sound transmission coefficient (STC) of three construction techniques is illustrated in figure 14.8. The sound transmission coefficient loss in figure 14.8 and noise criterion standards, NC in figure 14.11, page 310, should not be considered as equal. Sound transmission loss is a measure of airborne sound reduction as it passes through a sound barrier. Noise criterion standard is a curve which specifies the maximum permissible sound intensity of noise at various frequencies. The goal is to achieve a noise criterion level between NC 20 and NC 30, with NC 20 as the ideal and NC 30 as a maximum acceptable level.

Another requirement is to use raised floor construction with easily removed floor panels within and between the studio control, master control, and editing rooms to allow flexibility for cable arrangement when making changes. Equipment changes are constantly made in this high-technology area requiring maximum access and flexibility for cable routing.

Resource Facilities

To serve patrons well, a media center must have adequate and efficient facilities for the creation or delivery of services. The extent of these facilities is determined by the scope of the media services provided. Again, it is important that the media manager determine the *real* needs based upon patron requirements for services.

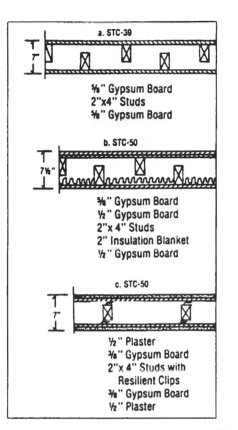

a. STC-39

⅜" Gypsum Board
2"x4" Studs
⅜" Gypsum Board

b. STC-50

7½"

⅜" Gypsum Board
½" Gypsum Board
2"x 4" Studs
2" Insulation Blanket
½" Gypsum Board

c. STC-50

7"

½" Plaster
⅜" Gypsum Board
2"x 4" Studs with
   Resilient Clips
⅜" Gypsum Board
½" Plaster

Figure 14.8. Sound transmission coefficient (STC) of typical nonhomogeneous multilayer walls. Reprinted with permission from the July issue of *Video Systems*. Copyright 1981, Intertec Publishing, Overland Park, Kansas.

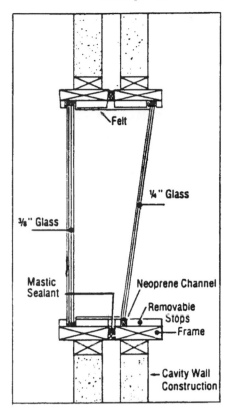

Felt

¼" Glass

⅜" Glass

Mastic
Sealant

Neoprene Channel

Removable
Stops

Frame

Cavity Wall
Construction

Figure 14.9. Typical double-glazed control room window. Reprinted with permission from the July issue of *Video Systems*. Copyright 1981, Intertec Publishing, Overland Park, Kansas.

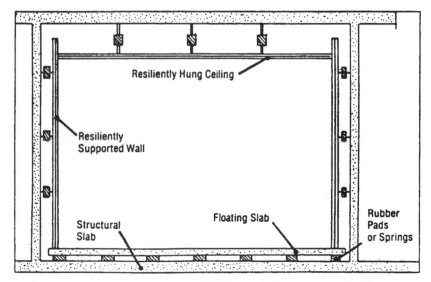

Resiliently Hung Ceiling

Resiliently
Supported Wall

Structural
Slab

Floating Slab

Rubber
Pads
or Springs

Figure 14.10. Floating room-within-a-room studio. Reprinted with permission from the July issue of *Video Systems*. Copyright 1981, Intertec Publishing, Overland Park, Kansas.

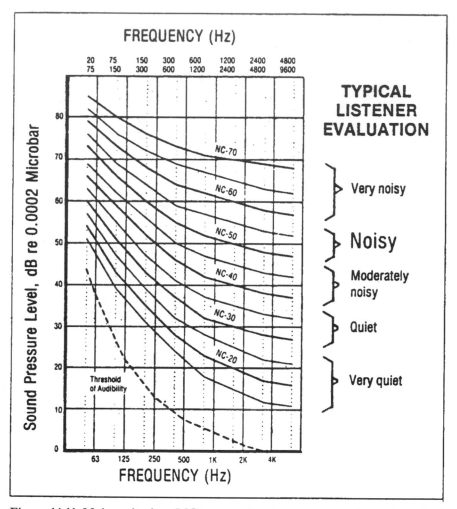

Figure 14.11. Noise criterion (NC) curves. Reprinted with permission from the July issue of *Video Systems.* Copyright 1981, Intertec Publishing, Overland Park, Kansas.

Collections

Typically, three types of media collections may be found in education and corporate institutions: print, nonprint or audiovisual, and equipment. Each requires facilities for acquisitioning, processing and cataloging, storing, maintaining, and circulating. The acquisition area needs to be large enough for staff to process incoming materials. The catalog area for patrons should be placed near the entrance and circulation counter of the facility. Only one public entrance/exit location should exist for security reasons. A commercial materials alarm security system is recommended for installation at the exit location to ensure that materials have been properly checked out; if they have not been checked out, the alarm sounds. Electrical power and data boxes must be provided for computers at the circulation counter and for each catalog terminal.

The shelving space for the collections should allow for a twenty-year net growth after weeding or removal of obsolete or worn-out materials. The floors in the collection areas must be adequate to carry the maximum possible book/film/video weight. The recommended minimum standard is 150-pound live load per square foot (Metcalf 1986, 327).

Nonprint collections of film and video require an area where the materials can be inspected and repaired using automated inspection equipment. Film inspection machines require, in addition to electrical power, exhaust venting to the outside to remove chemical fumes. Provision must also be made for film and video storage racks for materials being inspected and repaired. The area should be isolated from the circulation area to eliminate inspection equipment noise. Space for packaging materials for delivery to patrons should be located adjacent to this area.

While disagreements exist over intershelving print and nonprint materials, most media experts agree that the disadvantages far outweigh the advantages. Nonprint media should be stored in a vertical position, which is sometimes impractical on standard bookshelves. Many nonprint materials require equipment for viewing or listening, which means that appropriate equipment must be distributed throughout a building with intershelved collections. Finally, it is difficult if not impossible to maintain security for materials, as they can be removed from their containers and taken from the building. For these reasons, the authors believe such materials should be stored in separate, closed stacks. Equipment should be circulated from the same point as materials. Appropriate storage space should be located convenient to the service counter. Equipment cabinets should be built in four-foot modules with adjustable shelving for flexibility.

Equipment Repair

The equipment maintenance area requires a repair bench for each technician. Each bench should have multiple outlets for electrical power, data, an RF (radio frequency) signal for television, vacuum line, and compressed air. Space and shelving must be available for equipment waiting for repair. Space may also be provided for painting, welding, and fabrication, with each meeting current code requirements.

Media Development: Photo, Graphic, Video, and Multimedia

These media development facilities are an integral component of most media centers. In many institutions they may be shared with patrons; they were discussed under User Facilities earlier in this chapter.

TECHNICAL CONCERNS

The basic requirements of lighting, electricity, communication, and heating/cooling for a building are planned by the architect, with the input of the building's occupants. When special functional needs dictate that a change from standard practices is warranted, that change must be communicated to the architect. A media center does have many special needs.

Lighting

Light banks should be planned for placement above and between book and film shelves to provide proper light levels on the shelves. High-quality light with an intensity of fifty foot-candles on reading surfaces should be provided with some areas limited to thirty foot-candles to allow for individual light preferences. The less bright areas should be nearest to entrances to allow readers' eyes to adjust gradually as they enter. In lobbies, corridors, stairwells, and other nonreading areas, a light intensity of twenty foot-candles is adequate. In independent study areas, viewing rooms, and classrooms, lighting should be adjustable by a dimmer control or other means to allow for viewing of materials, but still allow note taking by students or an audience. In classrooms, the front light bank near the screen should have a switch so that it can be turned off when using various projectors. Fluorescent lighting is recommended to save energy. Lighting must be planned to meet the needs within each space. Data projection from computers requires much special attention: Ambient light falling on screens must be controlled and larger screens are generally needed due to the frequent lack of producers adhering to projection visibility standards.

Heating/Ventilating/Cooling

Heating, ventilating, and cooling must also be designed for the activities that occur in each space. In new or remodeled facilities, investigate the possibility of installing zoned thermostats that can be adjusted to match the activity taking place in different areas. In spaces where physical activity takes place, temperatures near 65 degrees F should be adequate, while study and other quiet activity areas require a higher temperature of 72 degrees F. One must also consider and provide for the existence of heat-producing equipment in a given space and for adequate ventilation to ensure that clean air is always present and that the amount of ventilation is sufficient for activities taking place within the space. Computer labs and television studios both require special study in regard to air conditioning needs. Even in moderate climates where temperatures rarely exceed 90 degrees F, air-conditioning and humidity control equipment are essential. The life of print and nonprint materials is shortened by inadequate temperature and humidity control. The ideal temperature for long-term storage of print and nonprint materials is between 45 and 60 degrees F, with humidity between 45 and 55 percent (Metcalf 1986, 327).

Electricity

Electric outlets must be conveniently placed for office and equipment use. Equipment voltage and current requirements must be noted. As stated earlier, the electrical needs in media development can be extensive and must be planned accordingly. The lighting grid in a television studio can require several hundred amperes of power. Therefore, power requirements and outlet placement must be carefully specified before electrical needs can be designed.

Acoustics

Acoustical treatment in both patron and staff areas within media center facilities is essential. Noise generated by workstations and equipment must be considered and controlled. The use of acoustical materials in ceilings and carpet on the floor is an effective way to lower noise in busy areas. Some research indicates that carpet is the single most important item but wall treatments are also effective. Walls can be set at irregular angles and surfaces decorated with finishes that reduce sound reflection. Noisy areas should be isolated from quiet ones by hallways and offices. Traffic patterns should be purposely designed to avoid creating crowded traffic routes within the center. Study all potential noise sources and develop plans to handle each source and type of sound. Pay particular attention to the design of heating and air-conditioning systems to ensure that the noise generated is not detrimental to the activity planned for different spaces.

Carpeting

In addition to controlling noise, carpet can also enhance the appearance of a media center. Carpet creates a warm and friendly atmosphere and is less fatiguing to walk on than hard surfaces. In schools with carpets in reading areas, children enjoy sitting and lying on the floor and in general are quieter than they are otherwise. Generous use of carpeting in media centers is highly recommended.

Communications

Twenty years ago the only communication tools installed in a media center were the telephone and often an intercom (that usually didn't work very well). Today, television and computers are considered important communication tools. Therefore, telecommunications systems must be provided to facilitate the use of telephones, computers, and video in classrooms. The present and future locations for telephones, computer terminals, and television receivers must be identified to enable communication cable routing to be planned. It is less expensive to install cables later if conduit or raceways have been built in initially. An alternative to conduit is cable trays above removable ceiling panels. Access to these trays is relatively easy, if the capability to add communications devices has been planned before the facility was built. Figure 14.12, page 314, shows the box configuration used in a new building to facilitate connections to electricity, video, data, and telephone.

Color

Behavioral research demonstrates that color influences attitudes, behaviors, and learning. Research indicates that red, orange, and yellow are warm, stimulating, and active colors, while blue and green are cool and restful colors. White is also a stimulating color and black instills a negative feeling. However, color affects individuals differently. Sinofsky and Knirk, in a review of research on the effects of color, summarized their findings:

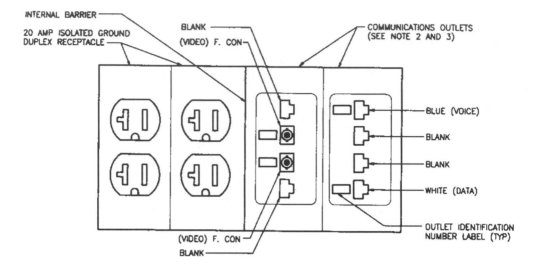

NOTES:
1. PROVIDE (2) 20 AMP ISOLATED GROUND DUPLEX RECEPTACLES.
2. PROVIDE COMMUNICATIONS OUTLETS. REFER TO COMMUNICATIONS FLOOR PLANS FOR TYPE AND QUANTITY OF COMMUNICATIONS OUTLETS REQUIRED.
3. PROVIDE BLANK INSERTS WHEN COMMUNICATIONS OUTLETS ARE NOT REQUIRED.
4. PROVIDE COMMUNICATIONS OUTLET IDENTIFICATION NUMBER LABEL FOR EACH ACTIVE OUTLET.

TYPICAL COMBINATION POWER/COMM. OUTLET BOX DETAIL ▽
SCALE: NONE

Figure 14.12. Combination power/communication box. Reprinted with permission of Central Washington University.

Social areas should have arousing hues (red, orange, or yellow).

The following combinations will increase visibility of signs and displays: yellow on black, white on blue, black on orange, black on yellow, orange on black, black on white, white on red, red on yellow, green on white, and orange on white.

In small, crowded rooms, lighter tones will create a feeling of spaciousness.

Choose colors that have the most favorable associations for the age or cultural group that will use the spaces.

Use specific colors for different room functions:

K–primary grades: tints of red, blue, yellow

Secondary classrooms/labs (requiring close visual and mental tasks): tints of blue-green, green, gray, beige

Dining areas: peach, pink, turquoise

Gyms, play areas: cool or neutral tones

Auditoriums: green, aqua, peach

Health services: green or neutral (1981, 19)

Work closely with the architects to develop a pleasing color scheme that will make the media center a pleasant place to work and visit. Walls, furniture, and carpet must be color coordinated. Colors and their intensity can be selected carefully to avoid oversaturation but still provide variety. An effective color scheme should evolve from matching room functions with recommendations on the use of color by an experienced decorator. Finally, the use of bold and colorful graphics can be effective in directing patrons to service areas.

INFORMATION INFRASTRUCTURE

The National Coordinating Committee for Technology in Education and Training (NCC-TET) (Yrchik and Cradler 1994, 32–34) has developed requirements to ensure that the National Information Infrastructure (NII) provides adequately for education and training. The NII will facilitate the transmission of information by voice, video, and data among groups across the nation. While these are national guidelines, every media services director needs to be aware of these nineteen requirements to ensure the institution is in harmony with the directions of education and training nationwide. The guidelines are:

1. Ensure that all Americans have affordable access to the National Information Infrastructure (NII).

2. Ensure that the NII is accessible in a variety of learning environments.

3. Develop a variety of sustained public and private partnerships and funding mechanisms to support education and training uses of the NII.

4. Make public and private information resources available to schools, institutions of higher education, training institutions, libraries, and arts and cultural institutions.

5. Coordinate NII-related education and training activities conducted by federal departments and agencies.

6. Develop and disseminate NII guidelines for education and training applications.

7. Identify and disseminate effective education and training applications of the NII.

8. Integrate applications of NII and related technologies into education reform plans.

9. Develop quality education and training applications for the NII.

10. Conduct research on the education and training applications of current and emerging technologies.

11. Promote training, professional development, and technical assistance for educators as an integral part of the development of the NII.

12. Support ongoing evaluation of the effectiveness and impact of the NII to inform policymakers and educators.

13. Emphasize interactive, broadband transmission of voice, video, and data for education and training.

14. Provide seamless interconnection among all relevant information networks and services.

15. Guide the development of voluntary standards that promote interoperability.

16. Ensure that the NII is easy to use.

17. Develop comprehensive directories of information resources and "navigation" systems for locating these resources.

18. Support user collaboration.

19. Create adequate measures to protect the security of resources on the network.

(Copyright 1994 by the Association for Educational Communications & Technology. Reprinted with permission.)

MEDIA FACILITY SPACE STANDARDS

New or additional space, equipment, and materials required by media centers do not come easy. In most institutions many programs request additional space and equipment simultaneously and budgets very rarely are adequate to fund all requests. How does a media manager strengthen his or her arguments for funding? The importance of identifying patron needs before facility planning begins has been noted. Patron needs must be clearly defined and used for expansion justifications just as they should be used to justify requests for the yearly budget. Statistics on past use should also be referred to for documenting additional space needs when the need for services has outgrown the available space. Established and accepted standards can also be used effectively to justify expansion needs. The American Association of School Librarians (AASL) and the Association for Educational Communications and Technology (AECT) have developed space recommendations for school media programs from kindergarten through grade twelve (AASL and AECT 1988, 132–39). The recommended space requirements are divided into functional service areas and list space relationships to other areas of the center and recommended space allocations for each functional area for schools with 500 and 1,000 students. For larger schools the spaces can be adjusted upward.

Two other sets of standards for establishing space needs for institutions of higher learning are worthy of discussion: California State College Library Standards and Standards for Media Services based upon research on "student media learning time," completed by Irving R. Merrill and Harold A. Drob and reported in *Criteria for Planning the College and University Learning Resource Center* (1977). The California State College Library Standards for institutions of higher education were based upon a consensus of a distinguished group of experts. The standards, while somewhat dated, have been well received and widely used. The California standards specify recommended shelving, reader, special materials, and staff spaces as follows:

Allow 0.10 sq. ft. per volume for book storage.

Allow 25 sq. ft. per reading station, with stations provided for 25 percent of FTE student expected enrollment.

Allow an additional 25 percent of the bound volume area for special collections (periodicals, maps, curriculum materials, etc.).

Collection size for colleges should be 30 volumes per FTE student for the first 5,000 students plus 20 volumes per FTE student beyond 5,000 students.

Collection size for universities should be 100 volumes per FTE student for the first 10,000 students, 75 volumes per FTE student for the second 10,000 students, plus 50 volumes per FTE student beyond 20,000 volumes.

The total floor area generated by number 1 through number 5 above should provide adequate space to include carrels, microfilm, and audiovisual collections (Metcalf 1965, 397–98).

The revised edition of Metcalf's work greatly expanded standards for library buildings. There are standards and guidelines for virtually any aspect of the design of an academic or research library in that source (Metcalf 1986). Clearly the California standards relate mostly to print-oriented libraries and provide very little support for nonprint collections. However, the first two items listed above can be used as a standard to justify space for audiovisual collections.

The standards developed by Merrill and Drob are limited to nonbook media resources (Merrill and Drob 1977). Evidence was collected from available studies, experiments, surveys, and research on the use of learning resources in universities. The data were compared with the results of a survey mailed to nine California universities and then checked with personal interviews in the nine universities. Merrill and Drob emphasize that no single media facility or program standard can reasonably be applied in higher education because institutions of higher education vary in size, curriculum, instructional strategies, and student backgrounds. Because of this assumption, they searched for a variable common to all institutions, and selected *student learning time,* defining it as

> the total time that a student devotes to his courses, including time spent in class, in the laboratory and in individual study. For a portion of this learning time, the student is under the stimulus and reinforcement of one or more kinds of learning resources (Merrill and Drob 1977, 51).

Merrill and Drob call the time that the student is under the stimulus and reinforcement of learning resources *percentage of learning time.* In media-oriented universities, the percentage of student learning time devoted to media resources is higher than in nonmedia-oriented institutions. According to Merrill and Drob, the Carnegie Commission on Higher Education estimates that the percentage of learning time devoted to the use of learning resources is between 10 and 20 percent for campus teaching. Ten percent was selected as the base for the development of their standards.

Another element in the Merrill and Drob standards requires explanation. Each type of service is divided into four levels or scopes; A, B, C, and D. *Scope* is defined as a range of activities offered by each type of service (see figure 14.13, page 318).

Students ⟍ Scope	1,000		5,000		15,000		27,500	
	FTE	ASF	FTE	ASF	FTE	ASF	FTE	ASF
A	0.012	3.7	0.004	1.2	0.002	0.6	0.001	0.5
B	0.027	6.7	0.007	2.0	0.003	1.0	0.002	0.8
C	0.050	11.7	0.013	3.5	0.006	1.7	0.004	1.2
D	0.076	18.4	0.018	5.0	0.008	2.4	0.005	1.7

FTE - Full Time Equivalent
ASF - Assignable Square Feet

Figure 14.13. **FTE/student and ASF/student ratios according to enrollment for scope of service.** From Irving R. Merrill and Harold A. Drob, *Criteria for Planning the College and University Learning Resource Center* (Washington, D.C.: Association for Educational Communications and Technology, 1977), 57. Used with permission.

The minimum activity qualifying as a campus-wide activity is designated as Scope A and the maximum activity as Scope D. Higher level scopes include all lesser levels.

Merrill and Drob, in addition to developing a set of media service standards, drew the following conclusions:

There is no single standard or typical resource center size that is appropriate for all colleges and universities.

As campus enrollment increases, the ratio of staff to students decreases and the ratio of assignable square feet devoted to resources decreases. This relationship is not linear.

Doubling the center staff from Scope A to Scope B may triple or quadruple the usefulness of the center.

No single FTE to space ratio can be applied to all resource center buildings on campuses (Merrill and Drob 1977).

Given this brief discussion and explanation of the development of the Merrill and Drob standards, the reader should find them helpful for justifying space. The standards are flexible and sensitive to different levels (scopes) of service programs and student enrollments.

PLANNING THE FACILITY

The most important phase of any building program is planning. Without careful and detailed planning, an architect cannot design a facility to meet one's needs. Inadequate planning is similar to asking a road builder to build a road without knowing where the road is to go. The steps in planning a facility are shown in figure 14.14. Successful media centers and other media facilities are designed to meet specific and unique needs of its media patrons. To identify these needs, a *needs assessment* must be completed.

PLANNING THE FACILITY

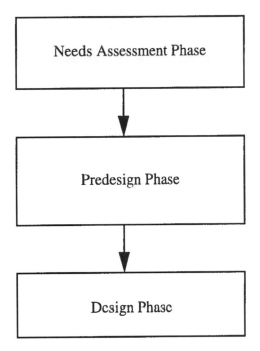

Figure 14.14. Planning the facility.

Needs Assessment Phase

The importance of this phase cannot be overemphasized. It is the base upon which the facility design is developed. Using the building of a new media center as a focus, a needs assessment identifies where and how the media center fits into the institution's organizational structure and what services will be needed if the center is to fulfill the institution's expectation of the center's mission (see figure 14.15, page 320). The needs assessment program can be condensed into the following six steps:

1. Determine the institution's mission and goals.

2. Determine the media center's mission and goals.

3. Determine the media center's program needs and objectives based on the mission and goals.

4. Identify the media center's patrons.

5. Determine the project's effect on the operational budget.

6. Determine the political implications.

NEEDS ASSESSMENT PHASE

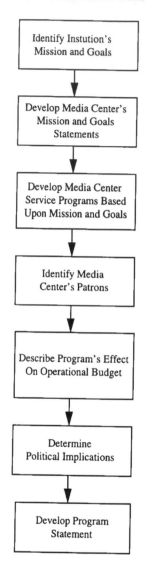

Figure 14.15. Needs assessment
phase for a media center.

An assessment program identifies new services that should be added as well as existing programs that should be considered for termination. A first step is to identify the institution's mission and goals. Then existing service departments should reassess their program objectives and determine if there are program or procedural changes to make that may alter space and space relationship needs. This analysis should result in a statement from each program unit of the total facility: technical services, public service, instructional or training development, media services, media development services, and all other program units who will occupy the building. The statement should justify the need for the space, list the objectives of the programs, identify the media center's patrons, and state the effect on the budget.

There are also political implications that must be recognized in the needs assessment. Is the existing funding climate such that funding realistically can be obtained now or would a delay of one, two, or three years be more appropriate? Identify other projects that will be competing for funding support. Are there both formal and informal leaders that are likely to support the proposed facility? Do not guess; these leaders must be identified and their opinions obtained. Is your relationship with administrators within the institution's organization adequate to get the necessary budget support? Can you get the support of managers of other service entities where new services may appear to compete? It is unavoidable that most institutions have political factors and issues that must be addressed before it is realistic to assume that support is available for building a larger facility.

The culmination of the Needs Assessment Phase usually results in the assembly of a document called a program statement or an academic prospectus. This document is reviewed by an institution's administration and, when funding is available, is given to a chosen architectural firm.

Predesign Phase

Only after the assessment phase and program statement have been completed and their findings indicate that a new facility or remodeling of an existing facility is justified should the predesign phase begin. The first step in the predesign phase is to determine the specific space requirements for each service component identified by the needs assessment. That information can then be transferred into functional specifications, which are statements describing what is to be accomplished in each unit of each program and for each space (see figure 14.16, page 322).

This step is followed by the development of detailed space specifications. It should include such information as the minimum number of square feet required, number of occupants, brief statement of function, equipment and furniture to be installed in the space, plumbing and electrical needs, and any special requirements. It also should include a description of how the various spaces must relate one to another within the unit. This is extremely important when several spaces are functionally related and must be adjacent to one another (see figure 14.17, page 323). Finally, an analysis of costs and some initial diagrams/drawings can be prepared.

Design Phase

After the needs have been identified and a program statement and a predesign are completed, they can be given to the architect to study before he or she begins to design the facility. Such detailed plans are vital to the architect. They are used to estimate the required size, shape, and location of each space within the design. The architect will then develop a preliminary design for review. If the relationship of spaces in the architect's preliminary design does not meet the functional and space specifications, insist that changes be made. A word of caution is needed here. When the project involves remodeling an existing building to serve a media center's identified needs, sometimes internal load-bearing walls exist that cannot be moved. Compromises must sometimes be made to obtain the best facility possible under the circumstances.

FUNCTIONAL SPECIFICATIONS:

Graphics. Space for computer graphics workstations, for mounting and laminating equipment, large tables for mounting work, transparency production equipment, silk-screen printing equipment, and for the making of signs, posters, covers, etc. Work space for two graphic artists plus student help.

Space Needed: 1,216 sq. ft.

Still Photography. Space to process black-and-white and color film, to house slide duplicating equipment and various copy camera setups, and space for finishing, sorting, and viewing of photographic materials. Also space for computer equipment (slide and flatbed scanners, a film recorder, etc.). Must be located adjacent to graphics room.

Space Needed: 1,283 sq. ft.

Video/Multimedia Production. Space for shooting, editing, assembly, and sound recording of video and multimedia productions. Should be located near the still photography laboratory for photographer convenience.

Space Needed: 1,200 sq. ft.

Audio. Space to process and duplicate audio materials with sound-proofed recording areas and a tape listening area.

Space Needed: 360 sq. ft.

Student Production Laboratory. Space to serve as a laboratory for student or staff production of materials for use in class projects, demonstrations, and reports. In addition to actual workstations, there will be stations to instruct users on the various processes involved. This area will include equipment and spaces for video, multimedia, graphic, photographic, and audio production.

Space Needed: 3,104 sq. ft.

Student Audio, Video, and Film Editing. Space where students and staff can edit audio, video, and motion picture films. This space must accommodate individuals or groups. Must be adjacent to student production laboratory.

Space Needed: 1,535 sq. ft.

Figure 14.16. Example of functional specifications.

SPACE SPECIFICATIONS

Room Name and Number: Graphics Workroom

Number Required: One

Area: 1,200 square feet

No. of Occupants: 7 stations @128 feet

Function: Space for graphics computers, mounting and laminating equipment, large tables for mounting work, and counter space for various kinds of equipment

Fixed Equipment: 1 wall clock
1 standing-height work counter (size: 25" x 26', Formica top, built in cabinets under and over)
1 standing-height work counter (size: 25" x 15', Formica top, built-in cabinets under and over)
1 exhaust hood to vent fumes outside

Movable Equipment: 1 refrigerator, 1 photocopier, 1 dry mount press, 1 large laminator, 4 graphics microcomputers, 1 laser printer (black & color), 1 scanner, 1 paper cutter (30" x 40"), 1 light table (4' x 6')

Services:
    Plumbing   Hot and cold water in 2 sinks built into cabinet counters
    Heating, Cooling,
       Ventilation   To maintain 72 degrees
    Electrical: Dedicated separate 110-volt, 20-amp circuits for dry mount press, laminator, and photocopier; other 110-volt, 20-amp circuits distributed around perimeter of room and recessed into floor
    Lighting   Diffused fluorescent ceiling lights, four separate zones with 2 levels per zone
    Communications: Data and telephone jacks located in four locations. Access to Internet and fast ethernet network at four computer locations (to be specified by owner)

Special Requirements: Should be adjacent to photography and video/multimedia production areas

Figure 14.17. Example of a space specification.

After the architect and client have agreed upon the completed preliminary design which fixes the load-bearing walls in place, the interior layout of each space can be determined. Who knows better than the library and media professional and other occupants of a building where the fixed and movable furniture and equipment should be placed? The location of the furniture and equipment will determine the location of plumbing and electrical wiring and therefore must be planned in advance. If the necessary equipment and furniture does not fit the space, adjustments can still be made by the architect.

An effective technique for developing interior space design is to use graph paper with grids that correspond to the architect's drawing scale. The scale usually is ⅛ inch equals 1 foot; however, the scale is determined by the size of the building. Trace the layout of the spaces on translucent grid paper laid over the architect's drawings. A fairly wide felt pen works well, as it emphasizes the walls. Next, identify all furniture and equipment that will be placed within the spaces. Obtain accurate measurements for these items through specification sheets, salespersons, or direct measurements from available equipment and furniture. Make simplified outline scaled drawings of each item on construction paper or stiff paper. Label each drawing and cut out as many as will be installed in the spaces. Use two cutout colors; one color should represent furniture and equipment to be installed immediately and another color to represent future purchases. All facilities should be designed for projected growth. This is prudent planning and helps to justify space for future growth.

The scaled cutouts representing the furniture and equipment that will be located in the spaces can now be placed on the grid paper and arranged and rearranged until things fit together and their location meets needs. Clearance space between furniture and/or equipment becomes evident through the use of the grid paper. One can tell at a glance if the areas between components are adequate. Adequate or inadequate expansion space also becomes evident through the placement of the colored scale cutouts. A limited-use area should be secured for this planning activity. The area should be reserved for this function only, as the cutouts are not pasted in place until an effective arrangement is found. In most cases, several arrangements should be developed, thus requiring several sets of scaled pieces representing equipment and furniture. The final selection can then be made and forwarded to the architect for integration into the physical and mechanical plans. The architect can now be held accountable because specific details regarding the facility to be designed have been provided.

The major steps in the design phase of planning a media center are as follows:

1. Determine specific needs for each service unit: work spaces; patron spaces; equipment, furniture, storage, and traffic patterns.

2. Finalize a functional specification for each space.

3. Finalize a detail specification for each space.

4. Determine the size of each component.

5. Make scale cutouts of all components.

6. Lay out several options.

7. Pick the best option.

8. Locate specific power, plumbing, and communication needs.

9. Give suggested layout to architect.

Relationship with the Architect

It is clear that a positive relationship must be developed with the architect. The architect must listen to the users of the building. Only the users can explain how the facilities are to be utilized. This is why very detailed preliminary planning is important, so that the architect will have specific information upon which to develop a building design.

In most organizations an institutional "facility planner" is assigned to coordinate all building construction projects. This person must be made aware of the value of media professional involvement in the preplanning and design of the building. The media manager must develop a positive relationship with the facility planner and provide him or her with pertinent information. Facility planners normally are responsible for many projects simultaneously. A quick and accurate response will develop the architect's or facility planner's confidence in the media professional's knowledge.

The facility planner also "tracks" or monitors the progress of the building construction through final inspection. The media manager should monitor the construction progress with the facility planner. It is easier to correct unforeseen problems during construction than after the building is complete.

MAXIMS OF FACILITY DESIGN

The following are worthy of consideration when designing media center facilities. The assessment, predesign, and design phases of a building project are busy times with ever-present deadlines. In addition to the design tasks, most media managers must continue to meet their daily media center management responsibilities. The busy manager would be wise to stop and ponder these maxims often during the planning process. The following short statements can serve as a checkpoint to refocus attention to important elements of facility design:

- Plan, plan, and plan some more.
- Learn from others; visit other media centers; do library and Internet searches.
- Form must follow function.
- Programs determine design.
- Plan for flexibility and change.
- Function supersedes aesthetics.
- The best economy is quality.
- Involve clients and staff in planning.
- Plan for convenience.
- Accessibility invites use.
- Plan for maximum control with minimum supervision.

- Function outranks windows.
- Get everything in writing.
- Expect everything to take twice as long as originally planned.
- Change orders mean money to the contractor—and additional costs to you.

SUGGESTED ACTIVITIES

1. Discuss the major tasks that a media manager should complete when designing media facilities.

2. List and describe the differences between three established standards that might be helpful when justifying media facilities.

3. Review several media equipment and furniture catalogs and/or sales brochures and list the size and power requirements of twelve items that are widely used in a media center.

4. Following the major design phase steps presented in this chapter, design a small hypothetical media service center that includes at least two media service functions such as collection and circulation, production of materials, television production, computer laboratory, student media production laboratory, or equipment circulation. Apply all of the steps that result in specifications and a tentative plan for an architect.

REFERENCES

American Association of School Librarians and Association for Educational Communications and Technology. 1988. *Information Power: Guidelines for School Library Media Programs.* Chicago: American Library Association, 132–39.

Brown, James W., Richard B. Lewis, and Fred F. Harcleroad. 1959. *A-V Instruction Materials and Methods.* New York: McGraw-Hill.

Jafari, Ali. 1996. "Video to the Desktop and Classrooms: The IUPUI–IMDS Project." *T.H.E. Journal,* 23, no. 7: 77–81.

Merrill, Irving R., and Harold A. Drob. 1977. *Criteria for Planning the College and University Learning Resource Center.* Washington, D.C.: Association for Educational Communications and Technology.

Metcalf, Keyes D. 1965. *Planning Academic and Research Library Buildings.* New York: McGraw-Hill, 397–98.

———. 1986. *Planning Academic and Research Library Buildings.* 2d ed. Philip D. Leighton and David C. Weber, eds. Chicago: American Library Association.

Nissen, Robert J., and Hubert Wake. 1981. *"The Basics of Studio Acoustics: Part 1: Noise Control." Video Systems,* July.

Sinofsky, Esther R., and Frederick G. Knirk. 1981. "Choose the Right Color for Your Learning Style." *Instructional Innovator,* 26, no. 3: 17.

Williams, C. Joseph, and Charles R. Crowell. 1993. "Providing Institutional Support for Educational Technologies." *T.H.E. Journal,* 20, no. 11: 114–18.

Yrchik, John, and John Cradler, principal authors. 1994. "The National Information Infrastructure: Requirements for Education and Training." *Tech Trends,* 39, no. 4: 32–34.

MEDIA RESOURCES

An Emerging Technology Classroom. Seattle Public Schools Instructional Broadcast Center, 28 minutes. Santa Monica, Calif.: Pyramid Media, 1996. Videocassette.

SELECTED BIBLIOGRAPHY

Allen, Robert L., and others. *Classroom Design Manual.* 3d ed. College Park, Md.: University of Maryland, 1996.

Anderson, Pauline. *Planning School Library Media Facilities.* Hamden, Conn.: Library Professional Publications, 1990.

Association for Educational Communications and Technology (AECT). *Standards for College and University Learning Resources Programs: Technology in Instruction.* 2d ed. Washington, D.C.: Association for Educational Communications and Technology, 1989.

Bozeman, William C., and Donna J. Baumbach. *Educational Technology: Best Practices.* Larchmont, N.Y.: Eye on Education, 1995.

Conway, Kathryn. *Master Classrooms: Classroom Design with Technology in Mind.* Research Triangle Park, N.C.: Institute for Academic Technology, 1993.

———. *Master Classrooms: Classroom Design with Technology in Mind. Research Methods.* New York: McGraw-Hill, 1959.

Hart, Thomas L. *Creative Ideas for Library Media Center Facilities.* Englewood, Colo.: Libraries Unlimited, 1990.

Iselin, Donald G., and Andrew C. Lemer, eds. *The Fourth Dimension in Building: Strategies for Minimizing Obsolescence.* Washington, D.C.: National Academy Press, 1993.

Klasing, Jane P. *Designing and Renovating School Library Media Centers.* Chicago: American Library Association, 1991.

Morris, Betty J., John T. Gillespie, and Diana L. Spirt. *Administering the School Library Media Center.* 3d ed. New Providence, N.J.: R. R. Bowker, 1992.

Organization for Economic Co-operation and Development. *New Technology and Its Impact on Educational Buildings.* Washington, D.C.: OECD Publications and Information Centre, 1992.

Sharpe, Deborah T. *The Psychology of Color and Design.* Chicago: Nelson-Hall, 1974.

Stuebing, Susan. *Campus Classroom Connections, Building with Information Technology: A Case Study Guide of Higher Education Facilities.* Newark, N.J.: Institute of Technology, 1994.

Wilson, L. *Assistive Technology for the Disabled Computer User.* Research Triangle Park, N.C.: Institute for Academic Technology, 1994.

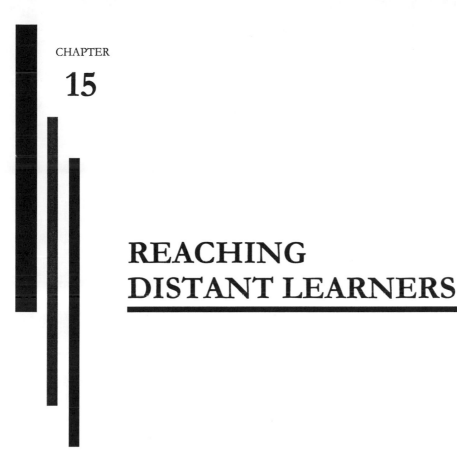

REACHING DISTANT LEARNERS

One important function of telecommunications is to provide a substitute for transportation; instead of moving people to ideas, telecommunications moves ideas to people.

Everett M. Rogers, *Communication Technology:*
The New Media in Society, 1986

OBJECTIVES

At the conclusion of this chapter you should be able to

1. List and describe early strategies used to provide instruction to distant learners.

2. Describe how each of the following delivery strategies can be used to reach distant learners:
   a. videotaped courses
   b. broadcast television
   c. cable television
   d. ITFS
   e. microwave
   f. satellite
   g. compressed video
   h. electronic text
   i. Web-based delivery
   j. desktop videoconferencing

3. Describe how the above delivery strategies can be used together to deliver instruction.

4. List and describe support services that are necessary for supporting distant learning services.

No media management text would be complete without a brief discussion on delivering instruction to distant learners—learners not located in close proximity to the normal classroom. The need for better-trained employees has made employees and management search for more economical ways to obtain or provide necessary training. Working people find it difficult and expensive to leave employment and move to another community to return to school. Others may not be able to move because of family obligations, children, physical disabilities, or cost. The cost of travel and time to send employees to workshops is high; in addition, sending employees to educational programs removes them from their normal productive tasks. Developing and operating training programs within institutions is also costly.

Many methods have been used to deliver instruction to distant learners. One of the first methods used by both public and private colleges and universities to reach distant learners was correspondence courses, which were designed around written materials, readings, exercises, and written tests. When the student satisfactorily completed a unit, the next in the series was sent until the course was completed. Radio has also been used for delivering instruction. Systematic use of radio in the classroom began as early as 1919 by WHA, the state-owned University of Wisconsin radio station (Wittich and Schuller 1957, 273). This was followed by stations in other states, but one of the most successful was the "Wisconsin School of the Air" which had 256,000 student listeners in 4,000 communities in 1955–1956 (Wittich and Schuller 1957, 275). Inservice training programs for teachers were also aired near the end of the school day.

The development of television for delivering instruction to distant learners paralleled that of radio. Television was first used for classroom delivery as early as 1946 (Stasheff 1947, 22–23), followed by inservice training for teachers. Its growth as an instructional delivery method is widespread and is the base upon which many distance education systems are now built.

Experimental programs called telelecture, using the telephone to deliver instruction, also developed. Telelecture consists of an amplified telephone and microphone system which allows students within a classroom to both listen and interact with a distant presenter. Telelecture has been used with varying degrees of success. The problem with telelecture soon became apparent—no visual images were possible unless they were prepared in advance and mailed for presentation at the site location. Cable television and satellite distribution and videoconferencing have brought the picture and sound capabilities jointly to the distant learner. Today we are utilizing computer networks and multimedia authoring systems to reach learners without regard to time constraints. The historical and technological bases for distance education are outlined in a chronology of devices and delivery modes (see figure 15.1, page 332).

Given this brief history of early attempts to reach distant learners, we will move on to discuss a wide range of delivery methods now available for delivering instruction to distant learners.

Print
1436

Internet/
Computer
Conferencing
1980s

Postal Service
1850s

Satellite Delivery
1980

Telephone
1875

Facsimile
1980

Radio
1895

Video
Conferencing
1980

Audio Tape
1945

Videodisc / CD-
ROM
1984 / 1985

Broadcast
Television
1953

Compressed Video
1988

Videotape
1960

Multimedia
1989

Audio Tele-
conferencing
1960

Wireless
Workstations
1996

Cable Television
1965

Computer Assisted
Instruction
1975

Smart Card
2000

Figure 15.1. Historical perspective of distance education delivery technologies.

DISTANT LEARNER DELIVERY VEHICLES

Videotape Delivery

Many institutions are successfully using videotape as a delivery form. Courses selected for taping are generally taught in a classroom modified for television recording with acoustic treatment, lighting designed for television, and remote-controlled mounted cameras (see figure 15.2). Multiple cameras are used to view and record both instructor and student activities. Instructor-developed illustrations are created for and viewed by a document camera, and other audiovisual materials are displayed as part of the instructor presentation and recorded as they occur. All class activities, including student interaction, become a part of the program lesson. Each day a recorded class session, including all handouts and assignments, is packaged and shipped to the remote viewers.

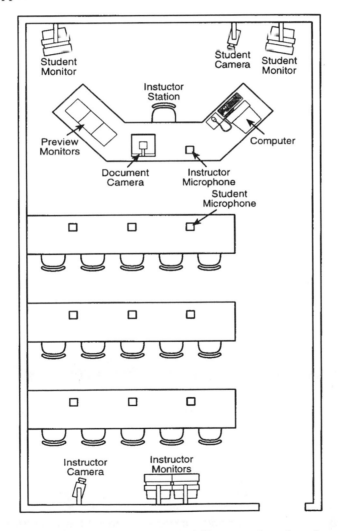

Figure 15.2. Diagram of a typical distance education classroom.
Reprinted with permission of Iowa State University.

Institutions have found several methods effective for student use of course materials. In some cases, programs are mailed directly to learner's homes for viewing and assignment completion. Another practice, used widely in business and industry, is for learners to meet in a classroom environment provided by the employer. An employed proctor makes the videotape and all materials available, administers tests, sends assignments and tests to the instructor for grading, and returns them to the students. Some corporations, realizing the long-term benefits to the company, pay their employees' tuition and allow them to attend class sessions on company time.

The videotape delivery method assures that learners obtain the same instruction, experience the same assignments, and are graded on the same criteria as students in the originating classroom. Some colleges and universities provide toll-free numbers, e-mail accounts, and Web sites for distant learners to use to contact their instructors during "office hours." According to research, distant learners perform as well or better than those in the originating classroom (Schlosser and Anderson 1994).

Broadcast Television

Both commercial and educational television stations have a long history of delivering instruction via *telecourses* to distant learners. Students register for each course, receive presentations by viewing the scheduled course program in their homes, complete reading and other assignments, and usually report to the college or university or some other group location for taking tests. Television stations charge the college or university a basic fee and may assess an additional fee for each student enrolled. The institution offering the course may prepare its own productions but most purchase and license finished course productions and provide the additional course materials. Some institutions are offering full degree programs via television or a combination of distance delivery technologies.

Cable Television

Cable television, as its name implies, is a closed system that uses cables as a delivery vehicle. Programs are transmitted through a cable instead of being radiated into the air. The signal follows the cable and is amplified along the cable route as required to maintain adequate signal strength. At each classroom or viewing area, the signal is "tapped" off and delivered by cable to a television receiver or receivers for viewing. The system should be designed and built with an adequate bandwidth to carry the number of channels required to meet existing and future needs. It is not unreasonable to plan for a cable system ranging from as few as 24 to as many as 500 channels. Broadband coaxial cable systems can be designed to carry television, data, and telephone signals with two-way television and remote control of video playback equipment. Fiber-optic cable can also be used to distribute television, data, and telephone signals. While fiber-optic cable is no more expensive than coaxial cable, tapping off and distribution equipment can be more costly in the long run. While fiber-optic cable can carry signals with less noise and signal loss over distance, it does not provide the connecting flexibility necessary for widespread distribution. It is ideal for long-distance transportation of signals from a single point to a single point when multiple channels and multiple taps are not required. Today, many campuses and organizations have developed cable or fiber-optic distribution systems for the dissemination of programming on multiple-channel education and entertainment networks.

Instructional Television
Fixed Service (ITFS)

Instructional Television Fixed Service (ITFS) systems are another way to reach distant learners. ITFS systems are sometimes referred to as narrowcast television. ITFS frequencies, or channels, are regulated like broadcast signals, and license and frequency assignments must be obtained from the Federal Communications Commission (FCC). Licenses are usually granted in blocks of two to four channels.

An ITFS system resembles other closed-circuit systems, except that the transmitter sends the signal on a high frequency that is not tunable on television receivers. A program source from cameras or a video playback unit is fed to the ITFS transmitter, which broadcasts the signal to a receiving antenna at the receiving site. The signal is then converted and distributed by cable to television receivers for viewing. The ITFS transmitter generates a 2,500-megahertz signal and superimposes upon it the program picture and sound. A transmitting antenna radiates the signal in all directions, or the antenna can be shaped to concentrate the signal in one direction to better serve specific sites. The useful range of an ITFS system depends upon the terrain, transmitter power, antenna height, and design. The signal travels on a line-of-sight path, and its effective distance is normally twenty to twenty-five miles. Because of its multiple-channel capability, ITFS can also be used for two-way transmissions. An ITFS system is inexpensive when compared to the cost of cable covering the same distance. ITFS also offers the privacy of closed-circuit television, but is limited in its channel capability. This method is ideal for delivering a limited number of programs each hour to learners concentrated within a twenty-mile radius.

Microwave

Microwave systems are used to transmit a signal from a single point to a single point over a distance of thirty to fifty miles. The picture and sound are superimposed (modulated) onto a high-frequency carrier, which is transmitted in a very narrow signal pattern by the transmitting antenna. The process can be repeated by many microwave stations until the signal is received at the desired site. As with ITFS, the signal moves on a line-of-sight path. The difference between microwave and ITFS is the signal pattern: a very narrow pattern for microwave aimed to a single point versus a signal radiating in a circular, or broad, pattern for ITFS. Microwave use is limited to point-to-point delivery.

Satellite

While cable and ITFS systems can reach learners economically when concentrated in urban centers and in small communities, it is difficult to deliver a signal to communities spread over a large state or region. Satellite downlinking, or satellite communications, has become a practical vehicle to deliver instruction economically to audiences located in large geographic areas. Satellite communication involves the transmission of a signal 22,500 miles into space to a geosynchronous satellite which receives, reprocesses, and transmits the signal back to earth. The signal can be received by a carefully aimed antenna dish on earth, transposed to a television receiver frequency, and viewed or transmitted to other locations within the receiving institution's area using any of the previously discussed distribution systems. Theoretically, the satellite signal can be received on half the earth's surface but in practice the satellite's signal covers only approximately one-third, or 140 degrees, of the area of the earth. Because of this broad coverage, a satellite system is ideal for distributing programs to learners distributed over an extremely large area.

The cost of satellite technology is not inexpensive. Uplink equipment to transmit a signal to the satellite ranges in cost from $500,000 to several million, plus expensive satellite time. Downlink stations on earth to receive the signal and transpose it are economical, costing from $500 (home use) to approximately $60,000 (commercial use). Downlinks in the $1,500 to $3,000 price range are adequate for most school and industrial training applications. Satellite time must be leased, with lease costs ranging from $300 to $500 per hour. As one can readily see, the cost of satellite use must be amortized over a large number of learners or multiple users.

A broad range of uses is being made of satellite communication in schools and the corporate world. One example is teleconferences, where top managers/consultants/resource experts provide a program to be viewed by personnel and/or learners in many locations across the country. Two-way audio provides for discussion among various sites. University courses are offered to learners scattered across the country. Institutions, individually and in consortia, are offering undergraduate and master degree programs in liberal arts, computer science, agriculture, and many other fields via satellite-based delivery systems. Business and industry consortia and public television entities are offering short courses, training modules and special update events to their constituents through uplink/downlink networks. Other groups and schools are providing upper-level high school courses to small school districts in rural areas that do not have the resources to provide such courses to their students. These are just a few of the present applications of satellite communications in providing information to distant learners.

Compressed Video

Due to the development of compression technology, it is possible to deliver digital television images over twisted pair cable, as well as coaxial and fiber-optic cable. Video compression involves processing the typical analog television signal digitally and transmitting it in a discrete and noncontinuous manner through codec links. International standards for compression technology were established in 1990 by the Consultative Committee on International Telegraph and Telephone (CCITT) for minimum performance levels that ensures equipment compatibility but allows some variance in equipment performance and price.

Videoconferencing using compressed video enables live, two-way auditory and visual signals to be transmitted simultaneously among sites which are equipped with a compatible system. Such systems include a codec (coder/decoder), receiving and transmitting hardware, and a transmission link. Compressed video transmissions are normally sent "point to point," meaning that digital signals are sent specifically from transmitting site to the receiving site or sites that are predetermined.

The major advantage of compressed transmission is that its "edited" signal demands less "space," or bandwidth, to send. Thus, videoconferencing can use standard telephone lines or less capacity on other cables. This makes it less costly than noncompressed systems. Reduced hardware and transmission costs appear to be the key value of this distribution technology.

Compressed video may, however, have limits on the quality. Motion may appear jerky, or after-images may linger on the screen. Usually, the greater the compression, the greater the picture degradation. However, as compression technology improves, it has become harder to detect video compression limits. Compression also can cause some slight difficulties in audio transmission. There may be a slight pause between the time someone actually speaks and when the audio is actually heard at the distance site. Learners, however, seem to adapt to this compression characteristic and it does not limit interaction.

Due to the ability of compressed video to use standard telephone lines, it provides distance education the opportunity for national and international distribution of programs. Numerous state distance education systems utilizing compressed video hardware are already in operation. States with large geographic distances, such as South Dakota, Wyoming, and Utah, have made effective use of this technology.

Electronic Text

Electronic text technologies that have potential for reaching distant learners are rapidly emerging. Electronic text services have existed for more than a decade, but recent technological developments and cost reductions have made their use more attractive as a distant learner delivery vehicle. Students, faculty, trainers, and administrators have already experienced some form of electronic text when they have used electronic mail, searched a database, or watched and read continuous news and weather summaries as they are presented on local cable news channels.

Electronic text is capable of using many forms of print and graphic information stored in computers and distributed over telephone lines, cable networks, broadcast transmission or satellite. This information is then accessed by users through special decoders connected to a television set.

Two terms are widely used to identify two different types of electronic text service. *Interactive videotex* is a two-way system where a user can both receive and send information. Because interactive videotex signals are transmitted via cable or telephone lines, the system has nearly unlimited text capacity. Viewers may receive the signal information on a television receiver equipped with a decoder, which demodulates the information and converts it to data or graphics for display. *Broadcast videotex,* also referred to as teletex, is a one-way system where a user can only select information. In broadcast videotex systems, the information is digitized and transmitted on a television broadcast transmission using unused horizontal lines. Each television picture in the United States consists of 525 horizontal lines displayed thirty times per second. However, some of these lines are not used, and videotex information is placed upon a few of these lines (lines numbered 10 through 16) (Alber 1985, 152). Interactive videotex has an advantage over broadcast videotex because it piggybacks upon standard television broadcasts and is therefore available in most homes. However, the six-line limit on the broadcast signal limits its capacity to several hundred pages, whereas interactive videotex using telephone or cable has nearly unlimited capacity.

There has been considerable experimentation with electronic text as a vehicle to deliver instruction to distant learners during the mid-1980s, sponsored by the Annenberg/EPB Project. Programs have been conducted by San Diego State University, the University of Wisconsin, the University of Nebraska, and WGBH-TV in

Boston through the Electronic Text Consortium. A major use of videotex today is closed captioning for hearing-impaired viewers of broadcast and cable television. This technology has become very useful to both entertainment and education.

Computers are rapidly becoming the preferred distance education tool, and networks are evolving as a major resource for distance learners. Computerized instruction has moved from the computer-assisted instruction (CAI) of the 1970s to computer-managed instruction (CMI), which provides broader objectives and capabilities in student sequencing and guidance. The development of networks, LANs, WANs, routers, CU-See Me software, the Internet, and the World Wide Web (the Web or WWW) has allowed distance educators to reach and communicate with learners faster and in ever-increasing geographically diverse areas. The use of e-mail, computer conferencing, telnet, Web course authoring, and specialized client/server systems has increased online distance education learning opportunities.

A number of institutions and companies are engaged in online courses and full degree programs via the Web. These systems and courses epitomize the trend toward student-centered active learning. The Open University of the United Kingdom, the National Science Foundation, and several consortia of higher education institutions are leading the way toward this future for individualized distance education.

While electronic text systems offer promise for distant learning, there exist some barriers to its success. Decoders and network hardware to provide access are expensive. Telephone line and network systems are not commonly available, and rates are often too high to make it feasible for learner use. Easy-to-use software and learner training and support need to become available on a widespread basis.

Desktop Videoconferencing

A relatively new distance learning technology is the use of two or more desktop computers to communicate in a multimedia fashion. At its simplest level, a video camera on the top of each monitor captures the participants. With appropriate software, the participants' images and audio, along with graphics and text, can be shared by all connected. At this level, a system costing around $1,500 or less per station allows relatively primitive live video images of the participants. More expensive systems in the neighborhood of $9,000–$30,000 per station allow better-quality images of participants and more reliable service. This is an evolving technology that improves annually.

National University in San Diego is one example of an institution having fairly extensive experience with this technology. The university uses it in a nursing degree program for one-on-one interaction between instructors and students at remote sites. Progress reports and interviews can be conducted without the extensive travel that would ordinarily be required.

Combination Services

The distant learner delivery vehicles discussed can and are being used in concert with each other. Each should be selected and used when it is most efficient for meeting specific needs. As an example, at Kirkwood Community College (Cedar Rapids, Iowa), a combination of delivery vehicles is used. A cable system distributes programs on campus, and a microwave system delivers programming to distant locations, where it is input into a local community cable system and/or transmitted to learners by ITFS. A satellite uplink could be added, if many learners were scattered across the United States or even over one-third of the earth. The employment of these various electronic delivery technologies, in combination with on-site attendance sessions, has been used successfully in various institutions and commercial organizations to upgrade or train staff. The use of appropriate vehicles in concert enables programs to be delivered to distant learners over a large geographic area at the most economical cost.

SUPPORTING
DISTANT LEARNER SERVICES

Providing adequate support services to distant learners and the instructors who provide those services is crucial if the outreach and training programs are to succeed. Programs have to be created and produced, selected and purchased, or recorded from classrooms. If distant learning programs are to be successful, the students enrolled must have the full support of the institution—admissions, counseling, library, and media resources. Before an institution or company embarks upon distant learning activities, it must carefully analyze the efforts required and the impact the program will have on its resident resources. In addition, the following concerns should be addressed:

- Instructors/trainers will need time to develop, reformat, and organize courses.
- Instructors/trainers may need additional incentives, such as royalties or release time.
- Instructors/trainers will need to acquire new skills for utilizing appropriate distant learning technologies and instructional methods.
- Instructors/trainers will need to have electronic services and software to hold "office hours" and provide for student interaction.
- Classrooms/laboratories and other support services will need to be located and made available in remote sites.
- Courses and programming for distant learning will need to be selected based upon needs assessment to assure enrollment.
- The most efficient delivery mode (technology system) will need to be selected.
- An appropriate fee structure and funding system will need to be developed for distance learning systems. It may not be on the same basis as a typical training event or campus course.
- Some form of face-to-face contact and group interaction activities need to be provided, if possible.
- Proctors need to be employed at group sites to provide logistical services, that is, to set up equipment, hand out papers, pick up papers, and administer tests.
- All phases of instruction/training will need to be monitored to ensure that organization or institutional standards are maintained.

ROLE OF THE MEDIA MANAGER

Distance education programs, like campus- or center-based programs, require the support of many groups and agencies. The media center and the media manager have a significant role and set of functions to perform in order for distance education and distant learners to be successful. Some of the support activities that a media manager should provide are:

- Manage operations and technical support for the electronic delivery methods and classrooms used by the distance education programs.
- Assist in the selection of the appropriate teaching tools and technology for the various distance education programs and clients.
- Provide instructional design and faculty development support for the staff members of distance education agencies.
- Develop and design distance education teaching materials, graphics, and support media.
- Coordinate the identification and licensing of appropriate teaching and media resources to be used in the distance learning systems.
- Act as a copyright and fair use specialist for the distance education faculty and support personnel.
- Cooperate in a learning team role with other agencies in the support and delivery of distance education programs.

SUGGESTED ACTIVITIES

1. List and describe the attributes of each of the following distant audience delivery vehicles and explain how each could best be used:

   a. videotape courses or presentations
   b. broadcast television
   c. cable television
   d. ITFS
   e. microwave systems
   f. the Web
   g. satellite communications

2. Lay out on a map how instruction, training, or information could be delivered to distant learners or employees in communities, branch campuses, or offices

   a. within the community
   b. widely distributed within a community thirty miles away
   c. to a branch campus or office thirty miles away
   d. to a branch campus or office sixty miles away
   e. to ten branch offices distributed across the United States

3. Describe the support services that a media center could provide to distant learning programs.

REFERENCES

Alber, Antone F. 1985. *Videotex/Teletex: Principles and Practices*. New York: McGraw-Hill.

Rogers, Everett M. 1986. *Communication Technology: The New Media in Society*. New York: Free Press.

Schlosser, Charles, and Mary Anderson. 1994. *Distance Education: A Review of the Literature*. Washington, D.C.: Association for Educational Communications and Technology.

Stasheff, Edward. 1947. "Television—Adjunct to Present Visual Materials in Public Education." *See and Hear,* 3, no. 3: 22–23, 38.

Willis, Barry, ed. 1994. *Distance Education: Strategies and Tools*. Englewood Cliffs, N.J.: Educational Technology Publications.

Wittich, Walter Arno, and Charles Francis Schuller. 1957. *Audiovisual Materials: Their Nature and Use*. 2d ed. New York: Harper & Row.

MEDIA RESOURCES

Breaking New Ground: Faculty Perspectives. Instructional Communications Systems, University of Wisconsin–Extension, 32 minutes. Madison, Wisc.: University of Wisconsin, 1995. Videocassette.

Communicating with Your Students. Penn State Television/WPSX-TV, 28 minutes. University Park, Pa.: Pennsylvania State University Media Sales, 1985. Videocassette.

Counseling for Adult Learners. Penn State Television/WPSX-TV, 28 minutes. University Park, Pa.: Pennsylvania State University Media Sales, 1985. Videocassette.

Distance Learning Series. Minnesota Satellite and Technology, 30–45 minutes. (Series of four programs). Los Angeles: First Light Video Publications, 1996. Videocassettes.

Distance Learning Today. RMI Media, 30 minutes. (Series of four programs). Washington, D.C.: Association for Educational Communications and Technology, 1996. Videocassettes.

Foundations and Applications of Distance Education. Iowa Distance Education Alliance, 7–18 minutes. (Series of nine programs). Washington, D.C.: Association for Educational Communications and Technology, 1995. Videocassettes.

SELECTED BIBLIOGRAPHY

Albright, Michael J., and David Graf. *Teleteaching: Distance Education Planning, Techniques, and Tips*. 2d ed. Ames, Iowa: Iowa State University, Instructional Technology Center, 1998.

Berge, Zane L., and Mauri P. Collins, eds. *Computer Mediated Communication and the Online Classroom*. Cresskill, N.J.: Hampton Press, 1995.

Boschmann, Erwin, ed. *The Electronic Classroom: A Handbook for Education in the Electronic Environment*. Medford, N.J.: Learned Information, 1995.

Cyrs, Thomas E. *Teaching at a Distance with the Merging Technologies*. Las Cruces, N.M.: New Mexico State University, Center for Educational Development, 1997.

Gilbert, John K., Annette Temple, and Craig Underwood. *Satellite Technology in Education.* New York: Routledge, 1991.

Hakes, Barbara T., Steven G. Sachs, Cecelia Box, and John Cochehour. *Compressed Video: Operations and Applications.* Washington, D.C.: Association for Educational Communications and Technology, 1993.

Minoli, Daniel. *Distance Learning Technology and Applications.* Boston: Artech House, 1996.

Mood, Terry Ann. *Distance Education: An Annotated Bibliography.* Englewood, Colo.: Libraries Unlimited, 1995.

Portway, P. S., and C. Lane. *Technical Guide to Teleconferencing and Distance Education.* San Ramon, Calif.: Applied Business Telecommunications, 1992.

Wagner, Norman. "Telecommunications and the Changing Nature of Instructional Delivery." *Syllabus* (June 1996): 10–12.

Willis, Barry. *Distance Education: A Practical Guide.* Englewood Cliffs, N.J.: Educational Technology Publications, 1993.

Wolcott, L. L. "The Distance Teacher as Reflective Practitioner." *Educational Technology,* 35, no. 1 (1995): 39–43.

Zvacek, S. M. "Effective Affective Design for Distance Education." *Tech Trends,* 36, no. 1 (1991): 40–43.

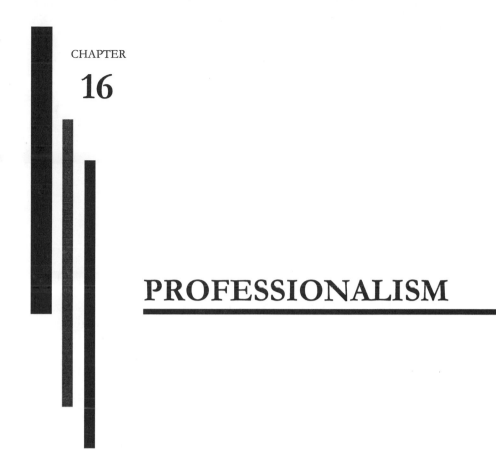

CHAPTER

16

PROFESSIONALISM

What are the characteristics of a profession? A profession has, at least, these characteristics: (a) an intellectual technique, (b) an application of that technique to the practical affairs of man, (c) a period of long training necessary before entering the profession, (d) an association of the members of the profession into a closely-knit group with a high quality of communication between members, (e) a series of standards and a statement of ethics which is enforced, and (f) an organized body of intellectual theory constantly expanding by research.

James D. Finn, "Professionalizing the
Audio-Visual Field," *Audio-Visual
Communication Review*, Winter 1953

343

OBJECTIVES

At the conclusion of this chapter you should be able to

1. Explain the value of a professional growth program.

2. List and discuss four specific professional growth activities that a media manager may develop that will provide for his or her continuous growth.

Media managers must be informed about the tools, materials, processes, procedures, issues, concepts, and scientific knowledge within the instructional media profession. They must be able to apply that knowledge to help others solve communication problems. Thus far in this text we have discussed that body of knowledge and how to apply it, but that is not enough if a person is to be effective as a media manager. The media manager must also be a professional.

What is a professional? In 1953, James Finn wrote the definition of a profession found on this chapter's first page. He was an early, staunch advocate for making the audiovisual (later media) field into a profession. He concluded at the time that he wrote the definition that only the first two criteria were met, and the field was not yet a profession. Over forty years later, much progress has been made in meeting the other four criteria of Finn's definition. Whether all have been completely met is debatable, but Seels and Richey, after reviewing the complete development of the media and technology field, make a strong case for professional status: "Instruction technology has moved from being viewed as a craft, to a profession, and now a field of study" (1994, 107).

After learning the body of knowledge necessary to obtain a position and becoming employed successfully as a media professional, how does a person remain current with the ever increasing new knowledge and technologies related to that profession? Where does the media manager turn for help and assistance when needed? With whom does the media manager interact to continue to be stimulated, excited, and enthusiastic about the work? Where are the seeds of new ideas generated? The answers should be obvious: Media managers must continue to study by developing a personal program for professional growth.

PROFESSIONAL GROWTH

The professional remains on the cutting edge of the media field. This is more difficult today than ever before, due to the complexity and the rapid change in various instructional technologies. The person who fails to stay current soon falls behind, loses his or her enthusiasm, and fails to generate ideas, and, therefore, will not survive. Through a continuous professional growth program, the professional grows as the body of knowledge in the field expands. There are many activities that one can develop or participate in for professional growth.

Study

One should never stop studying. The literature *must* be read faithfully. Identify the major periodicals that contain articles with instructional media-related issues and read them each month. These periodicals may not necessarily be from professional media associations. As early as 1953, James Finn also recognized the interdisciplinary nature of the audiovisual field.

> The audio-visual field is in the peculiar position of having its research carried on by workers in other disciplines using hypotheses unknown to many audio-visual workers, and reporting results in journals that audio-visual people do not read and at meetings that audio-visual people do not attend (Finn, 15–16).

That is, and probably will continue to be, the case as the content of the field will always be interdisciplinary in nature. Therefore, journals from other fields will have articles related to media applications. Locate periodicals that consistently have appropriate articles and add them to your monthly browse list. Remember, it is nice to know what the patrons you are serving are reading.

Be alert for new books that may provide helpful information. Appropriate subject areas include computer applications, telecommunications, instructional/training theory and practice, satellite applications, copyright, instructional design, psychology of learning, and futures studies.

Professional Associations

The value of belonging to and participating in professional associations cannot be overemphasized. Get involved in the committee and governance structure. Such involvement forces one to grow professionally, to think on one's feet, and to become informed about and conversant with issues. Good professional associations provide current information on issues via newsletters, and their journals are usually excellent and should be read faithfully. Journals may also provide an opportunity for the media manager to publish articles. Most institutions like to see their people publish. Publishing increases one's image as the media professional within the institution. Another benefit of belonging to professional organizations is the people one meets. Where else can one have contact with people who all have the same or related interests? It is through organizations that one can find out what is going on across the country, not only in program development but in the minds of fellow professionals. Here the emerging professional can touch base with leaders from across the country. Electronic mail and the Internet can be powerful tools to further this goal.

There are three main levels of professional organizations: state, regional, and national. All can be invaluable in providing professional growth activities for the media manager. It is usually easier to become active in the committee structure and governance of state organizations, as they are obviously smaller organizations. However, membership and involvement at all three levels are important. A word of caution is in order. Involvement in professional associations must never negate one's alliance or attention to one's institution and media service programs. Time requirements must be weighed carefully before professional association commitments are made. The approval of the institution's administration should be obtained before major commitments are accepted for professional association responsibilities and only after time factors have been thoroughly discussed. There is a real danger of media professionals becoming overinvolved in professional organizations to the detriment of their employing institution. This has sometimes led to unfavorable consequences to the individuals involved, e.g., job change, demotion, or dismissal.

Professional Conferences

Participation in workshops and conferences is an important professional growth activity. Again, workshops and conferences may exist at the state, regional, or national level. Workshops and conferences can be organized around a very specific topic covered in depth or can cover a wide variety of topics. State and national conventions are organized into hundreds of presentations, where national experts and others with in-depth expertise make presentations. Conventions provide the media manager an opportunity to attend ten to twenty presentations in one week. Most state and national conventions also arrange for an extensive exhibit of media materials and equipment. The exhibit areas of numerous media and technology national conventions display a veritable cafeteria of equipment and materials.

Another benefit of participation in workshops, conferences, and conventions is the contact with other media professionals. Here new friendships are developed, ideas shared, and new ideas generated. A network of personal contacts can be developed for future reference. For these reasons, participation at workshops, conferences, and conventions is an important part of a media manager's professional growth program.

Professional Information Pipeline

A professional expertise information pipeline is based upon one's listing of people who may be a valuable source of information. It can be a very precise resource bank with the people listed in specific areas of expertise—television production, instructional development, media facility design, and others. Such pipelines, or networks, are personal and may be of interest only to the media manager who developed them. They do not simply happen, but must be actively developed, cultivated, and kept up-to-date.

The value of establishing and maintaining contact with a group of such experts is being able to identify and call upon others when information is needed. The network saves time and can give authority to data and/or information. These same individuals can provide a source of inspiration and moral support when one seems to run into a stone wall. Sometimes an outsider with a fresh look at a problem can see a solution overlooked by those close to it. An information pipeline expands a media manager's information bank and is a useful professional growth tool. While writing letters and making telephone calls were the strategies of the past, electronic mail, fax transmission, and the Internet are powerful new pipelines of information.

SUGGESTED ACTIVITIES

1. Review professional journals and select 10 that include media-related information that will be of value to you. Select five of the 10 to include on your mandatory monthly reading list.

2. Identify the state, regional, and national professional associations that could be of value to you. Select and join one or more from each category. If you are still in school, student memberships are usually inexpensive.

3. Develop a list of media professionals by various categories that you believe would be of value to you to answer media management/logistical questions (professional expertise network). Actively correspond with them by telephone, traditional mail, and electronic mail.

REFERENCES

Finn, James D. 1953. "Professionalizing the Audio-Visual Field." *Audio-Visual Communication Review,* 1, no. 1: 6–18.

Seels, Barbara B., and Rita C. Richey. 1994. *Instructional Technology: The Definition and Domains of the Field.* Washington, D.C.: Association for Educational Communications and Technology.

SELECTED BIBLIOGRAPHY

Association for Educational Communications and Technology. *The Definition of Educational Communications and Technology.* Washington, D.C.: Association for Educational Communications and Technology, 1977.

Ely, Donald P., and Tjeerd Plomp. *Classic Writings in Instructional Technology.* Englewood, Colo.: Libraries Unlimited, 1996.

Hackbarth, Steven. *The Educational Technology Handbook: A Comprehensive Guide.* Englewood Cliffs, N.J.: Educational Technology Publications, 1996.

Morris, Betty J., John T. Gillespie, and Diana L. Spirt. *Administering the School Library Media Center.* 3d ed. New Providence, N.J.: R. R. Bowker, 1992.

THE
FUTURE

If the scientific advances of the past fifty years were wiped out tomorrow, we would hardly recognize the world we live in, but if all progress in educational practice during the past half-century were forgotten, the change would be minimal. . . . Will it be possible to erase the next fifty years of educational advances without changing education materially? I think not. Education is on the verge of momentous changes.

Raymond V. Wiman and Wesley C. Meierhenry, eds.,
Educational Media: Theory into Practice, 1969

OBJECTIVES

At the conclusion of this chapter you should be able to

1. Describe the process model that is used by many futurists to predict the future.

2. List ten technological or organizational changes that are likely to affect media service programs.

3. List ten socioeconomic changes likely to occur within the next ten years that may affect media services programs.

4. Discuss the effect that these technological, social, and economic changes may have on media service programs and on you as a media manager.

This chapter easily could have included a collection of facts and figures based upon the predictions of many of the recognized authors and futurists identified in the bibliography of this chapter. However, since the subject of this book is media management, facts and figures will be eliminated and the technological, social, and economical changes that can be expected in the next several decades will be generalized from the available data and predictions made from the selected authors. The serious media futurist student is encouraged to review the materials listed in the selected bibliography at the end of this chapter.

A media manager cannot remain static and content with the status quo, if he or she is to be successful. Society and all of its subsystems continue to change. The world is not the same as it was even five years ago. Ponder a moment the changes that have occurred in the instructional technology field in just the past three or four decades. Cable television was in its infancy. There were no two-way interactive systems, no portable videocassette players. There were no inexpensive computers in the classrooms or networking of computers or computerized library automated systems. Electronic special effects generators, character generators, and sophisticated nonlinear editing did not exist for producing high-quality television programs. Interactive video and multimedia systems were not even imagined. There were no semiconductor chips, integrated circuits, microchips, lasers, or fiber optics. All these and more are now here.

What about the future? Will as many technological changes occur in the next three or four decades as occurred in the previous similar period of time? Past history would indicate so—and even more. The creation of new knowledge increases exponentially and now doubles every few years. Futurists are predicting an increase in the rate of innovation unprecedented in human history, and refer to it as "spiral evolution." That would indicate that "we haven't seen anything yet"! What does this mean to the media manager? What changes are likely to occur in a media manger's programs, organizations, and in even his or her position responsibilities?

Before looking at the technological, organizational, social, and economic changes that may occur in the future, a lesson may be learned from the strategies that futurists use to predict the future. While many different strategies are used to make predictions, one strategy stands out that might serve media managers well when making decisions regarding the future. That strategy or approach, used by some futurists, is called the *process* model (figure 17.1).

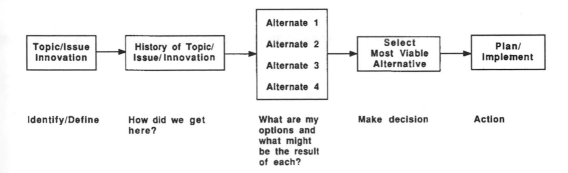

Figure 17.1. Process model used by futurists.

Process futurists believe that the future can be predicted through a process of looking at the past, developing alternative future changes, and picking the alternative that seems most likely to occur. Let us look at an example. What might the automobile look like in three decades? The process-oriented futurist would look at the automobile today, how it evolved, why it developed as it did, how it developed, manufacturing changes, and how it is used. The process futurist would then explore alternative changes that might occur in the next three decades, based upon the public's purpose for using automobiles, manufacturing technologies, economics, energy, and how each of these factors may impact the automobile. For each alternative automobile "shape," the process futurist would list very specific reasons why the alternative is likely to occur. Finally, the futurist would select the alternative that he or she believes is the most viable.

As the media manager attempts to develop plans for the future, the process model might serve well as a tool. The manager will need to make predictions prior to developing plans for the future. These plans should be based upon more than guesses. With application of the process model, viable alternatives can be developed and examined before a direction is selected.

ORGANIZATIONAL AND TECHNOLOGICAL CHANGES

The next three decades should bring exciting technological innovations to the media manager and media service programs. If the changes are equal to the past three decades, the changes are almost mind-boggling. A few of these technological changes of interest and importance to the media manager are described and projected by the following authors.

Dr. Frank B. Withrow of the NASA Classroom of the Future, in a recent *T.H.E. Journal* article (1997), described the impact and acceptance of new telecommunications technologies as comparable to those of the motion pictures of the 1960s. He explains that many people felt that moving pictures would dilute the educational process and "dumb down" the lessons children needed. However, he stated that, like the motion picture and the photograph before, telecommunication services will find their natural place in the education process. Withrow predicts that:

Modern telecommunications may be our legacy of sharing and conveying precise images of our human experiences.

Computers and telecommunications systems will remove time and geographic distance barriers from classroom attendance and participation. They will provide an increasingly better fit for our democratic value of quality education.

Digital technologies could impact our classrooms as great as did the writing process and the printing press.

Online course delivery through various technologies will reduce the cost of education while empowering students to guide their own learning agendas.

The twenty-first century may be depicted as the age of the mind, the brain, and telecommunications when compared to the past centuries.

Dr. Alfred Bork, University of California at Irvine, in discussing the future of computers and learning (1997) predicts that during the next twenty-five years of learning we will observe:

The development of highly interactive software and computer-based courses.

The effective use of voice-recognition software to operate the technology.

The development of pedagogical instructional designs and environments that will enhance the use of interactive software.

The significant expansion and improvement of at least two delivery technologies, CD-ROMs and networks, that will change the delivery capacities to distance learners.

The establishment of distance learning institutes and structures that have the characteristics of:

> degrees offered in many subject areas;
>
> some classes having 10,000 students each;
>
> much of the learning done in the home or place of employment;
>
> reduced costs per course or degree;
>
> study centers available which will provide human support to the individualized learning techniques;
>
> fewer teachers, more students; and
>
> programs operated by governments, companies, and international organizations.

Ely with Blair, Lichvar, Tyksinski and Martinez (1996) provide an analysis of trends identified in the literature on educational technology published in the mid-1990s. They identified the following eight trends:

Computers are pervasive in schools and higher education institutions, and virtually every student in a formal education setting has access to a computer.

Networking is one of the fastest growing applications of technology in education.

Access to television resources in schools is almost universal.

Advocacy for the use of educational technology has increased among policy-making groups.

Educational technology is increasingly available in home and community settings.

New delivery systems for educational technology applications have grown in major ways.

There are requirements that teachers must become technologically literate.

Educational technology is perceived as a major vehicle in the movement of education reform.

MacKnight (1995) reports on her interviews with a sample of academic leaders from private and public U.S. universities. Some of the opinions regarding future challenges and visions that surfaced in these interviews were:

Because of the high costs of the course development, some institutions will purchase courseware and applications tools rather than employ software designers.

More and more faculty will put their hard copy, slides, graphics, animations, QuickTime movies, simulations, and other materials created by their campus media centers onto diskettes for display by computer projection in the classroom. This may easily evolve into substantial collections of materials for each class, if not complete courseware.

Faculty will provide students with much more electronic access to their courses. Students' complete undergraduate or graduate programs might be put on CD-ROMs or some new emerging technology.

There will be a movement away from computer labs. Students will use more portable computers so they can work wherever they are at the moment. Campuses can then concentrate on providing rich resources on networks that students can connect to wherever they may be.

Computers will not be considered as capital expenditures, like buildings and major equipment, but a regular replacement cycle will be established. Computers that are purchased may be loaned or leased to students with rental or buy-back options.

Distance education will become a way to cut costs and provide better access to the institution.

The trend of shifting more and more learning from educational institutions to homes, businesses, museums, libraries, and other organizations will continue.

Albright (1992), in a chapter on the future of campus media centers, suggests the following organizational trends or directions for media centers:

The inclusion of a much broader concept of instructional technology that includes every aspect of the learning and teaching process. The future media center should include seven basic functional areas: (1) learning resources, (2) classroom technologies, (3) media development, (4) instructional and faculty development, (5) academic computing, (6) instructional telecommunications, and (7) research and evaluation.

The development of a media organization that includes centralization of services and a reporting structure to the chief academic officer or immediate subordinate in the institution or school.

The need for strong, effective leaders (media directors) that interact on a daily basis with the highest level of administrative staff and committees at the school or university.

The desire and requirement on the part of the media director to collaborate and cooperate across academic units and service agencies and to take a leadership role in equipping and preparing teachers or faculty for twenty-first-century teaching/learning processes.

The continued development of an emerging set of roles and services of these centralized media organizations will include:

> consultation services,
>
> technology (equipment) services,
>
> classroom management and learning environment advocacy,
>
> technology facilities and classroom design,
>
> multimedia and electronic image production,
>
> distance education support,
>
> instructional/faculty development, and
>
> technical training services.

Christopher Dede, a futurist and professor of education and information technology at George Mason University, predicts that significant advances in the multimedia and distributed learning technologies will be needed in order to keep up with the exponential growth of information in the future. He suggests that a scaling-up of current scattered, successful "islands of innovations," empowered by instructional technology, is needed in the twenty-first century to cause universal improvements in schooling.

Writers in *Learning with Technology*, edited by Dede (1998), project that several major shifts in developing and providing for technology will be needed to support future educational reform. The following actions are forecast by the authors in that work:

The massive infusion of needed school-based technology and professional development can be accomplished only through a distributed learning approach/model. An educational system is forecast in which students and teachers will function in a seamless environment of information technologies both in and out of the school.

Technology funding will be accomplished through reallocation of existing resources, not via add-on funding. In educational institutions, this will mean altering human resource configurations, instructional models, and organizational structures to release funds for technology acquisition.

Educators will change their pedagogical approaches and organizational structures in a fundamental way. Change will evolve through various bottom-up, middle-out, and top-down actions.

Parents and taxpayers will be convinced that new, technology-based strategies are needed in schools.

Educational technology will increase equity rather than widen current differences between the "haves" and the "have-nots."

Expectations of student performance will be increased and significantly changed by the systemic reform based on new strategies for learning through advanced technologies.

Dede (1992) also projects several major technical trends that will influence the future of learning:

The incorporation of hypermedia into multimedia, which will enable knowledge construction by learners.

A fusion of computers and telecommunications, which will lead to the development of highly realistic virtual environments that will be collaborative and interactive. Dede predicts a "meta-medium" that will immerse students in information-laden virtual worlds.

Visualization laboratories, asynchronous learning networks, virtual habitats and communities, knowbots and avatars are predicted as part of the information technology future.

SOCIOECONOMIC CHANGES

Changes will not be limited to technological and organizational areas. Social and economic changes will also occur in the United States with many, but not all, due to technological changes. These changes will undoubtedly affect the programs of media centers. Again, the media manager must be aware and alert to changes in the social and economic conditions of the country, state, and region. People will need to think globally instead of nationally, as the United States is part of a global economy.

Labor and Market

• With the improvements made in communications and transportation, the world is becoming one market and labor pool.

• A significant percent of American industry will continue to move overseas (owing to high labor and tax costs), resulting in fewer nonskilled jobs available in the United States.

• American industry that remains within the United States will become more efficient and technical through the use of robotics and computerization.

• The networked economy and e-commerce (conducting business over the Internet) will have profound effects on retail businesses.

• The job market in the United States will continue to shift to research, development, and service activities.

• The number of dual-income families will remain high.

• There will continue to be a change in the workplace, with a large percentage of the workforce working from their homes via telecommunications technologies, at least on a part-time basis.

Education

- Inflation-adjusted expenditures for education and training will remain at constant levels. The need to do more with the same financial resources will continue. Reallocation will be the practice of the early twenty-first century.

- There will be a continued shortage of teachers, and technology will play a large role in filling the needs of schools.

- Enrollments in schools will increase slowly, and school populations will continue to become more diverse.

- There will be more emphasis placed upon skills development and retraining.

- Improvements in digital technologies in print, data, audio, and video mediums will make the present concept of copyright laws and practices change dramatically.

Other

- The erosion of the family as a social base will continue.

- Third World nations will bypass the era of books and introduce a new era of electronic literacy to the masses.

- The rapid rate of obsolescence in technology will continue to affect its use and acceptance.

LIKELY EFFECTS ON THE USE OF MEDIA TECHNOLOGY

Technological, organizational, social, and economic changes will affect the application of media. In the past, such changes have always effected changes in education, training, business, and industry. The rapid development of media tools and mass-production techniques developed during World War II soon found their way into classrooms and industrial assembly lines after the war. Electronics developed for the space programs soon became widespread in miniaturized electronic equipment. Large and expensive computers developed to analyze large amounts of data are now small, inexpensive, and commonplace. The following are some of the likely effects that these changes may have in the future for media service programs. Such changes will occur not by choice, but by necessity because of social, economic, and technological changes throughout the world.

- Specific groups of professionals will become larger to meet educational needs in schools. These include

    instructional designers, who design validated instructional packages using media technologies based upon educational/training needs and objectives;

    instructional planners and consultants, who will coordinate teaching/learning activities within a variety of learning environments;

professional teachers, who coach, teach, and assist students within the learning environment; and

trained paraprofessional staff, who support learners and provide a variety of logistical support services to professional teachers.

- Conventional class structures and class size will be changed to meet each individual activity and the technology employed.
- The operational costs of education and training will be reduced through the use of technology, but capital costs will be high.
- Learning will be active, participatory, and interactive.
- High commuting and campus residence costs will force colleges and universities to deliver instruction to students in their homes and workplaces.
- Instruction will be delivered to postsecondary students using a combination of telecommunication technologies: interactive computer, telephone, video, and satellite.
- Educational course clearinghouses will be developed to serve as brokers for courses using high-quality interactive training materials and telecommunications delivery methods.
- The social and economic conditions and the continuous need for education and training will mandate a change to technology following the pattern experienced by industry.
- Business, industry, and private consultants will be able to exhibit products and services directly to customers via telecommunications systems anywhere in the world without leaving their school or institution.

SUGGESTED ACTIVITIES

1. Read two or more of the references in the bibliography of this chapter and analyze how their predictions may influence your media center.

2. Select a recent media innovation and apply the process model to help you determine if modification and implementation of the innovation could be of value to your media service program.

3. Select two technological changes that are likely to happen within the next ten years and analyze the likely costs/effects within your service program or institution if implemented.

REFERENCES

Albright, Michael J. 1992. "The Future of Campus Media Centers." *New Directions for Teaching and Learning,* 51, no. 3: 91–100.

Bork, Alfred. 1997. "The Future of Computers and Learning." *T.H.E. Journal,* 24, no. 6: 69–77.

Dede, Christopher J. 1992. "The Future of Multimedia: Bridging to Virtual Worlds." *Educational Technology,* 32, no. 5: 54–60.

Dede, Christopher J., ed. 1998. *Learning with Technology*. Alexandria, Va.: Association for Supervision and Curriculum Development.

Ely, Donald P., with Paul E. Blair, Paula Lichvar, Deborah Tyksinski, and Melissa Martinez. 1996. *Trends in Educational Technology 1995*. Syracuse, N.Y.: Information Resources Publications, Syracuse University.

MacKnight, Carol B. 1995. "Managing Technological Change in Academe." *Cause-Effect*, 18, no. 1: 29–31, 35–39.

Wiman, Raymond V., and Wesley C. Meierhenry, eds. 1969. *Educational Media: Theory into Practice*. Columbus, Ohio: Merrill.

Withrow, Frank B. 1997. "Technology in Education and the Next Twenty-five Years." *T.H.E. Journal*, 24, no. 6: 59–61.

MEDIA RESOURCES

The Future of the Media Center in Higher Education: Panel Discussion. Consortium of College and University Media Centers, 90 minutes. Ames, Iowa: Iowa State University, 1992. Videocassette.

The Future of the Media Center in Higher Education: Uplink. Consortium of College and University Media Centers, 90 minutes. Ames, Iowa: Iowa State University, 1992. Videocassette.

Mega Trends. Video Publishing House, 57 minutes. Schaumburg, Ill.: Video Publishing House, 1985. Videocassette.

A Network of People Linked By Technology—Distance Learning: Teaching the Teacher. Kirkwood Community College, 148 minutes. Cedar Rapids, Iowa: Kirkwood Community College, 1993. Videocassette.

Teaching the Future: Dr. Christopher Dede. WPSX-TV/Penn State Television, 29 minutes. University Park, Pa.: Pennsylvania State University Media Sales, 1992. Videocassette.

SELECTED BIBLIOGRAPHY

Anglin, Gary J., ed. *Instructional Technology: Past, Present, and Future*. Englewood, Colo.: Libraries Unlimited, 1995.

Batson, Trent, and Randy Bass. "Teaching and Learning in the Computer Ages." *Change*, 28, no. 2 (1996): 42–47.

Cornish, Edward, ed. *The Computerized Society: Living and Working in an Electronic Age*. Bethesda, Md.: World Future Society, 1985.

Craver, Kathleen W. *School Library Media Centers in the 21st Century: Changes and Challenges*. Westport, Conn.: Greenwood Press, 1994.

Cutcliffe, Stephen H., Steven L. Goldman, and others, eds. *New Worlds, New Technologies, New Issues*. Bethlehem, Pa.: Lehigh University Press, 1992.

Dede, Christopher J. "The Evolution of Distance Education: Emerging Technologies and Distributed Learning." *American Journal of Distance Education*, 10, no. 2 (1996): 4–36.

Enhagen, Linda, ed. *Technology and Higher Education.* Washington, D.C.: NEA Professional Library, 1997.

Kerr, Stephen T., ed. *Technology and the Future of Schooling.* Chicago: University of Chicago Press, 1996.

Lacy, Dan Mabry. *From Grunts to Gigabytes: Communications and Society.* Urbana, Ill.: University of Illinois Press, 1996.

Lindstrom, Robert L. "Meet Your Future: 13 Ways Presenting Will Change." *Presentations,* 12, no. 4 (1998): 65–73.

Messerschmitt, David E. "The Convergence of Telecommunications and Computing: What Are the Implications Today?" *Proceedings of the IEEE,* 84, no. 8 (1996): 1167–86.

Naisbitt, John. *Megatrends: Ten New Directions Transforming Our Lives.* New York: Warner Books, 1982.

Oblinger, Diana G., and Sean C. Rush, eds. *The Future Compatible Campus: Planning, Designing, and Implementing Information Technology in the Academy.* Boston: Anker Publishing, 1998.

———. *The Learning Revolution: The Challenge of Information Technology in the Academy.* Boston: Anker Publishing, 1997.

EPILOGUE

This completes our look at the theory and practice of managing media programs. It would be productive for the reader to now look at some real-world media centers and reflect on how elements of the theory and practice are applied in specific programs. Of course, firsthand experience is always most beneficial. Visiting actual media centers and observing, interviewing, and photographing can be an immense learning experience. But this is not always possible due to time and expense constraints. Conferences of media and technology associations frequently have sessions on innovative programs. However, using this method to gain a substantial amount of information on different programs is very time-consuming. The same can be said for reviewing journal articles featuring individual programs. As a substitute to these types of information gathering, we can access various print and electronic resources that each look at multiple media programs.

As a baseline, look at the book entitled *Learning Resources Programs That Make a Difference* (Schmidt 1987). Twenty-seven media programs were featured. Programs were included from four-year colleges and universities, community colleges, regional educational agencies, and K-12 school districts. A more recent source, *Educational Technology: Best Practices from America's Schools* (Bozeman and Baumbach 1995), provides profiles of 53 K-12 schools or school districts in the United States.

Web sites are another source of current, useful information. A site maintained by Michael J. Albright of the University of California at Monterey Bay provides descriptions of numerous college and university media centers in the United States, Canada, Australia, and Hong Kong. Its address is http://nms.monterey.edu/centers/. Another Web site is maintained by New Media Centers, a nonprofit organization that brings together media leaders in academia and the corporate sector. The corporate members of this organization help higher education media centers acquire and use new media technology. Information on members and their media programs is available at http://www.csulb.edu/~newmedia/ataglance.html.

The media and technology fields are changing so rapidly that it is essential that we constantly look to others for examples of the use of cutting-edge technologies and innovative uses of new strategies to improve services to our users. Let the search begin and continue on a regular basis.

REFERENCES

Bozeman, William C., and Donna J. Baumbach. 1995. *Educational Technology: Best Practices from America's Schools*. Larchmont, N.Y.: Eye on Education.

Schmidt, William D. 1987. *Learning Resources Programs That Make a Difference*. Washington, D.C.: Association for Educational Communications and Technology.

CLIENT NEEDS ASSESSMENT*

---

*Condensed version, 1987. California State University, Northridge, Instructional Media Center. Used with permission.

IMC Instructional Media Center

NEEDS ASSESSMENT

Specialization _____   Department _____

Status (check one): Full-time _____   Part-time _____   Faculty Rank: _____

Use the following scales in answering the questions which follow:

Awareness

Yes   No

Frequency of Use in the Past Year

1 = not at all
2 = 1-5 times
3 = 6-15 times
4 = 16+ times

Degree of Satisfaction

1 = Highly dissatisfied
2 = Somewhat dissatisfied
3 = Somewhat satisfied
4 = Highly satisfied

Importance to Instructional Program

1 = Not important at all
2 = Not very important
3 = Somewhat important
4 = Extremely important

I. Listed below are descriptions of the general services provided by the Instructional Media Center. If you are generally aware of the service, mark the *yes* response in the appropriate space and continue to mark appropriate responses on frequency of use, degree of satisfaction, and importance to the instructional program. If you are not generally aware of the service, mark *no* in the appropriate space and make no further responses that pertain to that service.

	Awareness	Frequency of Use in the Past Year	Degree of Satisfaction	Importance to Instructional Program
A. **Film and Video Distribution Services** Reservation and distribution of film, videotape, and media equipment, preview rooms and viewing carrels, assistance in locating specific instructional media	Yes No	1 2 3 4	1 2 3 4	1 2 3 4

B. Film Festivals
Assistance in the development and implementation of film festivals and special film showings

Yes No   1 2 3 4   1 2 3 4   1 2 3 4

C. Media Search Services
Computerized search services for films and videotapes

Yes No   1 2 3 4   1 2 3 4   1 2 3 4

D. Evening Delivery Services
Classroom delivery of films and media equipment to classes, Monday through Thursday, 4:30-10:00 p.m.

Yes No   1 2 3 4   1 2 3 4   1 2 3 4

E. Maintenance and Repair Services
Maintenance and repair of state-owned media equipment

Yes No   1 2 3 4   1 2 3 4   1 2 3 4

F. Media Equipment Consultation
Consultation on the purchase of new equipment and the design of new facilities for instructional media use

Yes No   1 2 3 4   1 2 3 4   1 2 3 4

G. Audio and Video Production Services
Development of video productions, slide/tape presentations, audio tapes, videocassette duplication of noncopyrighted materials, assistance in script writing

Yes No   1 2 3 4   1 2 3 4   1 2 3 4

H. Classroom Video Services
Walk-in videotaping for class projects, counseling, evaluation, videotaping of classroom sessions

Yes No   1 2 3 4   1 2 3 4   1 2 3 4

I. Photographic Services
Black-and-white printing and processing, slide photography and duplication, location and portrait photography

Yes No   1 2 3 4   1 2 3 4   1 2 3 4

J. Graphic Services
Dry mounting, laminating, poster graphics, illustrations, overhead transparencies

Yes No   1 2 3 4   1 2 3 4   1 2 3 4

	Awareness	Frequency of Use in the Past Year	Degree of Satisfaction	Importance to Instructional Program
K. Instructional Design Services Assistance in the design and development of instructional media, including interdependent and interactive video and computer-assisted instruction	Yes No	1 2 3 4	1 2 3 4	1 2 3 4
L. Grant Proposal Assistance Assistance in the development of research/project proposals that have a media component	Yes No	1 2 3 4	1 2 3 4	1 2 3 4
M. Faculty Training Program Training of faculty in the development and utilization of media, media workshops	Yes No	1 2 3 4	1 2 3 4	1 2 3 4

II. If funds were available, please indicate how important the following potential services would be to the instructional program:

	Importance to Instructional Program
A. Expanding services to include both daytime and evening delivery of media equipment to classrooms.......	1 2 3 4
B. Electronic distribution of media from the IMC to selected classrooms on campus..............	1 2 3 4
C. Training in computer-assisted instruction and interactive video................	1 2 3 4
D. Utilization of the Instructional Media Center facilities to assist faculty in improving teaching and instructional development skills...........	1 2 3 4
E. Implementation of computerized system for reserving films, videotapes, and media equipment...........	1 2 3 4

Comments and Suggestions:

Please make additional comments on any Instructional Media Center services provided and/or needed:

2

ORGANIZATIONAL PLANS OF EXEMPLARY PROGRAMS*

---

*From William D. Schmidt, *Learning Resources Programs That Make a Difference* (Washington, D.C.: Association for Educational Communications and Technology, 1987). Used with permission.

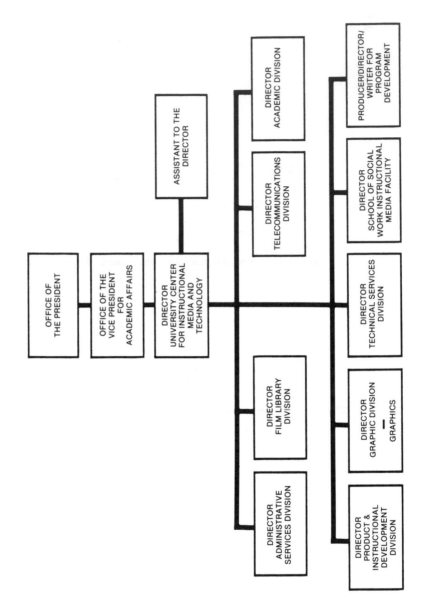

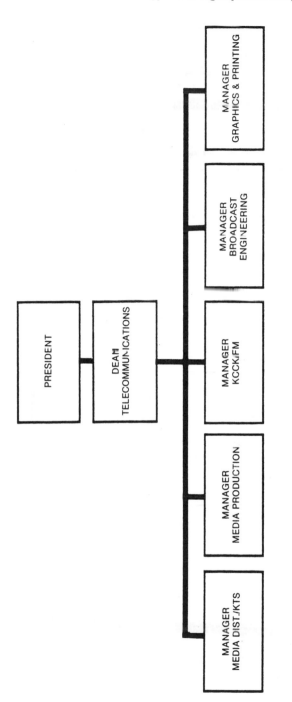

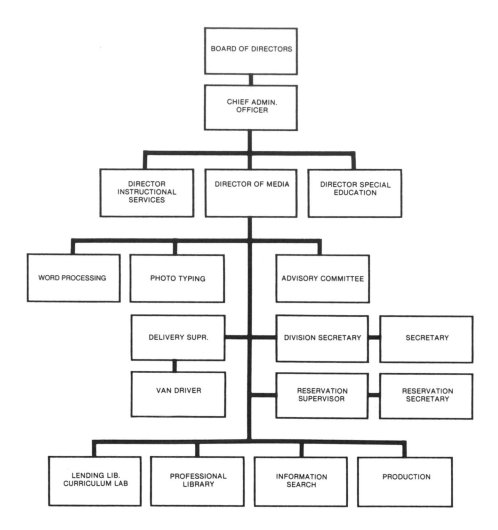

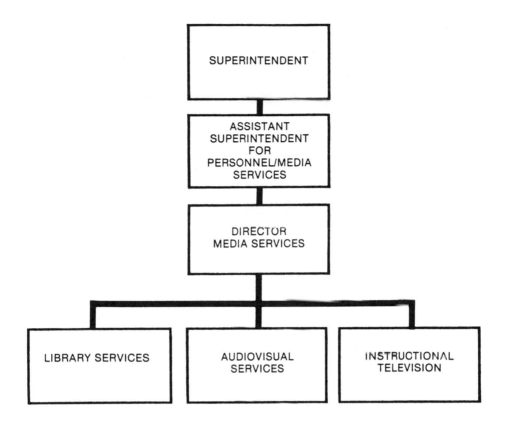

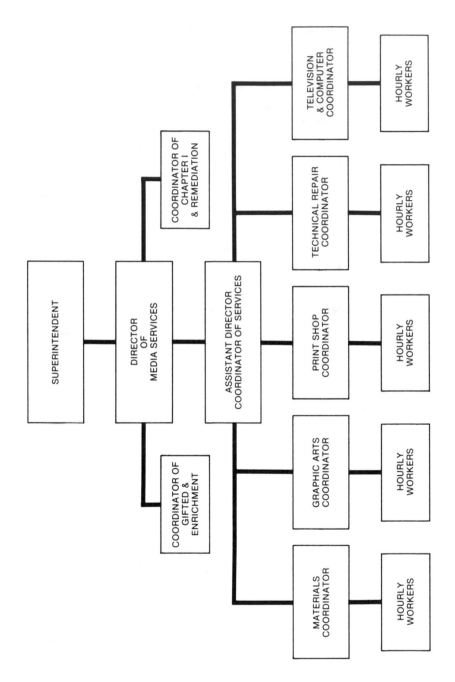

MEDIA SELECTION POLICIES

EDUCATIONAL SERVICE DISTRICT*

Purchase Procedures 1996

CRITERIA: We require that titles purchased:

- Be reviewed in at least one professional journal.

- Be specifically curriculum focused.

- Be reviewed by a committee consisting of a teacher, a nurse, and a parent (sex education titles only).

- Be free of sex, age, or race bias.

- Be of good technical quality (sound, visual image, color, editing, pacing).

- Be accurate, well written, and creative.

SELECTION PROCEDURES: Media is purchased for the multimedia collection only after a thorough examination in which the following questions are considered:

CURRICULUM

- Is this a subject area taught in the schools? At what grade level is this topic taught?

- How many titles do we already have in that subject area?

- Are they up-to-date and in good condition?

- How many times in one year are classes taught in this subject?

---

*Courtesy of Puget Sound Educational Service District, Burien, Washington.

REVIEWS

- Are there any reviews of this material in the professional journals? (*AFVA Evaluations, California Index, CD-ROM Professional, Video Rating Guide*, etc.).

- How many reviews, and do they agree?

- Have any of my colleagues in the media field seen this title? How did they rate it, and what are their reasons?

- Are the persons evaluating the materials qualified? Have they selection skills?

AWARDS

- Has this title won any awards?

- How many; what festivals? (CINE, American Film Festival, ALA Notable Films, Oscars, Emmys, etc.)

- If the media is based on literature, what awards has the story won? (Newbery, Caldecott, Pacific NW Young Readers Choice Award, Lewis Carroll Shelf Award)

COST

- What is the total budget for materials? How many times a year does the Co-op purchase? What percentage of the budget must pay for tax and shipping?

- Is the Co-op more concerned with purchasing quality or quantity?

- Do we need to replace any worn-out titles or buy duplicate copies?

- Is the material really worth the dollars? Will we get a return in circulation?

- Can a "deal" be negotiated with the vendor?

CIRCULATION

- Have the materials been shown on television: national broadcast or PBS?

- Is the popularity of the title such that more than one copy will be needed?

- Does the title have a limited appeal? How many grade levels will be able to understand and use the materials? Will the materials be used by a general audience or for a specific area only?

- How old is the title? Will it become dated fast or last for decades?

REQUESTS

- Who are the persons requesting materials: teachers, administrators, others?

- How many persons or districts have asked for this title?

- Would you buy this title if only one school wanted the material as opposed to many schools?

COMMUNITY

- What kind of community does the ESD serve (conservative, liberal, urban, rural, or what combinations)?

- What is the racial and economic mix?

- Will controversial materials be a problem?

- Does the ESD or local district have a controversial materials policy?

- What are the subjects and issues being requested by the service area?

MISCELLANEOUS

- In how many formats is the title available?

- What are the company contract restrictions (copyright/home video)? Can the title be loaned?

After all the above are considered, the Multimedia Director notes who have made the evaluations and what information has been provided to further show a need for particular materials (e.g., have they shown it to a class and what was the reaction?). What additional comments show the evaluators' careful attention? In other words, why is this particular title unique? Why should it be purchased instead of another?

UNIVERSITY*

University of Minnesota
University Film & Video Collection
Development Policy

Statement of Policy

The University of Minnesota University Film & Video (UFV) adopts the following procedures concerning the evaluation and selection of audiovisual resources for the educational, recreational, and cultural use of the university community, educational institutions, and nationwide patrons.

University Film & Video firmly believes in the patron's right to view all media, and supports the American Library Association's "Library Bill of Rights," the Educational Film Library Association's "Freedom to View," and AECT's "Statement on Intellectual Freedom." It is expected that patrons will select media resources from the UFV collection which relate to their own instructional goals and/or programming needs. It is also expected that these media resources be previewed by the user prior to use with a group. Since each patron's philosophy and goals reflect the uniqueness of the educational institution, group, or organization he/she represents, it is not expected that all media resources acquired by UFV would be appropriate for use by all patrons.

---

*Courtesy of the University of Minnesota, Minneapolis, University Film & Video.

Principles and Objectives of Selection

Media are to be selected that shall

a. Provide for the enrichment and support of the curriculum of public and private schools, universities and colleges, and the goals of community groups, taking into consideration the varied interests, abilities, and maturity levels of the patrons served.

b. Stimulate growth in factual knowledge, literary appreciation, aesthetic values, ethical development, political awareness, social development, and creativity.

c. Present a wide range of views representing the many sides of contemporary issues in order to promote critical thinking and objective evaluation. Selection of a media resource does not necessarily constitute agreement with the content.

d. As far as possible, to foster respect for minority groups by accurately reflecting contributions and achievements of women and men, as well as individuals and groups of various racial, social, ethnic, religious, and cultural backgrounds and which represent a pluralistic society.

e. Place the principle of freedom to view above personal opinion and reason above prejudice in the selection of media resources.

Responsibility for Selection

The Director of the UFV is responsible for the content of the collection. While selection involves many people (including subject specialists, faculty, and community persons), the responsibility for coordinating and recommending the selection and purchase of media resources rests with the certified media personnel.

Criteria for Selection

All media purchases will be consistent with the stated principles and objectives of selection. Guidelines for the evaluation and selection of media resources:

a. Consideration shall be given to the needs of the departments of University of Minnesota, the educational goals of the public and private school districts, and the needs of businesses and community clientele.

b. All acquisitions should be considered on the basis of overall purpose, timeliness or permanence, importance of the subject matter, quality of the production, availability and price, and requests from community members, faculty, students, and other patrons.

c. Media resource selections shall be considered on the basis of potential usage; current holdings in the same subject area; and representation of differing viewpoints, opinions, and beliefs.

d. Media resources shall be selected for their strengths rather than rejected for their weaknesses.

Procedure for Selection

In selecting media resources, the personnel shall evaluate existing resources according to selection criteria, and one or more of the following means:

a.   Preview of media resource

b.   Recommendation of professional, critical reviewers in library science, educational media, and specific curriculum areas

c.   Consultation with faculty, students, community persons, and subject matter experts

Donated, leased, or loaned titles shall be judged by the criteria outlined and shall be accepted or rejected on the basis of those criteria.

It shall be understood that selection is an ongoing process which shall include the removal of titles no longer appropriate and the replacement of lost and worn titles still meeting the needs of patrons.

Withdrawn titles in usable condition may be considered for trade-in or, if the content is deemed of historical or topical value, placed in archives. Otherwise, withdrawn titles shall be disposed of in a suitable and appropriate manner based on the discretion of the Director of UFV.

Procedures for Reevaluation of Media Resources

The right of any individual to free access to materials is basic to a democratic society and to the educational growth of its members. Occasional objections to media resources will occur, despite the quality of the selection process. In the event that media titles are questioned, UFV shall be prepared to uphold the freedom of access to information.

Response and procedure:

1.   Each objector shall be treated courteously and confidentially and asked to address an informal objection to the Director or designee.

2.   The Director and/or designee shall explain to the objector UFV's selection procedure, the selection criteria, and the qualifications of those persons selecting media resources, in addition to explaining the selection rationale for the objectionable title, its intended use, and any additional information deemed necessary at this initial stage.

3.   If the objector wishes the removal or restriction of the resource, he/she shall be directed to submit a formal "Request for Reevaluation of Media Resources" form to the Director. The objector shall complete one "Request for Reevaluation of Media Resources" form for each media title to which he/she objects.

4.   Use of the challenged media resource shall not be restricted during the reevaluation process.

5. Upon receipt of the completed and signed "Request for Reevaluation of Media Resources" form, the Director or designee shall refer it to a review committee for reevaluation of the media resource. A copy of the completed form shall also be sent to the appropriate Associate Dean within one (1) working day of receipt. The review committee shall be appointed by the Director within ten (10) working days of the request. This committee shall consist of two (2) appropriate U of M faculty members and one (1) CEE professional. The goal of the committee is to resolve the conflict over the resource in dispute.

6. The committee shall determine the extent to which the media resource meets the stated criteria for selection by consulting reviews, viewing the media resource, consulting users, and obtaining testimony from appropriate persons.

7. The committee shall prepare a written report of its findings to the Director within twenty (20) working days from the date of the first meeting. The Director shall make a decision based on the written report and shall notify the complainant and the appropriate Associate Dean of Continuing Education and Extension.

Policy Review

Ongoing review and evaluation are necessary to keep this policy vital and current. Therefore, it shall be the responsibility of the Director and Media Specialist to conduct a review of the Media Selection Policy at least once every five (5) years.

MEDIA CENTER AND LEARNING RESOURCES PROGRAMS STANDARDS AND RECOMMENDATIONS

A. LIBRARY MEDIA CENTER SPACE RECOMMENDATIONS*

*From American Association of School Librarians and Association for Educational Communications and Technology, *Information Power: Guidelines for School Library Media Programs* (Chicago: American Library Association, 1988), 132–39. Used with permission.

Table 1

Library Media Center Space Recommendations

Area/Function	Relationships/Considerations	Space Allocation in Square Feet	
		500 Students	1000 Students
Entrance/ Circulation	Near entrance—reserve section, work-room. Card catalog/online terminals, periodical/nonprint storage, equipment storage.	250-500	600-800
	Should have facilities for displays, copy machine, charge area. Program may warrant additional satellite areas for some services such as copy machine, microform readers, etc.		
Reading, brows-ing, listening, viewing, individual study, computing	Near card catalog/online terminals, reference area, magazines microform readers and periodical indexes. In elementary schools, the storytelling area should be located away from circulation area.	25-75% according to program requirements	25-75% Same
	Adequate shelving should be provided for 10 items per ft. At least 25% of the area should be available for student seating allowing 40 sq. ft. per student.		
	The instructional programs in some schools may require that ⅓ to ¾ of the student population be accommodated in the library media center. No more than 100 students should be seated in one area.		
	Mixed seating should include tables and chairs, carrels and lounge-type seating. Some seating should be provided in carrels or equipped tables. Carrels require approximately 16 sq. ft. floor space each to accommodate a computer and printer.		
	Provision should be made for electrical outlets, telephone, and TV reception. Electrical outlets should be switch-controlled at charge desk.		
	Consideration should be given to a flexible system for electrical cable, coaxial cable, and such as a cable duct under the floor or a floor. Computer terminals for database should be provided.		
Small group areas—listening and viewing	In addition to the facilities for individual listening and viewing in the carrels in the main library media areas, small group listening and viewing areas are often necessary. The areas should have electrical outlets, provision for television outlets, light control, wall screen (few if any windows), acoustical treatment.	150 1-3 areas	Same

Area/Function	Relationships/Considerations	Space Allocation in Square Feet	
		500 Students	1000 Students
Equipment storage and distribution	Near corridor, loading dock and elevator.	400-600	500-800
	Should have good control from work area.		
	Near production, carrel and viewing areas.		
	Should be in a secure area.		
	Cabinets with locks need to be provided for storage of equipment and supplies.		
	Should have electrical outlets.		
	Should have shelving and tables.		
Maintenance repair	Near loading dock, elevators, corridor, adjacent to equipment, storage and distribution.	150-300	Same
	Secure area.		
	Include workbench, electrical, and television outlets.		
	Storage for parts, lamps, equipment under repair.		
	Provision for necessary test equipment.		
Media production laboratory	Consider locating adjacent to equipment storage.	50-700	700-900
	Secure area.		
	Provide housing for equipment and materials used in production, and shelving and storage for supplies.		
	Requires refrigeration, sinks, running water, electrical outlets, and counter space.		
	Sound control is needed for audio production.		
	Plan space arrangements in terms of production methods used and work flow.		
Darkroom	The darkroom area should be adjacent to the media production laboratory. (A darkroom may be provided elsewhere in the school.)	150-300	Same
	Requires sinks, running water, electrical outlets, light locks, refrigeration, counter space, adequate ventilation.		

Area/Function	*Relationships/Considerations*	*Space Allocation in Square Feet*	
		500 Students	1000 Students
Conference areas	Locate in quiet and easily supervised area.	150 2-4 areas	Same
	An online search station should be placed near the conference rooms.		
	Should be acoustically treated and equipped with electrical and television outlets and a permanent screen.		
	At least one room should be equipped with a computer and one with a type-writer.		
	Should have movable walls to allow for combining areas.		
	May be used to house special collections which are used frequently.		
	Should be equipped with multipurpose use—see listening and viewing.		
	The listening and viewing areas and the conference areas can serve multiple functions.		
Multipurpose room	Adjacent to reference area, stack area, catalogs, and indexes.	700-900	900-1200
	Good visual control from main library media area and workroom is essential.		
	Space should be flexible and at least class-room size, and equipped for presentation using all forms of media.		
	Telephone jack for telephone conference and computer terminal.		
	Computer should be available.		
Work area	Near entrance, circulation, periodical/nonprint storage.	200-400	300-500
	Near instructional/group project area.		
	Should have access to corridor.		
	Desk space for library media professionals should be provided here or in an appropriate area of the library media center.		
	Provision for shelving, counters, cabinets, sink, running water, electrical outlets, telephone, copy equipment, and computer access.		
	Additional space may be required if cataloging is to be done in the school.		

Area/Function	Relationships/Considerations	Space Allocation in Square Feet	
		500 Students	1000 Students
Periodical storage	Near entrance, circulation, microform readers and reader printers.	250-400	400-600
	Copy equipment should be in close proximity.		
	Magazine indexes, such as *Magazine Index* or *Texts of Microfilm*, should be close to the magazine storage area.		
	Periodicals on microfilm should be provided to allow access to a larger collection in less space.		
	Cabinets should be provided to house microform. Compact shelving should be considered to save space		
Teacher/ professional area	Near classrooms, teachers' office, main library media area, quiet area.	500-600	600-800
	Plan for use as faculty group meeting or conference area.		
	Provide for listening and viewing and for selection and evaluation of new materials and equipment.		
	Emphasize lounge atmosphere.		
	Equip with telephone, computer, type-writer, listening and viewing equipment, professional journals and other resources.		
Computer learning laboratory	Adjacent to group project and instruction area.	600-800	800-1000
	Secure area.		
	Should have response capability.		
	Size of space may vary with nature of computer program.		
Stacks	Locate near reserve area, if appropriate.	400 minimum	400-600
	Consider location in relation to periodical storage.		
	Adequate lighting.		
	Provide for tables and seating as necessary, depending on types of materials sorted in stacks.		
	Include additional stack space as needed to store textbooks.		

Area/Function	Relationships/Considerations	Space Allocation in Square Feet	
		500 Students	1000 Students
Television studio	Should be convenient to media production.	1,600 studio 40' × 40' with ceiling, wide doors	Same
	Area must be soundproof.		
	Classroom facilities may be needed.		
	Studio capability may be provided instead at district level.		
	Consider as alternatives for school television production: mini-studios and portable videotape units.		
	Secure area.		
Audio studio	Should be located adjacent to television studio.	150 minimum	Same
	Area must be soundproof.		
	Provision for storage of equipment and supplies.		
	Secure area.		
Telecommunications distribution	Adjacent to television studio and equipment repair.	800 minimum	Same
	Provision for equipment necessary to distribute audio and visual programs— editing equipment room, TV, and audio.		
	Secure area.		

B. STANDARDS FOR
COLLEGE AND UNIVERSITY
LEARNING RESOURCE PROGRAMS*

LEVEL	PERSONNEL	FACILITIES	EQUIPMENT
Instructional Development Standards			
Minimal	Person with professional training in instructional development at master's level.	None required.	None required.
Basic	Professional with doctoral degree in instructional development or related field, plus clerical assistance.	Private office with adjoining conference and work space.	Additional office equipment; access to computer and production equipment.
Advanced	Additional instructional developer(s) as needed, with clerical assistance, to meet 95 percent of demand for service.	One office space per individual.	Additional office equipment as needed.
Faculty Development Standards			
Minimal	Person with professional training in college teaching, or at least five years' experience as a college teacher.	Part-time classroom or similar meeting space.	None required.
Basic	Professional with doctoral degree in higher education, college teaching, or related field, or a doctoral degree in an academic discipline and at least ten years' experience as a college teacher, plus clerical assistance.	Private office with adjoining conference and work space.	Access to computer terminal.

*From Association for Educational Communications and Technology and American Library Association, *Technology in Instruction: Standards for College and University Learning Resources Programs* (Washington, D.C.: Association for Educational Communications and Technology, 1989), 21–30, Used with permission.

LEVEL	PERSONNEL	FACILITIES	EQUIPMENT
Advanced	Additional faculty developer(s) as needed to meet 95 percent of demand for service, plus one clerical assistant for every three developers, plus one graduate assistant per developer as available.	One office per individual, plus facility for theatre-style presentations.	Additional computer access facilities and equipment, plus equipment for theatre-style presentations.

Creative Production Standards

Visualization Service:

Minimal	Person with professional training and/or experience in materials production.	Workroom with tables.	Dry-mount press, light table, laminator, paper cutter, and transparency maker.
Basic	Graphic artist/photographer with professional training, plus darkroom assistant.	Art production studio, darkroom, and finishing area.	Drafting tables, system for lettering, copy-stand and cameras; plus equipment for photo printing, finishing, and mounting.
Advanced	Graphic designer, photographer, and cinematographer with professional training, plus production, darkroom, and finishing technician(s).	Art studio, photo studio, cinema studio, and computer-generated graphics.	8mm and 16mm motion photography, color processing, and animation equipment.

Audio Service:

Minimal	Part-time assistance as required.	None required.	Audio recorders and related equipment.
Basic	Audio technician or equivalent.	Audio studio and control room.	Turntables, tape decks, audio mixers and related equipment, and audio disc.
Advanced	Full-time audio production professional(s) as needed to meet 95 percent of audio production requests.	Expanded audio studio.	Film sound equipment and upgraded broadcast audio system.

LEVEL	PERSONNEL	FACILITIES	EQUIPMENT
Combined Creative Services — Slide-Tape:			
Minimal	Work handled by personnel from visualization or audio service.	Facilities provided by visualization or audio service.	Equipment provided by visualization or audio service.
Basic	Part-time slide-tape professional as needed.	Work space, assembly/production room, and viewing area.	Two slide projectors, audiotape recorder/synchronizer, and dissolve controller.
Advanced	Professional slide-tape producer(s) as needed to meet 95 percent of requests for service.	Viewing area, facility for theatre-style presentations.	Additional projection control and audio equipment, and multi-image capability.
Combined Creative Services — Sound Motion Picture:			
Minimal	None required.	None required.	None required.
Basic	Part-time cinematographer.	Editing facility.	8mm and 16mm cameras and editing equipment.
Advanced	Producer shared with slide-tape service.	Shared cinema studio, plus sound editing and studio viewing area.	Animation equipment.
Combined Creative Services — Television:			
Minimal	Part-time technician as necessary to fill 95 percent of requests for service.	Storage space.	Portable equipment.
Basic	Television producer(s) as necessary to fill 95 percent of requests for service.	Television studio-control room complex.	Studio equipment, including two or more cameras, film chain, audio equipment, and basic post-production editing equipment, plus remote production capabilities.

LEVEL	PERSONNEL	FACILITIES	EQUIPMENT
Advanced	Additional professionally trained production crew, plus television staff as needed, including technicians, producers, writers, and engineers.	Television studio complex plus remote production and transmission capability.	Remote multicamera system, postproduction editing with character generator and AB roll capability, frame storage, and videodisc.

Equipment Distribution

LEVEL	PERSONNEL	FACILITIES	EQUIPMENT
Minimal	Distribution clerk and part-time assistant(s).	Office, storage, and equipment marshalling areas.	Equipment that is appropriate and adequate to meet 95 percent of requests for service.
Basic	Scheduling assistant as needed to provide service.	Expanded areas for offices, storage, and equipment.	Delivery vehicles suited to institution.
Advanced	Additional professional(s) for distribution services as needed, plus trained operator(s).	Expanded areas for staff and delivery personnel, including remote center distribution capability.	

Electronic Distribution:

LEVEL	PERSONNEL	FACILITIES	EQUIPMENT
Minimal	Electronic technician as needed.	Local or central (remote) distribution area.	Videotape recorders as needed, monitors, and head-end equipment.
Basic	Additional electronic professional(s) as needed.	Central electronic distribution/reception functionally located with television production control.	Institutional and video distribution, plus satellite down-link capabilities.
Advanced	Electronic engineer(s) and technician(s) as needed.	Expanded area.	Satellite up-link capabilities plus remote interconnection.

LEVEL	PERSONNEL	FACILITIES	EQUIPMENT
Microcomputer Accessibility:			
Minimal	One laboratory assistant per facility, plus access to computer specialist.*	Climate-controlled facilities (classroom, laboratory, or combination with office and storage space) with separate power circuits, plus controlled security, static control, and availability of discs, printer supplies such as ribbons, and printer paper.	Student microcomputer systems with single disc drive and graphics capability; instructor** station with two disc drives, printer interface, and printer; software programs as described in Standard 2.3.4.2; access to off-campus databases or computer from the microcomputer facility. All machines must have enough memory to run purchased software packages.
Basic	Two laboratory assistants per facility, plus access to computer specialist* and secretary.	Minimal facilities with additional offices and rooms for training sessions, plus check-out procedure for computer literacy materials and hardware.	Minimal level hardware/software, plus one printer and interface for every five student systems; two of each of several different brands of microcomputer systems to expand exposure to a variety of brands; multiple copies of software proportional to increased numbers of systems; local network in facility so users can share files, software, or peripherals; student access to computers or databases from locations other than computer facilities. All machines should have 25 percent more memory than at minimal level.

*The computer specialist typically would be the laboratory manager, with responsibility included for coordinating hardware maintenance and hardware/software replacement.
**Instructors should have one student contact hour per week for beginning users and two student contact hours per week for advanced users.

LEVEL	PERSONNEL	FACILITIES	EQUIPMENT
Advanced	Two or more laboratory assistants per facility, plus one full-time computer specialist*/programmer, one full-time secretary, and one laboratory administrator.	Basic facilities, plus electronic security system, power conditioning equipment, and skill classes for faculty and students.	Basic level hardware/software, plus interactive video equipment, robots, speech synthesizers, graphics tablets, light pens, music synthesis adapters, plotters, video digitizers, and other current developments; a variety of brands of each kind of software; hardware lines from facility to other locations for resource sharing to allow remote-site use of local area network; online messaging such as bulletin board system or computer conferencing for access by students and faculty; increased memory as needed to run new software.

Media Resources:

Minimal	Staff member(s), as needed.	Climate-controlled materials storage and checkout facility, including preview and viewing.	Film inspection equipment and preview equipment for all formats in use.
Basic	Professional staff member(s) and assistant(s) as needed.	Additional space as needed.	Film and video inspection and maintenance equipment.
Advanced	Technical staff member(s) and assistant(s) as needed.	Additional space as needed.	Additional equipment as needed.

LEVEL	PERSONNEL	FACILITIES	EQUIPMENT
Maintenance and Engineering Standards			
Minimal	Part-time technician(s) as needed.	Small repair shop.	Basic tools and test equipment.
Basic	Technician, plus field assistant(s) for cleaning and inspection.	Expanded repair shop.	Specialized tools and test equipment.
Advanced	Engineer(s) and technician(s) as needed to meet 95 percent of requests for service.	Expanded shop, office, storage, and construction areas.	Sophisticated electronic test equipment, plus equipment for device fabrication.

5

INSTRUCTIONAL MEDIA CENTER EVALUATION BY PATRONS*

MEMORANDUM

TO: Faculty and Administrators

FROM:

DATE:

RE: Instructional Media Center Opinionnaire

The Instructional Media Center has asked me to conduct its biennial survey on the quality of services and materials. This is part of the Center's efforts to evaluate its services and personnel on a systematic basis. Your cooperation is requested in completing and returning the questionnaire via campus mail to me at the Office of the Dean of Students by May 1, _____. *Note:* If you have not made use of the services offered by the Instructional Media Center, you have only to answer the first question, then return the questionnaire.

The Center is composed of five departments which offer the following services:

1. *Media Library.* Develops a collection of nonprint materials (films, filmstrips, audio tapes, transparencies, etc.) for the instructional program through consultation with the faculty and makes the collection available to the faculty. Major roles are: selection, cataloging, booking, and servicing the collection.

---

*Courtesy of Central Washington University.

2. *Television Services*. (a) Production of programs in the public schools in the state for instructional purposes. (b) Studio productions for ITV or segments of courses. (c) Recording and playback in classrooms for "mirror" experiences. (d) Recording commercial TV programs for later playback.

3. *Media Production*. Produces any materials (graphic, photos, slides, transparencies, etc.) for use in the instructional program. Promotional materials are also produced on a charge basis.

4. *Media Equipment*. Selects, inventories, maintains, and checks out audiovisual equipment to departments and faculty members for use in the instructional program.

5. *Instructional Computer Services*. Selects, inventories, maintains, and checks out computer equipment and materials to departments and faculty for instructional purposes.

I will tabulate the results and provide a summary of the data and comments to the Director of the Instructional Media Center. To preserve the confidentiality of your responses, your questionnaire will not be made available to the Director. In addition, I will make a summary of the results available to you if you provide your name and campus address.

Thank you for your cooperation.

INSTRUCTIONAL MEDIA CENTER OPINIONNAIRE

10. Have you made use of any of the services offered through the Instructional Media Center during the year?

_____ Yes

_____ No (If *no*, do not go on with the questionnaire. Return as is. (Thank you.)

Section I

Below are listed the four departments of the Instructional Media Center. Below the name of each department are selected items pertaining to the operation of the office on which your opinion is solicited. Using the scale below, mark (X) on the appropriate line to indicate your opinion or view on that item as it pertains to the department. If you have not requested services from a department, leave blank and go on to the next. The scale:

1 = Unsatisfactory
2 = Marginal
3 = Satisfactory
4 = Very good
5 = Outstanding
NA = Not applicable

Media Library Services
(Collection, i.e., films, film strips, audio tapes, etc.)

	1	2	3	4	5	NA
11. Quality of the collection........	___	___	___	___	___	___
12. Proficiency and performance of the booking/scheduling personnel...................	___	___	___	___	___	___
13. Proficiency and performance of the preview and rental personnel...................	___	___	___	___	___	___
15. Availability of materials when needed	___	___	___	___	___	___
16. Quality of the total service rendered by the department.....	___	___	___	___	___	___

Comments:

Television Services

	1	2	3	4	5	NA
17. Quality of productions.........	___	___	___	___	___	___
18. Quality of the collection........	___	___	___	___	___	___
19. Proficiency and performance of the professional and technical personnel...................	___	___	___	___	___	___
20. Proficiency and performance of the booking/scheduling personnel...................	___	___	___	___	___	___
21. Availability of the materials when needed................	___	___	___	___	___	___
22. Availability of the equipment when needed................	___	___	___	___	___	___
23. Quality of the total service rendered by the department.....	___	___	___	___	___	___

Comments:

Media Production Services

		1	2	3	4	5	NA
24.	Quality of materials produced...						
25.	Proficiency and performance of professional and technical personnel.....						
26.	Proficiency and performance of the clerical personnel.........						
27.	Time required for lab to produce the materials................						
28.	Quality of the total service rendered by the department.....						

Comments:

Media Equipment Services

		1	2	3	4	5	NA
29.	Proficiency and performance of the booking/scheduling personnel...........						
30.	General operating condition of AV equipment checked out of AV Library Pool by me........						
31.	General operating condition of AV equipment used from my building pool................						
32.	Availability of equipment when needed						
33.	Quality of the total service rendered by the department.....						

Comments:

Instructional Computer Services

	1	2	3	4	5	NA
34. Proficiency and performance of the booking/scheduling personnel	___	___	___	___	___	___
35. General operating condition of the computer equipment checked out of the equipment pool	___	___	___	___	___	___
36. General operating condition of computer equipment permanently assigned to my building. . . .	___	___	___	___	___	___
37. Availability of computer equipment when needed	___	___	___	___	___	___
38. Instructions received from media service staff as needed	___	___	___	___	___	___
39. Quality of the total service rendered by the department	___	___	___	___	___	___

Comments:

Section II

Following are a series of statements denoting areas in which student performance and achievement may be enhanced or developed by instruction. The use of audiovisual materials in the classroom is intended to assist and to facilitate the process. Please estimate your degree of agreement or disagreement with each statement as it pertains to your use of such materials in your classroom. Mark (X) on appropriate line using this scale:

1 = Unsatisfactory
2 = Marginal
3 = Satisfactory
4 = Very good
5 = Outstanding
NA = Not applicable

The Use of Audiovisual Materials in My Classes

	1	2	3	4	5	NA
40. Improved student thinking skills	___	___	___	___	___	___
41. Broadened interest in the discipline to which the class relates	___	___	___	___	___	___
42. Developed new viewpoints or appreciations	___	___	___	___	___	___
43. Increased interest in course content	___	___	___	___	___	___
44. Increased understanding of basic concepts in subject	___	___	___	___	___	___
45. Stimulated oral discussion in class	___	___	___	___	___	___

Section III

Below are statements which may characterize certain types of audiovisual materials, specifically films, slides, voice recordings, videotapes, etc. These prepared materials can convey information to a listener or viewer. Use the scale below to indicate your feeling about how well the materials you used achieved these desirable characteristics. A general opinion on all materials used is desired. The scale:

1 = Unsatisfactory
2 = Marginal
3 = Satisfactory
4 = Very good
5 = Outstanding
NA = Not applicable

	1	2	3	4	5	NA
46. Clearly interpreted abstract ideas and theories	___	___	___	___	___	___
47. Stressed important content	___	___	___	___	___	___
48. Offered clear and understandable explanations	___	___	___	___	___	___
49. Gave viewpoints and information other class materials did not contain	___	___	___	___	___	___
50. Were clear in presentation of concepts	___	___	___	___	___	___

Section IV

Please answer questions 51-56 *yes* or *no*.

_____ 51. Did your students benefit intellectually from the use of audiovisual materials?

_____ 52. Did the use of AV materials enable you to better explain difficult concepts?

_____ 53. Did the material improve your effectiveness as an instructor?

_____ 54. Would you recommend to a colleague that he/she make use of the Instructional Media Center?

_____ 55. Have you ever recommended to a colleague that he/she make use of the Instructional Media Center?

_____ 56. How do the services provided by the Instructional Media Center at your university compare with audiovisual services provided by other colleges where you may have taught?
   A. Worse
   B. Same
   C. Better
   D. Have not taught at other colleges

Section V

Please make any additional comments you wish to on the services offered by the Instructional Media Center.

DESIGN CASE HISTORY

Production:	The Magic of Business Week	**Year:**	1986

Designer: William D. Schmidt,
Central Washington University   **Length:** 17 minutes

Description of Completed Project: Videotape production

Client: The Association for Washington Business (AWB), Olympia, Washington

The Process Used to Design the Production:

THE IDEA: In 1986, the AWB requested another Business Week promotional production. This time they specified production on videotape instead of film, primarily to take advantage of being able to produce a large quantity of copies at low-per-unit cost.

Throughout the eleven years of Business Week sessions held each summer, many people found themselves describing Business Week as a bit of magic. The officials of Business Week wanted to have this new promotional production explore that magical concept. They and the designer agreed upon the objectives and the audiences:

THE OBJECTIVES: (1) To promote and raise money to support Business Week

(2) To explore what is the so-called magic of Business Week

THE AUDIENCES: (1) Service clubs

(2) Chambers of commerce

(3) Students and teachers in the state's high schools

THE RESEARCH: As the process of pinpointing the "magic" of Business Week appeared to be an elusive concept, a fairly ambitious schedule of interviews of students, teachers, business employees, and AWB officials was conducted each of four weeks during the summer of 1986. After interviewing on videotape about fifty people, a good sense of the substance of the magical concept emerged. Some of the most articulate and interesting recorded interviews were built into the design. The only additional research needed was to update Business Week statistical data. The specifications, treatment, and first page of the script for the 1986 Business Week design follow:

SPECIFICATIONS: **Production Length:** 12 minutes

Medium: Videotape (Master: 3/4" U-Matic, Copies: VHS; some of the original shots will be shot on 16mm film and transferred to videotape)

Timeline: Shooting (June–August 1986)

Editing (September–November 1986)

Completion (December 20, 1986)

Contacts: William D. Schmidt, 509-963-1842

Hal Wolf of AWB, 206-452-7894

THE TREATMENT: Open with narrator's voice over high angle shot panning general assembly (close-up shot gradually going to wide angle):

> "It would be a week unlike any they had ever experienced. High school students . . . teachers . . . business executives . . . business employees . . . from throughout the state of Washington. They came together to share a unique experience. Something some of them at week's end will call the magic of Business Week."

Music up over shots of interesting, appealing visuals (shots showing the excitement, joy, and magic of Business Week).

Cut to on-camera interviews of representatives of different groups giving their feelings about the magic of Business Week.

Back to narrator over shots of Business Week participants busy at work:

> "Not a vacation for students or the adult teachers and businesspeople, but an intensive week with daily activities from 7 A.M. to 9 P.M. A week with a special purpose: An opportunity for students and teachers to learn firsthand about our economic system—private enterprise."

Bring up Business Week song and, over visuals of Business Week activities, superimpose title "The Magic of Business Week." (This song will be composed and recorded by a CWU student. It will convey a general impression of what Business Week is all about.)

At the end of the song, narrator over shots of company meetings and general assemblies:

> "At the outset of the week, students know little about private enterprise. Businesspeople know little about students' attitudes toward business."

> "During the week groups work together on a computer simulation. Students make all the management decisions typical of the operation of a business for two years."

> "Business executives from across the state make presentations on topics ranging from how to start a business to day-to day operating principles to why businesses fail." (Shots of three presenters with name and company superimposed with short lip-sync segments of their presentations.)

Narrator over shots of three university campuses and Business Week activities:

> "The campus of Central Washington University in Ellensburg. Here's where Business Week started in 1976 and has developed through the years. Each year four separate Business Week sessions are held at CWU with usually two additional one-week sessions at other participating institutions."

> "Gonzaga University has hosted Business Week several years." (Music up while showing mixture of campus shots and Business Week activities.)

"Seattle Pacific University is one of the newer hosts for Business Week." (Music up while showing mixture of campus shots and Business Week activities.)

"Regardless of where it's held, the focus of each week's session is the same—much as it has been through the years."

Cut to on-camera interviews of key people talking about the focus of Business Week and how the program has developed through the years.

Bring up version 2 of Business Week song full, then under as Business Week students, teachers, and businesspeople tell about their Business Week experiences.

Music in lightly as narrator concludes:

"They come together in places like Ellensburg . . . Spokane . . . and Seattle. What kind of experience was it?" Enthusiastic group of students, teachers, and businesspeople on camera yell in unison: "Business Week is magic." Narrator continues: "Too much hype? Well, not really. It really is magic for everyone who helps to make the program work. This coming together has a profound and unique, if not magic, effect on all who attend Business Week. Don't let us be the judge. Participate yourself or help send a student to this year's Business Week."

Bring up version one of Business Week song and roll credits over rapidly changing stills of Business Week activities.

THE SCRIPT:
(1st page only)

1. CU of students listening to general session speech.

    > SOUND: Sound of business executive speaker up momentarily, then under.

2. General session presentation: Pan from students to teacher to business employee to business executive.

    > NARRATOR: (Voice-over)
    > IT WOULD BE A WEEK UNLIKE ANY THEY HAD
    > EVER EXPERIENCED. HIGH SCHOOL STUDENTS . . .
    > TEACHERS . . . BUSINESS EMPLOYEES . . . AND . . .
    > BUSINESS EXECUTIVES FROM THROUGHOUT THE
    > STATE OF WASHINGTON.

SOUND   Up full to hear business executive speaker momentarily, then under as narrator continues.

3. CU of students listening.

> NARRATOR: (Voice-over)
> THEY CAME TOGETHER TO SHARE A UNIQUE
> EXPERIENCE; SOMETHING AT WEEK'S END THEY
> WILL CALL THE MAGIC OF BUSINESS WEEK.

4. Shots of Business Week activities with emphasis on sharing—caring—communicating,
    shown with music of Business Week song.

> SOUND: (Vocal song) "It's magic . . . Business Week. No
> fantasy, but reality. It's magic . . . giving, caring,
> sharing, growing as one! Magic . . . Business
> Week. It's in the air, just take a look . . . Magic
> changing, working, striving, giving it all! Business
> Week! Telling the Private Enterprise Story!"

> Super title: THE MAGIC OF BUSINESS WEEK

5. Close up on interviewee before beginning to talk.

> NARRATOR: (Voice-over)

Author Index

Subject Index

Title Index

417